Dietrich's Ghosts

Dietrich's Ghosts

The Sublime and the Beautiful in Third Reich Film

Erica Carter

 Publishing

For Abi and Sam

First published in 2004 by the
BRITISH FILM INSTITUTE
21 Stephen Street, London W1T 1LN

The British Film Institute is the UK national agency with responsibility for encouraging the arts of film
and television and conserving them in the national interest.

Cover design: couch
Cover images: (front) Marlene Dietrich, by Wolff von Gudenberg, 1924, courtesy of Filmmuseum
Berlin – Marlene Dietrich Collection; (back) *Traumulus* (Carl Froelich, 1936), Carl Froelich – Tonfilm
Produktions; *The Scarlet Empress* (Josef von Sternberg, 1934), Paramount Productions; *Premiere*
(Géza von Bolváry, 1937), Gloria Film GmbH, courtesy of Fotoarchiv Stiftung Deutsche Kinemathek.

Set by Fakenham Photosetting Limited, Fakenham, Norfolk
Printed in the UK by The Cromwell Press, Trowbridge, Wiltshire

British Library Cataloguing-in-Publication Data
A catalogue record for this book is available from the British Library

ISBN 0–85170–883–8 (pbk)
ISBN 0–85170–882–X (hbk)

Contents

Preface and Acknowledgments

This book began life as a project for a study of Third Reich stars. In the event, the more comprehensive research to which that project led me became the backdrop for the rather larger study of Third Reich film offered here: a study that embeds the star system in the broader film-aesthetic discourses and practices of National Socialism. Numerous friends and colleagues have offered help, support and guidance along the way. They include, in no special order except reverse alphabetical, Ginette Vincendeau, Ulrike Sieglohr, Eve Rosenhaft, Loredana Polezzi, Richard Parker, John Osborne, Mica Nava, Anna Maria Mullally, Johannes von Moltke, Charlotte Klonk, Robert Kiss, the late Henning Harmssen, Deniz Göktürk, Geoff Eley, Margaret Deriaz, Jan Campbell, Charlotte Brunsdon, Tim Bergfelder, José Arroyo.

Anton Kaes, Joseph Garncarz, Richard Dyer and an anonymous reader saw earlier versions of the manuscript. My grateful thanks to all for helping me to let go of my first project, and for their warm encouragement in support of the history of film aesthetics this book now attempts. My colleagues in the Department of German Studies at the University of Warwick have given generously of their time and expertise, especially during my years as Warwick Research Fellow. A particularly important forum for the ideas explored in this book was the department's Kracauer reading group. Thanks in both contexts to Seán Allan, Stephen Lamb, Rob Burns, Helmut Schmitz and Georgina Paul.

This project owes its completion also to financial support from the Universities of Warwick and Southampton, and the British Academy, whom I thank most warmly for their generosity. I would also like to thank librarians and archivists at the following: in the UK, the University of the West of England, Bristol; the British Library at Colindale; the Imperial War Museum, London (with particular thanks to Brad King); the Modern Records Collection at the University of Warwick (with special thanks to Christine Woodland for her assistance with the Harmssen Collection); and the British Film Institute. In Germany, warm thanks to the following: the library of the Hochschule für Film und Fernsehen, Potsdam (especially Frau Lydia Wiehring von Wendrin and Frau Renate Göthe); in Berlin, the Bundesarchiv and Bundesarchiv-Filmarchiv, the Marlene-Dietrich-

Collection (now at the Filmmuseum Berlin), the Landesarchiv Berlin, the Renaissance-Theater, the (former) Stiftung Deutsche Kinemathek, and the Stiftung Archiv Akademie der Künste; in Frankfurt am Main, the Deutsches Filminstitut (DIF); in Wiesbaden, the DIF-Filmarchiv (with particular thanks to Herr Manfred Moos and Herr Matthias Knop), and the Friedrich-Wilhelm-Murnau-Stiftung, with special thanks to Frau Gudrun Weiss. Research into Hollywood perspectives on Marlene Dietrich's German reception was conducted in the Margaret Herrick Library at the Academy of Motion Picture Arts and Sciences, Los Angeles, California.

Illustrations are included courtesy of the BFI Stills Library (with special thanks to Sophia Contento); the *Fotoarchiv* Stiftung Deutsche Kinemathek Berlin (with thanks to Herr Wolfgang Theis and Herr Peter Latta); the Stiftung Deutsche Kinemathek Marlene-Dietrich-Collection Berlin (with thanks to Frau Silke Renneburg; the Landesbildstelle Berlin; and the Bundesarchiv Berlin-Lichterfelde.

The patience of my editor at the BFI, Andrew Lockett, has been immeasurable; I would like to thank him for his faith in this project, and for his careful guidance during my protracted delays. For support and encouragement throughout, thanks to Martin Pumphrey. For help on the dark days, and laughter elsewhere, thanks most particularly to Julia Wilcox and Linda Hoag, to Sally Welford, Olive Lewis, Nikki Eames and Howard Hall, Annie Bearfield, Andy Vine, Klaus Raymond-Wilcox, and to my family: John and Susan Carter, Chris Carter, Barbara Browning, Sara Parker and Abigail Carter.

EC, January 2004

List of abbreviations

ORGANISATIONS

ADF   Arbeitsgemeinschaft der Filmverleiher Deutschlands (Association of German Film Distributors)

BA   Bundesarchiv Berlin-Lichterfelde

BDM   Bund Deutscher Mädel (League of German Girls, the female Hitler Youth organisation)

DACHO   Dachorganisation der Filmschaffenden Deutschlands (Umbrella Organisation for German Film Practitioners)

DAF   Deutsche Arbeitsfront (German Labour Front)

DFA   Deutsche Filmakademie (German Film Academy)

FKB   Filmkreditbank (Film Credit Bank)

HFF   Hochschule für Film und Fernsehen, Potsdam

LBS   Landesbildstelle Berlin (now at the Landesarchiv Berlin)

MDC   Marlene Dietrich Collection, Filmmuseum Berlin

NSDAP   Nationalsozialistische Deutsche Arbeiterpartei (National Socialist German Workers' Party): the Nazi Party

OP   Oberprüfstelle (Central Censorship Office)

ProMi   Propaganda Ministry (RMVP)

RFK   Reichsfilmkammer (*Reich* Film Chamber)

RKK   Reichskulturkammer (*Reich* Chamber of Culture)

RMVP   Reichsministerium für Volksaufklärung and Propaganda (*Reich* Ministry for Popular Enlightenment and Propaganda)

RPK   Reichspressekammer (*Reich* Press Chamber)

SPIO   Spitzenorganisation der deutschen Filmindustrie (Confederation of the German Film Industry)

Ufa   Universum Film AG

JOURNALS AND NEWSPAPERS CONSULTED

AA   *8 Uhr Abendblatt, Berlin*

BLA   *Berliner Lokal-Anzeiger*

BN   *Die Bühne*

BT   *Berliner Tageblatt*
DAZ   *Deutsche Allgemeine Zeitung*
FK   *Film-Kurier*
FL   *Der Film*
FT   *Filmtechnik*
FLW   *Filmwoche*
FW   *Filmwelt*
HN   *Hamburger Nachrichten*
HT   *Hamburger Tageblatt*
KZ   *Kölnische Zeitung*
NZ   *Nationalzeitung*
PZ   *Preussische Zeitung*
RWZ   *Rheinisch-Westfälische Zeitung*
VB   *Völkischer Beobachter*

TRANSLATIONS

SECONDARY LITERATURE: FOOTNOTES

Where standard English editions exist, I have quoted the extant translation, and referenced the translator(s) in footnotes. All other translations from the original German are my own.

TITLES: WRITTEN PUBLICATIONS AND ORGANISATIONS

When books, articles and organisations are named in the main body of the book, the German title is used, followed by an English translation in brackets. Where standard English translations exist, I have used these. All other translations from the original German are my own.

FILM REFERENCES

The first reference in the text to German titles is given in the original German; English title translations and release dates follow in brackets. Subsequent references give the German title only. Where reference is made to treatments (draft proposals for possible titles), production dates are given in brackets, if it can be verified that the film subsequently went into production. For treatments for which no film title could be identified, only the English translation of the treatment title is given.

Introduction

On 13 March 1933, Joseph Goebbels was appointed by Presidential Decree as Germany's *Reich* Minister for Popular Enlightenment and Propaganda (Reichsminister für Volksaufklärung und Propaganda). From that date until his suicide on 30 April 1945, the Reichsminister was to preside over a film industry that occupied pride of place in his vision of a culture subordinated and subservient to the Nazi state. Small wonder then that it is the film medium that has come under the most intense scrutiny since 1945 from historians, political scientists and cultural commentators seeking critical purchase on the relationship between fascist ideology, Nazi politics, and culture in the fascist state. In the last six decades, we have learned much of film's nature and function within the Nazi regime. A first generation of works from the 1960s to the early 1980s used methods from the social sciences and political economy to investigate the institutional and ideological links between the Nazi state and the film industry. We know from those studies of the linchpin role allotted to film within the Nazi propaganda machine; hence, for instance, their focus on the early establishment of the *Reich* Film Chamber (Reichsfilmkammer, RFK), set up in July 1933 as an organisational arm of the Propaganda Ministry, and empowered to oversee the *Gleichschaltung* (co-ordination) of all fields of film-industrial practice under the control, via the Propaganda Ministry, of the Nazi state.[1] We know how *Gleichschaltung* was progressively implemented at the level of management via the *Reich* Film Chamber and the Film Department within the Propaganda Ministry, two bodies which operated in tandem to bring all sectors of the industry under state administrative control. At the level of finance, we know too that state control was initially gained through the Filmkreditbank (FKB), a financial operation established jointly by banks, industry bodies and the RFK in June 1933, controlled after 1934 directly by the RFK, and functioning therefore to secure the industry's financial dependence on Nazi state financial support. We know that Nazi managerial and financial control would later be cemented via the Ufi-Film GmbH, a 'giant holding company' through which the film industry in its entirety passed into state ownership in January 1942.[2] And we know, finally, how *Gleichschaltung* operated at the level of film-cultural production, first through the purging via the RFK of Jews and other figures deemed 'undesirable' on political or ethnic grounds; and second, through a complex apparatus of pre- and post-production censorship, including script monitoring by the Filmkreditbank, and pre-censorship of all scripts by the *Reich* Dramaturgical Office, the latter established in 1934 under a revised cinema law (*Reichslichtspielgesetz*) that Martin Loiperdinger for instance sees as enabling state intervention into film production on a 'massive' scale.[3]

To such first-wave historians as Gerd Albrecht, Jürgen Spiker, Joseph Wulf and others we owe, in sum, many of our insights into the highly ramified institutional apparatus that embedded film within the Nazi state.[4] Yet it has become something of a reflex in recent historiography to highlight the lacunae in these studies. Concerned as many early Third Reich film scholars were to highlight the links between state ideology and cinematic practice, they focused on a group of some forty to one hundred films that seemed clearly definable as political films, or propaganda. The remaining thousand or so productions of the Nazi years were relegated to the apparently less tendentious category of mass entertainment. Thus Gerd Albrecht, for instance, rejects as 'unsystematic' the classical entertainment genre distinctions, from musical to adventure movie, that had hitherto served to classify Third Reich films, and devises instead a genre schema that divides these titles into 'H-Filme' ('heitere Filme', or light entertainment), 'E-Filme' ('ernste' or serious films), 'A-Filme' (a rather dubious intermediate category of titles that fail to fit elsewhere) and 'P-Filme', the propaganda films that apparently fully realised the function of mass manipulation that the Nazi regime allotted to cinema. Albrecht's definition of 'P-Filme' as films not only publicly touted as state favourites through press coverage, *Prädikate* (quality ratings) and so on, but made with the 'manifest intention' of audience manipulation, is reproduced by such later writers as David Welch, in whose study the so-called *Staatsauftragsfilme* (state-commissioned films) figure prominently; or Erwin Leiser, for whom 'Nazi films' were clearly definable as those where 'Third Reich thinking is ... thickly laid on.'[5]

More recently, as Third Reich film history has shifted from this deterministic model, to what Sabine Hake calls 'more film-specific methods and inquiries', questions have been raised over the prioritising of films with apparently 'manifest' propagandistic intent. Obscured from view in earlier studies were what were certainly in numerical terms, and arguably also socio-culturally the more significant group of films intended for mass entertainment. What for instance of such titles as the Zarah Leander star vehicle *Heimat* (1938), the Marika Rökk revue *Frauen sind doch bessere Diplomaten* (*Women are the Better Diplomats*, 1942) or the musical *Der Weiße Traum* (*The White Dream,* 1944)? All are listed in Gerd Albrecht's survey of German box-office hits after 1930 as the most successful films of their respective years; yet they gain scant attention in many early histories of Third Reich film.[6] The box-office triumph of those films dubbed non-propaganda by previous histories, and thus ignored, as well as the relative unpopularity of some of the Nazis' most favoured propaganda vehicles (the public distaste for *Der ewige Jude/The Eternal Jew*, 1940, for example, is legend), has begged questions too about the criteria of selection of film titles for historical analysis. Are historians of Third Reich cinema only to be concerned with film in its ideological dimension? What of those more 'film-specific' issues of which Hake writes, from film-industrial developments, through textual aesthetics, to the questions of reception and spectatorship raised in film studies accounts of genre, stars and film spectatorship?

It is these and related questions that have been a repeated focus of the new Third Reich film history of recent years. Recent studio histories, for instance, situate the likes of Ufa or Tobis within a broader history of the national industry that explores both the German studios' intimate links with the German state, and at the same time, their status as commercial and industrial enterprises whose development followed not only the logic of national politics, but the economics of world cinema.[7] Important revisionist histories of Third Reich entertainment show a similar concern with cinematic specificity in their mobilisation of film studies methodology for a critical history of Third Reich popular aesthetics. Eric Rentschler's project, in his important *Ministry of Illusion*, is for instance to produce a critical re-reading of popular genre films that will see them no longer as 'ideological containers in which the Ministry of Propaganda packaged affirmation and falsehood', but rather 'as ambiguous and complex entities, as still resonant portrayals of an age's different inclinations and disparate wishes'.[8] Like the film historian Karsten Witte, to whose studies of Third Reich popular texts *Ministry of Illusion* is explicitly indebted, Rentschler's account of 'the form, address and appeal of Nazi films' aspires to embed the Third Reich film aesthetic in a larger history of popular desire ('an age's different inclinations and disparate wishes'). For him, as for those other writers who have worked to re-install the film text as the Third Reich film historian's first object of scrutiny, film histories of the period are best written through exemplary textual readings that situate key texts within a more expansive history of spectatorship and reception. Rightly critical of the mass manipulation paradigm that dominated early studies of 'Nazi film', such writers as Stephen Lowry and Linda Schulte-Sasse thus draw on psychoanalytic (Schulte-Sasse) or semiotic (Lowry) modes of textual critique to locate Third Reich film texts as complex and ambiguous entities that are certainly enmeshed within the political ideologies of their historical moment, yet which at the same time regularly exceed those ideologies through their 'heterogeneity', their 'internal contradictions' and their popular appeal.[9]

My own work in this volume owes many a debt to the new historiography scanned above: to scholarly studies, then, that have situated popular cinema – a German cinema of genres, stars, mass markets and popular fantasies and pleasures – at the heart of any analysis of Third Reich film. The mid-1990s works of Rentschler, Schulte-Sasse, Lowry and others paid long overdue attention to questions of textuality and spectatorship that were – problematically – barely addressed in early ideology critiques of so-called 'Nazi film'.[10] Similar issues are explored in *Dietrich's Ghosts*, most centrally in Chapter 3, on film exhibition, and in discussions from Chapter 4 on of the textual construction of popular auteurs and stars. Studies since Rentschler *et al.*, moreover (and the exemplary case here is Sabine Hake's *Popular Cinema in the Third Reich*), have amplified those 'text-based models' with contextual studies of Third Reich popular film as a 'social, cultural, economic and political practice': a practice with 'multiple functions' as industry, cultural institution, public sphere, social experience and 'fantasy machine'.[11] Again, I follow Hake in attempting below a study of Third Reich popular film contextualised within studio history (Chapter 1), an account of acting theory and practice (Chapter 2), a history of exhibition (Chapter 3), and (Chapter 4 to 7), a study of auteurism and the star system from 1933 onwards.

Unlike Hake, however, I privilege in this book an aspect of Third Reich popular film which, I suggest, has particular significance in the Nazi bid for ideological dominance in the arena of cinema. Recent histories, as the above quotations illustrate, highlight the heterogeneity of the material practices that together constituted popular film culture under National Socialism. That work offers a crucial corrective to earlier studies that conceived Third Reich film as a propaganda monolith unambiguously in thrall to fascist political ideology and the Nazi state. Thanks to the second-wave historiography I have briefly scanned above, Third Reich film is constituted today as an object of study with fluid boundaries temporally (hence the stress of such as Hake and Witte on film-historical continuities from Weimar to National Socialism), spatially (witness, for instance, the proliferation of recent works exploring the relationship of 'Nazi film' to Hollywood and vice versa),[12] and conceptually too, to the extent that the new film history operates across the totality of the cinematic field, from industry and studio practice, through textuality, to reception discourse and modes of spectatorship or textual address.

The history I propose in *Dietrich's Ghosts*, however, swims against some of the more markedly pluralist elements of this current historiographical tide. However disparate and internally contradictory, Third Reich film in all its diverse manifestations – as domestic and international industry, distribution network for foreign and indigenous product, exhibition sector, discourse and practice of reception – strove incontrovertibly after that 'production of consensual cultural values' which William Uricchio and Roberta Pearson identify in a different context as film's potential contribution to the maintenance of social order and popular consent. Uricchio and Pearson draw on the social theory of Antonio Gramsci, Raymond Williams and Pierre Bourdieu to suggest that film may work at certain historical moments not directly to legitimate political domination (as early accounts of Third Reich propaganda film suggest in the German case), but to construct and maintain what Gramsci termed hegemony.[13] Gramsci defined hegemony as 'the "spontaneous" consent given by the great masses of the population to the general direction imposed on social life by the dominant ... group'.[14] In this reformulation of Marxist cultural theory, social control and political dominance are thus achieved not only by the coercive exercise of state power, but also, indeed centrally, through cultural practices and institutions that construct a 'complex and interactive ... political consensus'.[15]

A cognate distinction has been drawn in the second-wave Third Reich film historiography of recent years. Revisionist histories from the mid-1990s on have shown how questionable in the National Socialist case (as indeed elsewhere) is the totalitarian conception of Nazi dominance as secured through the successful exercise of top-down ideological and political control.[16] But the illumination in those histories of the failures, fissures and internal contradictions that dogged the Nazi film-ideological project from 1933 on – the clash between Goebbels' promotion of apparently apolitical entertainment, for instance, and an NSDAP faithful that clamoured for films with overt propagandistic content; or audience appreciation of films and stars whose representational mode cut across and disrupted the ideological certainties of National Socialism – should not detract entirely from Nazism's drive for 'hegemony': its project, that is, to forge a common (*völkisch*, militarist, fascist) culture across the regime's multifarious domains of socio-cultural operation, including film.

Eric Rentschler reminds us in this context of Goebbels' 'orchestra principle', according to which '[w]e do not expect everyone to play the same instrument, ... only that people play according to a plan'. In cinema, Rentschler continues, the symphonic resonances between features, documentaries and newsreels, and 'an array of orchestrated diversions (radio programmes, mass rallies, gigantic spectacles, holidays and commemorations ...)', functioned to construct a cultural 'world' that somehow embodied what the National Socialists consistently referred to as the Nazi 'spirit' (*Geist*) or world-view (*Weltanschauung*).[17] Rentschler's comments draw attention to the tension ubiquitous in Third Reich film culture between cultural forces productive of heterogeneity, contradiction and difference, and the regime's drive for an ideological coherence achieved through the fusion of all socio-cultural activity into the cohesive body of a hierarchised, militarised and racialised *Volk*. Suggestively, he points here also to one significant force in Nazism's drive towards cohesion when he dubs the Nazi state 'a grand aesthetic construction' in which (and Rentschler cites Philippe Lacoue-Labarthe here) 'the political itself is instituted and constituted . . . in and as work of art'.[18]

THIRD REICH FILM AND THE FASCIST AESTHETIC

Like Rentschler, I take a cue from writers ranging from Walter Benjamin to Susan Sontag when, in the rest of this book, I investigate Third Reich film in its aesthetic dimension, and explore film aesthetics as a centripetal force that worked repeatedly (though certainly not always successfully) to recuperate cinematic practice ideologically for National Socialism. Thus Chapter 1 opens with references to two of Joseph Goebbels' most important speeches of the pre-war years: his first address to film industry representatives in March 1933, a fortnight after he assumed the post of *Reich* Propaganda Minister, and a second programmatic speech to film practitioners in the Berlin Philharmonie four years on, in March 1937. Here and in other pronouncements on the future of German film, Goebbels is emphatic in his demand for a film art that will effect exactly that fusion of the ideological and the aesthetic which was, for Benjamin, a defining characteristic of National Socialism. In a November 1933 speech at the official opening of the *Reich* Culture Chamber, Goebbels demanded, for instance, a 'fundamental marrying' of the fascist 'spirit of the heroic conception of life' with the 'eternal laws' of art, including film.[19] Witness also the *Reich* Minister's tautological plea in February 1934 for a view of the National Socialists as 'artists' who had 'liberated art' by 'artistic means' – a plea he will repeat at numerous turns throughout the consolidation period of National Socialist rule from 1933 to the outbreak of war.[20]

If we read Goebbels' pronouncements as manifest ideological messages, then their falsity seems clear. There are, of course, verifiable (and verifiably brutal) political, ideological, economic and social dimensions to the state interventions into German cinema – the institutional restructuring, the state regulation, and in particular the mass political and racial purging – that characterised Nazi film policy from the early years onwards. But there are more fruitful ways of reading Goebbels' claim that fascist hegemony could be established through a specifically aesthetic transformation of cultural institutions and cultural practice across all art forms, but especially film. Unpalatable as Goebbels' comments on fascist film politics as a 'work of art' may seem, they make two kinds of historical sense. Nazi interventions into German cinema displayed, first, numerous of the features that Benjamin identified in 1936 as characteristic of European fascism's aestheticisation of political life.[21] In the institutions of German film, as in other socio-cultural spheres, the rescripting of fascist politicisation as a work of art took place through public gatherings orchestrated around rituals of subservience to state authority and power. Hence, for instance, the Propaganda Minister's selection of premier cultural venues – the Dresden State Opera House, the Berlin Krolloper and Philharmonie – for his most significant speeches to industry representatives, cultural officials, and practitioners from the world of film. The function of Goebbels' speeches not merely as programmatic statements of fascist political intent, but as mass-cultural celebrations of German cinema's new submission to Nazi rule, was underlined by newsreel and press coverage that foregrounded the ceremonial character of these events – their opening to orchestral accompaniment, or the slow build to climax in the obsequious tributes that invariably preceded Goebbels' ascent to the podium to address the floor.[22] Similar public genuflections to the 'hand of the *Führer*' (actor Eugen Klöpfer, *verbatim*) were visible in the 'professions of faith' by film practitioners that peppered the trade and popular film press on such occasions as the Nazi 'election' triumph of 1936.[23] Indeed the very process of *Gleichschaltung* involved much more than the abstract institutional restructuring of all cultural sectors, including film. State co-ordination was simultaneously a process of repression and regulation, and a set of practices of cultural production that spawned and/or consolidated a network of professional bodies – such organisations as the Fachschule der Filmtheaterbesitzer (Technical School for Film Exhibitors), for instance, who met in public venues across the *Reich* to debate and celebrate their political contribution to the 'National Socialist reconstruction' of German film. A press officer from the *Reich* Culture Chamber could thus register with delight the 'unprecedented levels of activity and commitment' displayed by the Berlin-Brandenburg regional exhibitors' association through the array of lectures, public seminars and cognate events they had organised in pursuit of a 'qualitative enhancement' of exhibition practice after 1933.[24] Similar energy was displayed by creative practitioners intent on forging bonds between their own artistic efforts, and the political spirit of the times. Willy Fritsch's 1936 ditty, 'My election slogan runs/fight with our *Führer*/for labour and bread' may lack the gravitas of more formal declarations of political faith – from the film director and NSDAP member Karl Ritter, for instance, who called in one address to the *Reich* Film Chamber for a less frivolous celebration than Fritsch's of the 'great honour' bestowed on film practitioners by National Socialism's 'unique capacity to raise our will from the depths of superficial entertainment and the pursuit of commercial gain to the level of an artistic and state-political creation that ranks as an equal alongside the fine arts, as well as literature, music, and the tradition-bound art of the stage'.[25] These pronouncements by Fritsch and Ritter are, however, of a piece in their enactment of precisely that cultish celebration of the *Führer* principle which Benjamin situates at the core of National Socialism's aestheticisation of political life.

In *Dietrich's Ghosts*, my ambition is not, however, to attempt a full history of the processes whereby German fascism staged its political colonisation of the film industry as what Benjamin's contemporary, Siegfried Kracauer, might have termed a mass-ornamental spectacle of professional submission to Nazi power. Such a history would need to consider the internal industry events that mush-roomed across the lecture halls, concert houses and film theatres of the *Reich*, as film practitioners gathered for collective 'schooling' in a desired National Socialist transformation of German film; or the premiere evenings, gala events, festivals and film balls that littered the Third Reich film calendar, ostentatiously celebrating in their glittering mix of guests from industry and state the fusion of Nazi politics and film art. Attention would need to be paid, too, to the ritualis-tic vilification in the trade and popular film press of the victims of state regulation and repression in the domain of film: to press coverage of censorship decisions, for instance, that detailed the multiple offences against 'German pres-tige' purportedly perpetrated by such titles as Marlene Dietrich's 1933 *Song of Songs*. Despite the censors' excoriation of *Song of Songs*' 'distorted' and 'disfig-ured' portrait of Germany, the lavish reconstruction in published versions of their verdict of every 'base' and 'offensive' detail of image and narrative in the film locate censorship here not as a secret process of clandestine repression, but as an exhibitionist display of state repressive power in the arena of film.[26] Here as elsewhere – in the 1933 book burnings for instance, or exhibitions of 'degen-erate music' (1938) and 'degenerate art' (1937) – fascist cultural politics is enacted as a spectacular horror show displaying National Socialism's cultural 'others' ('kitsch' Hollywood production in the case of *Song of Songs*, modernist music, art and literature in other instances) for ritual denigration in carnivalis-tic celebrations of fascism's repressive power.

In this book, by contrast, I am concerned with a rather quieter mode in which German fascism enacted Benjamin's fusion of aesthetics and the political. My focus in ensuing chapters is less on Nazi film policy and politics, than on the specifically cinematic processes whereby creative and film-industrial practitioners worked to elaborate a politicised aesthetic for post-1933 German film. A word is in order here on the historical methodology on which my arguments draw. I am concerned in *Dietrich's Ghosts* with what Raymond Williams termed the 'complex of experiences, relationships and activities' that contributed to the 'lived hegemony' of National Socialism after 1933.[27] Williams' preoccupation with lived experience is mirrored in recent Third Reich social history, which similarly emphasises both the fluidity and heterogeneity of the social field under German fascism – its areas therefore of nonconformity, even cultural 'resistance' – and the function not only of the state repressive apparatus, but also of a culture of popular consent in extinguishing actual political opposition to the Nazi state. [28]

But I would add to these accounts the perception that it is in textuality – the written and spoken word, visual images, sounds – that this cultural 'complex' is realised, 'hegemony' created and recreated, undermined, reasserted, and perpetually transformed. Thus in *Dietrich's Ghosts*, I draw on a whole array of textual materials, from popular and trade press commentaries, through political speeches and internal studio, Propaganda Ministry and *Reich* Film Chamber files, scholarly and popular writings, and finally films themselves: 'texts', then, that I use to form a picture of the experiential and cognitive field within which shared knowledges, common meanings and values were articulated for post-1933 film. It hardly needs stressing, moreover, that we are dealing in this exploration of Third Reich cinema with an entirely hierarchical cultural domain. We know all too well the mechanisms of coercion whereby Nazi ideology asserted its dominance across all socio-cultural fields, including film. But I draw also on a second, and specifically film-cultural source for that naturalisation of the status quo which social theorists associate with the consolidation of political domination, in German fascism as elsewhere. Historians of Wilhelmine and Weimar film have frequently stressed the significance of what Sabine Hake, following Christian Metz, terms cinema's 'third machine': the apparatus of critical and theoretical writing on cinema that was integral to the development of the film medium in its early years. As Hake observes, it is discursive production around the film text that ultimately determines its broader socio-cultural location: its class position, as articulated through debates on high versus mass culture, its relation to audiences, its modes of spectatorship, and its relevance to state politics, and/or to revolutionary movements for political change.[29]

Scholarship on Weimar film theory in particular – on Siegfried Kracauer, Walter Benjamin, Rudolf Arnheim, Béla Balázs – has expanded exponentially in recent years in recognition of the dialectical interplay that Hake describes between creative practice and critical discourse in the production of an aesthetics of film. Until recently, however, film history has remained silent on the place of film theory in the larger cultural history of the film medium after 1933.[30] Goebbels' 1936 decree banning film criticism and replacing it with what he termed 'film commentary' (*Filmbetrachtung*) of an obsequiously laudatory kind, is assumed by many writers to have quashed film-aesthetic debate in toto, and located film as a medium in dialogue only with the ideological programmes of the Nazi state.

A rather different picture emerges, however, from contemporary surveys of the film-critical field. In 1940, Hans Traub published a comprehensive bibliography of existing scholarly and popular writings on film.[31] As Director of the

Ufa-*Lehrschau* (Ufa's Department of Education and Exhibition, described by the author as 'the only Institute yet to attempt a systematic overview of questions relating to every aspect of the film medium'),[32] Traub produced what remains today among the most authoritative available bibliographies of German print sources on film from 1895 to 1940. An important source for film historians after 1945, Traub's bibliography is significant also for its revelation of the complex, indeed pluralist nature of film-theoretical debate, even at the high point of Nazi hegemony in 1940. An opening section on 'cultural-political writings' certainly includes such unsavoury Nazi tracts as Carl Neumann's *Film-'Kunst', Film-Kohn, Film-Korruption* (*Film 'Art', Film Cohen, Film Corruption*), or Alexander Paul's *Der Film der Gegenwart und die Rassenfrage* (*Contemporary Film and the Race Question*). But in a subsequent survey of works on 'film dramaturgy and performance', Traub accurately reflects current critical preoccupations when he includes in his film-aesthetic pantheon such figures as Béla Balázs, Laszló Moholy-Nagy, Hans Richter and Rudolf Kurtz.

Post-1945 editions of Traub's bibliography show the 1940 version to have faithfully upheld Nazi censorship codes in its omission of Jewish writings, for instance, or other blacklisted books.[33] Nonetheless, the bibliography's broad scope (it includes not only scholarly works, but trade and industry publications, official reports, amateur film-making guides, fan literature and other popular ephemera) suggests that film-critical debate through the 1930s may have exhibited a diversity that only few histories acknowledge in their accounts of Third Reich film.

My attempt in *Dietrich's Ghosts* therefore has been at every turn to reconstruct something of the interplay that Third Reich cinema apparently sustained, even after Goebbels' 1936 Decree, between film theory, film criticism or 'commentary', the discrete film text, and broader systems of cinematic representation. My particular focus is on the efforts of film theorists after 1933 to elaborate for German cinema a film aesthetic that would legitimate and help creatively form a new National Socialist popular film art. Debates on film's relation to aesthetics, as I hope to show, were often heated and conflictual, pitting cultural conservatives (Joseph Gregor, Gottfried Müller, Fedor Stepun) against such 'modernist' figures as Bruno Rehlinger, Ernst Iros, or Günter Groll. For the former, film's claim to a status as legitimate art could be realised only if the medium drew for its formal construction on theatre's 'dramaturgical laws'. Thus the film director Wolfgang Liebeneiner, in his introduction to Gottfried Müller's 1941 *Dramaturgie des Theaters, des Hörspiels und des Films* (*The Dramaturgy of Theatre, the Radio Play, and Film*), insists that it is on 'the application to film of the eternally valid rules of dramaturgy' that 'the future', indeed 'the very existence of German film' depends.[34]

For the modernists, by contrast, film's future lay in the identification and application of inner laws deriving from the material specificities of the medium itself. Thus Bruno Rehlinger, for instance, followed the Weimar modernists, especially Rudolf Arnheim and Béla Balázs, in attempting to elaborate for film a modernised aesthetics grounded in montage, the close-up, and other 'grammatical' elements particular to what Balázs had termed the language of film.[35] Ernst Iros similarly opens his volume *Wesen und Dramaturgie des Films* (*The Nature and Dramaturgy of Film*, 1938) with a challenge to aestheticians, film practitioners and audiences to play their part in elaborating what remained, he claimed, an underdeveloped aesthetics of film. The sound film, he wrote, had returned film to its early reliance on cheap sensation, which he saw as represented among other phenomena by the cult of the star.[36] In what was by far the most extensive of late 1930s revisions of Weimar film aesthetics, Iros traced traditions in eighteenth- and nineteenth-century aesthetics that might permit him to elaborate 'aesthetic values and standards' which would in turn lend 'grammatical discipline' to the infant medium of film.[37] Writing at the high point of German cinema's success as a popular mass medium, Béla Balázs had pleaded for film theory as a mode of meaning production (*Sinngebung*) that would equip film for 'self-defence' against the 'chaos' of a culture devoid of 'soul'.[38] For Iros, too, aesthetic theory was to provide for film what he termed a form of 'armour' against the emotional volatility and rampant sensationalism of mass culture in general, and in particular of film.[39]

In *Dietrich's Ghosts*, I draw not only on Iros, but on the range of contemporary critics and theorists for whom his work is symptomatic, committed as all these writers were to film-theoretical production as 'armour' against a cinematic system perceived as rooted dangerously on the one hand in Weimar modernism, on the other in the 'un-German' spectacle of Hollywood film. Diverse as the writings to which I refer may appear, they share two common features. The first is their shared recourse to Weimar film theory, in particular the writings of Richter, Arnheim and Balázs, as the most sophisticated available antecedents for a new aesthetics of German film. The ambivalence evoked by the likes of Hans Richter (whose writings on rhythm Rehlinger, among others, much admired), or Balázs, whose work on the film grammar and the close-up enjoyed similarly influential status among Third Reich writers, was countered in post-1933 writing, I set out secondly to show, by rhetorical slippages that shifted Weimar film theory from its modernist connections, and resituated the film medium phantasmagorically within the lost utopia of idealist art. For Siegfried Kracauer – a figure of whose writings for the *Frankfurter Zeitung* Third Reich critics were surely aware – modern mass culture had rendered 'naïve' the 'misuse of concepts such as personality, inwardness, tragedy, and so on – terms that in themselves certainly refer to lofty ideas, but that have lost much of their scope, along with their supporting foundations, due to social changes'.[40] Critics after 1933, by contrast, railed against the modernism of surfaces defended by Kracauer as modernity's most authentic representational mode. In place of what the *Reichsfilmblatt* editor and prominent critic Felix Henseleit called the 'gold and silver of superficial events', Third Reich film theory aspired to reconstruct an idealist film art organised around 'content' and what Henseleit called those 'compelling ideas' that 'manifest themselves from time to time in works of art' – here, specifically in film.[41]

KANT THROUGH THIRD REICH EYES

We arrive, at this point, at a further methodological move that I make in *Dietrich's Ghosts*. At various points in this book, I return to Kant – specifically to Kant's aesthetic theories, as elucidated in his *Kritik der Urteilskraft* (*Critique of the Power of Judgement*, 1790), and his *Betrachtungen über das Gefühl des Schönen und Erhabenen* (*Observations on the Feeling of the Beautiful and the Sublime*, 1764) – and offer readings of Third Reich cinematic phenomena through neo-Kantian eyes. There is a twofold rationale for what may at first sight seem a surprising recourse to a figurehead of German Enlightenment in a study of German fascism on film. The turn to Kant arises, firstly, out of my attempt throughout this book to reconstruct, via the panoply of textual materials that provide the discursive context for Third Reich film, what the anthropologist Mary Douglas might call cinema's 'thought collective': its founding assumptions, symbolic distinctions and correspondences, the metaphorical constructs and narrative tropes through which practitioners, theorists and audiences alike conceptualised and experienced cinema after 1933.[42] Inside that collective world, I have encountered not only that pervasive nostalgia for pre-twentieth-century modes of aesthetic experience of which Kracauer writes, but a nostalgia also (and Kracauer observes this too) for a critical vocabulary that could frame contemporary aesthetic experience within the idealist categories of the beautiful and the sublime.

In what follows, then, I am in the first instance making what Douglas might recognise as an anthropological move towards an understanding of Third Reich film within the terms of the critical discourse of its time. But there is also a second impulse underpinning my location of *Dietrich's Ghosts* within the framework of the beautiful and the sublime. True, within the plural and internally contradictory field of Third Reich film-critical debate, the aesthetics of sublimity was regularly challenged, in particular by calls for a popular (*volkstümlich*) realism that foregrounded not the grandiose or the terrible, but the familiar, the local and the known. The privileging of a realism with a human face that might overcome the 'cult of surface phenomena' associated with Weimar and Hollywood film, was visible not only in film-critical debates, but in film genres and star images cast in a representational mould that I do not discuss at length in *Dietrich's Ghosts*.[43] Signal absences from this book include therefore Heinz Rühmann's comedies of the 'little man'; the girl-next-door romances of Ilse Werner; or the rough-and-tumble backstage musicals of the Hungarian 'heart-with-paprika' star Marika Rökk.

But there are reasons for this omission. Sabine Hake writes that the category of the *volkstümlich* with which Rühmann *et al.* were associated was mobilised by 'film critics, journalists, scholars and officials from the Propaganda Ministry' not to describe a 'film-specific' representational mode, but as a category of film *reception* that was most highly prized for its 'elevation of the motion-picture audience to a model of the racial community, the *Volksgemeinschaft*'.[44] Ideology and the aesthetic converge in the *volkstümlich*, in other words, through the capacities of both to convey an experience of belongingness to race and nation. In the course of this book, we will see in repeated evocations of the cinematic beautiful and the sublime a similar impulse to encapsulate an experience of fusion with the Nazi racial state. But my shift from the popular, to these apparently more elevated registers of aesthetic experience, allows a perception of one ideological dimension of Nazi film art that is not centrally addressed in debates on the popular/*volkstümlich* in film art. Already in Kant (as we see in more detail in Chapter 5), 'beauty' was seen to display a capacity to produce social cohesion through its promotion of pleasure in a social order that mirrored the harmony and aesthetic order of the beautiful in Nature. The emphasis discernible in Kant on the socio-political dimensions of the aesthetic had made his work, moreover, a focus of fierce ideological struggle long before the appropriations I trace below of Kant's aesthetic theory for National Socialist film art. Already at the turn of the century, such left-liberal thinkers as Hermann Cohen and other 'Marburg neo-Kantians' had built their plea for an 'ethical-humanitarian socialism' around a Kant whose writings they considered emblematic of the 'cosmopolitan humanity' of German Enlightenment. Early theorists of the racial *Volk* (Max Hildebert Boehm, Bruno Bauch) focused analogously (if perversely) on a rather different Kant, conceived this time as the bearer of an idealist tradition that stressed the 'integrative force of German intellectual and cultural history'.[45]

STRUCTURE OF THE BOOK

This, moreover, is the Kant we encounter in *Dietrich's Ghosts* as the origin – perversely again – of a *völkisch* aesthetic for Third Reich film. In Chapter 1, I show for instance how the appropriation of Kantian idealism for *völkisch* nationalism occurred in Third Reich film through a racialisation of the genius myth. Look-

ing first at internal industry reforms that aligned the studios in structural terms
with Goebbels' project for a new National Socialist film art, I suggest that both
ideology and industry practice cohered around the concept of the artistic 'personality' as both a leader figure in the political-ideological sense, and as the
embodiment of a racialised version of the genius figure. Here, I use two specific
instances – the managerial reconstruction of the studios around new 'artistic
committees' (*Kunstausschüsse*) after 1936, and the project for a German Film
Academy from 1937 on – to exemplify what are, I suggest, broader efforts to
construct a German industry in thrall to the 'personality principle' as the ideological pivot for a reconstructed Third Reich film art. That exploration of
'personality' continues in Chapter 2, as I move on to show how the resurrection
of idealist aesthetics for film occurred also through a re-theorisation of actorly
performance as an ideal fusion of actorly 'soul' and dramatic form. Performance
practice in both theatre and film, I suggest, was framed theoretically by a physiognomic conception of the actor's face and body indebted in part to Béla
Balázs, but recuperating Balázs for National Socialist film art via a mélange of
race theory and bourgeois aesthetics that, again, had at its heart the 'personality
principle' to which I allude in Chapter 1.

The relation of aesthetics to the ideologico-political is not, however, confined
to aesthetic theory's function as a legitimating discourse for artistic practices that
occur in a separate and discrete realm (Third Reich acting theory as ideological
support to specific performance modes, and so on). It is a peculiarity of Kant's
Kritik der Urteilskraft that he describes the sublime in particular in metaphors
of the body and of objects in space – thus the sublime 'vibrates', and takes effect
in the body insofar as it makes us, 'considered as natural beings, recognise our
physical powerlessness'.[46] Yet at the same time, he insists that the experience of
sublimity does not depend on, indeed it negates bodily sensation; for 'that is
sublime which pleases immediately by its resistance to the interest of the
senses'.[47] In Chapter 3, I set out to explore how Third Reich cinematic practice
attempted a resolution of this tension in idealist aesthetics between body and
mind through an organisation of cinematic space (the cinema auditorium) that
dissolved the body of the spectator into the sublime body of a fantasised *Volk*.
My focus here is on the way in which changing exhibition practices – new pricing policies, cinema refurbishment, innovations in the dramaturgy of film
programmes, and so on – reorganised the space-time relations of film reception
in ways designed to generate an audience experience of film spectatorship both
as an encounter with high art, and as an experience of fusion within the *Volksgemeinschaft in nuce* that was the cinema audience.

Moving on to Chapter 4, I consider as a further instance of the redefinition
of film within the terms of a neo-Kantian aesthetic the place in Third Reich film

of the personality in his manifestation as film auteur and star. I argue through-out this book that it was through specific aesthetic strategies that film practitioners after 1933 sought to evince in film audiences attitudes of awe, admiration and reverence that are central not only to Kantian aesthetics, but also to fascist politics in the cultural domain. Thus Chapter 4 considers issues of film style, first in relation to the textual construction of Carl Froelich as auteur-personality, and second, of the actor Emil Jannings in his performance for Carl Froelich's *Traumulus* (*Little Dreamer*, 1936): a film whose Romantic-pictorial *mise en scène*, I suggest, positioned Jannings as the focus for an experi-ence of what I term fascism's masculinised '*völkisch* sublime'.

Chapter 5 shifts from masculine to feminine, from Germany to Hollywood, and from the sublime to the beautiful in its consideration of one of Third Reich film's most troublesome figures of ambivalence, the émigré star Marlene Diet-rich. Despite her 1930 emigration, her refusal to return to Germany, and her embracing in 1939 of US citizenship, Dietrich remains important in two senses for a study of Third Reich film. The continuing popularity of her Hollywood films among 1930s German audiences offers, first, a symptomatic reminder of the ambiguities surrounding industry and audience relationships with Holly-wood throughout the Nazi regime's formative years. Recent studies of Hollywood in Germany have shown how pervasive was Hollywood's influence as German film's main market competitor, and as a source of visual and narra-tive models for German cinema – including for German stars.[48] Dietrich's transnationalism, her status simultaneously as German and American star, Hol-lywood femme fatale and Weimar vamp, situated 'Marlene' herself as a source of ideological trouble (why *would* she not return?), and located her image as a prime focus for Third Reich aesthetic debates on a specifically German mode of film stardom. In a study of Dietrich's German reception, I set out therefore in Chapter 5 to show how contemporary criticism mobilised the aesthetic cat-egory of the beautiful, in an effort, in the face of a Dietrich who stubbornly refused to return to Germany, to recuperate her symbolically at least for Ger-man film art.

The political dimensions of that aesthetic reclamation are already evident in Kant's third *Critique*. For Kant, as I indicated above, beauty was allied to social order in the sense that it restored to social subjects an experience of pleasure in the harmonious affective totality that arises from an encounter with the beauti-ful in art. Third Reich commentary on Dietrich, I contend, sought a similar politico-ideological stabilisation when it attempted to relocate her image within a discourse of the beautiful in German film. It is indicative not only of the ideo-logical ambivalence of the Third Reich's film-aesthetic project, but of the fundamental ambiguity that surrounds all aesthetic experience that these efforts at an ideological recuperation of Dietrich apparently failed. Not only did Dietrich herself refuse to return to Nazi Germany, re-entering the country only at the end of the war as a US citizen and troop entertainer for 'enemy' GIs; that the *image* of Dietrich and her émigré compatriots also remained a source of trouble for Third Reich film aesthetics is evidenced, I propose in Chapter 6, by the surfacing in German star representation after 1933 of a sequence of 'Dietrich's ghosts': uncanny doubles of émigré actors and stars exiled or purged from the industry after 1933. It has often been observed that Third Reich stars were modelled in part as replicas of Hollywood counterparts, 'Germanicised American' prototypes of a hybrid star aesthetic, as Karsten Witte once described them.[49] As facsmilies or doubles of American counterparts, stars like Marika Rökk, Jenny Jugo or Viktor de Kowa encapsulated the continuing ambivalence surrounding German responses to US stars. Hollywood stars were admired for their spectacular quality, but denigrated also for their status as inauthentic, serially produced doubles or replicas, the manufactured products of a film industry oriented around profit, not art. German stars fashioned in Hollywood's image therefore always risked embodying a profane commercialism that Third Reich film commentary abhorred. But German stars were uncanny doubles also in a second, psycho-symbolic sense, representing as they often did an imagined return to German screens of figures 'repressed' through mass purges and censorship. Thus the star on whom I focus in Chapters 6 and 7, Zarah Leander, was famously touted as a substitute for two departed Weimar idols, Greta Garbo (who had left for Hollywood after starring in G. W. Pabst's *Die Freudlose Gasse/The Joyless Street*, 1925), and Marlene Dietrich.

These concluding chapters offer an account of Leander, then, that both explores her status as 'Dietrich's ghost', and at the same time investigates how she became (more successfully than Dietrich) the emblem of a star aesthetic of a supposedly specifically German kind. The key feature of Leander's star persona was not, as in Dietrich's case, the 'beauty' of her image, but rather a unique, contralto-baritone singing voice that Third Reich critics celebrated as touching artistic heights unprecedented in German sound film. This emphasis on vocal performance, I finally propose, locates Leander as the cinematic vehicle for a post-Kantian sublime that is both cognate with, and distinct from the 'sublimity' identified as the subject-effect evinced by Froelich and Jannings in Chapter 4. It is, I suggest in Chapter 7, Leander's femininity that allows her to function, in the late 1930s reception context of accelerating militarisation and the outbreak of war, as the conduit for sublimity in its more terrifying aspect, as the sublime experience of war.

What I suggest in Chapter 7 is, then, that Leander's voice entered, in the late 1930s, a savage dialogue with those visual and aural representations (newsreels, press coverage, radio and so on) with which it was juxtaposed in the specific reception context of early wartime popular film. A final comment must be made here on periodisation. My readings of Leander and other Third Reich stars have critical purchase on the aesthetics of film production and reception *primarily*, and in some cases *only* in the specific reception context of the late 1930s and early 1940s. Two factors demand that strict delimiting of historical period. First, my emphasis throughout *Dietrich's Ghosts* is on the aesthetic as a set of somatic, imaginative and cognitive experiences that arise through the conjunction in determinate historical moments of historically particular film-aesthetic apparatuses and artistic modes. Outside the context of a dramaturgy of film programming that positioned her films as the climax to newsreel coverage of war, Leander's singing voice on film, for instance, has historically evoked quite different modes of spectatorial response from the sublime violence I here describe. Witness, for instance, the important studies of Leander's significance for gay audiences in Germany and elsewhere – studies that regularly stress the historical particularity of that response, and its specific relation to conditions of reception in the post-war period from 1945 onwards.[50] Leander did not, furthermore, retain after 1941–2 her status as Dietrich's most plausible substitute in Third Reich film. Future studies of Third Reich stars might well trace other figures (Marika Rökk is one) whose mounting popularity after 1940 demonstrates a shift in popular aesthetics away from the 'sublimity' embodied by Leander, and towards a more vulgar, spectacular or sensationalist mode. Certainly – and this is the second factor determining my periodisation here – Germany's changing political and military fortunes after 1939 produced concomitant film-aesthetic shifts, briefly (1939–42) to what Karsten Witte terms a looser, more ideologically permeable creative mode, later – after Stalingrad and the shift in gear to 'total war' – to an (entirely anti-Kantian) celebration of mass-cultural spectacle in such titles as *Kolberg* (1943–4), *Münchhausen* (1943) and *Die Frau meiner Träume* (*The Woman of my Dreams*, 1944). Film policy, too, shifted focus after 1939–40 from overblown projects for a new film art, to a more pragmatic emphasis on mass entertainment; hence, for instance, the demise of the German Film Academy, and the gradual withering of film-theoretical debate on a new aesthetics for Third Reich film. The fate of the 1930s film theorist Ernst Iros is emblematic here. After a long career in Germany, first as a minor author and journalist, late as a film practitioner (he worked as story editor-in-chief for Emelka), he began writing his *Wesen und Dramaturgie des Films* in 1934, basing the work on his lectures at the Munich Acting and Film School from the mid-1920s on. In 1935, however, Iros was refused a licence to work in the German industry; he departed shortly afterwards for Switzerland, where he lived as an exile until his death in 1953.[51] In Germany, Iros and his contemporaries were supplanted from the late 1930s onwards by film theorists and critics (Fritz Hippler, Otto Kriegk) whose focus was centrally on the ideological, not the aesthetic dimensions of Third Reich film. This shift in the conceptual landscape of Third Reich film is, then, a final reason for the limited historical reach of *Dietrich's Ghosts*. The book begins in 1930, but extends no further than Zarah Leander's greatest German success, *Die grosse Liebe* (*The Great Love*, 1942). It will be for readers and other historians to assess the value for studies of Third Reich film's later years of my account of National Socialism's cinematic beautiful or (*völkisch*, gendered) sublime. That account is framed, as I explain above, within a larger survey of Nazism's early 1930s project for a new film art; and it is to that project, as well as to its philosophical underpinning in the personality principle, that we now turn.

NOTES

1. *Gleichschaltung* is commonly, though rather unsatisfactorily translated as 'co-ordination', and refers to the process whereby all public institutions were made subject after 1933 to NSDAP control.
2. Cited in David Welch, *Propaganda and the German Cinema 1933–1945* (Oxford: Clarendon, 1983), pp. 36–7. Among the best English-language overviews of these processes of institutional restructuring is Julian Petley's *Capital and Culture. German Cinema 1933–45* (London: BFI, 1979), pp. 47–94.
3. Martin Loiperdinger, 'State Legislation, Censorship and Funding', in Tim Bergfelder, Erica Carter and Deniz Göktürk (eds), *The German Cinema Book* (London: BFI, 2002), p. 152.
4. See Gerd Albrecht, *Nationalsozialistische Filmpolitik. Eine soziologische Untersuching über die Spielfilme des Dritten Reichs* (Stuttgart: Ferdinand Enke, 1969); idem, *Der Film im Dritten Reich. Eine Dokumentation* (Karlsruhe: Schauburg, 1979); Jürgen Spiker, *Film und Kapital* (Berlin: Volker Spiess, 1975); Joseph Wulf, *Theater und Film im Dritten Reich. Eine Dokumentation* (Frankfurt am Main, Berlin and Vienna: Ullstein, 1966); also Erwin Leiser, *Nazi Cinema*, Gertrud Mander and David Wilson (trans.) (London: Secker & Warburg, 1975, orig. 1968); David Welch, *Propaganda and the German Cinema*, Francis Courtade and Pierre Cadars, *Histoire du Cinéma Nazi* (Paris: Eric Losfeld, 1972).
5. Leiser, *Nazi Cinema*, p. 19. The term 'manifest intention' is from Welch, *Propaganda and the German Cinema*, p. 44.
6. Sabine Hake, *Popular Cinema of the Third Reich* (Austin: University of Texas Press, 2001), p. vii; Gerd Albrecht and Deutsches Institut für Filmkunde (eds), *Die Großen Filmerfolge. Vom Blauen Engel bis Otto, der Film. Die erfolgreichsten Filme vom Beginn des Tonfilms bis heute* (Ebersberg: Edition Achteinhalb, 1985), pp. 33, 41 and 45.

7. See, for example, Klaus Kriemeier, *Die Ufa-Story. Geschichte eines Filmkonzerns* (Munich: Hanser, 1992); Erika Wottrich, *Deutsche Universal. Transatlantische Verleih- und Produktionsstrategien eines Hollywood-Studios in den 20er und 30er Jahren* (Munich: edition text+kritik, 2001); Jan Distelmeyer (ed.), *Tonfilmfrieden/Tonfilmkrieg. Die Geschichte der Tobis vom Technik-Syndikat zum Staatskonzern* (Munich: edition text+kritik, 2003).

8. Eric Rentschler, *The Ministry of Illusion. Nazi Cinema and its Afterlife* (Cambridge, MA and London: Harvard University Press, 1996), p. 15.

9. Linda Schulte-Sasse, *Entertaining the Third Reich. Illusions of Wholeness in Nazi Cinema* (Durham and London: Duke University Press, 1996), p. 12; see also Stephen Lowry, *Pathos und Politik. Ideologie in Spielfilmen des Nationalsozialismus* (Tübingen: Niemeyer, 1991).

10. An important exception here is Julian Petley, who drew in his 1979 *Capital and Culture* on the structuralist ideology critique of Althusser, Lacan and Poulantzas to explore 'the heterogeneity of ideological representations' in Third Reich film: see Petley, *Capital and Culture*, p. 21 and *passim*.

11. Hake, *Popular Cinema*, p. ix.

12. See, for example, Lutz Koepnick, *The Dark Mirror. German Cinema between Hitler and Hollywood* (Berkeley and Los Angeles: University of California Press, 2002); Markus Spieker, *Hollywood unterm Hakenkreuz. Der amerikanische Spielfilm im Dritten Reich* (Trier: Wissenschaftlicher Verlag, 1999).

13. William Uricchio and Roberta Pearson, *Reframing Culture. The Case of the Vitagraph Quality Films* (Princeton: Princeton University Press, 1993), p. 6.

14. Antonio Gramsci, *Selections from the Prison Notebooks of Antonio Gramsci*, Quintin Hoare and Geoffrey Nowell-Smith (trans. and eds) (New York: International Publishers, 1971), p. 12: cited in Uricchio and Pearson, *Reframing Culture*, p. 8.

15. Uricchio and Pearson, *Reframing Culture*, p. 8.

16. For a helpful overview of historical debates on the concept of totalitarianism and its application to National Socialism, see Ian Kershaw, *The Nazi Dictatorship*, (London: Arnold, 2002), fourth edition, chs 1 and 2.

17. Rentschler, *The Ministry of Illusion*, p. 20.

18. Ibid., p. 21; Philippe Lacoue-Labarthe, *Heidegger, Art and Politics*, Chris Turner (trans.) (Oxford: Blackwell, 1990), p. 64.

19. Joseph Goebbels, speech at the official opening of the *Reich* Chamber of Culture, 15 November 1933. Quoted in Gerd Albrecht, *Der Film im Dritten Reich*, p. 267.

20. Speech in the Krolloper to the *Reichsfachschaft Film*, 9 February 1934. Quoted in ibid., p. 267.

21. Walter Benjamin, 'The Work of Art in the Age of Mechanical Reproduction', in idem, *Illuminations*, Harry Zohn (trans.), Hannah Arendt (ed.) (London: Fontana, 1992, orig. 1936), pp. 234–5.

22. See, for example, the trade journal *Der Film*'s account of Goebbels' speech in the Berlin Kaiserhof, 28 March 1933, in 'Es besteht kein Anlaß zur Unsicherheit', *Der Film* (FL), 4 April 1933.

23. 'Filmkünstler bekennen sich zum Führer', *Film-Kurier* (FK), 26 March 1936.

24. Hans Steinbach, 'Der Theaterbesitzer auf der Schulbank', in Landesverband Berlin-Brandenburg-Grenzmark, e.V., *Filmtheaterführung. Die Vorträge des ersten Schulungsjahres 1934/5 der Fachschule der Filmtheaterbesitzer* (Berlin: Neue Film-Kurier Verlagsgesellschaft, 1935), p. 7.

25. Karl Ritter, 'Vom Wesen der Filmkunst', in Oswald Lehnich (ed.), *Jahrbuch der Reichsfilmkammer 1938* (Berlin: Max Hesses, 1938), pp. 49–50.

26. 'Oberprüfstelle über *Song of Songs*', FK, 16 March 1934.

27. Raymond Williams, *Marxism and Literature* (Oxford: Oxford University Press, 1977), pp. 112–13; cited in Uricchio and Pearson, *Reframing Culture*, p. 20.

28. The groundbreaking work here was Detlef J. K. Peukert, *Inside Nazi Germany. Conformity, Opposition and Racism in Everyday Life*, Richard Deveson (trans.) (Harmondsworth: Penguin, 1987).

29. Sabine Hake, *The Cinema's Third Machine. Writing on Film in Germany 1907–1933*. (Lincoln and London: University of Nebraska Press, 1993), especially Introduction, pp. ixff.

30. Two signal exceptions to this rule are Hake, *Popular Cinema* and Kurt Denzer, *Untersuchungen zur Filmdramaturgie des Dritten Reiches* (unpublished doctoral thesis, University of Kiel, 1970).

31. Hans Traub and Hanns Wilhelm Lavies, *Das deutsche Filmschrifttum. Eine Bibliographie der Bücher und Zeitschriften über das Filmwesen* (Leipzig: Hiersemann, 1940).

32. Ibid., p. 15.

33. An updated edition of the bibliography was published in 1980 under the editorship of Herbert Birett: see Hans Traub, *Das deutsche Filmschrifttum* (Stuttgart: Hiesermann, 1980).

34. Wolfgang Liebeneiner, 'Spielleiter und Dichter', in Gottfried Müller, *Dramaturgie des Theaters, des Hörspiels und des Films* (Würzburg: Konrad Triltsch, 1962, orig. 1941), pp. 21–2.

35. See Bruno Rehlinger, *Der Begriff Filmisch* (Emsdetten: Lechte, 1938).

36. Ernst Iros, *Wesen und Dramaturgie des Films* (Zürich and Leipzig: Max Niehaus, 1938), p. 4.

37. Ibid., p. 5.

38. Béla Balázs, *Der sichtbare Mensch oder die Kultur des Films* (Vienna and Leipzig: Deutsch-österreichischer Verlag, 1924), p. 13.

39. Iros, *Wesen und Dramaturgie*, p. 5.

40. Siegfried Kracauer, 'The Cult of Distraction', in idem, *The Mass Ornament. Weimar*

Essays, Thomas Levin (trans. and ed.) (Cambridge, MA and London: Harvard University Press, 1995), p. 326.

41. Felix Henseleit, 'Gestern und heute', in idem, ed., *Der Film und seine Welt. Reichsfilmblatt-Almanach 1933* (Berlin: Photokino-Verlag, 1933), pp. 20–22.

42. Mary Douglas, *How Institutions Think* (London: Routledge & Kegan Paul, 1987), p. 12. Douglas is here borrowing a term from the philosopher of science Ludwig Fleck.

43. Quote from Hake, *Popular Cinema*, p. 181.

44. Ibid., p. 173.

45. I am indebted to Charlotte Klonk for drawing my attention to Christian Tilitzki's detailed account of ideological appropriations of Kant after 1918: see Tilitzki, *Die deutsche Universitätsphilsophie in der Weimarer Republik und im Dritten Reich* (Berlin: Akademie Verlag, 2002), pp. 478, 486 and *passim*.

46. Immanuel Kant, *Critique of the Power of Judgement*, Paul Guyer (trans. and ed.), Eric Matthews (trans.) (Cambridge: Cambridge University Press, 2000, orig. 1790), p. 145.

47. Ibid., p. 150.

48. See Koepnick, *The Dark Mirror*, and Spieker, *Hollywood unterm Hakenkreuz*; also Karsten Witte, *Lachende Erben, Toller Tag* (Berlin: Vorwerk 8, 1995), pp. 102–21.

49. Witte, *Lachende Erben*, p. 112.

50. See Alice Kuzniar, '"Now I have a Different Desire": Transgender Specularity in Zarah Leander and R. W. Fassbinder', in idem, *The Queer German Cinema* (Stanford: Stanford University Press, 2000), pp. 57–87; and Brian Currid, '"Es war so wunderbar!" Zarah Leander, ihre schwulen Fans, und die Gegenöffentlichkeit der Erinnerung', *montage/av*, vol. 7, no. 1, 1998, pp. 57–93.

51. See Martin Schlappner, 'Vorwort', in Ernst Iros, *Wesen und Dramaturgie des Films*, (Zürich: Die Arche, 1957), second edition, pp. 24–6.

I

Film as Art: A Cinema of Personality

When the National Socialists seized power in Germany in January 1933, the nation's film industry was in a state of commercial and cultural crisis. Already ten years earlier, currency reform and changes in quota law had shaken the economic foundations of German film production by exposing the industry for the first time since the end of World War I to serious competition from abroad. The advent of the sound film in the late 1920s further destabilised an already weakened industry. The total costs of the transition to sound – which included for example the re-equipping, or sometimes the wholesale rebuilding of studios, restaffing with new personnel, the refurbishment of film theatres, and rising costs for the production of export copies – have been estimated at between 50 and 55 million *Reichsmark* for the transitional period 1927–8 to 1932.[1] The prospects for recouping figures of this magnitude from box-office takings, moreover, were slim. In the depression years of 1929 to 1932, audience figures in Germany declined by an estimated 25 per cent, producing a 'wave of company liquidations' in the period immediately preceding Nazi rule.[2]

Helmut Korte's conclusion, in his study of the feature film in the last years of the Weimar Republic, is that the National Socialists in 1933 encountered a 'severely financially weakened and ... largely compliant film industry that ... looked to the state for decisive intervention, indeed for "salvation"'.[3] That perception is certainly supported by accounts of the first major public encounter between regime and industry, a meeting that took place on the occasion of Goebbels' speech as newly appointed *Reich* Minister for Propaganda and Popular Enlightenment in the Berlin Kaiserhof on 28 March 1933. Goebbels' address to an audience comprising 'prominent figures from all sectors of the film industry and filmmaking', as well as a vociferous band of activists from Alfred Rosenberg's Kampfbund für deutsche Kultur (League of Struggle for German Culture), was preceded by obsequious welcoming speeches from key film industry figures. Carl Froelich, whom we will meet again in his capacity as film director later in this chapter, spoke in the Kaiserhof as President of the

Dachorganisation der deutschen Filmwirtschaft (Umbrella Organisation for the German Film Industry: DACHO). Froelich named 28 March as a 'memorable day' in the history of German cinema, marking as it did the first public commitment of a German government to 'the art of film'. Apparently more contentiously (there are reports of heckling), Ludwig Klitzsch, Director-General of Ufa, promised a 'willingness to cooperate' on Ufa's behalf, while the Nazi Adolf Engl, representing the Reichsverband deutscher Filmtheater (Reich Association of German Exhibitors) – an organisation that had, in his words, 'always considered itself a mediator of cultural values' – committed German exhibitors to 'championing' the ideas of the new state.

Opening speeches at the Kaiserhof event, then, emphasised the need for cultural and aesthetic transformation within the context of the Nazi state as prerequisites for the revival of German film. That these contributions were mere scene-setting for the Reichminister's entrance (the trade journal *Der Film* called the opening speeches 'dry' in both content and form) became evident when Goebbels himself finally took to the podium.[4] His initial naming of 'the current crisis' as 'ideal' not 'material' in nature was, admittedly, hardly innovative. Attempts at an idealist reform of the film medium dated back to the cinema reform movements of the 1910s and 1920s, and had found echoes in late Weimar debates over film-as-art versus film as commerce or kitsch. But Goebbels galvanised his audience – *Der Film* reports rapturous applause – when he reframed these older categories of film-aesthetic debate within a more emotive opposition: art versus *danger*. 'I want to use a number of examples,' he began, 'to show what it is that makes a film artistic, and what makes it dangerous'.[5]

In Third Reich film historiography, Goebbels' speeches are often used to preface studies of policy shifts within the broader scenario of Nazism's ever tighter political and ideological control of German cinema. To this purpose, the Kaiserhof address lends itself well. It is among the earliest public records of Goebbels' intention – phrased here, with characteristically treacherous understatement – to 'intervene' in the film industry and to 'regulate' the 'effects' of film in its more 'dangerous' manifestations.[6] The rapid *Gleichschaltung* of the industry, the racial and political purging of film personnel that this entailed, the revision of film legislation (the 1920 *Reichslichtspielgesetz*) to make provision for pre-production censorship alongside the already generous censorship privileges accorded to the German state: all this was presaged, albeit often in the vaguest of terms, by the Kaiserhof speech.[7]

In what follows, however, I want to focus on a second and often critically underestimated aspect of the Kaiserhof event. When, towards the end of the speech, Goebbels recognises film as subject to 'the inner laws of art itself', this is more than mere sophistry, a ploy to disguise his (undoubtedly malign) ideological intent. This demand for an aesthetic rebirth of German cinema – a demand that found echoes in all areas of film-cultural debate through the 1930s – was certainly on one level what the film historian Klaus Kreimeier terms a 'rhetoric of legitimation' for the state-controlled film industry of the Third Reich.[8] At the same time, as I seek to demonstrate in this book, the transformation of aesthetic practice to which Goebbels and others 'rhetorically' aspired was also a material and determining element in the Nazis' achievement of state control in the arena of film.

In the opening four chapters, then, I proceed from an assumption borrowed from Walter Benjamin, which is that what was historically innovative in National Socialism was its forging of an intimate bond between aesthetics and the political.[9] Benjamin's contention was realised, I will argue, in Third Reich film through a variety of transformations in film production and reception that aimed to establish German cinema as the apotheosis of Nazism's new national popular art. The Nazis' organisational restructuring of German cinema through the 1930s is commonly assumed to have occurred in two stages. In the first phase, covering a four-year period roughly from 1933 to 1937, the Nazis' attention focused on extending state control of the industry through a combination of organisational restructuring (*Gleichschaltung*), state funding via the Filmkreditbank, political and racial purging, tightened censorship and other measures. In a second phase, the emphasis shifted towards the establishment of a state monopoly through a gradual, and initially covert, nationalisation of the industry via the Cautio Treuhand trust company.[10]

In each of these phases, however, as I seek to show, restructuring at the level of political economy went hand in hand with cultural policies designed to realise Goebbels' goal of a rejuvenated film art. That the state functioned after 1933, not merely as a repressive apparatus exercising totalitarian control over the film industry, but also as the source of a series of generative measures designed to stimulate modes of artistic production that were consonant with fascism's aesthetic aims, is demonstrated, I will argue, by numerous policy initiatives from mid-decade on, including the promotion of creative practitioners to powerful managerial positions within the industry, training initiatives to bring on a new generation of creative personnel, and interventions into exhibition practice designed to mould public taste to the shapes and patterns of an (apparently) quintessentially German film aesthetic.

Again, Goebbels' speeches are illuminating here. In his 1937 address to the *Reich* Film Chamber – an annual event in which the Propaganda Minister reviewed past 'progress' and specified future plans – he presents his own vision of a two-phase development in Nazi film policy after 1933 when he asserts:

The task that faces us now is no longer organisational in nature. Last year, I was able to demand that artists be made members of company boards. Easy enough! The year before that, I could demand that scripts be ready at an earlier point, and that production continue throughout the year ... The year before that, I could say, 'We must raise box office figures by 50 or 60 million.' This is hardly difficult! But this time around, we face programmatic demands of an artistic nature.[11]

Goebbels has already specified earlier in this address the force on which he will draw to meet the 'programmatic' artistic demands to which he now gives precedence: 'Even in film, as in all other fields, it is true to say that any work can in the long term be sustained only by personality. In the long run, it is towering, fascinating and magnetic personality that sustains film.'[12]

The 'programmatic' restructuring of German cinema as a high art form from the mid-1930s on was to pivot, then, around the 'towering ... personality' as its fulcrum and centre. What then are we to make of the concept of personality mobilised here? What are its origins, its ideological ramifications, and it specific role in 'sustaining' the art of film?

FILM, PERSONALITY AND GENIUS

Though there has been extensive scholarship on the 'cult of personality' surrounding Hitler, few studies exist of 'personality' (*Persönlichkeit*) as a core concept in Nazism's reorganisation of cultural discourses and practices at every level – and for our purposes most significantly, in film.[13] Film-aesthetic writings of the 1930s, for instance, repeatedly centre on 'personality' as the quality that will in future distinguish German film art from Hollywood kitsch, indeed that will engineer a much desired aesthetic elevation of the film medium *tout court*. For such disparate figures as Joseph Gregor, for whom film could never aspire to the aesthetic status of theatre, and the modernist and film enthusiast Ernst Iros, in his *Wesen und Dramaturgie des Films* (*The Nature and Dramaturgy of Film*), 'personality' was the quality that would at last raise film to high art status. What Iros dubs the 'personality style' that imprints itself as what he oxymoronically calls 'content-filled form' on film art, is for Gregor a quality that has as yet been only glimpsed, never fully realised in film:

Nowhere ... have I yet been able to identify a poet [Dichter], a personality whose creation towers as far above the whole monstrous handiwork that is film as does the primitive drama of Shakespeare above his *Hamlet*, his *Midsummer Night's Dream* or his *Henry IV*. Only with the appearance of such a figure could the machine that is film acquire some higher legitimation. Such a personality would not so much draw new material into film, as use his uncontested capacity to embrace the world entire to erect a poem for the eyes and ears – a work in relation to which the comedies of a René Clair, or Chaplin's tragi-comedies, would be mere dim premonitions.[14]

The German term *Persönlichkeit* as used by Gregor and Iros differs from the English 'personality' in important respects. In the Anglophone tradition, 'personality' refers to the inner qualities of discrete individuals; as Richard Sennett stresses, personality inevitably 'var[ies] from person to person', it is the product of 'emotion and the inner nature of the person feeling'.[15] The term derives its individualist emphasis from its embedding within a long tradition of English empiricism, in which philosophical problems – issues concerning the nature of the self, its relation to the external world and so on – have conventionally been addressed as 'questions of a factual kind to be answered by psychology'.[16] The genealogy of the German *Persönlichkeit* is quite different. The term has its origins in German idealism: in Kant's 'metaphysical concept of the soul as an unobservable substance underlying ... particular mental states', or Hegel's notion that 'all finite persons are absorbed into an absolute' which transcends the individual.[17] This idealist conception of 'personality' as the transcendent quality that allows individuals to overcome social fragmentation and 'embrace the world' is evident not only in Gregor, Iros and other Third Reich film theorists; it was from the mid-19th century onwards a core concept in conservative discourse on German culture and its necessary transformation. Idealist philosophies of the subject experienced a revival from the 1880s on; and, as Geoffrey Field points out, late nineteenth-century race theorists, most particularly the Wagner disciple Houston Stewart Chamberlain, worked hard to intertwine the philosophical neo-idealism of such figures as Dilthey, Windelband or Rickert with contemporary theories of race. In Chamberlain's *Foundations of The Nineteenth Century* (1899), for instance, neo-idealism was refocused to incorporate a racialised vision of the transcendent subject as an embodiment of a 'vague, mystical ... Teutonic Spirit'.[18] As Chamberlain explicitly claims, it is through the medium of personality that what he calls 'Teutonic individuality' achieves fusion with the higher entity that is the racialised *Volk*. As he writes (with characteristic obscurity): 'if personality is the highest gift which we children of earth receive, then truly the individuality of our definite race is one of those "best" things. It alone carries along all separate personalities, as the ship is borne by the flood.'[19]

Chamberlain's work enjoyed considerable influence under National Socialism. His cultural theories were enthusiastically embraced by early Nazism's principal ideologue, Alfred Rosenberg; Nazi publicists 'made him the subject of numerous essays, speeches, radio programmes ... books [and even] doctoral dissertations' after 1933; his most influential works were republished in new popular editions; and so on.[20] The influence of Chamberlain's writing, including his 1925 *Race and Personality* is evident, too, in Hitler's *Mein Kampf*. Itself a heady pot-pourri of idealist philosophy, *völkisch* cultural history, race theory and other elements, *Mein Kampf* includes a chapter on 'Personality and . . . the Folkish State'. Here, Hitler echoes such forbears as Hegel and Meinecke when he writes of personality as the 'bearer of the state'.[21] In Hitler's *völkisch* vision, however, the racialised *Volk* replaces the Hegelian state as that metaphysical totality which transcends individual experience and lifts 'man' to a higher realm. The essence of 'man', Hitler writes, is to be found in 'blood components', and it is through mutual racial ties of 'blood' that 'personality' is bonded to the community of the nation.

The biological analogy continues with Hitler's social Darwinist comments on personality as the highest form of a humanity rigorously stratified by hierarchies of race. Vilifying 'the Jew' most particularly for his 'eternal efforts to undermine the position of the personality . . . in the host peoples', the demagogue continues, 'the folkish philosophy is basically distinguished by the fact that it not only recognises race, but with it the importance of the personality'. A cultural order built around the 'personality principle' is thus necessarily authoritarian and hierarchical, since it must 'make sure that the leadership and the highest influence in this people fall to the best minds'.[22]

In existing film histories, it is the *'Führer* principle' that is often invoked to describe the restructuring of the German film industry after 1933. Following the creation of the *Reich* Film Chamber (RFK) and its incorporation in September 1933 into the *Reich* Culture Chamber (RKK) – itself directly subject to Goebbels' authority – a situation emerged a in which 'organisationally the Führer principle prevailed', since 'the RFK was in the last analysis answerable to Goebbels and the RMVP'.[23] Julian Petley's analysis here is flawless. Yet a return not only to Hitler's *Mein Kampf*, but to the numerous Third Reich treatises on 'personality' in the racial state, suggests the need for a different critical vocabulary if we are to situate Nazi film – as this study aims to do – within the panoply of cultural discourses that surrounded and secured popular assent for Nazism's restructuring of industry and audience after 1933.

The popular purchase of Hitler's concept of personality as the 'bearer' of the racial state is in part evidenced by the popularity of *Mein Kampf* before and after 1933. Total sales during Hitler's lifetime are estimated at 8 to 9 million, with a readership far in excess of this, if account is taken of the book's status as a school primer, a must-read for party fellow-travellers, and even (after 1936) a recommended official present from registrars to bridal couples.[24] A more specific resurgence of interest in what Hitler terms 'the personality principle' is attested, moreover, by the proliferation of titles on that topic penned by conservative cultural commentators from the mid-1920s onwards. In the wake of Chamberlain's 1925 *Race and Personality*, Ludwig Klages' *Persönlichkeit. Einführung in die Charakterkunde* (*Personality. An Introduction to the Study of Character*, 1928) and Eduard Spranger's *Lebensformen. Geisteswissenschaftliche Psychologie und Ethik der Persönlichkeit* (*Life Forms. A Humanities Perspective on the Psychology and Ethics of Personality*), a seventh edition of which was published in 1930, Nazi ascendancy opened the floodgates to a new generation of *völkisch* writers (Schottky, Rothacker, Hehlmann and others) who followed Chamberlain and Hitler in situating personality as a core organising principle of the racial state.[25] As the Catholic novelist and apologist for 'personality', Albert von Trentini, put the case in 1935, there had dawned a new epoch of what he called '*Gattungspflege*' (cultivation of the species). 'Historically speaking', he continues, 'there are today ... no more individual problems ... but only problems of the collective'. In this context, what is urgently required are 'personalities' with the capacity to become the 'representative individual expression [and] the voice of that which is essential to the species'.[26]

In a later example of the genre, Permanent Secretary Franz Schlegelberger makes the same connection from personality to race when he references *Mein Kampf* on the 'idea of personality' as the foundation of the 'folkish state', then continues: 'The individualist seeks freedom and individuality in the community. The personality has attained freedom within the community and works for his people (*Volk*) as the herald of its essence.'[27] As Schlegelberger further notes, now directly citing *Mein Kampf*: 'A philosophy of life which endeavours to reject the democratic mass idea and give this earth to the best people ... must logically obey the same aristocratic principle within this people ... Thus it builds, not upon the idea of the majority, but upon the idea of personality'.[28]

In the film industry after 1933, *Mein Kampf*'s racialised 'aristocratic principle' as articulated here was realised on the one hand by organisational restructuring to bring all sectors under the Propaganda Minister's control. As Julian Petley notes, the *Reich* Film Chamber, first established in July 1933, and incorporated into the *Reich* Culture Chamber in September of that same year, implemented *Mein Kampf*'s personality principle by subordinating all sectors of the industry to Goebbels' direct control. Indeed, Petley observes, 'the RFK's *raison d'être* lay in Goebbels' determination to exercise sole responsibility over the future development of the film industry'. Since membership of the RFK was obligatory for industry workers, it also served, on the other hand, as a 'particularly efficient means' of racial and political purging.[29] A first wave of Jews, along with Left political activists and other regime scapegoats had in any case already been forced into emigration, unemployment or worse (some were sum-

marily murdered) in successive waves of political terror in the early months of
1933. The definitive decision on the exclusion of Jews and foreigners from film
was announced in a Propaganda Ministry decree of 28 June 1933, according
to which any film industry worker was to be 'a German citizen and of German
extraction'.[30] Further anti-Jewish purges followed in the wake of the Nuremberg laws in 1935, and the anti-Jewish pogroms of *Reichskristallnacht* in 1938.
Measures included not only the exclusion of Jews from work in the industry,
but a series of orders between 1935 and 1938 banning them from participation
in German film as audience members.[31]

Thus by the end of the 1930s, German cinema, like all public institutions,
had come to embody *in nuce* the racially purified and hierarchical cultural order
that *Mein Kampf* envisages. But the position of the 'personality' in cinema
specifically deserves further elaboration. Goebbels, of course, was taken to
embody in his own person the authoritarian leadership and mythical connection to the *Volk* that were the key requirements of the personality principle. But
in film, as in other areas of cultural life, 'personality' was embodied too in a
series of 'towering' figures whose stature derived not from political, but from
cultural labour in the service of the *Volk*. In the racialised philosophy of personality as it developed from the late 19th century onwards, the creative artist
was allotted a special place as what Houston Stewart Chamberlain terms a
'specifically creative mind' – a genius. For Chamberlain, 'when we are dealing
… with a purely creative activity, then Personality is everything'. But 'Personality' is only the general category applied to exceptional men. Creative artists
and writers, in Chamberlain's world-view, occupy a subset of personality, which
is 'genius'. 'No less a thinker than Kant', Chamberlain continues, 'draws our
attention to the fact that the greatest discoverer in the sphere of science differs
only in degree from the ordinary man. The Genius, on the other hand, differs
specifically.'[32]

In his *Foundations of the Nineteenth Century*, Chamberlain is quick to seek
legitimacy for his theory of genius in such illustrious antecedents as Kant and
Goethe. And indeed, he is right to claim that the modern idea of genius was an
eighteenth-century creation designed to define 'men who have everlastingly
enriched our intellectual store by powerful creations of their imagination'.[33] In
the German literary and philosophical tradition, the idea of genius first gained
widespread currency in the *Geniezeit* (genius epoch) from 1760 to the mid-
1770s. Literary historians have traced the emergence of the cult of genius to a
variety of cultural-historical shifts from the mid-18th century on, including the
gradual independence of writers from the aristocratic courts, and the development of a bourgeois reading public that provided the economic and cultural
basis for autonomous literary production. The genius concept flourished in this

period, claims Jochen Schmidt, as a prop that lent ideological legitimacy to the newly independent author; and it was embraced most eloquently by Goethe, who wrote critically on the notion of genius, but also functioned in his early drama and nature poetry as a material embodiment of the genius figure.[34] Goethe's 'Ode to Prometheus' in particular provides in the Prometheus image an enduring metaphorical figure that 'grounded the new individual conscious-ness in the individual's own productive capacity'.[35] At the same time, the poem is significant as one of a series of early works that established Goethe himself as an exemplary model of this Promethean figure of genius.[36]

When, however, Houston Stewart Chamberlain invokes Goethe as one inspi-ration for his own genius myth, his allegiance is not to the 'radical individualism' of Goethe's early work.[37] Chamberlain's debt instead is to a long tradition in German cultural philosophy that embeds the idea of genius first in ideas of nation, then of race. As Michael Beddow has observed, the 'chief critical topic' in mid-eighteenth-century Germany was 'the absence of a native literary culture and the prospects of creating one'. The idea of genius was thus tied from the beginning to a preoccupation with nation. For Goethe's early mentor Herder, for instance, original genius was always dependent on a break with outmoded, 'foreign' classical. Herder, by contrast, lauded the work of Homer, Pindar, Shakespeare and Ossian as examples of original genius; for these writers exhibited, he claims, an 'uncultured directness' deriving from their rootedness in vernacular language and popular or folk cultural traditions.[38]

In Herder, then, the 'people' (*Volk*) is invested with 'the creative energies of genius';[39] hence the importance attached both by Herder and the early Romantics (Arnim, Görres, Jakob Grimm) to folk myths, songs and fairy tales as expressions of popular genius. It was not, however, until the mid-19th cen-tury that the term acquired the racial overtones it gains in Chamberlain's *Foundations*. Gobineau, in his *Essai sur L'Inégalité des Races Humaines*, was the first writer of influence to embed the genius concept in biology when he argued for a hierarchy of races with the 'Aryan' at its head, and claimed that the Aryan race alone was truly creative. An enthusiastic disciple of Gobineau, Chamber-lain in turn clearly prefigures Nazism's racialised inflection of genius when he writes:

> Nothing is so convincing as the consciousness of the possession of Race.... Race lifts a man above himself: it endows him with extraordinary – I might almost say supernatural – powers, so entirely does it distinguish him from the individual who springs from the chaotic jumble of peoples ... and should this man be perchance gifted above his fellows, then the fact of a Race strengthens and elevates him on every hand, and he becomes a genius ...[40]

It was this concept of genius as the distilled essence of race that Nazism adopted and adapted not only from Chamberlain, but from that whole host of cultural commentators from the early 20th century onwards who despaired of what Spengler termed the 'decline of the West', and sought in the genius figure a source of messianic deliverance. As Jochen Schmidt again points out, two lines of development can be traced in the cult of genius from the turn of the century until fascism. On the one hand, political Romantics from Spengler to Carl Schmitt proselytised for what Egon Friedell termed a German leader of genius, a 'personality cast in Caesar's mould', a 'steel hard man of Race' who alone could effect Germany's desired political transformation from post-Versailles defeat to the European supremacy that was its destiny.[41] As the NSDAP rose to prominence through the 1920s and early 30s, party ideologues, foremost among them Goebbels, meticulously crafted an image of Hitler as precisely that 'steel hard' Aryan genius invoked so passionately by Friedell. Thus even in 1941, when the 'Hitler myth' was beginning to crumble, Goebbels still claimed of Germany under Hitler that 'we are experiencing the greatest miracle in all history: the building of a new world by a man of genius!'[42]

It is, however, a second line of development in the genius myth that more directly concerns us here. From its inception, the bourgeois conception of genius had attributed to the artist a special capacity to embody the essence of nation and, later, race. Hitler's own (mediocre) artistic talents were thus regularly invoked in support of his claim to supremacy; for, as Goebbels wrote in his 1929 novel *Michael*, 'the statesman is also an artist [since for him] the *Volk* is nothing more nor less than is the stone for the sculptor. *Führer* and mass: this is no more nor less a problem than is paint to a painter.'[43]

The *Führer*, then, is a creative artist moulding the mass and bringing it under his sway. That this vision of the creative process as an act of totalitarian appropriation in which the (male, Aryan) artist as a 'personality' of 'genius' bends his material to his will, became paradigmatic for film-creative practice in the early years of the Reich is demonstrated, moreover, by that series of material transformations in film production and reception after 1933 to which we now turn our attention. In his racist perversion of Herder's concept of folk literature and nation, Goebbels, as is well known, allotted to film the function of a new national popular art that would express the racial essence of *Volk*. The centrality of the Aryan personality or genius to Goebbels' conception is illustrated by three linked developments in film policy and practice after 1933. The first was a process of organisational restructuring that promoted 'creative' figures to positions of industrial power and influence. Initially, posts for 'film advisors' (*Dramaturge*) were created within the Filmkreditbank (FKB) and the Censorship Office; in terms of their impact, however, the artistic committees formed at the managerial heart of the major studios are of greater interest. Second, the mid- to late 1930s witnessed various experiments in the (racial) selection and breeding of cinematic genius, examples of which are explored below in my discussion of the Filmnachweis (Office of Film Licensing) and the short-lived German Film Academy, 1937–9. Finally, the early Nazi period witnessed a planned restructuring of cultural discourse around the category of film art, and the promotion in particular of 'personality' and 'genius' not only through the genius films that have been the subject of much recent film history, but through the star system (see Chapter 2), the recontextualisation of film reception (Chapter 3), and a textual aesthetic that placed at its centre the auteurist director or star (Chapter 4).

Let us turn, then, to the first of the organisational transformations outlined above: the selection of key personalities to channel and regulate German film at the pre-production stage, especially through the monitoring and control of script submission and development.

THE 'PERSONALITY' AS CULTURAL OFFICIAL: DRAMATIC ADVISORS AND THE ARTISTIC COMMITTEES

In a recent work on Weimar cinema, Thomas Elsaesser follows Bordwell, Staiger and Thompson among others in insisting that it is managerial models as much as the control of stock that determine structures of power and authority within film industries. In their studies of classical Hollywood, Bordwell *et al.* tell the story of the Hollywood studios in terms of a shift from what they call the director-unit system, in which directors had overall artistic and financial control, to a producer-unit system that 'functioned by giving a head of production control and responsibility over all of a studio's annual product output'.[44]

Elsaesser uses this model to show how Ufa – as the German studio most directly comparable to the Hollywood majors – sustained until well into the 1920s a system in which director-units under such figures as Fritz Lang, E. A. Dupont, F. W. Murnau and others worked 'under conditions of great autonomy and freedom from interference or supervision'.[45] After Ufa's financial collapse in 1927, Hugenberg's subsequent acquisition of the company and the installation of Ludwig Klitzsch as Director-General, the studio finally shifted, suggests Elsaesser, to a central producer system along Hollywood lines. The centralisation of production after 1927 in producer-units managed by a small handful of commercial heads leads Elsaesser, indeed, to conclude that the key caesura in the economic history of German film occurred in 1927, not 1933. As he observes: 'Even before the Nazi takeover in 1933, the transformation of the German film industry from a twin-track artistic film/prestige production cinema to a mainstream entertainment cinema was well on the way.'[46]

Elsaesser certainly convincingly shows how internal restructurings within Ufa and other bodies paved the way for a Third Reich industry geared to the indigenous production of mass entertainment. But the story he tells of managerial transformation does not stop in 1933. From the beginning, Goebbels had aimed to insert at pivotal points in the production process key cultural figures – 'personalities' – whose job was not merely to block material ideologically repugnant to the regime, but to inflect the finished product 'artistically' towards National Socialism's desired aesthetic and ideological norms. The institutional restructuring of censorship in the regime's early years is a case in point. A key innovation of the reformed *Reichslichtspielgesetz* of 1934 was the creation of the post of Reichsfilmdramaturg (*Reich* Film Adviser). The first *Dramaturg* was Willi Krause, an NSDAP member and former journalist on Goebbels' paper *Der Angriff*. His role was to assess and comment on scripts at every stage of the production process, from the submission of the first treatment, through to the shooting script and beyond. The 1934 legislation, in other words, invested in the Reichsfilmdramaturg key directorial powers, beginning with 'advice' to scriptwriters on 'rewriting the material', and extending to 'assistance' of film industry personnel in 'all dramaturgical questions'.[47]

As Martin Loiperdinger has noted, the extension of censorship in the 1934 law to offences against 'artistic feeling' marks, along with the powers invested in the Reichsfilmdramaturg, a decisive break in the history of German film censorship; for

the new authorities defined their relationship to the film industry not only negatively, in terms of a defence against danger. Instead, they presented the industry with a demand for the active state promotion of films that corresponded to the ... National Socialist world-view.[48]

The impulse that Loiperdinger identifies towards the 'active state promotion' of Nazi cultural values in film was, admittedly, only tangentially visible in other areas of film policy in the early to mid-1930s. True, Goebbels' speeches regularly referenced the 'artistic' mission that was allotted under National Socialism to film. True also that there were gestures towards a programme of 'artistic' reform, even within institutions more obviously geared to the tightening of state financial and political control. Thus the Filmkreditbank, set up in May/June 1933 and state-owned by 1934, had its own dramaturgical office charged – analogously to the Reichsfilmdramaturg – with monitoring scripts and treatments at the pre-production stage, and empowered to demand changes on 'artistic' as well as ideological grounds. Further common destinations for treatments from aspirant scriptwriters and directors were the Film Office within the Propaganda

Ministry, as well as the President's Office in the *Reich* Film Chamber. Though neither had as its central function either script commissioning or development, internal correspondence shows that the *Reich* Film Chamber President in particular functioned as a conduit to the industry for manuscripts deemed valuable not always explicitly on ideological grounds, but also for their adherence to what were presented as aesthetic norms. The RFK's dismissal of a treatment from one Max Krause as 'removed from life [*lebensfremd*]' and 'unnatural', or its diatribes against 'sentimentality', 'kitsch' or 'inauthenticity' in the manuscripts it processed suggest that RFK functionaries understood their role to include not only the ideological policing of film, but just as significantly the guardianship of a 'fundamentally honest', 'artistic', 'authentic' and 'popular' (*volkstümlich*) aesthetic.[49]

But it was not until the late 1930s that Goebbels' fantasy of a film industry driven by creative personalities and their aesthetic impulses achieved programmatic status in full-blown initiatives for managerial reform. The turning-point was formally announced by Goebbels in his March 1938 speech to the *Reich* Film Chamber. Germany is living, thunders the Propaganda Minister, through 'a time that so cries out for talent, that so clearly demands personalities, that has such a heightened need for men with the courage and strength to shoulder responsibilities ... that we are faced not with a moment for discussion, but for action'.[50]

In reality, what Goebbels terms in this speech the 'programmatic' installation of creative personalities at the heart of the production process had already begun more than one year earlier. What the Propaganda Minister represents here as the 'entry march of German film practitioners into the boardrooms, their banners high', is a reference to the creation from 1937 on of *Kunstausschüsse* (artistic committees) at the heart of the four major studios Ufa, Tobis, Bavaria and Terra.[51] The way to the artistic committees had been paved by Terra, which, according to Goebbels, had in the course of 1936–7 appointed 'three respected film artists' to its board of directors.[52] In his 1937 speech to the Film Chamber, Goebbels seized on Terra's initiative as a model that could pave the way for a departure from a mode of film production geared principally to the profit motive. In his view, 'purely commercial tendencies have obscured and hampered the development of the artistic element in film to such a degree that today, we are more justified in speaking of film as industry than as film art'.[53] The answer, Goebbels now suggested, lay in a restructuring of management which, while retaining the centralised power structure of the producer-unit system, would remove managerial authority from the money men, and invest it instead in 'personalities' of creative genius: 'men ... seized by an inner obsession with film art'.[54]

By 1938, then, and at Goebbels' behest, 'artistic committees' with wide-ranging decision-making powers had been installed at top managerial level within the major studios.[55] The Ufa studios are a case in point. In May 1937, the company acquired what Klaus Kreimeier terms an 'entirely transformed' board of directors whose members included the producer-director Carl Froelich, Hans Weidemann from the Propaganda Ministry film department, actors Mathias Wieman and Paul Hartmann, director-producer Karl Ritter, and Eugen Klöpfer, known both for stage and screen acting, and for his official functions as Vice-President of the *Reich* Theatre Chamber and as manager (*Intendant*) of one of Berlin's foremost theatres, the Volksbühne.[56] In line with Goebbels' demand for increased decision-making powers for creative personnel, these newcomers to the Ufa board were simultaneously appointed to the newly established artistic committee. Under the chairmanship of Froelich, the committee's role was to lend artistic direction to the Ufa output by assessing treatments and scripts submitted to the studio, commissioning work from established scriptwriters or directors, and planning strategically for the studio's future artistic programme. The *Kunstausschuß* reported directly to Ludwig Klitzsch, and gained further decision-making authority by the co-option onto the committee of the Ufa production chief, Ernst Hugo Correll, and of the then Reichsfilmdramaturg, Ewald von Demandowsky.

THE UFA ARTISTIC COMMITTEE

We saw above how, in the racialised version of the genius myth adopted by National Socialism, the creative personality functioned simultaneously as bearer of the artistic 'idea', and as the individual voice of a collective essence of race, state and nation. The 'personality', in other words, became such under National Socialism both by his (*sic* – of which more later) allegiance to a racially conceived German aesthetic, and by his prominence in the Nazi public sphere as a representative of state and nation. Precisely those roles were fulfilled by the five 'creative' figures on the Ufa committee. Eugen Klöpfer was well known on stage and screen before 1933 for his roles as heroic types and historical Titans. By the late 1930s, his status as actor-personality in Goebbels' sense was evidenced in part by the critical accolades he gained for his acting talent. In Joseph Gregor's *Meister der deutscher Schauspielkunst* (*Masters of the German Acting Art*), for instance, Klöpfer was assigned a place in the German pantheon as a 'peasant son' whose 'healthy memory of the *Heimat* soil' bonded him to the 'heart' of the *Volk*.[57] At the same time, Klöpfer's positions at the *Reich* Theatre Chamber and the Volksbühne, his roles in major propaganda titles, including von Ucicky's *Flüchtlinge* (*Refugees*, 1933), and his naming as State Actor (Staatsschauspieler) in 1937, established him in public discourse as a prototype of precisely that 'fanatical' artist of genius whom Goebbels sought to elevate.

The status of Wieman, Hartmann and Ritter was similar. Wieman's reputation as an actor embodying an austere Germanic masculinity in such films as
Das blaue Licht (*The Blue Light*, 1932) and *Patrioten* (*Patriots*, 1937) led him to
be awarded the title of State Actor in 1937, the same year in which he joined
the Ufa board. Alongside Paul Hartmann, whose most notable Third Reich
role was as Bismarck in Wolfgang Liebeneiner's 1940 biopic, Karl Ritter was
perhaps the most politicised of this illustrious group. Though all of them combined Nazi allegiance with their commitment to a *völkisch* artistic heritage,
Ritter was the most prominent as a party member and apologist for fascism.
Having joined the NSDAP well before 1933, he was hired by Ufa in that year
to produce a string of propaganda titles, starting with Steinhoff's *Hitlerjunge
Quex*, 1935. As a director, Ritter made the soldier genre his own with such titles
as *Unternehmen Michael* (*Enterprise Michael*, 1937) and *Pour le mérite* (1938).
At the same time, he proselytised for a new German cinema that would be
'created by the film artist, not the businessman'. He saw this dream realised
not least through the artistic committees, whose role in prising control from
the producers corresponded entirely to Ritter's call for an end to the 'commercial period of our film development', and to the 'dictatorship' of industry
over art.[58]

The committee chairman, Carl Froelich, boasted a career similarly marked by
a mix of film-making activity and political collaboration. Already a prominent
figure in the Weimar industry, Froelich joined the Nazi party in 1933, and was
awarded a personal professorship by Hitler in 1937. In 1939, his status as regime
collaborator was confirmed by his appointment as head of the *Reich* Film Chamber. Committee minutes reveal, moreover, that it was under Froelich's
directorship that some of the bitterest struggles were fought within Ufa to
achieve Karl Ritter's desired displacement of 'businessmen', and to replace them
with creative practitioners who would seek to realise Nazism's ideological project by transforming Ufa's aesthetic agenda. In the minutes, references abound
to Goebbels' desire for a new film art; thus for instance in one especially heated
discussion of a script for *Der Durchbruch* (*Breakthrough*), co-authored by the
actor and *Kunstausschuß* member Mathias Wieman, von Demandowsky reminds
a recalcitrant Correll of Goebbels' wish that artists become the 'vanguard'
of contemporary film production. Already a thorn in the side of the regime,
Correll sounded regular financial warnings over the lavish productions planned
by the *Kunstausschuß* in the service of art. In the case of *Der Durchbruch*, the
committee bowed to Correll's commercial misgivings, and delayed the project
pending full costing – though Carl Froelich could not resist closing the meeting
with a sharp reminder of the *Reich* Minister's continuing demand for 'good,
artistic film'.[59]

In other instances, it was the political considerations aired in particular by von Demandowsky that stayed the committee's hand. There is evidence, for example, that it rejected scripts at his bidding on political or racial grounds, and acquiesced (albeit sometimes only temporarily) in his interventions into such issues as casting or script development.[60] On issues apparently specific to film aesthetics, by contrast, film practitioners on the committee enjoyed a freer hand, and records show how diligently they strove to achieve a Ufa style consonant with the tastes and sensibilities of National Socialism. For the two years from its founding to the outbreak of war, the committee apparently saw treatments and scripts for all potential or actual Ufa productions. From their discussions, there emerges a picture of a group straining to realise in practice Goebbels' vision of works imbued with the values of the 'towering, fascinating and magnetic personality'.[61] In some cases, 'personality' was explicitly invoked as the standard against which a manuscript should stand or fall. Thus a proposed Beethoven biopic, *Die unsterbliche Geliebte* (*Immortal Lover*), was trounced by Froelich for its debasing of 'our spiritual German heroes' through trivial dialogue; and an early treatment for what was to become Traugott Müller's *Friedemann Bach* (1941) was rejected for its similar failure to represent in properly tragic terms the 'fate' of this 'man of genius'.[62] 'Personality' surfaced as an issue, too, in debates on casting – and this not only in the genre of the genius film. In one clearly heated exchange on casting for Karl Ritter's 1939 comedy *Die Hochzeitsreise* (*The Honeymoon*), the director himself defended his desire to cast the Austrian Angela Salloker in a leading role on the grounds that 'the casting of Françoise Rosay in the role of the mother makes it imperative to engage a strong actorly personality in the daughter's role'. That even female actresses could in exceptional circumstances attain 'towering' status as prominent representatives of the actor's art is evidenced not only by Hartmann, Weidemann and Froelich's further comments on both Rosay and Salloker, the former of whom they see as meeting the requirements of literary art (*Dichtung*) through her 'marvellous command of the actor's art'.[63] The same criteria of aesthetic judgment were applied when the committee debated new roles for Zarah Leander, by this time Ufa's most prized up-and-coming female star. A proposal to cast Leander in a remake of Hans Behrendt's 1931 musical *Gloria* met with general derision, since Leander 'tower[ed] head and shoulders', both metaphorically and physically, above this film. Carl Froelich's own plans to cast Leander as the lead in his female version of a genius film, the Mary, Queen of Scots biopic *Das Herz der Königin* (*The Heart of the Queen*), receive, by contrast, general acclaim, representing as they did a chance at last to confront Leander with a challenge whose 'true greatness' befitted her artistic status.[64]

But it was not only in discussions of the biographical or genius genre, nor even solely in relation to casting, that the significance of 'personality' for the artistic committee's cultural project became visible. As Carl Froelich phrased the issue in his comments on a proposal for a biopic of Beethoven under the direction of Detlef Sierck, the representation of genius demanded 'a wholly new film style' – a style that 'renders bearable' the representation in film of the genius principle.[65] Goebbels himself, in his 1938 *Reich* Film Chamber speech, had framed his comments on personalities of genius in a more wide-ranging peroration on the 'nature and character' of film as art.[66] Goebbels here echoed such contemporary film theorists as Günter Groll, Ernst Iros and Bruno Rehlinger when he called for a new cinematic realism that distinguished itself in both content and form, on the one hand from a degenerate naturalism, and on the other, from the 'kitsch' illusionism of the Hollywood style. Attacking commercial cinema for its modernist splitting of the film image between 'illusion' and 'reality', appearance (*Schein*) and essence (*Sein*), Goebbels called instead for an idealist regeneration of cinematic realism that would situate filmic representation as a 'condensed', 'heightened' and 'concentrated' distillation of the *völkisch* 'soul'. As Goebbels concluded: 'The strength and indeed the roots that are the source from which we can draw the impulse to create our own artistic style and our own conception of art lie in the soul of the *Volk*.'[67]

Records of internal discussions within Ufa's artistic committee show its members struggling to realise in their day-to-day decisions Goebbels' call for a mode of *völkisch* realism that might restore German cinema's shattered links with the soul of its people. Some manuscripts were praised therefore for their return to mythic and folk art forms; hence Ludwig Klitzsch's demand for a rewrite of the thriller *Pharao* that might transform the film from 'a barely credible low-quality thriller' into 'a mystical film whose effects would stem from the mysterious magic that still emanates today from the graves of the pharoahs'.[68] Other committee members echoed Goebbels in their praise of 'clarity', 'simplicity' or 'linear' narrative construction. Treatments were dismissed for the excessive ornamentation that made them 'implausible', 'tasteless', 'kitsch'; by contrast, in their search for an art cinema for and of the *Volk*, the committee valued work that was morally untainted ('decent'), yet also 'human' and thus 'close to life'. Above all, film-artistic quality was measured in terms of a neo-Kantian reception aesthetic that valued film as the 'sublime' vehicle of the 'great inner experience' evinced by 'poetry' (*Dichtung*) of 'quality' (*Niveau*).[69]

I referenced earlier Elsaesser's comment on the importance of studies of internal management structures as a way of charting changing modes of production in the history of German film. Internal documents from the Ufa artistic committee, I want finally to suggest, show how that committee sought strategically to roll back the shift from 'artisanal' to 'commercial' production modes that Elsaesser identifies in the late 1920s. Goebbels' aim in creating the artistic committees was to displace power and authority in the production process from the producers (most particularly from Ufa production chief Ernst Hugo Correll), and to invest it instead in cultural practitioners who were at the same time functionaries or fellow-travellers of the Nazi state.

The political allegiances of such figures as Froelich, Ritter or Klöpfer should not blind us, however, to the cultural project in which they were also quite clearly engaged. Recent histories of Third Reich film have focused increasingly on the correspondences between, say, the Ufa popular genre output, and its Hollywood equivalents. Eric Rentschler has, for example, noted the 'reliance of the era's cinema on classical Hollywood conventions', as well as the admiration that German practitioners sustained for Hollywood's 'professional craft, seemingly inexhaustible talent, and ... technical prowess'.[70] By way of contrast, minutes from the proceedings of the Ufa artistic committee begin to demonstrate how intense was the effort from within the industry to establish for German cinema standards for a different mode of 'classical' realism. Realism in the positivist tradition to which Hollywood was heir rested on the assumption that language – film language, in the Hollywood case – was a descriptive and denotative medium whose function was to convey in its full immediacy the 'knowledge of things'.[71] In the idealist tradition espoused in Nazi cultural thinking, by contrast, the function of (film) language was to convey knowledge of the essence and 'soul' of the *Volk*. As Third Reich film commentary repeatedly stressed, the specific features that would differentiate this *völkisch* realism from its positivist counterpart escaped precise formulation, since, as Günter Groll insisted, the 'essence of film' lay not in its material or formal qualities, but in its capacity to express 'creative life-feeling'.[72] Nonetheless, there do emerge from the artistic committee's deliberations the beginnings of a set of formal precepts that might govern the actual practice of film construction. We have seen in the committee's comments its prioritising of 'clear' and 'simple' linear narrative over 'kitsch' ornamentation and 'superficial' spectacle. Other elements include its insistence on the primacy of dialogue over the image, or its preference for theatrical forms (what it called 'robust drama') over some at least of the conventional genres of the entertainment film.[73]

It is beyond the scope of this study to draw conclusions on the ultimate effectiveness of the Ufa artistic committee's attempted imposition of its aesthetic precepts on particular films. Much more research is needed on chains of command within the studios, on the precise negotiations that took place during production and post-production with directors, actors, editors and others, and most centrally, on the relationship between the management's aesthetic dictates and film texts in their finished form. For now, it is worth noting that such shifts as can be observed in films of the Nazi period away from classical Hollywood, and towards a more characteristically German national style are (of course) the products not only of the interventions of functionaries in one committee, the Ufa-*Kunstausschuß,* but of very diverse efforts across the film industry to bring their practices into line with Goebbels' call for a national popular film art. As Kurt Denzer has demonstrated, Third Reich film theory, in the (relatively diverse) works of such figures as Gottfried Müller, Ernst Iros, Bruno Rehlinger, Günter Groll and others drew in the Nazi period on pre-1933 traditions in film theory and criticism, but inflected them radically towards Goebbels' mode of film-cultural nationalism.[74] Film practitioners too, both amateur and professional, explored in trade publications and discussion events the practical means to realise a distinctive national film style for the new Germany. Practitioner clubs and associations – the Klub für Kameratechnik e.V., the Verband der Kameraleute Deutschlands e.V., the Verband Deutscher Lichtspielvorführer e.V., the Verband filmschaffender Tonmeister Deutschlands e.V. and others – debated in a variety of fora, from evening seminars to the professional press, the specific national qualities of a whole plethora of technical practices and stylistic traits: tracking versus static camera, ensemble versus star lighting, back projection and other trick devices versus cinematic naturalism, and so on.[75]

But it is in a second 'programmatic' initiative by Goebbels that we find most clearly realised his aspiration for a German cinema that situated the *völkisch* 'personality' at its creative centre – and that is in what was to be for the last two pre-war years the Propaganda Minister's pet project, the German Film Academy.

THE GERMAN FILM ACADEMY AND THE RACIAL SELECTION OF GENIUS

We began to see in my discussion of the artistic committees how, even in the early years of the regime, the Propaganda Ministry and the Film Chamber gained control of the industry not by repression alone, but by a series of generative measures designed to foster among film practitioners the *völkisch* artistic modes that Goebbels and others demanded. But one special anxiety dogged the exponents of fascist film-cultural revolution, and that was the issue of so-called *Nachwuchs,* or new talent for German film.

The question was, of course, especially acute for a film industry that had passively complied with the persecution of its finest creative practitioners. In the years following the Nazi seizure of power in 1933, the industry experienced a massive haemorrhage of qualified personnel, which conservative estimates place at around 1,000, almost exclusively German-Jewish directors, producers, scriptwriters, cinematographers, costume designers, actors and technicians, who fled the Nazi terror and sought exile abroad. As Jan-Christopher Horak comments, this forced migration was but 'the first step of a politics of exclusion, persecution and mass-murder that would end in the death of 6 million'. Yet the murderously efficient racial purging of German cinema (already by summer 1933, Jewish employees had vanished entirely from the sector) met with negligible protest or resistance. Faced with the choice of collaboration or emigration, the vast majority of film practitioners chose the former; indeed as Horak further observes, a meagre 5 per cent of 'Aryans' chose to follow their endangered colleagues to the major exile destinations: Austria, Hungary, France, Britain, Holland and, above all, the US, where Hollywood absorbed an estimated 25 per cent of German exiles after 1933.[76]

The Propaganda Ministry under Goebbels was initially slow to respond to the crippling talent shortage that was a product of the regime's own racial madness. In the first five Nazi years, initiatives to train badly needed new personnel were largely *ad hoc*, emanating from individuals and offices within the Ministry and the Film Chamber whose official duties lay elsewhere. Thus for instance the Filmnachweis (Office of Film Licensing) within the RFK – an office that played a key role in the political and racial purging of the industry by regulating contractual arrangements between production companies and creative personnel – gradually assumed responsibilities as an 'advice centre and employment agency for film practitioners'.[77] Under the direction of Fritz Alberti, the Filmnachweis ran regular auditions and seminars for actors, directors, screenwriters, composers, designers, cinematographers and others, in an effort to 'open up opportunities for [new] talent' and thus 'fulfil [the office's] higher mission'.[78]

By 1937–8, however, Goebbels had conceived a more grandiose plan for the nurturing of new creative personnel. In his 1938 speech to the RFK, the Propaganda Minister specified:

> What is at issue here is ... the planned cultivation of people of whose skill we are convinced, and whom we consider important for the future. [W]hat is required to produce a highly qualified new generation is not so much fine words or programmes launched on the crest of an emotional wave, but rather systematic cultivation and education in an Academy built for that purpose and staffed by men who rise to the task before them because they have made a profession of so doing .... [79]

With these words, Goebbels launched his latest favoured project, an Academy of German Film. In his biologist vision, the Academy that was his new dream would, by the application of eugenic principles of racial selection and 'systematic cultivation', produce a generation of practitioners equipped both racially and culturally to fulfil his 'programmatic' demands for a new film art. Action in that direction was swift. On 4 March 1938, Goebbels laid the foundation stone for what was for a short time – until the outbreak of war eighteen months later – to be the ProMi's flagship project: the German Film Academy (Deutsche Filmakademie).

Proposals for an academy of German film art had circulated throughout the early years of the regime, and gained influential support from both industry and state. In an early blueprint for what was initially titled the Deutsches Institut für Filmkunde (German Institute for the Study of Film), Ufa's Director-General, Ludwig Klitzsch, was described as having 'harboured plans for many years of creating a film research institute whose work in universities and technical institutions of higher education would be intimately connected to its role in training new generations of film practitioners'.[80] Previous attempts at film-industrial training had been scattered and fragmentary, limited either to short-lived Weimar experiments in film actor training (the Ufa Film School, opened in 1926, or the German Film School – Deutsche Filmschule – in Munich, 1921–34), or to film studies initiatives at university level in departments of theatre or news media studies, as well as in such scientific disciplines as had relevance to film technology and economic development.[81] The Deutsche Filmakademie, by contrast, was for the first time both to unify these geographically disparate film training initiatives, and build bridges between scholarly research and practical training at all industrial and creative levels.

The lavish illustrated booklet that accompanied the inauguration specified in some detail how this fusion of art and science, theory and creative practice was to be achieved. The Film Academy was organised in three faculties: the Faculty of Film Art (described by Ludwig Klitzsch as 'necessarily the most significant'), the Faculty of Film Technology and the Faculty of Film Economics.[82] Each of these was run by a skeleton staff comprising the faculty head (the film director Wolfgang Liebeneiner, in the case of Film Art) together with departmental heads; but it was serviced by a large population of visiting lecturers, all of whom were active, and many prominent both in the RMVP hierarchy, and (more often) in relevant sections of the film industry. The Film Art Faculty, for instance, boasted among its pool of potential lecturing staff Fritz Hippler from the RMVP, as well as such seasoned practitioners as the actor Paul Hörbiger, art director Erich Kettelhut, and even – until his banning from film work in 1939 – the leftist director Werner Hochbaum. The glittering array of further names said to have promised collaboration with the Faculty of Film Art underlines the Film Academy's status as a prominent initiative for industry and Propaganda Ministry

alike; witness the inclusion in this star line-up of such figures as the Ufa
Production Chief Ernst Hugo Correll, directors Willy Forst, Carl Froelich, Veit
Harlan, Luis Trenker, actors and actresses Heinrich George, Rudolf
Klein-Rogge, Viktor de Kowa, Maria Koppenhöfer, Harry Piel, or such legendary
names from other creative fields (scriptwriting, art direction, musical compo-
sition, etc.) as Thea von Harbou, Otto Hunte, Rochus Gliese, Theo Mackeben,
Walter Röhrig and Hermann Warm.[83]

The chief significance of the Deutsche Filmakademie from our perspective in
this book derives, however, from the systematic effort it represents to create as
the cornerstone of German film art a model community geared to the racial
selection and cultivation of artistic genius. In terms of its internal organisation,
the Academy was, first, a model in microcosm of a cultural sphere dominated
by the personality principle and led by figures of genius. Each of the three faculties was hierarchically organised under a single director: Wolfgang Liebeneiner
for Film Art, the engineer and television pioneer Rudolph Thun for Film Technology, and for Film Economics, the economist and co-director of the
Filmkreditbank, Günter Schwarz. Nazi ideological and organisational control
of the faculties via these three directors was secured by the appointment of
Wilhelm Müller-Scheid as DFA President. Having worked formerly as Director
of Propaganda in Hessen-Nassau, then as Chief of the *Reichspropagandaamt*,
Müller-Scheid took the role of ideological policeman for the Academy, and
described as his priority the 'schooling [of] the students intellectually and in
terms of their world-view [*Weltanschauung*]'.[84]

Student recruitment under Müller-Scheid's direction proceeded, moreover,
according to the strictest principles of racial selection. Among the documents
required for application were completed questionnaires on racial origin, as well
as birth and marriage certificates reaching back over three generations of the
applicant's family and, where applicable, that of her/his spouse.[85] Müller-
Scheid himself concisely summarised the Academy's social-Darwinist vision of
the racial selection of creative excellence when he demanded that 'every applicant desiring future acceptance into the Academy must ... show traces of
genius'.[86]

This is not to say, however, that genius was perceived as merely inborn. As the
Academy's crammed timetable shows (Figure 1), the syllabus reflected the fascist conception of the man of genius in its emphasis on a combination of physical
drill and ideological training, these latter designed, in tandem with practical seminars in the cinematic disciplines, to fashion its pupils in the image of precisely
that 'steel-hard man of Race' that we saw championed above by Friedell, Chamberlain and others. The Academy's principal figureheads, Müller-Scheid and
Liebeneiner, were to function, meanwhile, as models of the creative genius type

Allgemeine Pflichtvorlesungen und Übungen für die ordentlichen Studierenden aller Fakultäten						
Zeit	Montag	Dienstag	Mittwoch	Donnerstag	Freitag	Sonnabend
8³⁰ — 9³⁰	Gymnastik und Sport	Gymnastik und Sport	Bild- und Tontechnik (8³⁰—10⁰⁰) Thun/Etzold	Gymnastik und Sport	Gymnastik und Sport	Musik (8³⁰—10⁰⁰)
10 — 11³⁰	Literatur mit Vortrag und Rezitation	Allgemeine Filmwirtschaft Schwarz (10⁰⁰—10⁴⁵) Geschichte und Grundzüge des Filmrechts Roeber (10⁴⁵—11³⁰)	Gymnastik und Sport (10³⁰—11³⁰)	Bildende Kunst Gudenrath (10⁰⁰—10⁴⁵) Filmtheaterkunde Quadt (10⁴⁵—11³⁰)	Geschichte und Weltanschauung Schneider	Gymnastik und Sport (10³⁰—11³⁰)
11⁴⁵ — 13¹⁵	Vorführung von Filmen mit Aussprache Filme vom Beginn des Stummfilmes bis zur Gegenwart					
13¹⁵ — 15	Gemeinsame Mittagspause					
17 — 18⁴⁵			Das Entstehen eines Films unt. besond. Berücksichtigung des Zusammenwirkens der künstlerischen u. technischen Kräfte Liebeneiner			

Filmkünstlerische Fakultät				Semester: 1 Lehrgruppe: Dramaturgie a) Dramaturgen		
Zeit	Montag	Dienstag	Mittwoch	Donnerstag	Freitag	Sonnabend
8³⁰ — 13¹⁵	Siehe Stundenplan oben					
13¹⁵ — 15	Gemeinsame Mittagspause					
15 — 15⁴⁵	Einführung in die Photographie Beck	Wesen und Geschichte des Films Kalbus	Die Welt des Sichtbaren und Hörbaren Fürst		Kulturgeschichte des deutschen Bauerntums von der Frühzeit bis zur Gegenwart Bruger	
16 — 16⁴⁵	Grundfragen der Filmdramaturgie Gressieker	Aufbau einer Jahresproduktion (Cyclus)		Grundlagen der Filmbildgestaltung und des praktischen Bauens Kettelhut		
17 — 17⁴⁵		Kostümkunde Bruhn Heereskunde u. Uniformkunde Knötel	Das Entstehen eines Films unt. besond. Berücksichtigung des Zusammenwirkens der künstlerischen u. technischen Kräfte Liebeneiner	Grundfragen der Filmregie Liebeneiner	Die Gestaltung der Wirklichkeit in Kulturfilm und Wochenschau Hippler	
18 — 18⁴⁵	Der Herstellungsgang eines Films v. d. Idee bis zur Theaterkopie Hochbaum	Die Anschauungswelt des Filmbildners — der Mensch und seine Umwelt Sohnle			Dramaturgische Übungen Gressieker	
19 — 19⁴⁵	Photographisches Praktikum Weitzenberg	Photographisches Praktikum Weitzenberg	Photographisches Praktikum Weitzenberg		Voraussetzungen der Filmmusik Fürst	

Figure 1: excerpt from *Deutsche Filmakademie* Timetable, 1938

for general emulation. In contemporary press coverage, Müller-Scheid himself was variously described as a war hero ('[he] spent four-and-a-half years at the very vanguard of the World War battle front'), a 'playwright and theatrical poet' (his *Ein Deutscher namens Stein/A German Named Stein* was especially successful): a man, then, who 'met all the prerequisites for the task of infusing the Academy in a very real sense with the spirit of National Socialism'.[87] Indeed, in his 'intimate bond with artistic creation', Müller-Scheid's talents were seen to be surpassed only by those of State Actor, film director and head of the Film Art Faculty, Wolfgang Liebeneiner.[88] As *Der Deutsche Film* reported in 1938,

> In the person of Wolfgang Liebeneiner, the German Film Academy has appointed a young artistic personality who is unique both in his precipitous rise to prominence and in his refusal to compromise on any artistic question. Liebeneiner has shown himself to be a man of multiple talents, not only as a film actor, as stage actor and director, but more recently, as a film director. He has mastered each and every film genre; each of his films has risen above the merely mediocre. If we further consider the fact that the almost unprecedented successes of this young artist have deprived him of none of his appetite for hard work, his modesty, his artistic enthusiasm and his 'youth' in the best sense of that word, then we must acknowledge that no better man could have been found to confront the difficult task – a task, indeed, never before encountered in quite this form – of educating a new generation of film artists.[89]

This paean of praise to Liebeneiner incorporates the usual roll-call of features that comprise the Third Reich artistic personality. Though 'unique', Liebeneiner is no Romantic individual lost in interiority, nor is he Enlightenment man committed to the analytical dissection of the object world. Liebeneiner as portrayed here is the fascist man of steel, who 'masters' that world through 'hard work' and an 'uncompromising' willingness to shoulder artistic duties. Years later, the writer-director Peter Pewas would defend his former Academy colleague Liebeneiner on the grounds of his 'unsurpassed reputation' among students. As Pewas claimed, 'he was never a Nazi, not in any sense of that word'.[90] What Pewas misses here, of course, is Liebeneiner's structural function within the Academy as a 'personality' whom students were called upon to emulate. That the will to personality was a key structuring force in artistic production as construed by the DFA becomes, moreover, further visible if we consider the Academy's organisation of the cinematic disciplines. Of the three faculties, Film Art was widely viewed as the most significant; thus, for instance, it was 'creative film artists' of 'above average talent, if not of genius' in whom Müller-Scheid, in an article marking the DFA's opening, declared himself interested.[91]

PERSONALITY AND GENIUS AS SOCIAL FANTASIES

Researching the further development of the German Film Academy after 1938 is a frustrating business. What survives of Goebbels' late 1930s venture is a lavish inaugural booklet, transcripts of speeches at the opening ceremony, a handful of press reports and interviews on the Academy's 'significance and role', and on the principles of its future development.[92] Sketches and photographs of the finished building show a forbidding, monumental structure: classical portals framed by four-storey stone blocks, courtyards and gardens more reminiscent of military parade grounds than exercise yards for a centre of cultural excellence. On closer inspection, however, even the photographs have the eerie quality of the simulacrum. These are photographs of architects' models, provisional images of a characteristically sterile architectural site for the future 'cultivation' of artistic genius.

These images' non-referential quality is telling; for indeed, the Academy was never realised in the form planned by Goebbels, Müller-Scheid and others. When the foundation stone was laid in Babelsberg-Ufastadt in March 1938, a completion schedule of '1–2 years' was projected. In November 1938, teaching began in provisional buildings; but by November of the following year, Germany was at war, and the German Film Academy running into the sand. Tuition in the various film disciplines continued throughout the war in Babelsberg, but neither the ambitious building programme nor the integrated curriculum envisaged in 1938 was ever realised.

The Academy remained therefore a male fantasy in Klaus Theweleit's sense: a fascist projection, emanating largely from Goebbels, of what Theweleit terms a 'totality-machine', a microcosm of a perfect society whose 'fundamental reference' was to 'indefinitely progressive forms of training' – in the case of the Film Academy, the training of artistic genius. It is, however, precisely the German Film Academy's fantasy status that renders it significant for this present study. In Linda Schulte-Sasse's illuminating analysis of Nazi film, she draws for her film readings on theories of social fantasy from Slavoj Žižek, Chantal Mouffe and Ernesto Laclau. In the post-structuralist paradigm those writers establish, any vision of society as a harmonious whole – visions of the kind we see embodied in the Film Academy – is always illusory; for 'societies are marked by ruptures that prevent the utopian visions that hold them together from ever being realised'. In response to those fundamental ruptures or blockages, Schulte-Sasse continues, societies 'invent social fantasies ... to mask the impossibility of the ideals by which they identify themselves'.[93]

Schulte-Sasse's readings of Third Reich historical and genius films show how Nazism's 'social fantasy' of wholeness was realised in film texts through their organisation around two central symbolic figures: the 'Jew' as the 'material embodiment of the very qualities supposedly hindering social perfection', and on the other hand, the 'positive fantasy of the Leader', the latter realised in figures of creative genius in such Third Reich titles as *Friedemann Bach* (1941) and *Friedrich Schiller – Triumph eines Genies* (*Friedrich Schiller – Triumph of a Genius*, 1940). What is suggested by the case of the German Film Academy is that Schulte-Sasse's 'social fantasy' of racial purity and organic wholeness was a structuring principle not only of the film text, but also of the cultural institutions generated by the Third Reich project for a new film art. The brief history of the Academy offered above illustrates, too, how Nazi cultural institutions, analogously to Schulte-Sasse's films, pitted the (racialised) figure of the mere entertainer against racially 'pure' and masculinised figures of genius. Thus while the Academy 'had no place' for the 'semi-educated opportunists' represented among other groups by aspirant stars, it 'open[ed] its doors to all those in whom we can perceive an above-average talent, if not ... genius'.[94]

In that context, moreover, priority was given to film actor training. The Academy saw itself as unique in its efforts to train actors specifically for film, and represented actor training in its inaugural booklet as a 'among the most interesting' elements of a larger programme geared to 'laying the foundations for authentically German film creation'.[95]

In the next chapter, I want then to consider more closely the symbolic opposition that held currency among other places in the German Film Academy between stars on the one hand, and on the other, film actors in an authentically German tradition. How did the film actor of genius differ in her/his identity as public figure from the star? And what was the performance mode that marked out the film actor as an 'authentically German' opposite to the (Hollywood, Jewish) star?

NOTES

1. Figures from Jürgen Spiker, *Film und Kapital. Zur politischen Ökonomie des NS-Films*, Vol. 2 (Berlin: Volker Spiess, 1975). October 1927 is generally seen to mark the beginning of the sound era, with the screening of Alan Crosland's *The Jazz Singer* in New York. By 1929, German studios lagged far behind the US in the development of sound, with only eight sound titles produced in that year. That figure rose dramatically in subsequent years, from 101 in 1930, to 132 in 1932: see Wolfgang Mühl-Benninghaus, *Das Ringen um den Tonfilm. Strategien der Elektro- und der Filmindustrie in den 20er und 30er Jahren* (Düsseldorf: Droste, 1999), p. 190 and *passim*.

2. See Helmut Korte, *Der Spielfilm und das Ende der Weimarer Republik. Ein rezeptionshistorischer Versuch* (Göttingen: Vandenhoek & Ruprecht, 1998), p. 94. Figures are from Spiker, *Film und Kapital*, pp. 55ff; see also Mühl-Benninghaus, *Das Ringen*, p. 356.

3. Korte, *Der Spielfilm*, p. 94.

4. 'Es besteht kein Anlaß zur Unsicherheit', *Der Film*, 4 April 1933. The article reports in some detail on the event, though it quotes only extracts from Goebbels' speech, since the full text had already appeared in the daily press.

5. Goebbels' speech in the Berlin Kaiserhof, 28 March 1933. Reproduced in full in Gerd Albrecht, *Nationalsozialistische Filmpolitik. Eine soziologische Untersuchung über die Spielfilme des Dritten Reichs* (Stuttgart: Ferdinand Enke, 1969), pp. 439ff.

6. Ibid., pp. 439–50.

7. The term *Gleichschaltung* is commonly, though rather unsatisfactorily translated as 'co-ordination', and refers to the process whereby all public institutions were made subject after 1933 to NSDAP control. The texts of the 1920 and 1934 *Reichslichtspielgesetz* are reproduced in Albrecht, *Nationalsozialistsche Filmpolitik*, pp. 510ff. An English translation of the 1934 version appears in David Welch, *The Third Reich. Politics and Propaganda* (London and New York: Routledge, 1993), pp. 159ff.

8. Klaus Kreimeier, *Die Ufa-Story. Geschichte eines Filmkonzerns* (Munich: Hanser, 1992), p. 300.

9. In Benjamin's words, 'The logical result of Fascism is the introduction of aesthetics into political life. The violation of the masses, whom Fascism, with its *Führer* cult, forces to their knees, has its counterpart in the violation of an apparatus which is pressed into the production of ritual values.' His further comment that 'All efforts to render politics aesthetic culminate in one thing: war', is of particular pertinence to Chapter 7 of this book, where I investigate the 'sublime' experience delivered to cinema audiences in Germany by the spectacle of the *Blitzkrieg*. See Walter Benjamin, 'The Work of Art in the Age of Mechanical Reproduction', in idem, *Illuminations*, Harry Zohn (trans), Hannah Arendt (ed.) (London: Fontana, 1992, orig. 1936), pp. 234–5.

10. Among the most lucid and comprehensive English-language accounts of this restructuring process is Julian Petley's *Capital and Culture. German Cinema 1933–45* (London: BFI, 1979), Ch. 3.

11. Speech by Joseph Goebbels at the second annual conference of the RFK, in Oswald Lehnich (ed.), *Jahrbuch der Reichsfilmkammer 1938* (Berlin: Max Hesses, 1938), pp. 25–6. Goebbels makes specific mention here of the two initiatives discussed later in this chapter: the appointment of creative practitioners to managerial positions within the studios via the establishment of *Kunstausschüsse* – artistic committees – from 1937 on, and the 'systematic' nurturing of rising talent through the creation of the Deutsche Filmakademie.

12. Ibid., p. 18.

13. On Hitler as charismatic personality, see Ian Kershaw, *The Hitler Myth. Image and*

Reality in the Third Reich (Oxford and New York: Oxford University Press, 1987);
Kurt Sontheimer, *Anti-demokratisches Denken der Weimarer Republik. Die
politischen Ideen des deutschen Nationalsozialismus zwischen 1918 und 1933*
(Munich: Nymphenburger, 1962), especially pp. 268ff, 'Der Ruf nach dem
Führer'; Jochen Schmidt, *Die Geschichte des Genie-Gedankens 1750–1945*
(Darmstadt: Wissenschaftliche Buchgesellschaft, 1985), vol. 2, pp. 194ff.

14. Joseph Gregor, *Das Zeitalter des Films* (Vienna and Leipzig: Reinhold, 1932)
    second edition, p. 188; Ernst Iros, *Wesen und Dramaturgie des Films* (Zürich and
    Leipzig: Max Niehaus Verlag, 1938), p. 759.

15. Richard Sennett, *The Fall of Public Man* (London and Boston: Faber & Faber,
    1986), p. 152.

16. Anthony Quinto, 'Psychologism', in Alan Bullock and Oliver Stallybrass (eds),
    The Fontana Dictionary of Modern Thought (London: Fontana, 1977), p. 508.

17. Idem, 'Personalism', in Bullock and Stallybrass, *Modern Thought*, p. 465; also
    idem, 'Transcendence', in Bullock and Stallybrass, *Modern Thought*, p. 642.

18. Geoffrey C. Field, *Evangelist of Race. The Germanic Vision of Houston Stewart
    Chamberlain* (New York: Columbia University Press, 1981), p. 284.

19. Houston Stewart Chamberlain, *Foundations of the Nineteenth Century*, John Lees
    (trans.) (London: The Bodley Head, 1910, orig. 1899), vol. II, p. 227.

20. Field, *Evangelist of Race*, p. 2.

21. Adolf Hitler, *Mein Kampf*, Ralph Manheim (trans.) (London: Hutchinson, 1974,
    orig. 1925/6), second edition, p. 402.

22. Ibid., pp. 403–9.

23. Petley, *Capital and Culture*, p. 57.

24. D. C. Watt, 'Introduction', in Hitler, *Mein Kampf*, p. xv.

25. Ludwig Klages, *Persönlichkeit. Einführung in die Charakterkunde* (Potsdam: Müller
    & Kiepenhauer, 1928); Eduard Spranger, *Lebensformen. Geisteswissenschaftliche
    Psychologie und Ethik der Persönlichkeit*, (Halle [Saale]: Niemeyer, 1930), seventh
    edition; Johannes Schottky, *Die Persönlichkeit im Lichte der Erblehre* (Leipzig:
    Teubner, 1936); Erich Rothacker, *Die Schichten der Persönlichkeit* (Leipzig:
    Ambrosius, 1938); Wilhelm Hehlmann, *Persönlichkeit und Haltung. Rede gehalten
    auf der Tagung des NSD-Dozentenbundes der Martin-Luther-Universität Halle-
    Wittenberg am 13.Februar 1940* (Halle: Niemeyer, 1940).

26. Albert von Trentini, *Erziehung zur Persönlichkeit. Ein Zyklus in acht Betrachtungen*
    (Munich and Berlin: Oldenbourg, 1935), p. 27.

27. Franz Schlegelberger, *Der Weg zur Persönlichkeit. Vortrag gehalten am 26.April 1938
    vor den Rechtswahrern des Reichsschulungslehrgangs 1938 auf der Reichsschulungsburg
    Erwitte in Westfalen* (Berlin: Franz Dahlen, 1938), p. 13.

28. Hitler, *Mein Kampf*, p. 403. Quoted in Schlegelberger, *Der Weg zur Persönlichkeit*,
    p. 5.

29. Petley, *Capital and Culture*, pp. 57–8.

30. See Boguslaw Drewniak, *Der deutsche Film 1938–1945. Ein Gesamtüberblick* (Düsseldorf: Droste, 1987), p. 64.

31. The *Reich* Chamber of Culture (RKK) issued an edict on 12 November 1935 banning Jews from visiting 'theatres, cinemas, concerts, exhibitions etc.'. Cited in Joseph Walk (ed.), *Das Sonderrecht für die Juden im NS-Staat*. (Heidelberg: C. F. Müller, 1996), second edition p. 255. For details of the further tightening of the RKK ban after 1935, see BA R55/1416 2–20.

32. Chamberlain, *Foundations*, vol. I, p. xxxix.

33. Ibid.

34. Schmidt, *Die Geschichte des Genie-Gedankens*, vol. 1, pp. 1–5. On the literary history of the genius concept, see Michael Beddow, 'Goethe on Genius', in Penelope Murray (ed.), *Genius. The History of an Idea* (Oxford: Blackwell, 1989), pp. 100–3.

35. Schmidt, *Die Geschichte des Genie-Gedankens*, vol. 1, p. 2.

36. See also Goethe's 'Ganymed', 'Mahomets-Gesang', and *Götz von Berlichingen*, as discussed in Beddow, 'Goethe on Genius', p. 102.

37. Quote from ibid., p. 106.

38. Ibid., pp. 99ff.

39. Schmidt, *Die Geschichte des Genie-Gedankens*, vol.2, p. 213.

40. Chamberlain, *Foundations*, vol. I, p. 269. For an excellent account of the progressive fusion from the mid-19th century onwards of race theory with cultural debates on genius, see Schmidt, *Die Geschichte des Genie-Gedankens*, pp. 213–55.

41. Egon Friedell, *Kulturgeschichte der Neuzeit*, 3 vols (Munich: Biederstein, 1927–31). Cited in Schmidt, *Die Geschichte des Genie-Gedankens*, p. 202. Schmidt places Friedell in a line of descent from Thomas Carlyle, whose 'On Heroes, Hero-Worship and the Heroic in History' (1841) he translated into German.

42. Joseph Goebbels, radio broadcast, 19 April 1941, quoted in Schmidt, *Die Geschichte des Genie-Gedankens*, p. 209. Ian Kershaw identifies the German advance into Russia in June 1941, the disastrous retreat of German troops in the face of the Russian winter, and the declaration of war on the United States on 11 December 1941 as turning points that triggered the growth of a 'silent majority increasingly critical of the Nazi regime', and a concomitant decline in the strength of the Hitler Myth. See Kershaw, *The Hitler Myth*, pp. 169ff.

43. Joseph Goebbels, *Michael. Ein deutsches schicksal in Tagebuchblättern* (Munich: Eher, 1931), second edition, p. 31, cited in Schmidt, *Die Geschichte des Genie-Gedankens*, p. 207.

44. Thomas Elsaesser, *Weimar Cinema and After. Germany's Historical Imaginary* (London; Routledge, 2000), pp. 117ff.

45. Ibid., p. 119.

46. Ibid., p. 132.

47. *Reichslichtspielgesetz*, 16 February 1934. Quotations are from David Welch's translation, in Welch, *The Third Reich*, p.159.

48. Martin Loiperdinger, 'Filmzensur und Selbstkontrolle', in Wolfgang Jacobsen, Anton Kaes and Hans Helmut Prinzler (eds), *Geschichte des deutschen Films* (Stuttgart: J. B. Metzler, 1993), p.4 90.

49. Quotations from RFK correspondence September 1936 to September 1941, including letter of rejection from RFK to Max Krause, 2 August 1937, BA R56 VI/5a 13; internal RFK memorandum re. Wilhelm Leitschuh's script *Für Dich, Geliebte, sei's getan* (*Let it be Done for You, my Love*), 14 August 1937, BA R56 VI/5a 255; letter to RFK President Lehnich from script editor Hilde Kohze, 2 November 1937, BA R56VI/5a 88; letter from RFK to scriptwriting hopeful Hans Werner Müller, 18 November 1939, BA R56 VI/5a 450; letter from RFK to 'Party comrade' Curt Muscat, 21 March 1941, BA R56VI/5a 466.

50. Speech by Joseph Goebbels at the second annual conference of the RFK, in Lehnich (ed.), *Jahrbach 1938*, p.14.

51. That initiative was announced in Goebbels' speech to the 1937 RFK conference; see 'Rede des Reichsministers Dr Josef Goebbels auf der ersten Jahrestagung der Reichsfilmkammer am 15. März in der Krolloper, Berlin', in Gerd Albrecht (ed.), *Film im Dritten Reich. Eine Dokumentation* (Karlsruhe: Schauburg, 1979), p. 45.

52. Ibid., p. 55.

53. Ibid., p. 43.

54. Ibid., p. 45.

55. My own research for this chapter focuses exclusively on the Ufa artistic committee. For an insight into the workings of the cognate committee at Terra, see Pressedienst der Terra-Filmkunst, *Der Kunstausschuss der Terra-Filmkunst. Gespräch mit Karl Hartl, H. Paulsen, H. George, W. Liebeneiner und Th. Loose* (Berlin: Terra-Filmkunst, 1937).

56. See Kreimeier, *Die Ufa-Story*, pp. 305–6.

57. Joseph Gregor, *Meister der deutscher Schauspielkunst. Krauß, Klöpfer, Jannings, George* (Bremen and Vienna: Carl Schünemann, 1939), pp. 33–5.

58. Karl Ritter, 'Vom Wesen echter Filmkunst', in Lehnich (ed.), *Jahrbuch 1938*, p. 50.

59. Ufa *Kunstausschuß* minutes, 14 October 1938, BA R1091 5252 396–397. This episode appears to have been one of many examples of friction between Correll and the Propaganda Minister or his camp followers. Already in 1936, Goebbels had informed Ufa Director-General Klitzsch of his displeasure at Correll's reluctance to accept party dictates, and Correll's Ufa contract was eventually terminated in spring 1939; see Kreimeier, *Die Ufa-Story*, pp. 300ff.

60. For example, see von Demandowsky's airing of political 'misgivings' over a treatment for the thriller *Geliebte Feindin* (*Beloved Enemy*), which the committee subsequently rejected (BA R109I/5252 365), or his reminders to the committee of

Goebbels' wishes in respect of aesthetic issues (BA R109I/5252 395), as well as casting (one might surmise in this context that the Propaganda Minister was the moving force behind von Demandowsky's unexplained – and later countermanded – decision to reject Zarah Leander as the lead for Viktor Tourjansky's *Der Blaufuchs* [Arctic Fox, 1938], and to replace her with the Czech actress Lida Baarova, Goebbels' current favourite and alleged lover: see BA R109I/5252 355).

61. Goebbels in Lehnich (ed.), *Jahrbuch 1938*, p. 18.

62. BA R109I/5252 522 and 430. *Die unsterbliche Geliebte* never went into production under the Third Reich, but was eventually completed under the direction of Veit Harlan in 1951.

63. BA R109I/5252 446.

64. BA R109I/5252 469 and 364.

65. BA R109I/5252 522.

66. Joseph Goebbels in Lehnich (ed.), *Jahrbuch 1938*, p. 7.

67. Ibid., p. 24.

68. BA R109I/5252 504.

69. BA R109I/5252 430 (Podehl, on the need for clarity and human qualities in *Friedemann Bach*, Traugott Müller, 1941); BA R109I/5252 446 (Froelich, on simplicity and linearity in *Die Hochzeitsreise/The Honeymoon*, d. Karl Ritter, 1939); BA R109I/5252 504 (Wieman, on implausibility in a treatment for *Die Rache des Pharao/The Revenge of the Pharaoh*, which was never made under this title); BA R109I/5252 448 (Ritter on 'concessions to taste', 'proximity to life', and 'inner experience' in *Die Hochzeitsreise*); BA R109I/5252 469 (Riedel, on a proposed remake of Hans Behrendt's *Gloria*, 1931); BA R109I/5252 505 (Wieman on the 'sublime' in a proposed adaptation of the popular novelist John Knittel's *Der blaue Basalt/Blue Basalt*); BA R109I/5252 447 (Hartmann, on *Die Hochzeitsreise*).

70. Eric Rentschler, *The Ministry of Illusion. Nazi Cinema and its Afterlife* (Cambridge, MA and London: Harvard University Press, 1996), pp. 23 and 103.

71. See Ian Watt's account of the philosophical underpinnigs of literary realism in his *The Rise of the Novel. Studies in Defoe, Richardson and Fielding* (Harmondsworth: Penguin, 1963), p. 33.

72. Gunter Groll, *Film. Die unentdeckte Kunst* (Munich: C. H. Beck, 1937), p. 7.

73. BA R109I/5252 411 (on a treatment for the proposed *Wien-Film* production *Es lebe Astoria*).

74. Kurt Denzer, *Untersuchungen zur Filmdramaturgie des Dritten Reiches* (unpublished doctoral thesis, University of Kiel, 1970), pp. 177ff.

75. Translations, in the order in which the German titles appear, are: Club for Camera Technology, Association of German Film Cameramen, Association of German Projectionists, and Association of German Film Sound Engineers. See also Chapter 2, pp. 73–6.

76. Jan-Christopher Horak, 'Exilfilm, 1933–1945', in Wolfgang Jacobsen, Anton Kaes and Hans Helmut Prinzler (eds), *Geschichte des deutschen Films* (Stuttgart: Metzler, 1993), p. 101. In this 1993 piece, Horak suggests a figure of 2,000 film personnel in toto who sought refuge outside Nazi Germany after 1933. That figure is reproduced, though without reference to statistical sources, in Helmut Asper's *'Etwas Besseres als den Tod . . .'. Filmexil in Hollywood. Porträts, Filme, Dokumente* (Marburg: Schüren, 2002), p. 20. In an earlier work, however, Horak gives a more conservative estimate of 900 exiled film personnel, basing that figure on statistics from Günter Peter Straschek's 1975 *Westdeutscher Rundfunk* documentary *Filmemigration aus Nazi-Deutschland*: see *Fluchtpunkt Hollywood. Eine Dokumentation zur Filmemigration nach 1933*, 2nd Edn (Münster: MaKs, 1986), second edition.

77. Oswald Lehnich, 'Das entscheidende Filmjahr 1937', in Lehnich (ed.), *Jahrbuch 1938*, p. 35.

78. Felix Henseleit, 'Kraftquellen deutschen Filmschaffens. Der Filmnachweis und seine höhere Mission' (orig. m/s, 1938), BA/R56VI/5a 2.

79. Goebbels, in Lehnich (ed.), *Jahrbuch 1938*, pp. 25–6.

80. Oskar Kalbus and Hans Traub, *Wege zum Deutschen Institut für Filmkunde* (brochure, n.d., c. 1934–5), HFF C532.

81. Ibid., p. 11.

82. 'Feierliche Grundsteinlegung der Film-Akademie und des Arbeitsinstituts für Kulturfilmschaffenden. Ansprache des Generaldirektors Ludwig Klitzsch', in Lehnich (ed.), *Jahrbuch 1938*, p. 155.

83. Deutsche Filmakademie (ed.), *Deutsche Filmakademie mit dem Arbeitsinstitut für Kulturfilmschaffen* (inaugural brochure) (Babelsberg-Ufastadt: Deutsche Filmakademie, 1938), HFF T443.

84. Wilhelm Müller-Scheid, cited in Frank Maraun, 'Kostümgestalter und Trickfilmzeichner gesucht! Abteilung Bildende Künste: ein Lehrgebiet der filmkünstlerischen Fakultät', *Der deutsche Film* 5, 1938, p. 126.

85. Deutsche Filmakademie (ed.), *Deutsche Filmakademie*, p.80.

86. Wilhelm Müller-Scheid, 'Zur Eröffnung der Deutschen Filmakademie', *Der deutsche Film* 5, 1938, p. 117.

87. Gabriele Müller-Schwarz, n.t., *Filmwelt*, 7 October 1938, cited in Peter Gallasch, 'Im Hintergrund ein überdimensionaler Schirmherr. Vor 44 Jahren legte Goebbels den Grundstein zur Deutschen Film-Akademie in Babelsberg', *Filmkorrespondenz* 15, 20 July 1982, p. 2. See also Ilse Wehner, 'Die deutsche Filmakademie', *Der deutsche Film 2*, 1938, p. 35; Wilhelm Müller-Scheid, *Ein Deutscher namens Stein*, unpublished manuscript (Berlin: Theaterverlag A. Langen/G. Müller, 1935). Müller-Scheid's Nazi ideological credentials were impeccable; he had joined the SA in 1931, and took up a post in 1933 as *Gaupropagandaleiter* (Area Propaganda

Chief) for the RMVP, with responsibility for the RMVP regional office in Hessen-Nassau. See Joseph Wulf, *Theater und Film im Dritten Reich. Eine Dokumentation* (Frankfurt am Main, Berlin and Vienna: Ullstein, 1966), p. 335.

88. Quote from *Filmwelt*, 7 October 1938, cited in Peter Gallasch, 'Im Hintergrund', p. 2.

89. Ilse Wehner, 'Die deutsche Filmakademie', p.118.

90. Ulrich Kurowski, interview with Peter Pewas, in Wolfgang Jacobsen (ed.), *Babelsberg. Ein Filmstudio, 1912–1992* (Berlin: Stiftung Deutsche Kinemathek Argon, 1992), p. 244.

91. Müller-Scheid, cited in Maraun, 'Kostümgesta Iter', p. 126.

92. The best contemporary overview of the project is Ilse Wehner 'Die deutsche Filmakademie'.

93 Linda Schulte-Sasse, *Entertaining the Third Reich. Illusions of Wholeness in Nazi Cinema* (Durham and London: Duke University Press, 1996), p. 6.

94 Müller-Scheid, cited in Maraun, 'Kostümgestalter', p. 126.

95. Deutsche Filmakademie (ed.), *Deutsche Filmakademie*, p. 33.

2

The Actor in the Cinema of Personality

ACTORS VERSUS STARS

It was not initially in aesthetic terms that the star system was identified as a cinematic object ripe for the transformation National Socialism sought to achieve in
German culture after 1933. The first imperative confronting industry and state
from the early 1930s onwards was for the economic regeneration of a national
film sector suffering the multiple effects of sluggish markets, rising production
costs, and a decline in export markets following the advent of sound. Details of
that crisis, and of regime and industry responses, are well documented in existing histories of early 1930s film.[1] Less often noted is the prominence of stars
and related issues in trade and industry discussions of what one trade journal
identified as German film's 'fight for its very future' in the early Nazi years.[2]
Though neither rising production costs nor shrinking markets were attributable
entirely to misplaced investment in stars, *Der Film* and cognate titles pointed
repeatedly to rampant inflation in star fees as one cause of film industry crisis
from the late 1920s. Under such headings as 'Star fees prevent recovery', or
'The monstrosity of stardom', critics of the star system campaigned vigorously
in the trade press for state and industry regulation to stem the 'madness' of esca-
lating fees and salaries for German stars.[3]

The efforts of apologists for a planned film economy to block rising expendi-
ture on stars were, however, in vain. The decade 1930–40 saw continuing
inflation of fees and wages, particularly for the most prominent among German
stars. Among the highest paid, for instance, was Hans Albers, the quadrupling
of whose fee from RM5,000 to 20,000 per film in 1933–4 had been an early
focus of critical outrage. By 1939, however, Albers' average of RM120,000 per
film – a 600 per cent increase from 1934 – was by no means the only example
of the German industry's refusal throughout the 1930s to stage that 'twilight of
the [film] idols [*Götzendämmerung*]' which *Der Film* had demanded in 1934.[4]

Tables 1 to 3 below offer a useful snapshot of stars' economic status in the
pre-war industry. Following the outbreak of war, and the subsequent imposition

of a national wage freeze across all economic sectors from autumn 1939, the *Reich* Propaganda Ministry instigated a comprehensive survey of income levels across the spectrum of actorly employment in German film. As the tables show, it was a feature of the national industry that actors were contracted predominantly on a daily basis, with fees calculated pro rata against a sliding scale of lump sum rates for single films. Single-day rates ranged from RM150 for bit parts to RM2,000 for prominent figures barred by other commitments from full-time studio contracts for their work in film. Thus, for instance, such stage luminaries as Werner Krauss and Heinrich George were paid daily rates of

Table 1: Actors' fees October 1939, expressed in equivalent RM per film title

Fee per film title (RM)	Total actors surveyed	Actors paid on pro rata daily rate	Actors under studio contract	Percentage of actors under contract
under 20,000	209	201	8	4
20–25,000	23	19	4	17
25–30,000	10 (13)	8 (8)	2 (5)	20
30–40,000	10 (11)	9 (10)	1	10
40–50,000	10	5	5	50
50,000 +	14	1	13	93
Total	276	243	33	12

Source: See Table 3

Note: Figures in brackets include actors also listed by Raether in other fee categories. Actors named twice or more are included in Tables 1–3 in the highest fee category in which they are named.

Table 2: Actors under studio contract – fees per film up to RM50,000

Fee per film (RM)	Actors receiving maximum fee in this category	Actors receiving fees below maximum in this category (fee per film in RM)
Under 20,000	Fritz von Dongen, Herta Feiler, 'Krista' Söderbaum, Mathias Wieman	Albert Hehn (10,000), Albert Matterstock (15,000), Herma Relin (3,000), Ilse Werner (15,000)
20–25,000	Ewald Balser, Paul Javor, Hilde Krahl, Ferdinand Marian	
25–30,000	Gusti Huber, Hans Söhnker	
30–40,000	Olga Tschechowa	
40–50,000	Ingrid Bergman, Willy Birgel, Karl-Ludwig Diehl, Willy Fritsch, Brigitte Horney	

Source: See Table 3

Table 3: Actors under studio contract – fee per film at RM50,000+

Actor	Fee (RM)
Hans Albers	120,000
Gustav Fröhlich	50,000
Willi Forst	70,000
Benjamin Gigli	132,000
Gustav Gründgens	80,000
Emil Jannings	125,000
Jenny Jugo	80,000
Viktor de Kowa	50,000
Pola Negri	75,000
Heinz Rühmann	80,000
Luis Trenker	60,000
Paula Wessely	120,000
Zarah Leander	150,000

Source, Tables 1–3: Reichsministerium für Volksaufklärung und Propaganda: Memorandum Arnold Raether
to *Oberregierungsrat* (senior government official) Kohler, 13.10.1939: Bundesarchiv R55/949.

RM1,000 and RM2,000 respectively to secure their release from more binding
contracts in theatre. 'Unknowns' of the likes of Johannes Bartel, Frauke Lauter-
bach, Vera von Langen or Edith Oss trailed behind on daily rates below RM200,
rising to RM400–500 for more promising young talent, including Heidemarie
Hatheyer, Kirsten Heiberg, or the already (relatively) well known Carola Höhn.[5]

Despite the hardships induced at the lower end of the income scale by contractual instability and occasionally meagre fees, there remained however, as
the Ministry survey clearly shows, a sizeable contingent among German actors
who continued by 1939 to enjoy both the security of studio contracts, and fee
levels above RM20,000 per film. Even lesser figures among the group recognisable as major stars by virtue both of the pay they attracted and their
contractual status, could apparently command gross annual salaries of
RM40,000 or above. Ferdinand Marian, for instance, who starred in a succession of romantic melodramas and thrillers before taking the lead role in Veit
Harlan's *Jud Süss* (1940), could earn, at the rate of RM25,000 per title, a com-
fortable RM50,000, even from the two run-of-the-mill crime films in which he
starred in 1939. *Robert Koch* (1938) appears in RMVP figures to have secured
for Emil Jannings over double that amount (RM125,000), while German cinema's favourite comic, Heinz Rühmann, stood to gain a cool RM160,000 from
his two 1939 titles, *Paradies der Junggesellen* (*Bachelors' Paradise*), and *Hurra, ich
bin Papa* (*Hooray, I'm Papa*).

Compare these figures with reported monthly salaries of RM300 for lesser
theatre performers, and of well under RM200 for industrial workers, and it
becomes clear that film stars remained throughout the 1930s (and to the dis-

gust of conservative critics) figures of opulence and luxury, potent symbols of a wealth of which the majority among their audience could only dream.[6] Continuing wage inflation after 1933 was due in part, ironically perhaps, to the strong market position stars attained precisely as a result of the political triumph of a regime with whose cultural values the star system seemed so at odds. Internal purges, and the emigration of film personnel exposed to persecution on racial or political grounds, drastically reduced Germany's available pool of acting talent from 1933. Studio records show such sought-after figures as Hans Albers or Pola Negri capitalising on their strong bargaining position in this period of diminishing supply, in Negri's case by refusing even the most prestigious of roles, in Albers', by garnering such privileges as the right to select his own scriptwriter and director, as well as to define the parameters of advertising and public relations for his forthcoming films.[7]

As the Propaganda Ministry statistics confirm, the Third Reich industry boasted by 1939 an (almost) full complement of male and female stars to fill the staple roles of German-language genre film: the lusty man of action (Hans Albers), the Viennese charmer (Willi Forst), the young lover (Viktor de Kowa), the fresh-faced comedienne (Jenny Jugo), the vampish femme fatale (Pola Negri), and so on – not forgetting, of course, Ufa's highest-paid star, the Swedish revue-turned-film-star Zarah Leander, to whom we return in more detail in Chapter 6.[8] Tables 2 and 3 suggest, moreover, that neither the five studios still operative in 1939 – Ufa, Tobis, Terra, Bavaria and Wien-Film – nor the state institutions that oversaw the industry (the *Reich* Film Chamber and Propaganda Ministry) had succeeded in restraining the star wage inflation that had so exercised industry observers from the early 1930s. More accurately perhaps, they had barely tried. Certainly, existing records document the continued use by studios of large financial incentives to win over major stars. In April 1935, Lilian Harvey was offered significant concessions – a fee of RM125,000, 80,000 of it payable in sterling to her British address – to secure her return from a three-year sojourn in Hollywood and London to work on the Ufa musical *Capriccio* (a title eventually shot under Karl Ritter's direction, and released by Ufa in 1938).[9] That same spring, Willy Birgel was wooed by Ufa with the promise of an eventual doubling of his salary from RM8,000 to RM16,000 per film, provided he agreed to a two-year contract binding him to the studio for the six titles in which he was to star between 1935 and 1937.[10] By 1936, Birgel's fee had been revised upwards to a maximum RM24,000 per film, while Zarah Leander, Birgel's co-star in the Detlef Sierck title *Zu neuen Ufern* (*To New Shores*, 1937), was won for Ufa with the promise of RM200,000 for her first three titles, an unprecedented 70 per cent of which was payable in krone to a bank account in her Swedish home.[11]

The continuing upward curve of star fees and salaries (including in Zarah Leander's case a staggering annual increase of RM100,000 between 1937 and 1939) attests to a sustained official tolerance of fee inflation, at least in the case of major stars.[12] Even the outbreak of war failed entirely to halt this upward trend; in late 1939, the Propaganda Ministry noted numerous infringements of the wage freeze in contracts with such middle-range stars as Paul Dahlke, René Deltgen and Camilla Horn, but conceded in internal memoranda that full implementation of the freeze remained impossible, since 'any kind of standard wage tariff for cultural activity' was a 'near impossibility'.[13]

As historians of Third Reich film have often observed, official tolerance of rising costs for major stars bespeaks a recognition by both industry and state of the key role the star system played in German film-industrial regeneration after 1933. That recognition was grounded in part in the economic impera-tive to recapture audiences for cinema in general, and in particular for German film, which remained squeezed by foreign competition, especially from Hollywood, until import bans from the late 1930s onwards secured the domestic market for indigenous product and home-grown stars. Alongside their economic function as audience magnets, stars were seen, moreover, at least by regime ideologues, as figures of identification securing popular com-pliance with the ideological programmes of the Nazi regime. Thus, for instance, in one account of film spectatorship by the *Reich* Film Dramaturg Fritz Hippler, star identification could produce, alongside that 'personal association of the spectator with the main protagonist which arises during the course of the film', a simultaneous 'striving to emulate' the behaviour of the star. Citing the case of female stars whose influence on 'ideals of beauty' is decisive, Hippler continues,

> it is impossible to overemphasise the importance of casting choices for film roles. It is not only the case that this or that woman must please the audience in her role in this or that particular film. No indeed; for if that woman is selected on the proper basis of her external *habitus* in combination with her inner qualities and attributes, and if she is successfully deployed in a variety of films, then she can decisively, though quite unconsciously influence general levels of taste . . .

Hippler's startling conclusion that the female star, in shaping 'ideals of beauty among large numbers of men', could serve the pro-natalist 'population policies' of the regime, locates his theory of star identification more as a fascist fantasy of audience control, than as a usable insight into the reality of star reception after 1933.[14] In fact, as more recent studies habitually stress, Third Reich star images were marked by an acute ambivalence that hampered any effort to har-

ness stars to the ideological project of National Socialism. It is indeed the con-
viction of scholars from Klaus Kriemeier and Stephen Lowry, to Sabine Hake,
Marc Silberman and Lutz Koepnick that efforts to reconstruct the star images
of such ambiguous figures as Hans Albers or Willi Fritsch, Lilian Harvey or
(especially) Zarah Leander to serve propaganda ends ended almost inevitably
in 'dismal failure'.[15]

Those recent studies emerge, as I have observed elsewhere, from a new film
historiography that draws on minute, micro-archival research, alongside textual
study, in an effort to arrive at a fully contextual study of German film.[16] A study
of contextual material in respect of Third Reich stars pinpoints, however, a further field of enquiry that returns us to National Socialism's aspiration for a
transformed film art. For numerous contemporary commentators – film theorists, critics, ideologues, practitioners, political appointees – stars were to be
seen neither primarily as commodities deployed on domestic film markets, nor
as ideological filters for the regime, but rather – to quote one influential critic,
Fedor Stepun – as 'core issue[s] for the totality of film aesthetics'.[17] Harking
back, among other antecedents, to early German movements for cinema reform,
Third Reich commentators repeatedly identified stars as emblematic of what
they claimed was a 'new' film aesthetic for the 'new era' of National Socialism.
Thus, while such journalists and theorists alike were keen to gesture towards the
ideological issues considered so fundamental by Fritz Hippler and his ilk, their
writings segued regularly into arguments for a new aesthetic that might define
at last the specificity of stars in German film. In one 1935 article in the trade
organ *Film-Kurier*, the critic Heinz Wemper, to quote one example, certainly
begins by citing Hans Grimm's racist apologia for German imperialism, *Volk
ohne Raum* (Volk *without Space*) to support his view of contemporary stars as
'unnatural' figures of opulence who sustained an existence only 'at the expense
of other comrades among the *Volk*'. Here again, however, stardom's crime is
located less in its ideological infringement of *völkisch* principles, than in its con-
travention of a film aesthetic that suppresses the cinematic artwork's commodity
nature, and privileges instead its status as auratic art – a film art that, for Wemper, 'has been and is today still possible only if the businessman remains in the
background for the duration of the creative process'.[18]

STARS AND PERSONALITY

I suggested in Chapter 1 that film's aesthetic transformation after 1933 pivoted
around the concept of the 'personality' as the motor of reconstruction for a
nationally specific, *völkisch* film art. A quote from Heinz Siska's popular study
of 'the magical world of film' illustrates how this assertion of 'personality' operated in the case of stars. In Germany, Siska contends,

attitudes to film actors in Germany have been transformed in recent years. We are perhaps more considered than other peoples, less susceptible to the bluffs of external presentation. Quite the reverse; the more public interest [in Germany] centres on a particular actor, the more it is considered important to establish whether this is an artist whose other merits are complemented by his status as *Persönlichkeit*.[19]

What, then, were the qualities that established an actor as a *Persönlichkeit* – not 'just' a star – in the public mind? In his seminal study of stars, Richard Dyer draws on Weber's notion of charisma to discuss the relationship between the social order and the star image. Charisma as defined by Weber is 'a certain quality of the individual personality by virtue of which he is set apart from other men and treated as endowed with supernatural, superhuman, or at least superficially exceptional qualities'.[20] Quoting Alberoni, Dyer suggests that the difference between the star and the political personality, in the Hollywood context at least, resides in the star's status as a figure devoid of institutional or political power. Indeed stars are adored not for their socio-political status, but for their perceived ordinariness, their status as superlative examples of what are nonetheless plausible everyday individuals. A whole apparatus of representation, from studio publicity and merchandising, through to newspaper and magazine coverage, popular biographies, fashion and advertising, thus uses images from the most intimate corners of stars' private lives to create figures who are 'usual in appearance ... psychologically credible in personality [and] individuated in image'.[21]

For generations of film scholars, Dyer's work has been hugely illuminating for studies of the social function of stars in Western democracies, societies ideologically organised, as is the Hollywood star system, around the bourgeois individual as their stabilising centre. The function of the 'personality' in the corporatist *völkisch* state was rather different. Already before 1933, German star commentary had drawn on existing discourses of art to situate stars as personalities of creative genius. Under Nazism, as we have seen, ideas of genius gained a racial and political inflection, not least in celebrations of the *Führer* as a prototypical genius figure. Public representations of stars in this context constructed a vision of actorly 'charisma' that derived not – as in Dyer – from stars' status as extraordinary versions of ordinary individuals, but from their position as leadership figures embedded in a hierarchically organised Nazi state. Stars were accordingly exhorted to take prominent roles in the *Volksgemeinschaft* by assuming public responsibilities that served the interests of *Volk* and state. Public appearances at premieres in provincial as well as metropolitan cinemas, for example, were encouraged as a means of disseminating to film audiences across the *Reich* the message that 'a common bond binds all those who work in

German film; [for] in the end the individual can only prosper if the collective does also'.[22] Significant events in the annual film calendar – the Berlin Press Ball, the Venice Biennale – further cemented symbolic links between film acting and *völkisch* public identity. Zarah Leander's first public concert in Berlin, for instance, took place during the 1939 Press Ball, and was attended by 'numerous personalities from government, party, military, diplomatic service, economy, science and art', including among others Joseph and Magda Goebbels, *Reich Press Chief* Otto Dietrich, Ufa Director-General Klitzsch, Tobis Director-General Paul Lehmann, and such 'well-known film industry faces' as Kristina Söderbaum, Dorothea Wieck, Hilde Weissner, Heinrich George, Paul Hörbiger and many more.[23] The recruitment of stars to numerous state and military initiatives, ranging from the winter aid programme to military service; their elevation to managerial and bureaucratic positions within a state-controlled industry, as well as their lionisation with numerous state prizes and honorary titles – some ('Professor' and 'State Actor') awarded by the *Führer* in person – reinforced the public association of stars and state-political charisma: an association that, for Dyer, is largely absent from the Hollywood star system in its classical mode.[24]

The importance in the fascist public sphere of the ritual event has often been noted; and the example of the Press Ball is one indication that the star *Persönlichkeit* was as much a product as were political personalities of public rituals of *völkisch* identity formation. But distinctions between the Hollywood star and the Nazi *Persönlichkeit* were evident, too, in less obviously political forms of public presentation. In popular representations from star biographies to the illustrated press, the collective embedding of the actor-personality was signalled symbolically by three recurrent metaphors. For the most avid fascist supporters, the metaphor was military: the star as a 'soldier of art' who is 'open to his people and his time', willing to 'risk stepping down from the stage' to become one element in the 'troop' that was the folk community.[25] Others drew on the motif of work as the ethical imperative binding the people to a common cause, and wrote of actors as craftsmen applying their 'iron industry' to the construction of a common culture for the German nation.[26] For others again, it was race, *ethnos* or regional identity that bound the actor-personality to the nation: hence for instance Joseph Gregor's obsessive tracing, in his *Meister der deutsche Schauspielkunst,* of actors' roots in region, nation and the *Heimat* soil.[27]

In all these figurings of the actor-personality as a focus of collective emulation, there was, however, a common thread. It was not, as we have seen, in narratives of personal experience and/or by processes of psychic identification that the actor-personality forged bonds with the audience or the *Volk* at large. Instead, it was in his very body that the actor achieved identity with what Emil Jannings, for instance, termed the 'great qualities of the German *Volk*'.[28] In the fascist public sphere, collective identity was in any case formed around what the French fascist Pierre Drieu la Rochelle termed the 'values of the body': values that fuelled the 'revolution' of 'totalitarian fascism and Hitlerism' and offered to modern man (*sic*) 'a double restoration, corporeal and spiritual'.[29]

In cinema, it is, of course, in the actor's performance that the body is fore-grounded; and it is in contemporary discussions of actorly performance that this relation of the body to the *völkisch* collective was most vividly developed. What, then, are the specific features of acting in post-1933 film that may help us ident-ify more clearly the function of the embodied 'personality' as a focus of collective identification?

FILM ACTING AND THEATRE

Screen acting, as Peter Krämer and Alan Lovell have noted, has until recently been a neglected area in film studies and film history. Krämer and Lovell's own edited collection addresses that imbalance with several contributions on acting history, including Cynthia Baron's study of Hollywood in the so-called studio era from 1930 onwards. Baron focuses in particular on acting theory and formal studio training; and she dates the latter from the early 1930s, when the decline in theatre audiences and the closure of many venues in the face of competition from film reduced 'traditional training grounds for Hollywood actors'. The stu-dios responded by hiring their own acting experts (dialogue directors and drama coaches), and establishing actor training programmes on the lots. Thus accord-ing to Baron, 'by 1939 all of the major studios had actor training programmes', and were exploring new techniques in voice production and diction, as well as the use of body, gesture and facial expression specifically for film.[30]

In Germany, as elsewhere in Europe, the relationship between film and theatre was rather different. Certainly, as in the US, theatre suffered economi-cally from the impact of film. As early as 1912, the *Deutscher Bühnenverein* (German Theatre Association) published a memorandum citing 29 provincial and metropolitan theatres that had succumbed to competition from the nick-elodeon (*Kientopp*), and calling for a defence of the theatre sector on the grounds of its cultural superiority to film.[31] During the Depression years 1929–32, however, both theatre and film were equally threatened. The 'wave' of cinema liquidations referenced in the opening to Chapter 1 was paralleled by shortened seasons and closures in theatre too. Thus according to one calcu-lation, German theatres 'accounted for a total of 1,567 "theatre-months" during the 1932–3 season, down 25 per cent from 1,957.5 in 1929–30'.[32] Importantly, too, the Nazi takeover in 1933 brought with it not, as in the US situation, a weakening, but an ideological strengthening of ties between theatre and film. As one contemporary commentator observed, the Nazis aspired to replace econ-

Table 4: Acting – training routes into film, c. 1936

	Theatre	Dance	Variety	Opera/ Operetta	Sport	Cabaret	Circus	Radio	Film	Total
Actresses	83	8	1	–	–	–	–	–	8	100
Actors	171	–	–	8	6	5	1	1	–	192
Total	254	8	1	8	6	5	1	1	8	292

Source: Walther Freisburger, *Theater im Film. Eine Untersuchung über die Grundzüge und Wandlungen in den Beziehungen zwischen Theater und Film* (Emsdetten: Lechte, 1936), p. 69.

omic competition with an education of public taste that would bring equal benefits to all ailing cultural sectors; thus the question of competition between theatre and film was 'in the end to be resolved ... within the framework of a general education of German man [*der deutsche Mensch*]'.[33]

In film, this was seen to involve, among other things, a return to traditional and highbrow theatrical genres as sources of adaptations for the German screen. Walter Freisburger notes, for instance, in his 1936 study of theatre and film an initial steep decline in the early 1930s in the use of modern drama and theatrical comedy as sources, as well as a return after 1933 to classical drama as a genre model for film.[34] Studies by Freisburger and others suggest, too, that theatre remained (unlike in North America) the major training ground and talent pool for German film from 1933, at least until the founding of the German Film Academy in 1937. Among Freisburger's sample of 100 actresses and 192 actors for his survey of mid-30s film, 83 per cent of women and 89 per cent of men were theatre-trained. Among the women, only 8 per cent, and none among the men, began their acting career directly through film (see Table 4). Importantly, too, even the biggest screen stars were often active in theatre throughout their film career. Freisburger tells an early anecdote of Eugen Klöpfer, who he claims was arrested in 1924 on his way to 'film for Reinhardt in Italy', and 'forcibly returned' to fulfil theatrical commitments at one metropolitan theatre.[35] A decade on, the ability to run parallel careers in the theatre and film remained the signal quality that distinguished the film star from the actor-personality or 'genius'. In Joseph Gregor's pantheon of 'German actors who today most radiantly represent our acting art', all four – Werner Krauss, Eugen Klöpfer, Emil Jannings, Heinrich George – were as prominent in theatre as in film, which latter, according to Gregor, they 'elevated' through their special gift for theatre art.[36] Gregor's choice of older men as models of acting art was not unusual, for 'personality' demanded both maturity, and sublime powers to which – as we see in Chapter 4 – men were considered best suited to aspire. Even women, however, could achieve through theatre acting the 'depth' that personality demanded. The screen diva Olga Tschechowa wrote of the woman as film actress that she might retain through theatre work 'a capacity for fully-rounded performance', and thus demonstrate that 'beyond external appearance, a personality is present'.[37] For Rudolf Bach, similarly, in his study of 'of the woman as actress', women could most successfully transcend 'external appearance and phenomenal form [*Erscheinung*]' if they mastered 'the art of theatre, which consists in its very nature in immediate physical human presence'.[38]

The technical source of the theatre actor's excellence, admittedly, remained obscure. Though many actors began their careers with drama training, actor biographies emphasised time and again the need for apprenticeships in repertory; for, in Bach's words again, 'in the initial stages especially, nothing is more important than to perform, to perform and to perform again'.[39] This emphasis on practice, not theoretical training, as the proper mode of professional initiation again runs counter to the Hollywood case. Baron cites as evidence of the increased US emphasis on actor training from 1930 on the appearance of numerous acting manuals 'authored by individuals who were integral to the network of actor training programmes in Hollywood'.[40] That development is apparently absent in the German case. Hans Traub's 1940 bibliography of German print sources on film (see Introduction) is striking, for the virtual absence of acting manuals in the strict sense. Alongside a plethora of titles from the 1910s and 20s on career pathways to film acting, only two works on diction from the late 1930s, Walter Kuhlmann's *Schule des Sprechens* (*School for Speaking*) and Hans Lebede's *Erziehung zum Sprechen* (*Learning to Speak*) are practical guides of the kind Baron references for the Hollywood case.[41] Indeed, practitioners writing on acting countered the pragmatism of Hollywood manuals with idealist celebrations of actorly 'soul' that dismissed as vulgarly materialist any reference to performance technique. As Mathias Wieman would later write, film in particular, through its use of close-up, was uniquely equipped to 'render visible and communicable the most microscopic and delicate stirrings of the soul'. And yet, continued Wieman, 'if you ask me what exactly I have in mind here, I can only reply that this is something I do not wish to put into words'.

With his concluding, 'I wish only to try and try again to say it in film', Wieman repeats Rudolf Bach's threefold emphasis on practice as the actor's sole route to perfection. Paradoxically, however, this foregrounding of bodily praxis points not towards an absence of acting theory, but rather situates Third Reich performance in a nationally specific theoretical and ideological tradition that locates the actor as the embodiment of 'the new man of our century ... the soldier of art'.[42] The Hollywood studios' practical acting guides found their German counterparts not in the smattering of diction manuals cited above, but in a whole philosophical literature that linked the body in performance to National Socialism's conception of the actor as embodied representation of the *völkisch* soul.

ACTING AND PHYSIOGNOMY

In Richard Dyer's *Stars*, reference is made to Béla Balázs' notion of the 'eternal ineffability of the face as the window to the soul'. This account is problematic, Dyer observes, on the theoretical grounds that 'how we read (and produce) facial expressions is deeply dependent on conventions of various kinds: filmic ... artistic ... and cultural'. On the other hand, Balázs is important 'because he gives expression to a widely held view, namely that the close-up reveals the unmediated personality of the individual'.[43]

I want to add in what follows a further, and specifically historical dimension to this argument for a recuperation of Balázs in the context of a study of stars. The author of two major film-theoretical works prior to 1933, *Der sichtbare Mensch* (*Visible Man*, 1924) and *Der Geist des Films* (*The Spirit of Film*, 1930), Balázs stands as a representative of a much broader philosophical tradition in Weimar and Third Reich film theory: a tradition whose emphasis is most evident in writings on acting for film. In his own comments on the film actor, Balázs specifies the nature of that tradition when he writes, citing Goethe:

> For no animal has ever existed that has had the form of one animal and the species [*Art*] of another; rather, each animal always has its own body and its own meaning [*Sinn*]. It thus necessarily follows that every body determines its own nature ... [And] if this is so, as indeed it always is so, then there is such a thing as physiognomy. [44]

As Massimo Locatelli has noted, Balázs' references here and elsewhere to phys-iognomy situate his film theory as a 'homage' to early Romantic aesthetics and philosophies of identity.[45] The specific debt here is to Lavater, a religious thinker and philosopher whose four-volume *Physiognomische Fragmente zur Beförderung des Menschentums und der Menschenliebe* (*Essays on Physiognomy Designed to Pro-mote the Knowledge and the Love of Mankind*) triggered a modish concern in the late 18th century with precisely those readings of face and body as 'windows to the soul' that, as Dyer points out, also preoccupy Balázs. An early precursor of German Romanticism, Lavater devoted years to developing elaborate typologies of gesture and face that would demonstrate how indivisible was the relation between the body's surface, and the spirit that infused corporeal form. His com-mitment to Romantic conceptions of the immanence of soul or spirit in material form located him as an important forerunner of such figures as Novalis in the early 19th century. But Lavater's influence was also felt in numerous German writings on film. The paucity of manuals on acting technique was counterbal-anced in late 1930s and 40s Germany by a rash of publications on the relation between actorly gesture and inner being, including Wolfgang Berkefeld's

Untersuchungen zur Theorie der Schauspielkunst (*Studies in the Theory of the Art of Acting*, 1937), Wilhelm Böhm's *Die Seele des Schauspielers* (*The Soul of the Actor*, 1941) and the director Arthur Maria Rabenalt's *Mimus ohne Maske. Über die Schauspielkunst im Film* (*Mime without the Mask. On the Art of Acting in Film*, 1945).[46] Though Rabenalt claims of his book, published as it was in the wake of German defeat in 1945, that its precepts 'ran strictly counter to the conceptions of the Nazi film leadership', its preoccupation with the film actor's capacity to 'descend to the very depths of a particular state of the soul' reveal the rooting of *Mimus ohne Maske* in physiognomy, and thus in a metaphysics of acting that had become by the mid-1940s the dominant tradition of thinking on acting in Third Reich film.

Again, the contrast with Hollywood is illuminating here. According to Dyer, Maltby and others, two 'broad schools of thought' (Dyer) underpinned Hollywood acting in the classical period. The first, deriving from the eighteenth- and nineteenth-century writings of Diderot and Coquelin, stressed the necessary distinction between performance technique and the presentation of character. Here, the actor in performance remained dispassionate, not feeling a character's emotion, but focusing instead on the 'technical devices' that produce the effect of that emotion for the audience. The second, later school of thought, associated initially with Stanislavski, and later with Hollywood 'Method', encouraged the performer to explore her/his own psychology, using internal reserves of memory and affect in order to 'live the character s/he plays as fully as possible and ... base the performance on how s/he feels inside'.[47]

Dyer's characterisation of the two practices as, for the former, 'acting from the outside in' and, for the latter, ' acting from the inside out' throws into sharp relief the distinction between the performance theories he references, and the physiognomic tradition that informed writings by Böhm, Berkefeld, Iros, Rabenalt and their peers. Two central tenets informed philosophies of performance in the German tradition. The first involved a rejection of the inside versus out, mind versus body opposition that structures both the Diderot and Stanislavski schools. Against both 'acting from the outside in', and 'from the inside out', Berkefeld, for example, posed a concept of acting as a struggle for synthesis between inside and outside, being and form. Berkefeld cites the actor Werner Krauss in support of his case that 'actors who are aware of themselves and of their presence on stage are not actors in the true sense'. Instead, the actor's body on screen must become the immanent expression of what Berkefeld's cynosure, Ludwig Klages, termed 'soul, the soul [as] the very meaning of the body's phenomenal form'.[48] In other writings, that demand for an idealist fusion of soul and form received a racist inflection; hence for instance Edmund Schneider's insistence, in his 'structural-psychological' account of actorly psychology, on the 'Jewishness' of some actors' preoccupation with technique, convention and form.[49] Universally, however, what Third Reich theorists identified as the modernist split between content and form was pilloried as a feature of the star phenomenon in film. Ernst Iros, for instance, wrote of the 'sin against art that is the star system', and railed against its 'formal ornamentation' and 'excessive will to personal style'. In what Iros goes on to term 'technical style' (Dyer's acting from the outside in), as well as 'inauthentic, pseudo-individual style' (acting from the inside out), 'forms become detached, as it were, from their very soul, and rigidify as lifeless graven images'.[50]

The writings of Iros and his contemporaries emerged contemporaneously with the German Film Academy, and represent an attempt to provide, along with the Academy itself, a specifically German alternative to Hollywood acting theory and training. Iros' preference in this context is for what he terms the 'personality style'; and his comments on possible routes to the creation of personality (not stardom) in film highlight a second common preoccupation that surfaces repeatedly in the Third Reich metaphysics of screen acting. The 'sin' of stardom, with its excessive stress on 'individualist cravings for admiration', can be avoided, Iros suggests, and 'personality' achieved, by a return to synthesis as the organising principle of creative practice in film. As we saw in Chapter 1, 'personality' in Third Reich film commentary, like its sub-category 'genius', was a term rooted in conceptions of the creative artist as the privileged bearer of collective cultural identity. It was, in other words, through her/his rooting in the collective that the actor achieved the 'synthesis' that Iros demands: and the collective bonding of the actor-personality specifically was to be achieved in one of three ways.

First, especially for writers who stressed the proximity of the film medium to theatre, it was the ensemble that was to be the guiding motto of actors in film. As the journal *Film-Kurier* put it in a 1935 essay on 'The star monstrosity: its consequences and possible counter-measures', 'any connoisseur of acting knows that it is never the individual actor (the star) who creates success, but always the ensemble *in toto*!'[51] Wilhelm Böhm echoed that sentiment in his monograph on the actor's 'soul' when he wrote that: 'Stardom of any kind, any assertion of superiority over the ensemble ... is wrong. In the ensemble, the stature of the minor actor increases, as he gains a sense of the values represented by the great figures alongside whom he stands.'[52]

Studio employment practices in part reflected this privileging of the ensemble over the star. Admittedly, there was no studio equivalent of the repertory company in provincial theatre. Most leading actors were contracted to studios only for the duration of the film's production, and only the most successful – figures of the stature of Hans Albers, Zarah Leander, Willi Fritsch – were engaged for two or more films, and thus became part of a studio's stable or ensemble. For the majority of stars, flat fees were negotiated per film, while minor actors worked at daily rates negotiated with the studios, and overseen by the Propaganda Ministry (see Tables 1–3).[53]

On the other hand, studios and Propaganda Ministry alike repeatedly emphasised the need for a promotion of German cinema's ensemble ethos. Star salaries, as we saw above, were the subject of often heated debate, and stars were regularly exhorted – or coerced – to cut their cloth to meet the financial needs of the film-making collective. Each studio, moreover, retained a regular team of actors that could be drawn upon at any time: figures like Fritz von Dongen, Albert Hohn, Albert Matterstock or Herma Relin, now barely remembered, but whose ubiquity in minor roles contributed to the ensemble character of Third Reich genre film.

Press commentary too eschewed the extravagance and excess of star acting, and polemicised regularly in favour of the constrained and decorous style associated with ensemble acting for stage and screen. Allied to this was the second feature that, in the writings of Third Reich drama critics, linked the actor-personality to the collective, and this was her/his commitment to the performance style that Arthur Maria Rabenalt termed the '*Mimus*', or 'mime'.[54]

Rabenalt's observations on 'mime' refer to theatrical traditions from classical antiquity that were widely cited in Third Reich acting theory as models for the contemporary screen. The 'mimes' were traced by Rabenalt and others to Greek and Roman theatre, where they were taken to represent a tradition that was both popular, and antipathetic to the formal self-consciousness so despised in Third Reich theories of dramatic form. The mime in the classical context was a repertory form centring usually on 'everyday domestic situations or ... burlesqued versions of myth'. It differed from classical comedy and tragedy among other things in its performance mode; thus unlike Roman tragedy, for instance, in which 'all the actors were male, wore masks and probably doubled in roles', the mimes renounced the mask, and instead emphasised the expressive powers of the body and facial expression.[55]

In German acting theory from the late 1930s on, two elements of the mime were highlighted as features to be emulated by actors striving after integration with the folk soul. In the first instance, it was the mimes' geographical mobility that was identified as a source of their model status. For the long-time opponent of film, Joseph Gregor, the medium could be redeemed in part by the mime, which 'is and remains film's strongest element'. The performer in mime, Gregor continues, was a 'wandering player, almost a circus artiste'; and his analogy of the contemporary actor with the mime leads him to stress for the modern context the importance of an actor's 'wandering years' – the decades of provincial repertory that Gregor considered formative both for legendary

theatre greats (Mitterwurzer, Matkowsky, Kainz), and for the towering personalities (Krauss, Klöpfer, Jannings, George) who are the subject of his *Meister der
deutscher Schauspielkunst*.[56]

This stress on provincial experience as an antidote to the false glamour of the
metropolitan stage and screen was echoed in press accolades to film stars attend-
ing premieres at local and regional screens, as well as in the studios' emphasis
on 'theatre tours' as integral elements in star publicity.[57] But there was a further
feature that more securely rooted the mime of 1930s acting theory in the collective soul, and that was its renunciation of formal convention, and in particular
the mask, in favour of the actor's body and face as the prime focus of audience
attention. Repeatedly, post-1933 writings on acting denounce the 'sensation',
the 'affectation' (*Manier*) and 'excessive extravagance' which they associate both
with Weimar theatre, and with contemporary star acting in the Hollywood style.
'The mime', by contrast, is mobilised to evoke an ancient performance tradition
that apparently erases style and form, and presents the body instead as an
unmediated representation of 'inner life'. As Rudolf Bach observes:

> Every art form is of course inner life transformed as entirely as possible into
> aesthetic form. But this is most comprehensively true of theatre … [in which] what
> is decisive is the ability to render visible and accessible to the senses [a] whole
> interior world. … This is the basic drive that animates the actor: the drive we call
> the mime.[58]

Though Bach's main reference is to theatre, he concedes that the mime may
infuse film acting too when he writes of Paula Wessely in her debut film role
(*Maskerade/Masquerade*, 1934) that she achieves there 'a breakthrough to a
human and artistic reality', and thus lends to her film image, as to her body in
theatre the 'pure power of being itself'.[59] Bach's comments show clearly how
'the mime' is invoked in 1930s acting theory to reference idealist notions of the
actor as a vessel for essential being and soul. But Bach leads us too to a third
and final actorly principle that situates the body in Third Reich film theory as a
representative of collective soul. I noted in Chapter 1 the emphasis placed in
the recent revisionist historiography of Third Reich film on the notion that 1930s
and 40s German film replicated in its formal construction many classical Hollywood conventions. As Eric Rentschler suggests, German film-makers 'openly
admired the professional craft … and … technical prowess behind American
movies' – an admiration Rentschler sees reflected for example in Paul Martin's
Glückskinder (*Lucky Kids,* 1935), a remake of Capra's *It Happened One Night*
(1934) that 'relied on foreign patterns of recognition yet still proudly bore the
appellation "made in Germany"'.[60]

PERSONALITY AND PERFORMANCE

What is suggested by readings of 1930s film theory is that the national flavour Rentschler detects, even in such avowed Hollywood homages as *Glückskinder,* results among other things from German cinema's characteristic treatment of actorly performance in film. Though no single film style can be identified as dominant in Third Reich film, certain precepts of formal organisation do recur across film texts and film commentary of the period: precepts that distinguish German cinema from its Hollywood rival in part by their treatment of the actor's body in film. The first – discussed in more detail in my study of Carl Froelich's *Traumulus* (*Little Dreamer*, 1936) in Chapter 4 – involves a disavowal of offscreen space, and a penchant instead for a use of the camera frame as the limit of performance and the boundary of meaning. Karsten Witte has noted how, in the Third Reich revue film for instance, the actor/singer/dancer's body is regularly contained within architectural sets and a symmetrical frame, and the spectatorial focus thus shifted to the performer's whole body as the shot's organising centre (Figure 2).[61] That this containment of meaning (as well as, as Witte points out, of visual pleasure) within the limits of the camera frame was promoted as a structuring principle not only of the revue film, but of narrative cinema in general, is illus-

Figure 2: Zarah Leander in *Premiere* (1936)

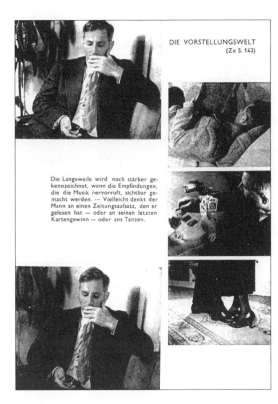

DIE VORSTELLUNGSWELT
(Zu S. 143)

Die Langeweile wird noch stärker ge-
kennzeichnet, wenn die Empfindungen,
die die Musik hervorruft, sichtbar ge-
macht werden. -- Vielleicht denkt der
Mann an einen Zeitungsaufsatz, den er
gelesen hat — oder an seinen letzten
Kartengewinn — oder ans Tanzen.

Figure 3: acting bored – Alex
Strasser, 1937

trated by contemporary film-making manuals that demand of the film-maker –
as one Alex Strasser puts it – 'that every thought, every internal and external cir-
cumstance ... be given visual expression'. In that context, as Strasser's further
comments indicate, the body of the actor becomes the immanent representation
of what he calls 'processes of the soul': a principle bathetically illustrated in
Strasser's book with a sequence in which an actor portrays an 'inner state' of
boredom with an understated but meaningful yawn (Figure 3).[62]

Strasser's privileging here of the performing body over the cinematic apparatus as a source of 'soul' is repeated across the spectrum of the professional press
in the 1930s, which regularly extolled the specific national qualities of cinematic
practices that masked the medium's technological nature. In cinematography,
the fast track was considered characteristic of Hollywood, and anathema to German practitioners; thus the journal *Filmtechnik* caricatured the refrain of
US cameramen as 'How many miles did you dolly today?'[63] New 'American'
techniques in back projection and camera mobility (large craning movements,
for instance) were simultaneously admired by German practitioners, and
attacked as evidence of an indecent penchant for 'tempo' and 'technical extravagance'.[64] Even amateur publications, from the monthly magazine *Film für alle*

(*Film for All*), to handbooks in the Wilhelm Knapp series *Filmbücher für alle*
(*Everyman's Film Books*), exhorted hobby film-makers to strive after 'inner
authenticity', while at all costs avoiding those contemporary techniques (modernist montage, for instance) that 'disturb the eye and provoke in the spectator
feelings of discomfort and disorientation'.[65]

The relevance to Third Reich acting of this downplaying of cinematic technique is illustrated most clearly by debates on lighting in the 1930s technical
press. Universally, so-called ensemble lighting was the preferred German
alternative to the US habit of back and top lighting for 'halo effects' in star representation in particular.[66] In films by prominent exponents of the new German
film art, this produced a curious visual underemphasis, even of Germany's most
favoured stars. Figure 4 is a shot of Ingrid Bergman taken from her only film
made in Germany, Carl Froelich's *Die vier Gesellen* (*The Four Companions*,
1938). Designed to launch Bergman as a new addition to Ufa's star stable, the
film is notable for the absence of top, back and fill lighting that Hollywood
would later use to imbue Bergman with the aura of a star (Figure 5).[67]

This absence of star lighting in *Die vier Gesellen*, as in numerous other contemporary titles, illustrates how lighting conventions in 1930s German film
conspired with pictorial framing, unemphatic or static camera and slow montage to create a film-making context in which the actor's performing body was

Figure 4: ensemble lighting for Ingrid Bergman in *Die vier Gesellen* (*The Four
Companions*, 1938)

Figure 5: star lighting for Bergman in *Casablanca* (1942)

the principal resource on which s/he might draw in her/his effort to represent
the collective 'soul'. As we saw earlier, formal instruction in performance techniques that might produce the actor's body as an unmediated representation of
inner being was rare. From the philosophical literature of acting aesthetics, as
well as in some contemporary autobiographical testimony, we can nonetheless
glean some insight into the specific demands made of actorly performance in
Third Reich film. Again, it is Ernst Iros who is most prolix in formulating an
approach to what he terms the 'personality style'. Iros writes as follows of what
he calls 'filmic gesture' – a term that includes for him not only the gestural use
of the body (hand or arm movement, posture, etc.), but also movement within
the *mise en scène*, as well as facial expression:

> In order to experience the idea imagined by the [scriptwriter as] a poet of the
> image [*Bilddichter*], the film actor must read the visual score [*sic*] ... in a state of
> the greatest immediacy and unhindered by acts of abstract or conceptual thinking.
> The unmediated and concrete idea that is the imaginative product of an original
> creative experience thus serves as the originary source of [the actor's] performance
> gestures; for that experience projects itself directly, and with no detour through
> abstract thinking, onto the emotions and experience of the film actor.[68]

For Iros, then, the art of film performance involves in the first instance an act of aesthetic reception: a reading of the script as a form of 'visual poetry'. The product of this encounter with the script-as-poetry is a dynamisation of the actor's inner world; the actor is literally 'moved' both imaginatively to recreate the writer's original creative experience, and to use that experience as an impetus to the creative production of 'gesture'.

I pointed earlier in this chapter to the debt 1930s and 40s acting theory owes to early Romantic philosophies of identity, and especially to physiognomy as a practice that reads the soul through phenomenal form. But it is to a second Romantic tradition that Iros' comments above can be more clearly traced. We will see in Chapter 4 how writing on acting by Iros' contemporaries (my example here is Richard Bie on Emil Jannings) recalled the early Romantic landscape painting of Caspar David Friedrich, Carl Gustav Carus and others in its description of the actor's body as a 'landscape of the soul'. The quote from Iros above shows how he too was influenced by early Romantic accounts of the creative process. In Caspar David Friedrich's conception, for instance, art came into being through 'visionary seeing and imagination'. 'Close your bodily eye', Friedrich proposes, 'so that you may first see your picture with your mind's eye. Then bring to the light of day what you have seen in the dark, so that it may reflect back on others from outside to inside.'[69] Artistic production in Friedrich's account, in other words, is the result of precisely that imaginative reconstruction of an originary creative experience that Iros would describe a century later as central to acting for film. Iros is, moreover, not alone in this invocation of Romantic conceptions of artistic creativity as models for film. In an essay on 'the nature of the actor', Rudolf Köppler writes similarly of 'gesture' as the product of a 'mood [*Stimmung*]' that 'proceeds from the soul and overwhelms the body', producing an 'authentic' performance mode that 'surges forth from the total experience of the soul'.[70]

For other 1930s writers, it was the pre-Romantic sublime that was more clearly the inspiration for their conception of performance. The subjects of Edmund Schneider's survey of the actor as a psychological type thus recall not Friedrich, but Kant in their description of performance as the product of an encounter with the script as representation of the 'sublime'. According to Kant, what is produced in an encounter with the sublime is a mobilisation of the soul in which the perceiving subject is at first moved, then willingly subordinates her/himself to the superior power evinced by sublimity.[71] Among Schneider's respondents, the 'movement' that Kant references is variously described as a state of 'intoxication', of 'excitement [*Erregung*]' and of 'extension of inner being', all of which result from the actor's encounter with 'the sublime works of literary art'.[72] In a later autobiographical reflection, the film and stage actress Käthe Dorsch reproduces the same emphasis on the necessary subordination of the actor's self to sublime works of literary genius when she claims to base her acting on an experience of 'all the possibilities of existence': an experience accessible, moreover, only when she 'relinquishes her own self' and involves herself body and soul in the process of imaginative creation that is actorly performance.[73]

As Dorsch and Schneider's comments indicate, the metaphysics of acting that ghosts through the writings of Iros, Böhm, Bach and others provided in 1930s Germany a discursive frame through which actors could represent their practice as a contribution to the collective drive after 1933 for the recreation of film as national popular art. As Mathias Wieman saw it for instance, the actor's art was a contribution to what Adolf Hitler called National Socialism's 'sublime mission' to create 'authentic art' from the raw material of German film.[74] For Olga Tschechowa, similarly, the new Germany had imposed a 'higher duty' on the actor or actress to become the symbolic representative of 'an art that has been returned to the *Volk*'.[75] In acting practice, moreover, celebrations of the actor's body as a physical manifestation of the sublime spirit or soul of a new *völkisch* art do appear to have produced in some performers an increasingly restrained and static acting mode: a mode that we shall see represented later in this book by developments in the performance style of key actors (Jannings and Leander) that seemed designed to contain the ambivalence of bodily gesture within the boundaries of a sculptural body as representative of inner essence or 'soul'. The physical constraint that the 'personality style' imposed on Third Reich performance is evident, too, in the numerous references in writing on acting to 'iron discipline' and the work ethic, as well as to the dangers of an excessive emphasis on technique or form. Such formalist preoccupations were considered the product not only of modernist decadence; they undermined the very ideological foundations of acting as an expression of (masculine, Aryan) racial essence. That access to the personality style was differentially distributed according to gender and race is indicated by regular comments on the 'Jewishness' of some actors' preoccupation with form, as well as by warnings from such as Tschechowa that 'the actress in particular must be wary of superficiality in all its forms [since this is] a danger to which actresses who see external appearance as the basis of their profession, have often fallen prey'.[76]

In Chapter 4, I discuss Emil Jannings as a figure whose Teutonic pedigree and masculinity are among the attributes that locate him as a source of that sublimity, which was the Third Reich actor's ideal. Jannings himself claimed a capacity to represent the 'eternal' and transcendent qualities that are a feature of the sublime when he wrote of his various roles as key personalities in history (*Ohm Krüger*, *Robert Koch*) that 'to perform [these roles] is to imbue the unique and the historical with a sense of destiny and the eternal'.[77]

Jannings presents himself here as an actor-personality who escaped the dangers of stardom by fashioning himself as a vessel for the sublime experience of authentic art. We have seen both here and in Chapter 1 how the strivings of such as Jannings after transcendent art were framed within much larger initiatives for industry reorganisation and artistic training: initatives that aimed to situate the artistic personality at the centre of the creative process in film. In Chapter 3, we move on to investigate similar shifts in film reception, considering here how both state and industry restructurings of film exhibition from 1933 onwards aimed to transform star reception from the 'vulgar' indulgence of the pleasures of spectacle, and towards an aesthetic encounter with the *völkisch* sublime.

NOTES

1. See, for example, Helmut Korte, *Der Spielfilm und das Ende der Weimarer Republik. Ein rezeptionshistorischer Versuch* (Göttingen: Vandenhoek & Ruprecht, 1998), especially pp. 90ff; Wolfgang Mühl-Benninghaus, *Das Ringen um den Tonfilm. Strategien der Elektro- und der Filmindustrie in den 20er und 30er Jahren* (Düsseldorf: Droste, 1999).
2. Betz, 'Stargagen verhindern Gesundung', *Der Film*, 25 August 1934.
3. Ibid.; also, Heinz Wemper, 'Das Starunwesen. Seine Folgen und möglichen Gegenmassnahmen', *Film-Kurier*, 1 July 1935.
4. Betz, 'Stargagen'.
5. RMVP internal memorandum: Arnold Raether to Oberregierungsrat Kohler, 13 October 1939: BA R55/949, pp. 56ff.
6. Salary figures for theatre personnel from Alan E. Steinweis, *Art, Ideology and Economics. The* Reich *Chambers of Music, Theater, and the Visual Arts* (Chapel Hill and London: University of North Carolina Press, 1993), p. 152. For industrial wage levels, see Detlev J. K. Peukert, *Inside Nazi Germany. Conformity, Opposition and Racism in Everyday Life*, Richard Deveson (trans.) (Harmondsworth: Penguin, 1989), p. 115.
7. Minutes of Ufa board, BA R1091/1139, 7 February 1936 (on Pola Negri), and BA R1091/1065, 4 March 1935, on Hans Albers. Pola Negri is reported here as having refused the role of Frau Garvenberg in Detlef Sierck's *Schlußakkord* (1936), on the grounds of more pressing engagements in Russian film.
8. Ingrid Bergman's presence in Table 2 underlines the force of my '(almost) full' here. Bergman played in one German title, Carl Froelich's *Die vier Gesellen* (1938), before departing for Hollywood to play in a 1939 remake of her Swedish success *Intermezzo* (1936). The citing of Bergman in this Propaganda Ministry memorandum as a star still active in the German industry (and indeed efforts to secure her return continued until as late as 1941: see BA R109 I/5465, doc. 14) situates her as one of the numerous émigré artists whose rejection of the German

industry was long denied or disavowed by the regime. I return in Chapters 5–7 to the numerous figures of Bergman's ilk whose emigration or exile after 1933 created a German star system haunted by a pervasive sense of lack – despite the impressive panoply of German star figures these tables reveal.

9. Minutes of Ufa Board, BA R1091/1071, 2 April 1935.
10. Ibid., BA R1091/1065, 12 March 1935.
11. Ibid., BA R1091/1031b, 10 November 1936 (Leander) and BA R109 I/1031b, 4 November 1936. On similar concessions for Hans Albers and Willy Fritsch see Klaus Kreimeier (ed.), *Die Ufa-Story. Geschichte eines Filmkonzerns* (Munich: Hanser, 1992), pp. 338ff.
12. Leander's fees rose to a total of RM300,000 for the two titles in which she starred in 1938 – hence the figure of RM150,000 in Table 3 – and RM400,000 for 1939. Source: Internal memorandum to Ufa Director-General Ludwig Klitzsch, BA R1091 I/2874, 17 August 1939.
13. Internal memorandum, RMVP personnel department: BA R55/949, Doc. 94, 7 December 1939. Other actors named as exacting raised fees were Heli Finkenzeller, Ernst Legal, Theodor Loos, Peter Voss, Albert Lippert and Charlotte Schultz.
14. Fritz Hippler, *Betrachtungen zum Filmschaffen* (Berlin: Max Hesses, 1942), p. 95.
15. Kreimeier, *Die Ufa-Story*, p. 340. On the ideological ambiguity of Leander's image, see, for example, Lutz Koepnick, 'Engendering Mass Culture: Zarah Leander and the Economy of Desire', in Koepnick, *The Dark Mirror. German Cinema between Hitler and Hollywood* (Berkeley, Los Angeles and London: University of California Press, 2002), pp. 72ff; Marc Silberman, 'Zarah Leander in the Colonies', in Knut Hickethier and Siegfried Zielinski (eds.), *Medien/Kultur. Schnittstellen zwischen Medienwissenschaft, Medienpraxis und gesellschaftlicher Kommunikation* (Berlin: Volker Spiess, 1991), pp. 247–53; Claudia Lenssen, 'Zarah Leander. Operation Zarah', in Lenssen, *Blaue Augen, Blauer Fleck. Kino im Wandel von der Diva zum Girlie* (Berlin: Filmmuseum Potsdam/Parthas Verlag, 1997), pp. 8–47.
16. See 'Introduction', in Tim Bergfelder, Erica Carter and Deniz Göktürk (eds), *The German Cinema Book* (London: BFI, 2002), pp. 5ff.
17. Fedor Stepun, *Theater und Kino* (Berlin: Bühnenvolksbundverlag, 1932), p. 51.
18. Heinz Wemper, 'Das Starunwesen'.
19. Heinz W. Siska (ed.), *Wunderwelt Film. Künstler und Werkleute einer Weltmacht* (Heidelberg, Berlin and Leipzig: Hüthig, n.d.), p. 18.
20. Max Weber, *On Charisma and Institution Building*, S. Eisenstadt (ed.) (Chicago and London: University of Chicago Press, 1968), p. 329: cited in Richard Dyer, *Stars*, (London: BFI, 1998), second edition, p. 30.

21. Dyer, *Stars*, p. 22.

22. 'Der Filmstar ist persönlich anwesend', *Film-Kurier*, 1 June 1934.

23. 'Berliner Presseball 1939. Es war eine rauschende Ballnacht', *Film-Kurier*, 30 January 1939.

24. See also Martin Loiperdinger's designation of Kaiser Wilhelm II as 'the first German film star', and his claim that similar strategies of cinematic representation were in play in early cinema both for star entertainers of the likes of Asta Nielsen, and for 'emperors, kings, presidents, military figures, in other words for high-ranking representatives of state power'. Martin Loiperdinger, 'Kaiser Wilhelm II. Der erste deutsche Filmstar', in Thomas Koebner (ed.), *Idole des deutschen Films* (Munich: edition text+kritik, 1997), p. 42.

25. The term 'soldier of art' is Mathias Wieman's from his 'Der Mensch im Film', in Siska, *Wunderwelt Film*, p. 73; see also Walter Falk, 'Schauspieler und Soldat. Ein Kapitel Standesehre', *Die Bühne*, 1 March 1936, p. 132.

26. Siska, *Wunderwelt Film*, p. 19; Joseph Gregor, *Meister der deutscher Schauspielkunst. Krauß, Klöpfer, Jannings, George* (Bremen and Vienna: Carl Schünemann, 1939), p. 5.

27. Gregor, *Meister der deutscher Schauspielkunst*, p. 34 and *passim*.

28. Emil Jannings, 'Die grösste Aufgabe', in Siska, *Wunderwelt Film*, p. 57.

29. Pierre Drieu la Rochelle, 'The Rebirth of European Man', in Roger Griffin (ed.), *Fascism* (Oxford: Oxford University Press, 1995), pp. 202–3.

30. Cynthia Baron, 'Crafting Film Performances. Acting in the Hollywood Studio Era', in Alan Lovell and Peter Krämer (eds), *Screen Acting* (London and New York: Routledge, 1999), p. 33 and passim.

31. See Walther Freisburger, *Theater im Film. Eine Untersuchung über die Grundzüge und Wandlungen in den Beziehungen zwischen Theater und Film* (Emsdetten: Lechte, 1936), p. 73.

32. Figures from Alan Steinweis, *Art, Ideology and Economics. The Reich Chambers of Music, Theater, and the Visual Arts* (Chapel Hill and London: University of North Carolina Press, 1993), p. 16.

33. A. Funk, *Film und Jugend* (Munich: Ernst Reinhard, 1934), p. 169: cited in Freisburger, *Theater im Film*, p. 77.

34. Freisburger, *Theater im Film*, p. 81.

35. Ibid., p. 74.

36. Gregor, *Meister der deutscher Schauspielkunst*, p. 5.

37. Olga Tschechowa, 'Die Frau als Filmkünstlerin', in Siska, *Wunderwelt Film*, pp. 82–4.

38. Rudolf Bach, *Die Frau als Schauspielerin* (Tübingen: Rainer Wunderlich, 1937), p. 7.

39. Ibid., p. 9.

40. Baron, 'Crafting Film Performances', p. 35.

41. Walter Kuhlmann, *Schule des Sprechens. Atmung, Stimm- und Lautbildung, Rechtlautung, Betonung* (Heidelberg: C. Winter, 1939); Hans Lebede, *Erziehung zum Sprechen. Im Anschluss an die neuen Lehrgänge* (Frankfurt am Main: Moritz Diesterweg, 1938): cited in Hans Traub and Hanns Wilhelm Lavies, *Das deutsche Filmschrifttum. Eine Bibliographie der Bücher und Zeitschriften über das Filmwesen* (Leipzig: Hiersemann, 1940), p. 53.

42. Wieman, 'Der Mensch im Film', pp. 67–73.

43. Dyer, *Stars*, p. 15.

44. Quote from Goethe's Anteil an *Lavaters Physiognomischen Fragmenten, in Goethes Werk* (edition commissioned by Grand Duchess Sophie von Sachsen) (Weimar: Hermann Böhlan, 1896), p. 348: cited in Béla Balázs, *Der sichtbare Mensch oder die Kultur des Films* (Vienna and Leipzig: Deutsch-österreichischer Verlag, 1924), p. 71.

45. Massimo Locatelli, *Béla Balázs. Die Physiognomik des Films* (Berlin: Vistas, 1999), p. 82.

46. Wolfgang Berkefeld, *Untersuchungen zur Theorie der Schauspielkunst auf dem Boden der Forschungen von Ludwig Klages* (Dresden: Dittert, 1937); Wilhelm Böhm, *Die Seele des Schauspielers* (Leipzig: E. A. Seemann, 1941); Arthur Maria Rabenalt, *Mimus ohne Maske. Über die Schauspielkunst im Film. Essay* (Düsseldorf: Merkur, 1945). Though not published in book form until the end of the Third Reich, Rabenalt's work was a version of an article for the *Neue Wiener Tageblatt*, 29 March 1944, and thus – despite Rabenalt's protestations to the contrary in his 1945 preface – represents views in tune with the then current thinking on acting.

47. Dyer, *Stars*, p. 132. See also Richard Maltby, *Hollywood Cinema. An Introduction* (Oxford: Blackwell, 1995), p. 263.

48. Quotes from Alfred Mühr, *Die Welt des Schauspielers Werner Krauss* (Berlin: Brunnen, 1927), pp. 14–15, and Ludwig Klages, *Grundlegung der Wissenschaft vom Ausdruck* (Leipzig: J. A. Barth, 1936), fifth edition, cited in Berkefeld, *Theorie der Schauspielkunst*, p. 6.

49. Edmund Schneider, 'Empirisch-strukturpsychologische Untersuchungen über den Schauspieler' *Zeitschrift für angewandte Psychologie*, vol. 42, no. 4, 1932, p. 300. Schneider's article draws on research interviews with twenty-six actors and actresses, and uses E. R. Jaensch's typology of psychological tendencies to categorise his subjects as 'idealist', 'synaesthetic' or 'hysterical'. At this point (1932), neither Jaensch nor Schneider was overtly ideologically committed to fascist anti-Semitism; this comment on the 'Jewishness' of a preoccupation with form is certainly rooted, however, in those widely held conceptions of racial identity that were the breeding ground for fascist anti-Semitism – conceptions that held sway across ethnic divides (thus Schneider's 'Research subject 16', from

whom this comment derives, was himself a Viennese Jew). On Jaensch's typology, see also Ulfried Geuter, 'Nationalsozialistische Ideologie und Psychologie', in Mitchell G. Ash and Ulfried Geuter (eds), *Geschichte der deutschen Psychologie im 20. Jahrhundert* (Opladen: Westdeutscher Verlag, 1985), pp. 146–71.

50. Ernst Iros, *Wesen und Dramaturgie des Films* (Zürich and Leipzig: Max Niehaus, 1938), pp. 236 and 358.

51. Heinz Wemper, 'Das Starunwesen. Seine Folgen und mögliche Gegenmassnahmen', *Film-Kurier*, 1 July 1935.

52. Böhm, *Die Seele des Schauspielers*, p. 63.

53. See Boguslaw Drewniak, *Der deutsche Film 1938–1945. Ein Gesamtüberblick* (Düsseldorf: Droste, 1987), p. 70: also BA R55/949 23ff, RMVP internal memo from Director of Personnel to Geobbels, 22 September 1939, re. star fees.

54. Rabenalt, *Mimus ohne Maske*.

55. Oscar Brockett, *History of the Theatre* (Boston: Allyn & Bacon, 1977), pp. 22 and 69.

56. Gregor, *Meister der deutschen Schauspielkunst*, p. 26 and *passim*.

57. See for example minutes of the Ufa Board, 24 April 1935, R1091/1030a 1071.

58. Bach, *Die Frau als Schauspielerin*, p. 7.

59. Ibid., pp. 78–9.

60. Eric Rentschler, *The Ministry of Illusion. Nazi Cinema and its Afterlife* (Cambridge, MA and London: Harvard University Press, 1996), pp. 103 and 114.

61. Karsten Witte, *Lachende Erben, Toller Tag* (Berlin: Vorwerk 8, 1995), pp. 200ff.

62. Alex Strasser, *Filmentwurf, Filmregie, Filmschnitt. Gesetze und Beispiele* (Halle: Knapp, 1937), pp. 75 and 143.

63. 'Amerikanische Kameraleute über 'Verfolgungswahn'', *Filmtechnik*, 6 April 1935, p. 78.

64. On crane, see 'Neuer Kamerakran', *Filmtechnik*, 7 April 1934, pp. 82–3; on tempo, 'Amerikanische Kameraleute über ''Verfolgungswahn''', *Filmtechnik*, 6 April 1935, p. 78; on technical extravagance, Heinz Umbehr, ''Aufnahmetechnik neuer Filme. *Hermine und die Sieben Aufrechten*', *Filmtechnik*, 26 January 1935, pp. 13–14.

65. H. C. Opfermann, *Die Geheimnisse des Spielfilms. Ein Buch für Filmer und Leute, die gern ins Kino gehen* (Berlin: Photokino-Verlag, 1938) p. 68, and Alex Strasser, *Filmentwurf, Filmregie, Filmschnitt*, p. 86.

66. A. von Barsy, 'Die Grundtypen der Freilichtbeleuchtung', *Filmtechnik*, 1 October 1936, p. 172.

67. Ufa files suggest that some in the studio continued for many years to nurture hopes of Bergman's return: see June 1941 Ufa internal memorandum from overseas division (*Auslandsabteilung*) reminding Herr von Reith in personnel that 'Frau Bergman moved from Sweden many years ago [and] has made films with a variety of American producers', R109I/5465 14.

68. Iros, *Wesen und Dramaturgie*, p. 267.
69. Quotes from Sigrid Hinz, *Caspar David Friedrich in Briefen und Bekenntnissen* (Berlin: Henschel, 1974), p. 94; Birgit Verwiebe (trans.), in Françoise Forster-Hahn, Claude Keisch, Peter-Klaus Schuster and Angelika Wesenberg, *Spirit of an Age. Nineteenth-century Paintings from the Nationalgalerie, Berlin* (London: National Gallery, 2001), p. 66.
70. Rudolf Köppler, 'Vom Wesen des Schauspielers', *Die Bühne*, vol. 7, 1937, p. 166.
71. Immanuel Kant, *Critique of the Power of Judgement*, Paul Guyer (trans. and ed.), and Eric Matthews (trans.) (Cambridge: Cambridge University Press, 2000), p. 131. Although all quotations from Kant are taken from this edition, I have retained in the body of the text the title *Critique of Judgement*, since this is the title by which the work is best known, and there remains some debate among translators as to the proper rendering of the German *Urteilskraft*.
72. Schneider, 'Empirisch-strukturpsychologische', pp. 293, 294, 297 and 302. Although Kant does follow Edmund Burke in representing aesthetic experience as in part 'corporeal' (Kant, *Critique of the Power of Judgement*, p. 159), he does not use Schneider's term *Erregung*. Here as elsewhere in Third Reich theory, the appropriation of Kant must be seen as inflected through traditions in aesthetic theory, especially nineteenth-century empathy theory, as well as through those Nazi ideological discourses that affirm the values of the body over those of the intellect or imagination.
73. Käthe Dorsch, in Bach, *Die Frau als Schauspielerin*, p. 12.
74. Wieman in Siska, *Wunderwelt Film*, p. 73.
75. Tschechowa in Siska, *Wunderwelt Film*, p. 82.
76. Ibid.
77. Jannings in Siska, *Wunderwelt Film*, p. 57.

3

The New Film Art: Exhibition

CINEMA AS THEATRE: THE DRAMATURGY OF RECEPTION

In September 1935, Wilhelm Siegfried, chairman of the Berlin-Brandenburg section of the *Reich* Association of German Film Theatres and Director of a technical college (*Fachschule*) providing in-service training for exhibitors, wrote the following in his preface to a collection of lectures from the college's opening year:

> With the breakthrough to the new state of today came a fundamental change in the position of film in Germany. In accordance with film's significance as a cultural force, it has been developed and elevated, with vigorous support from the state, to the status of an autonomous art form.

> The general position of exhibition sites and of their owners has undergone concomitant and equally fundamental change. 'Cinemas' have become 'film theatres' – theatres of the people. No longer are those who run them destined to … remain mere 'cinema owners'; their task is to transform themselves into 'theatre directors of the people' [*Volksintendanten*].[1]

We saw in Chapter 1 how the supposed degradation of German film art through the Weimar years was countered after 1933 by state and industry initiatives to reorient production around the creative capacities of *Führer*-figures of genius. Underpinning those efforts, as we also saw, was a theory of artistic personality that, though rooted in Enlightenment conceptions of the bourgeois individual, was recast under Nazism to accord with *völkisch* philosophies of personality as expressive of biological and racial essence. In this third chapter, we will consider how these shifts in film production towards a racialised recuperation of film as bourgeois art were paralleled by a reshaping of the reception context designed to foster in audiences the proper reverence for the new film art and its creative personalities, especially directors, actors and stars.

As in film production, exhibition practitioners too sought legitimation for their reforms in *völkisch* adaptations of classical aesthetics. Wilhelm Siegfried's call for a transformation of cinemas into 'theatres of the *Volk*', for example, resonated loudly with similar demands across the field of contemporary film-aesthetic debate. The Weimar modernists – Kracauer, Benjamin, Balázs – had already recognised and (cautiously) celebrated film's potential as mass popular art. Thus for the leftist Balázs, for instance, film as a 'mental technology of expression and communication that is accessible to us all, and thus constitutes a culture', gained its 'enormous significance ... not least because this is a culture that for the first time in history has not remained the monopoly of the ruling classes'.[2] Among the conservative aestheticians who rose to prominence after 1933, responses to the mass character of cinema were more ambivalent. While recognising in film the artistic expression par excellence of a modernity they themselves sought to embrace, writers like Fedor Stepun, Joseph Gregor, Ernst Iros or Friedrich Munding echoed early cinema reformers in their railing against the cultural disorder induced by film's indulgence of mass desires. For the Russian émigré and anti-Bolshevist Stepun, for instance, film was both an inevitable component of modern life – 'modernity', he writes, 'has in the very depths of its unconscious and unequivocally embraced the film medium' – and was to be denounced for its appeal to base desires and for the 'primitive eroticism of the majority of films'.[3]

Three years after Stepun, Friedrich Munding writes similarly of a 'crisis' in film engendered by its appeal to the 'amorphous and immutable mass'. For Munding, however, as for other Nazi sympathisers, there is in the new political status quo the promise of film's redemption. Since 1933, he continues, the *Volk* to whom film appeals has cast off its guise of formlessness and become instead the 'incipient bearer of metaphysical developments'. The 'soul' of the *Volk* is in its essence capricious, torn between desires for 'higher' and 'lower' aesthetic pleasures. Authentic art, however, bends the *Volk* to its will by addressing the 'metaphysical need that it [the people] has always possessed'. Citing as examples the medieval mystery plays and the songs of Hans Sachs, Munding demands of film that it become a popular art in the pre-modern sense; and his effusive anti-modernism is, in the Third Reich context, more than empty rhetoric.[4] Such celebrations as Munding's of the power of film to bypass modernity and rekindle archaic connections between *Volk* and art provided the paradigm for numerous pragmatic interventions into film reception after 1933. Two years after the Nazi seizure of power, the Director of the Berlin Institute for Film Research (Institut für Filmforschung) A. Hinderer, for instance, had similar recourse to the rhetoric of *völkisch* essence to ground his research into German film audiences and national popular taste. Allotting to film, as Munding had done, pride

of place as the quintessential popular art, Hinderer explained in a 1935 address
to film exhibitors that:

> Film ... forms the word in shapes that are those of visual perception; it ...
> represents a liberation from the conceptual world. Even sound film is an art
> defined by wordlessness. Wordlessness, however, is the deepest, the ultimate
> quality possessed by man ... for wordlessness, the inexpressible, contains within
> itself our last remaining connections to the cosmos, to unity and to the very depths
> of our world. We have no words that can express this; the highest forms of words
> that we know are in the end only images. Yet it is in this realm of the inexpressible
> that our deepest affinities are to be found ... And this, ultimately, is what explains
> the proximity of film to the *Volk* ... [5]

In earlier chapters, we saw how Nazi philosophies of identity dispensed with the
modernist vision of a fundamental disjuncture between the self and its linguistic or
visual representation. Drawing on traditions from eighteenth-century physiognomy
to contemporary race theory, Third Reich theorists of personality conceived of cultural representation as the unmediated expression of a racially defined essence.
Hinderer, in his work both as a theoretician and as a pioneer of Third Reich audience research, was one of many film aestheticians who set about exploring the
implications of this foundationalist philosophy of representation for an understanding of film spectatorship. Hinderer's work mirrored that of more prominent
theoreticians – Gregor, Iros, Rehlinger – in its attempted binding of German film
to specific inner laws (in Hinderer, the anti-logocentric laws of the visual image)
that rooted cinema in a *völkisch* cultural order. Weimar film theory had stressed
film's capacity to absorb the viewer into its representational world; as Kracauer put
it, 'one forgets oneself gazing'.[6] That vision of cinema as an apparatus for the sub-
suming of the self within representation resulted, as Miriam Hansen has observed,
from specific developments in textual and exhibition practice through the 1910s
and 20s – the emergence of the long narrative film, the reduction to a minimum
of non-filmic activities (live variety, musical performance), and so on. These both
facilitated the 'absorption of the viewer into narrative space' and 'corresponded to
an increased derealization of the theater space – the physical and social space of
the spectator'.[7] In early cinema, Hansen contends, the presence in the film theatre
of flesh-and-blood mediators between film and audience – lecturers, musicians,
sound-effect specialists – was one of numerous elements that constructed film viewing as an experience of 'immediacy and participation' by emphasising 'the
presentness of the performance and the audience'.[8] The emergence of narrative
film and its representational concomitants, by contrast – centred composition, continuity editing, close framing and the like – suppressed awareness of the cinema

space. In so doing, importantly, it 'eliminated the conditions' for that awareness of social (local, ethnic, class and gender) identities which, argues Hansen finally, were fostered by the more interactive spectatorial mode of early film.

Hinderer's quote above is one example, by contrast, of widespread efforts in the early Nazi period to dislodge the spectator from her/his absorption into pro-filmic worlds, and to reinstate the cinema as a public space for the enactment of a shared cultural identity: the identity of the *Volk*. Two sets of developments were of significance here. First, a whole raft of reforms in cinema exhibition from 1933 onwards reconfigured both the physical space of the cinema, and the temporal relations of film spectatorship, producing the cinema itself as a *mise en scène* for the collective performance of *völkisch* identity. This dramaturgical recomposition of the film viewing experience was accompanied, as I show in Chapter 4, by shifts in the textual aesthetics of popular genre film, and an embracing in particular by auteur-directors of an aesthetics of sublimity: a mode designed to produce not spectatorial immersion in the filmic text, but a more distanced attitude of awe and contemplative appreciation. It was that awe before the sublime, I will finally suggest, that was the reception mode deemed proper to the actor-personality: a mode fostered, moreover, by that reconfigur-ing of the reception context after 1933 to which we now turn our attention.

SPACE-TIME TRANSFORMATIONS OF SPECTATORSHIP

In his illuminating study of theatre and drama theory after 1933, Uwe-Karsten Ketelsen observes how Third Reich dramatists drew on turn-of-the-century the-atrical neo-classicism to recreate the theatre as a place of quasi-religious collective experience. In Nazi writing on tragedy, for instance, 'tragedy and its representation are understood in the broadest sense as religious phenomena. The effects of tragedy extend beyond the limits of the stage; tragedy can indeed only attain its full significance if the theatre audience too is wholly drawn in and becomes ... a kind of creative participant in the drama.'[9]

The active audience whom Ketelsen references is, of course, in no sense the critically enlightened collective that was the desired product of, say, Brechtian modernism. Rather, Third Reich drama strove after a theatre of the emotions that 'dissolved the individual into larger experiential entities' by involving her/him in a shared enactment of collective identity. Dramatic representation was thus not simply propagandistic, designed to 'exert a lasting influence on the spectator and to coerce her/him into predetermined ways of thinking'.[10] Theatre spectatorship, suggests Ketelsen, was creatively productive, and engendered in particular an emotional (not intellectual) symbiosis among audience members participating in a collective encounter with what one contemporary commenta-tor dubbed Nazism's 'theatre as experience [*Erlebnis*]'.[11]

This notion of theatrical reception as a performative activity in which the audience participates in the affect-laden enactment of a collective drama, has resonances too in the arena of film reception after 1933. For Ernst Iros, for instance, film realised Kant's conception of art as the vehicle for 'aesthetic ideas' that are distinguished from 'intellectual ideas' (*Vernunftideen*) by their refusal to be encapsulated in conceptual form. Film's indebtedness to symbolic, rather than abstract conceptual representation, allows it to 'fill ... conceptual skeletons with life', thus allowing 'affective and experiential access to what is represented'.[12]

Iros' notion of a cinema of experience was pervasive in Third Reich writing on film. Film succeeds, it is claimed, when it 'shatters' (*erschüttert*), 'grips' (*fesselt*), 'moves' (*rührt*);[13] film reproduces in the audience those same sensations of shock and emotional disturbance that were the product of the 'colossal political transformation' that they experienced in 1933.[14] The political allusion is apposite, reminding the reader as it does that German film's objective, as defined by the period's prescriptive aesthetics, was not the production of emotion pure and simple, but the reconstitution in the cinema auditorium of a particular structure of affect and experience – a structure that mirrored the experiential patterns which accompanied Nazism's transformation of socio-political experience. As Friedrich Munding put it, the new German cinema was to disavow the 'hectic tempo' and 'optical sensation' of earlier cinematic modernity, and offer instead films whose measured pace and economy of material produced in the audience the same 'collectedness and concentration' they encountered in mass rallies or political parades – each of which, like film, functioned to offer its participants a collective experience of the unity of the *Volk*.[15]

We saw in Chapter 2 how, for the theoreticians who set out after 1933 to reformulate idealist aesthetics for a theory of cinema, film reception was understood as an aesthetic experience facilitating access to the truths of nation and *Volk*. It was not, moreover, the single film text that was conceived as the site of production of an experience of *Volk*; instead, cinemas themselves were widely understood as the three-dimensional *mise en scène* for a collective performance of *völkisch* identity.

SPACE

In classical dramaturgy, it is the dramatic unities of space and time that lend to the drama its thematic and affective coherence. In Third Reich exhibition practice likewise, it was to the reconfiguring of the space-time relations of cinemagoing that exhibitors and policymakers first turned their attention. Let us look first at some of the more striking developments in the spatial organisation of cinemas after 1933.

Figure 6 is a sketch from the industry journal *Filmtechnik* showing a refurbished medium-sized (650-seat) cinema in the Berlin suburbs in July 1936. Redesigned by a prominent cinema architect of his day, Heinrich Möller, the Rex-Kino in Berlin-Haselhorst has much in common with similar refurbishments of its day (see Figures 7–9). The wave of cinema makeovers began, of course, in the late 1920s and early 30s with the hugely costly refurbishment of cinemas for sound. In the four years prior to 1933, the total number of sound cinemas in Germany was estimated to have risen from around 220 in December 1929, to 4,700 by December 1933.[16] Numerous commentaries on poor sound quality in industry journals after 1933 indicate, moreover, how ever-present, even by mid-decade, was the imperative for technical upgrading.[17] At the same time, cinema refurbishment acquired from 1933 onwards a more pronounced role in the aesthetic and ideological reconstruction of the cinemagoing experience. For the government architect Werner Gabler, for instance, writing in December 1933, what is expected of the modern cinema is more than technical perfection; for the film theatre has a 'cultural responsibility ... that cannot be overestimated, [which is to] provide a dignified space in which a gathering of listeners [*sic*] can submit without external distraction to the shared impressions the performance delivers'.[18]

The design of the Berlin Rex-Kino, like the other sketches that accompany it here, highlights some of the ways in which the redesigned cinemas of the early to mid-1930s fulfilled their 'cultural responsibility' to their audience and to the nation. The new audience in the film theatre as 'theatre of the *Volk*' was to become a model in microcosm of what National Socialism termed the 'folk community' (*Volksgemeinschaft*), a mythical racialised community bound by ties of blood and soil in which, as the social historian Richard Grunberger puts it, 'all social and political divisions could be solved in the great national equation'.[19] Of course, the erasure of social division through the revival of primordial racial bonds was not synonymous with social equality; for the second aspect of the folk community was its emphasis on hierarchies of blood, rank and title: the supremacy therefore of the Aryan over the Jew, of the soldier over the lay citizen, man over woman and so on.

Figures 6–9 begin to illustrate how this fantasy of *Volksgemeinschaft* was written into the redesigned cinemas of the early sound era. In the refurbishments of the late 1920s and early 30s, most cinemas retained boxes for persons of special rank, plus raised seating that might – as in the Rex-Kino – be little more than tiered seating at the back, or might extend, in such larger houses as the Dresden Ufa-Palast, to a theatre-style gallery, balcony or circle. After 1933, the Nazi state undertook a series of interventions into pricing designed to ensure that the spatial disposition of audience members in this new generation of cin-

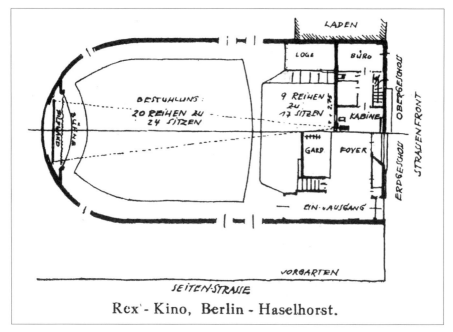

Figure 6: Rex-Kino, Berlin-Haselhorst, December 1936

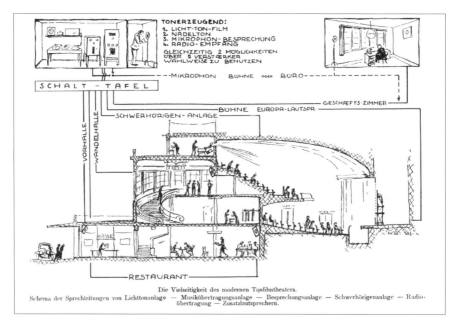

Figure 7: 'The multiple dimensions of the modern sound cinema', *Filmtechnik* 1932. The diagram shows how sound is transmitted from projection box to auditorium, as well as transmission routes for music, voice (via public address system), radio, and direct to headphones for audience members with hearing difficulties

Figure 8: the cinema as dignified space 1 – Ufa-Palast am Zoo, Berlin, 1936

Figure 9: the cinema as dignified space 2 – Tauentzien-Palast Berlin, 1936

emas mirrored the hierarchised socio-cultural order of the fascist *Volk*. Pricing regulations introduced after 1933 imposed strict guidelines on criteria of eligibility for quality seating. In the first instance, state price controls aimed to counter what was widely seen as the artistic degradation of German cinema culture over the preceding decade. By early 1933, cinemas nationally had reached their supposed nadir as fun-palaces for cheap mass entertainment. Competition for dwindling audience shares had produced a veritable frenzy of price-cutting among exhibitors. Despite the best efforts of local and national exhibitors' associations, as well as distributors and local price cartels, prices fell in the early 1930s to as low as 10 Pfennigs per show, as cinemas fought to sustain their share of a market threatened by 'complete unprofitability'.[20]

In the absence of state intervention in the early months of 1933, the industry responded at local and regional level with initiatives for price regulation and control. In major metropolitan centres – Berlin, Hamburg, Cologne and elsewhere – exhibitors' and distributors' associations together with the Spitzenorganisation der deutschen Filmindustrie (SPIO), formed local coalitions to combat price cutting and thus stabilise the ailing exhibition sector. In Berlin, the Association of Independent Cinema Owners collaborated with SPIO and the distributors' organisation ADF to become the first city to establish a rigid scale of ticket prices ranging from 60 Pfennigs to RM1 according to seating category (stalls, circle, etc.), cinema type (premiere, first- and second-run and repertory theatres) and purchaser status (adult normal, adult unemployed, child, etc.) (see Table 5). Other regional and local coalitions followed Berlin's lead; thus when, in September 1933, the *Reich* Film Chamber finally imposed mandatory price controls, it was doing little more in economic terms than consolidating and extending nationwide the industry's own locally and regionally based anti-competition measures.

The price structure imposed by the RFK had, however, not only economic but also cultural implications. On the one hand, as it followed SPIO in raising ticket prices across the board (the new minimum was 60, as opposed to the previous 10 Pfennigs), the RFK rescued cinema from the proletarian stigma attached to the 'giveaway prices' (*Schleuderpreise*) that were the pre-1933 norm.[21] At the same time, price reforms ensured a spatial disposition of audience members that reflected the cultural hierarchies of the folk community. The RFK ruling of September 1933 stipulated that, within the average price range of 60 Pfennigs to RM1, the maximum number of seats offered at the lowest price should not exceed one-third of the total. While this helped re-establish cinemagoing as a respectable cultural practice, the RFK's further ruling that price differentials be set at a minimum of 20 Pfennigs ensured that the 'correct' distance was maintained between differently ranked audience members.[22] The

Table 5: Minimum ticket prices for Berlin cinemas[1]

	Premiere cinemas[2]	First-run cinemas[3]	Second-run cinemas	Repertory cinemas	Total
Total cinemas in this category	12	84	93	174	363
Minimum ticket price[4]	RM1	RM0,80	RM0,70	RM0,60	–
Concessions (children, unemployed)[5]	RM0,50	RM0,40	RM0,30	RM0,25	–

Source: 'Eintrittspreise-Klassifizierung der Berliner Lichtspielhäuser', FK, 22 April 1933; 'Die Preisreform in Berlin', FK, 25 April 1933; 'Einheitliche Regelung der Eintrittspreise', FK, 14 August 1933.

Notes:

1. Agreed by resolution of the *Verband selbständiger Filmtheaterbesitzer* Berlin (Chair: W. Siegfried); April 1933.
2. Ufa-Palast am Zoo, Gloria Palast, U.T.Kurfürstendamm, Capitol, Marmorhaus, Tauentzien-Palast, Universum, Ufa-Pavillon, Mozartsaal, Titania Steglitz, Primus-Palast, Atrium.
3. First- and, to a lesser extent, second-run houses were clustered in middle-class districts, especially Charlottenburg, Wilmersdorf, and Schöneberg. Charlottenburg also boasted large numbers of repertory houses (thirty in all) playing re-runs of older titles, but these less prestigious venues were concentrated also in working-class districts (Neukölln, Wedding, Moabit, etc.).
4. Further 10Pfg reductions were permissible at the discretion of exhibitors for specified daytime performances.
5. From 25 April 1933, concessions were granted to the unemployed only for performances before 7p.m., and on production of a dole card. From August 1933, concessions were granted nationwide to SA, SS and *Stahlhelm* members, who were permitted, provided they wore uniform, to take seats in the price category immediately above their actual entry fee.

simultaneous offer of special deals exclusively for army, navy, SS, SA and *Stahlhelm* (League of Frontline Soldiers) personnel – with the important proviso that they wear uniform – further contributed to a general functionalising of the cinema auditorium as a visual and spatial representation of the cultural hierarchies of a militarised *Volk*; and the seal was set on that development by more brutal state controls on cinema audiences after 1933. From the mid-1930s, the Staatssicherheitsdienst (SD – the secret police arm of the SS) began collecting regular reports from local informers and spies on all aspects of everyday life in the *Reich*, including cinemagoing. In the latter context, deviant behaviour – hissing at Nazi dignitaries in the newsreels, for instance, or altercations between uniformed Nazis and other audience members – was reported to the SD and defaulters dealt with.[23] Efforts at racial purging, meanwhile, began with the establishment of cinemas for Jews only in the early 30s, and culminated the day after *Kristallnacht* (the Crystal Night pogroms) in November 1938 in an edict from Goebbels banning Jews from all 'presentations of German culture', including films.[24]

The shift in prevailing conceptions of cinema audience that these and other developments entailed is exemplified, again, in Werner Gabler's commentary on film theatres in small and medium-sized towns from December 1933. Gabler's interest in provincial cinemas as a model for future development mirrors a general box-office drift from 1933 onwards away from large-scale metropolitan cinemas and towards middle-range, medium-priced theatres.[25] This reassertion of cinemagoing as a provincial and petit-bourgeois pursuit not only echoes the general trend so often noted under National Socialism towards an enthroning of petit-bourgeois cultural practice as the norm. At the same time, it again highlights the significance of spatial relations in achieving the regime's desired transformation of its audience from the untutored metropolitan mass of the Weimar period, to the ordered, disciplined, racially purified and hierarchised provincial cultural community that was the fantasy addressee of much of German film from 1933 onwards. Expressing his contempt for the 'profligate use of space and luxury décor' of the 'urban picture palace', Werner Gabler formulates the advantages of the provincial model thus:

> It is one of the characteristics of small-town theatres that, almost without exception, it is seats in the gallery and in boxes that are requested. Precisely because the majority of audience members know each other, there exists a desire for theatre seating to be ranked according to the public and social position of its occupants. This retention of established custom is perhaps not at all as old-fashioned or antisocial as it may at first appear; for the theatre auditorium that is properly organised in this way offers a mirror image of the people [*Volk*] and the inhabitants of its home town. . . . [26]

Gabler's comments clearly demonstrate how significant was the part played by the spatial reconfiguring of the filmgoing experience in broader transformations of film spectatorship from 1933 onwards. In the provincial cinemas that are Gabler's desired cultural norm, the cinema audience becomes part of the spectacle of *völkisch* unity that was to become a prime source of visual pleasure for film spectators under National Socialism.

What conclusions flow, then, from this brief study of cinematic space for our broader enquiry in this chapter into film spectatorship? A preliminary answer lies in changing modes of film reception from Weimar to the Third Reich. When modernist film theory in Germany first engaged issues of film spectatorship, it did so in terms of film's contribution to the wider perceptual and psychic shifts that human subjectivity underwent in the transition to twentieth-century modernity. Walter Benjamin, for instance, saw film as a prime vehicle for the 'shock' that he considered one of the quintessential psychic modes of modern experience.[27] For Béla Balázs too – as he set out to demonstrate most particularly in *Der Geist des Films* – the development of the moving image involved a fundamental transformation of human perception, and thus of subjectivity itself.

> To those, therefore, who complain of the degradation of the art of film, let it be said that, even in the midst of the basest kitsch, there has nonetheless developed an optical culture of the highest kind. The language of film . . . has been continually and inexorably refined, and the perceptive faculties of even the most primitive of audiences have followed in its wake.[28]

Unlike his contemporary, Arnheim, Balázs perceived in sound cinema the potential to further film's dialectical progress towards aesthetic perfection. By augmenting silent cinema's 'whole rich culture of visual expression' with an exploration of 'our acoustic environment', sound film, he claimed, could 'open up a new sphere of experience' and thus redeem film as legitimate art.[29] Balázs is worth citing at length here because, in his phenomenological commitment to an understanding of film as a vehicle for a whole plethora of new modes of subjective experience – aural, visual, psychic, somatic – he prefigures later Third Reich calls for a revived 'cinema of experience'. Yet at the same time, post-1933 film commentators à la Gabler radically refuse Balázs' commitment to an 'opening up' of subjective experience. Instead, the impulse we glimpse in the spatial reorderings of the filmgoing experience discussed above, is towards a channelling of visual and aural perception into the rigidified structures of *völkisch* aesthetic form. From the very moment of crossing the threshold of the cinema auditorium, the Third Reich spectator is engaged as witness to the spectacle of an audience reconstructed as racially purged and hierarchically ordered *Volk*. At the same time, her/his bodily presence as a material participant in the public enactment of a folk identity shifts her/his relation to the film medium itself. Where Balázs' spectator – like that of Christian Metz forty years on – dissolves into an identity with the camera and surrenders her/his subjectivity to the cinematic apparatus ('the camera takes my eyes and transports them with it into the very centre of the image itself'),[30] the spectator in Third Reich film theory dissolves first into the body of the *Volk*-in-miniature that is the cinema audience.

This prior absorption into the fantasy space that is the *völkisch* audience has significant potential implications, as we shall see later, for processes of identification with Third Reich film narrative, and specifically with its characters and stars. But let us look first at a second means by which this material absorption of the spectator into the folk body occurs, namely through the temporal reconfiguring of the film viewing experience after 1933.

TIME: CINEMA PROGRAMMING AND RHYTHM

In his late Weimar cultural history of the film medium, *Das Zeitalter des Films* (*The Age of Film*), the drama theorist Joseph Gregor polemicises in the following vein against the revue genre that is the stock-in-trade of contemporary popular film:

> The core principle of construction of the ... revue is that of visual magnificence; there is no literary core, nor even the most superficial entertainment. What is injected into these images is not drama, but rhythm, whether in the form of

purely rhythmically constructed ballet (the chorus line), or of popular song. Once again we see how close is the link between empty optical impressions, and rhythm.[31]

Gregor was a leading figure among those cultural conservatives who, even as late as the early sound era, fought a rearguard action against the soulless and degenerate medium of film. His comments on rhythm, however, have their roots in a more celebratory film-aesthetic tradition. Once again it was Balázs whose concern with film's capacity to embody modern experience in aesthetic form ('for every art form involves a particular relationship between human beings and the world, a particular dimension of the soul'), led him to laud what Gregor decries as the rhythmic properties of film. In his work on the 'grammar' of montage, for instance, Balázs notes how film's nature as an art of the *moving* image enables it – uniquely, he claims – to embody and render meaningful the chaotic rhythms of modern experience.[32] This is an age, claims Balázs, in which 'we have learned to see more quickly'; and, as for his contemporary Hans Richter (whose influence Balázs cites), the rhythm established by montage, camera movement and direction, the tempo and duration of movement within the frame, or by the rhythmic structuring of scenes and sequences, is for Balázs the equivalent in representation of the 'movement that is life'.[33]

For writers under Nazism, the Weimar modernists' work on rhythm offered a useful tool for their pro-fascist reformulation of the aesthetics of film. In their struggle for conformity with fascism's recasting of modernity in the image of what Klaus Theweleit calls the 'totality-machine' of the military troop, Third Reich film theory drew on Richter and Balázs to formulate a vision of a cinema that moved in tandem with the 'steel-hard rhythms of our time'.[34] In the new film 'dramaturgy' after 1933, film as an art form with privileged access to what the Marxist Romantic Balázs had termed a 'dimension of the soul' was to undergo an aesthetic revision that would fit it at last to fulfil the function that Balázs assigned it as 'the popular art art form (*Volkskunst*) of our century'.[35] For the Weimar theorists, of course, it was in modernism that film would discover the forms that embodied the twentieth-century soul; witness for instance Richter's enthusiasm for contrapuntal editing as the 'richest' form of rhythmic construction, or Balázs' celebration of Walter Ruttmann as the acknowledged master of rhythm in montage.[36] Third Reich 'reactionary modernists', by contrast, abhorred much Weimar film modernism for its disjunctive time schemes, its formal disharmony, its metropolitan tempo. Ernst Iros and Wolfgang Berkefeld, for instance, drew on the 'ecological Romanticism' of Ludwig Klages to represent rhythm per se as a primordial and 'thought-free' experience that 'arises not from the mechanical construction of objects, but from the organic law of life'.[37] Since the rhythm that underpins all life contains, in its organic harmony, the 'impulse towards synthesis', so too must film strive after those 'elements of plenitude and harmony' through which it achieves the wholeness that mirrors 'life'.[38]

In a contemporaneous essay on film dramaturgy, Wolfgang Liebeneiner – film director, actor and Director of the Faculty of Film Art in the German Film Academy – similarly stresses the importance of a 'harmony of image, word and music' in film; and he too names rhythm as the 'moment of excitation that transmits itself like an electric current directly to the unconscious of the spectator'.[39] For those such as Iros, Berkefeld and Liebeneiner, in other words, the pioneering work on rhythm by Balázs, Richter and their peers lays a foundation on which they will construct a differently ideologically inflected account of Third Reich cinematic temporality and film spectatorship. Film in the eyes of these later writers was significant for its spectators not primarily as a source of symbolic meaning and self-definition through identification. Instead, the rhythm of film was one of many of the medium's 'organic' features that forged a bond between the spectator, and the rhythmic movements of a social totality that marched to the iron beat of National Socialism.[40]

In Liebeneiner's hyperbolic formulation, the harmoniously rhythmic film text for which he argues fulfils 'the old Germanic longing to incorporate the whole world in a single work of art, and to conjoin all art forms in one single vast experience [*Erlebnis*]'.[41] Rhythmic harmony, then, is considered the prerequisite for the collective 'Germanic' experience that was Third Reich film reception. It is this impulse towards rhythmic reconstruction, moreover, that underpinned a series of state interventions after 1933 into cinema programming: interventions that focused on the purging from German cinemas of the 'scandal' of the double bill.

As in the US, the double bill had emerged in early 1930s Germany as a response to economic crisis in film exhibition. The period from 1928–9 had witnessed what the journal *Film-Kurier* termed an 'illusory blossoming' of cinemagoing in Germany.[42] In the five years from 1925 to 1930, the total number of cinemas increased by 30 per cent, from just under 3,900 to over 5,000.[43] When world depression struck in autumn 1929, there began a bitter struggle in this over-inflated cinema sector for viable market shares of a dwindling film audience. As box-office figures tumbled (total ticket sales fell by 115 million from 1928–9 to 1932–3, an estimated decrease of some 32 per cent),[44] exhibitors fighting to stay afloat adopted ever more desperate commercial measures, including price-cutting and the double bill.[45]

The double bill gained widespread popularity in the early 1930s as a response to market crisis from small and medium-sized cinemas in particular. In larger theatres, live variety was reintroduced during this period as a middlebrow form already popular among the middle-class audiences on whom these luxury houses depended.[46] Smaller venues, by contrast, lacked resources for live performance of this kind, and courted their more impecunious audience with bargain-basement prices, and double bills comprising two full-length features alongside advertising, actuality and other shorter forms.

For German producers and distributors, the implications were financially disastrous. The double bill reduced by exactly half the monies available to exhibitors to pay film hire for any given film; the result was price war among distributors, and a crippling reduction in producers' capacity to recoup costs through box-office receipts. By 1931–2, therefore, the film press and trade associations were actively campaigning against the 'scandal' of double bills, whose placing in a single programme of two such prestige titles as Luis Trenker's *Der Rebell* (*The Rebel*) and Hans Behrendt's *Grün ist die Heide* (*Green is the Heath*, both 1932) was said to be hastening industrial ruin for film in Germany.[47]

In ways that are by now familiar, however, the battle against the double bill was waged as much on cultural as on economic grounds. The disgrace of programmes featuring, for example, Hollywood's social realist *I am a Fugitive from a Chain Gang* (Le Roy, 1932) alongside Carl Lamac's 1931 romantic comedy *Die Tochter des Regiments* (*The Regiment's Daughter*) was seen to reside not only in their deflation of the market value of German product, but in the coarsening of public taste that the double bill supposedly represented.[48] Echoing the arguments of early twentieth-century cinema reformers, late Weimar commentators denounced the double bill as an offence against good taste and public education. In one attack on the 'monstrosity' that was the double feature, *Film-Kurier* fulminated:

> When a trade squanders its best wares in this fashion, and in so doing not only denies its audience any powers of discernment ... but also merely educates them in the ways of mass consumption, then we should consider that trade unworthy of the risk-taking involved in quality product.[49]

Measuring the double bill against criteria of aesthetic construction derived more from theatrical than cinematic tradition, its critics excoriated this mode of programming for its excessive length (the spectator was sustained, claimed one Wolfgang Abshagen in 1933, in a constant state of titillation that rendered unattainable that state of 'spiritual recovery and relaxation' induced by quality entertainment); for the over-stimulation afforded by an excess of dramatic climax in the double feature; and for the aesthetics of dissonance that underpinned its 'un-organic' juxtaposition of incompatible titles.[50]

The policy response was swift, and came initially from within the industry, before the *Reich* Film Chamber implemented a final ban in September 1933. As early as April 1932, a commission of the industry's own self-regulating body, the SPIO, passed a resolution exhorting affiliated associations, as well as non-affiliated distributors to comply with a proposed ban on the double bill as of 15 May 1932. SPIO's relative weakness among the plethora of competing film-industrial associations was demonstrated, however, by widespread non-compliance with the ban. In April 1933, under the combined auspices of the Berlin-Brandenburg Association of Independent Film Theatre Owners and the Straussberger Platz Entertainment Association, the double feature was successfully outlawed, but in Berlin only. It was left to the *Reich* Film Chamber to impose from 15 September of that year a nationwide moratorium on a practice it condemned as the 'ruination' of German film, an 'automatic, soulless overindulgence of the metropolitan audience in particular' that represented 'not only an economic issue . . . but a question of cinema culture and thus of the culture of the *Volk*'.[51]

In what sense, however, did this shift to the single feature meet the demands of the film theorists for the 'plenitude and harmony' that was to characterise audience responses to Third Reich film? That question is best answered if we conceive the 1933 programming reforms as a restructuring of the rhythm of audience experience in the act of watching film. To an extent, programming structures still varied after the September 1933 reforms according to cinema size and status. Thus first-run houses might for instance run variety acts as an adjunct to the filler programme, while second-run theatres were restricted to newsreels, documentaries (*Kulturfilme*) and adverts alongside occasional comedy or other entertainment shorts.[52] The common thrust of programming policy across all cinema types after 1933 was, however, towards a programme whose predetermined length and 'organic structure' produced in the audience the 'inner coherence' (*innere Sammlung*) that was the desired effect of film spectatorship. The double bill had produced, it was widely argued, a regime of cinematic experience organised around an 'oversaturation' with sensual (visual and aural) pleasures.[53] This had been a modernist culture of excess that emphasised division and disjuncture over integration; witness the double bill's unwieldy juxtaposition of clashing genres and national styles, or early 1930s cinema's splitting of the audience along lines of class (cinema had become, it was claimed, a largely proletarian pursuit), of regions (hence the widespread references to cinemagoing as a metropolitan mass pursuit), and of gender (by 1933, women were estimated to make up 60–70 per cent of the film audience, and film was widely touted as the female leisure pursuit par excellence).[54]

In post-1933 cinema, by contrast, the aesthetic integration of individual programme elements was to produce in the audience an impression of its own wholeness and 'inner coherence'.[55] Though there were some discussions of the need for closer parallels in film style between the filler programme and the main feature, what Linda Schulte-Sasse has termed Third Reich cinema's 'illusion of wholeness' was primarily to be achieved at the exhibition level through a structuring of the cinema programme that orchestrated audience responses in line with the rhythms of a desired experience of inner synthesis.[56] The newsreels and documentary shorts that preceded the main feature were designed to serve therefore both as a prelude to the long feature film, and, through their stylistic difference from narrative film, to impose a well-defined structure on a programme typically of two to two-and-a-half hours duration.

The experiential transformations that this restructuring engendered are usefully illuminated by one contemporary account of a filmgoing experience in the sumptuous Hamburg Ufa-Palast. Writing in summer 1939 for the British film journal *Sight and Sound*, the English journalist Winifred Holmes described as follows her trip to see the Zarah Leander blockbuster *Der Blaufuchs* (*Arctic Fox*):

> First we see advertising films such as we come across sometimes in our own provincial cinemas. Then a propaganda film – what the householder should do with empty tins.[57] ... After that ... there is an instructional film made by a professor of natural history on the subject of the increasing stages of intelligence in nature from a toad to a monkey. This turns out to be a superb film. Excellently planned, beautifully photographed and well cut and edited ... Now at last – the news-reel. I shall be able to put my finger for a moment on the pulse of the ordinary folk of Germany, judging as one can here in England by the emotion of the audience displayed whenever a public figure or event comes on the screen – boos, cheers, hissing and clapping which always accompany a news-reel when it deals with politics.
>
> But to my surprise there is silence ... The good citizens in the cinema just watch the spectacle as a spectacle and take no active part in its emotion ... [After the interval] we are treated to a long variety programme. There's a cinema organ; then a troubador with a guitar singing in American; then a trapeze and tightrope act – almost a strip-tease – and lastly 16 performing poodles. My chances of seeing the feature are rapidly diminishing, but the poodles are fun. ... The audience is wideawake now and amusing itself hugely and audibly.
>
> I look uneasily at my neighbour's watch and murmur something about the Hauptbahnhof. She understands vaguely that I have a train to catch and after that looks at her watch every five minutes. This makes me so nervous that soon I sneak

out after seeing only a short footage of the feature film. Is it tabu to go out between intervals? I wonder, looking at the shut doors. Well, I'll pretend to feel ill if anyone stops me . . . [58]

It was in the year of Holmes' Hamburg visit that Wolfgang Liebeneiner wrote of the 'old Germanic longing to incorporate the whole world in a single work of art'. That longing, as Holmes' account illustrates, was satisfied through the construction not just of the film text, but of the whole reception context as a Wagnerian *Gesamtkunstwerk* in which film programmes were structured no longer according to the 'automatic' rhythms of mass entertainment, but the 'organic' patterns of Nazi art. Holmes' programme, for instance, has a five-part structure: prologue (adverts and propaganda), the *Kulturfilm* or educational documentary, the newsreel, variety acts, and finally the main feature. That structure itself lends to cinema spectatorship the structural balance and temporal extension that, as Corinna Müller has pointed out, had in previous phases of German film history been considered the prerequisites for the acceptance of film as legitimate art. In her history of film's transition from mass cultural to prestige bourgeois form from the early to mid-1910s, Müller attributes determining significance to the emergence of films whose length and internal organisation reflected established theatrical norms. The classical drama, notes Müller, was structured in five acts and was of extended duration: two and a half hours at minimum, and longer for the dramatic productions of Goethe, Schiller and other genius figures.[59]

In the Third Reich context, the programme itself mimics the five-act structure of classical drama: a structure which, according to one early twentieth-century drama critic, Heinrich Stümcke, organised the theatregoing experience at a pace and in a rhythm that allowed the audience 'to immerse itself *reverentially* in the work of art'.[60] There is, of course, a clear distinction between the theatrical experience Stümcke describes, and Holmes' account of cinemagoing in the Third Reich. In the Imperial context to which Stümcke refers, audience responses were regulated textually by the five-act dramatic structure, and socially by common codes of taste and artistic appreciation. After 1933, by contrast, social conventions governing proper modes of audience reception were reinforced or supplanted by the disciplinary regulation and control of audience response. Holmes comments, for instance, on the 'tabu' of leaving the cinema between intervals; and indeed, the outlawing of the double bill was accompanied by a phasing out of the rolling programme, and the imposition of set times for cinema entry and exit.[61] Holmes further notes that the newsreel heckling she knows from British picture houses is wholly absent from her Hamburg experience. This is hardly surprising, given the stringent policing of cinemas, as of all public spaces in Nazi Germany, and the suppression of expressions of popular disaffection or dissent.[62] It is only in putatively apolitical moments of popular entertainment (here, Holmes' '16 performing poodles' and the like) that audience emotion can be publicly expressed in energetic applause, explosions of mirth or other 'huge and audible' expressions of pleasure.

SPECTATORSHIP TRANSFORMED?

In the course of a two-and-a-half-hour programme, then, what Liebeneiner and others would have termed the 'rhythm' of audience experience is modulated, the public expression of pleasure alternately promoted and suppressed both by conventions governing audience organisation, admission and exit, and by an apparatus of surveillance that includes SD spies in the audience, SS officers in their boxes, and perhaps even the ushers whom Winifred Holmes fears will stop her leaving to catch her train. Importantly, the complex spatial, temporal and ideological reconfiguring of cinematic experience captured briefly in Holmes' account transforms the relationship between viewing subject and text in the act of film spectatorship. In the various interventions into film exhibition and reception discussed above, we witness an effort to return film reception to a fantasised primordial bond between the work of art and the collectivity. Accounts of spectatorship by film theorists from the heyday of cinematic modernity between the wars had focused above all on transformations in individual subjectivity in the act of watching film. For Béla Balázs, for instance, film, like all the visual arts, was of significance not for its intrinsic aesthetic worth, but because it opened to the human subject whole new vista of perceptual development. Drawing a parallel between film and Impressionist art, for instance, Balázs claimed that 'one can in no sense talk here of an aesthetic development. But the perception of perspective and of the atmosphere of the air is nonetheless a great development [whose] substrate is the subject, the human subject. . . .'[63]

There is after 1933, by contrast, both in the material and theoretical reformulation of cinematic experience, an effort to position film as a force not for Balázs' creative transformation of the human subject, but for its dissolution into a position of subordination within the hierarchical collectivity of the *Volk*. Ernst Iros, for instance, saw himself as following Kant (and by implication disavowing his phenomenological predecessors from Balázs to Kracauer) when he derided film's capacity to appeal to and transform the human senses. The senses, he claims, are of use only for the 'perception of material phenomena' – a category from which, we may conclude, film is excluded, since for Iros, the senses must be abandoned in any encounter with art in favour of a mobilisation of the 'soul' (*Seele*). Only this latter, he continues, can grant access to the 'invisible life at work below the surface of the phenomenal world'.[64] Access to that 'invisible life' is gained in part through an experience of the 'rhythm' that suffuses both art and life; hence, as I have tried to argue above, the significance of formal changes in the film programme that lend it the proper rhythm and tempo for an appreciation of film as art. But the metaphysical fusion of 'art' and 'soul' after which Iros and his contemporaries apparently strive is achieved also only through a wholesale evacuation of the human subject, a 'surrender to an Other' that is the prerequisite for 'that state of dissolution that frees us from our consciousness and "fuses" us with the work itself'.[65]

In Winifred Holmes' account of her own 1939 cinematic 'experience' there emerges a picture of a film programme that situates the main feature at the end and climax of the programme, and thus as the apotheosis of the aesthetic *Erlebnis* that is film spectactorship. Holmes herself, of course, can give no account of the Third Reich feature, thwarted as she was in her efforts to experience *Der Blaufuchs* and its stars. In the next chapter, therefore, we revisit narrative film before the war, and explore more closely the implications for the reception history I am attempting here of a Third Reich model of the film spectator as participant in the scenario that Iros outlines of submissive 'surrender' to the experience of film, a scenario already in part realised, as I have shown, in the spatial and temporal organisation of German cinema and film reception after 1933.

NOTES

1. Wilhelm Siegfried, 'Vorwort', in Landesverband Berlin-Brandenburg-Grenzmark (ed.), *Filmtheaterführung. Die Vorträge des ersten Schulungsjahres 1934/35 der Fachschule der Filmtheaterbesitzer des Landesverbandes Berlin-Brandenburg-Grenzmark e.V. im Reichsverband Deutscher Filmtheater e.V.* (Berlin: Neue Film-Kurier Verlagsgesellschaft, 1935), p. 5.

2. Béla Balázs, *Der Geist des Films* (Halle: Knapp, 1930), p. 5.

3. Fedor Stepun, *Theater und Kino* (Berlin: Bühnenvolksbundverlag, 1932), p. 12.

4. Friedrich Munding, 'Krisis des Films', *Film-Kurier* (FK), 30 December 1935.

5. A. Hinderer, 'Die Bedeutung des Films', in Landesverband Berlin-Brandenburg-Grenzmark (ed.), *Filmtheaterfuhrüng*, p. 61.

6. This is Miriam Hansen's translation, from Siegfried Kracauer, 'Langeweile' (Boredom), in idem, *Das Ornament der Masse* (Frankfurt am Main: suhrkamp, 1963), p. 322. See Hansen, *Babel and Babylon. Spectatorship in American Silent Film* (Cambridge, MA and London: Harvard University Press, 1991), p. 112.

7. Ibid., p. 83.

8. Ibid., p. 43, citing Norman King, 'The Sound of Silents', *Screen*, vol. 25, no. 3, May–June 1984, pp. 2–15.

9. Uwe-Karsten Ketelsen, *Heroisches Theater. Untersuchungen zur Dramentheorie des Dritten Reichs* (Bonn: Bouvier, 1968), p. 185.

10. Ibid., p. 187.

11. E. W. Möller, 'Wandlungen des deutschen Theaters', *Hochschule und Ausland* XIII, 1935, p. 48. Cited in Ketelsen, *Heroisches Theater*, p. 184.

12. Ernst Iros, *Wesen und Dramaturgie des Films* (Zürich and Leipzig: Max Niehaus, 1938), p. 121.

13. 'Zurück zum ersten Film!', FK, 5 November 1934.

14. Interview with Hans Schlenk, Director, *Residenztheater* Munich, FK , 8 April 1935.

15. Munding, 'Krisis des Films'.

16. Figures from A. Jason, 'Kinotheater und Tonfilmkinos in Europa 1926–1933', *Film-Kurier*, 23 December 1933. See also Wolfgang Mühl-Benninghaus, *Das Ringen um den Tonfilm. Strategien der Elektro- und der Filmindustrie in den 20er und 30er Jahren* (Düsseldorf: Droste, 1999), p. 190.

17. A lively debate on sound technology was conducted in the trade journals *Filmtechnik* (FT) and *Der Film* (FL); see, for example, 'Der schlechte Ton', FT, 19 March 1932, p. 1; 'Der schlechte Ton im Lichtspielhaus', FT, 17 August 1932; Rudolf Arnheim, 'Fragen an den Tonmeister', FT, 27 May 1933, pp. 137–8; Alfred Schneider, '10 Jahre deutscher Tonfilm', FT, 16 August 1933, pp. 209–11; E. von Lölhöffel, 'Schöpferische Mitarbeit der Tonfilmtechnik', FT, 9 May 1936, pp. 87–8; 'Rückblick auf 1937 in Deutschland', FT 1, 1938, pp. 13–19; and from *Der Film* (FL): E. von Lölhöffel, 'Tonfilmtechnik dient dem Kinobesucher', FL, 20 October 1934; 'Schallplattenwiedergabe im Tonfilmtheater', FL, 11 February 1939; J. W., 'Wer Augen hat, zu sehen und Ohren, zu hören', FL, 5 August 1939.

18. Werner Gabler, 'Lichtspielhäuser in Klein- und Mittelstädten', FT, 23 December 1933, p. 300.

19. Richard Grunberger, *A Social History of the Third Reich* (Harmondsworth: Penguin, 1991), p. 67.

20. 'Wahl des erweiterten Vorstandes. Debatte zum Spio-Plan – und die Eintrittspreise!', FK, 1 January 1933.

21. For a snapshot from the trade journal *Film-Kurier* of the piecemeal developments across the *Reich* that led to the RFK ruling, see 'Immer wieder: Die Schleuderpreise', FK, 23 January 1933; 'Wahl des erweiterten Vorstandes. Debatte zum Spio-Plan – und die Eintrittspreise!', FK, 1 February 1933; 'Eintrittspreise-Klassifizierung der Berliner Lichtspielhäuser', FK, 22 April 1933; 'Die Preisreform in Berlin', FK, 25 April 1933; 'Eintrittspreisregelung in Köln', FK, 17 May 1933; 'Preisregelung in Hamburg getroffen', FK, 3 June 1933; 'Einheitliche Regelungen der Eintrittspreise für ganz Deutschland', FK, 14 August 1933.

22. 'Einheitliche Regelungen der Eintrittspreise für ganz Deutschland', FK, 14 August 1933.

23. Heinz Boberach (ed.), *Meldungen aus dem Reich. Die geheimen Lageberichte des Sicherheitsdienstes der SS 1938–1945* (Herrsching: Manfred Pawlak, 1984), especially pp. 116, 690, 712, 740, 759–60, 978, 1024–5, 1179.

24. See Boguslaw Drewniak, *Der deutsche Film 1938–1945. Ein Gesamtüberblick* (Düsseldorf: Droste, 1987), p. 635.

25. See Alexander Jason, 'Der Filmtheaterbesuch in den Jahren 1932–1933', FK, 8 February 1934.

26. Gabler, 'Lichtspielhauser'.

27. On the 'shock effect of the film', see Walter Benjamin, 'The Work of Art in the Age of Mechanical Reproduction', in idem, *Illuminations*, Harry Zohn (trans.), Hannah Arendt (ed.) (London: Fontana 1992, orig. 1936), p. 232; and on shock as the perceptual mode that is most characteristic of modernity, see idem, *Charles Baudelaire. A Lyric Poet in the Era of High Capitalism.* Harry Zohn (trans.) (London: Verso, 1997), pp. 114ff.

28. Balázs, *Der Geist des Films*, p. 7.

29. Ibid., pp. 142–5. See by way of contrast Rudolf Arnheim, *Film as Art* (Berkeley, Los Angeles and London: University of California Press, 1971, orig. 1957), pp. 1–2.

30. Balázs, *Der Geist des Films*, p. 9. Compare Christian Metz' suggestion that '[i]nsofar as it abolishes all traces of the subject of the enunciation, the traditional film succeeds in giving the spectator the impression that he is himself that subject, but in a state of emptiness and absence, of pure visual capacity.' Metz, 'Story/Discourse: Notes on two kinds of voyeurism', in Bill Nichols (ed.), *Movies and Methods* Vol. II (Berkeley, Los Angeles and London: University of California Press, 1985), p. 548.

31. Joseph Gregor, *Das Zeitalter des Films* (Vienna and Leipzig: Reinhold, 1932), p. 63.

32. Balázs, *Der Geist des Films*, p. 47.

33. Ibid. See also Béla Balázs, *Der sichtbare Mensch oder die Kultur des Films* (Vienna and Leipzig: Deutsch-österreichischer Verlag, 1924), p. 124. See also Hans Richter, *Filmgegner von heute – Filmfreunde von morgen* (Berlin: H. H. Richter, 1968, orig. 1929), p. 34.

34. Iros, *Wesen und Dramaturgie*, p. 109.

35. Balázs *Der sichtbare Mensch*, p. 11.

36. Richter, *Filmgegner von heute*, p. 41: Balázs, *Der Geist des Films*, p. 58.

37. Iros, *Wesen und Dramaturgie*, p. 107. The term 'ecological Romanticism' is from Andrew Bowie, 'Critiques of Culture', in Wilfried van der Will and Eva Kolinsky (eds), *The Cambridge Companion to Modern German Culture* (Cambridge: Cambridge University Press, 1998), p. 150.

38. Iros, *Wesen und Dramaturgie*, p. 108.

39. Wolfgang Liebeneiner, 'Die Harmonie von Bild, Wort und Musik im Film', in Oswald Lehnich (ed.), *Jahrbuch der Reichsfilmkammer 1939* (Berlin: Max Hesses, 1939), p. 150.

40. Liebeneiner (ibid.) formulates the issue of harmony between the rhythms of pro-filmic and extra-filmic realities thus: 'Wherever the harmony of image, word and music with the inner processes that are the stuff of film has imposed a common rhythm on every last dimension of the inner and outer worlds of human beings, sweeping them in the process into hitherto undreamed of new experiences and sensations: this is when film reaches its highest stage of development.'

41. Ibid., p. 155.

42. Josef Kugel, 'Wir alle sind schuld! Ehrliches Theaterbesitzer-Bekenntnis zum Zweischlagerprogramm', FK, 27 April 1933.

43. Figures of 3,878 and 5,059 respectively are given by Walter Möhl, *Das deutsche Filmtheatergewerbe unter besonderer Berücksichtigung der Zusammenschlußbewegung* (Berlin: Lichtbildbühne, 1937), p. 37.

44. Ibid., p. 33.

45. For a comparative view of US exhibition practices in respect of the double bill, see Richard Maltby, *Hollywood Cinema: An Introduction* (Oxford: Blackwell, 1995), pp. 65ff.

46. For a contemporary account of this mix of variety and film in a large Hamburg first-run cinema, see Winifred Holmes, 'Hamburg Cinema. A Typical German Programme', *Sight and Sound*, no. 8, 1939, pp. 18–20.

47. The two titles ran side-by-side in a Gelsenkirchen double bill in January 1933. See 'Skandal in Gelsenkirchen', FK, 31 January 1933.

48. 'Schluß mit dem Doppelprogramm', FK, 22 April 1933. Hollywood productions often ran alongside German titles in the double bill; thus its eventual outlawing in September 1933 can be seen in part as a protectionist measure against Hollywood market penetration. See Wolfgang Abshagen, 'Es müssen 1000m-Beifilme geschaffen werden', FK, 22 April 1933.

49. 'Skandal in Gelsenkirchen', FK, 31 January 1933.

50. Abshagen, '1000m–Beifilme; Hans Cürlis, 'Das Zweischlager-Programm – wie es der Kulturfilmproduzent sieht', FK, 26 April 1933; Bruno Esbold, 'Zweischlager-Programm muss restlos verschwinden', FK, 25 April 1933.

51. 'Die Frist bis 15. September. Filmkammer-Beschlüsse sind Befehle – keine Anweisungen', FK, 22 August 1933.

52. See Esbold, 'Zweischlager-Programm', and 'Wie möchten Sie das Beiprogramm haben', FL, 26 August 1939.

53. Esbold, 'Zweischlager-Programm', and 'Vom Publikum aus betrachtet. Keine Träne für das Zweischlager-Programm', FK, 20 July 1933.

54. Gertrud Broich, 'Zauber der filmischen Organisation', in FL, 24 December 1932. This special issue contains articles on women in film by, among others, the bourgeois feminists Gertrud Bäumer and Marie-Elisabeth Lüders, film star Asta Nielsen, director Leontine Sagan, and scriptwriter-director Thea von Harbou.

55. 'Vom Publikum aus betrachtet. Keine Träne für das Zweischlager-Programm', FK, 20 July 1933.

56. Linda Schulte-Sasse, *Entertaining the Third Reich. Illusions of Wholeness in Nazi Cinema* (Durham and London: Duke University Press, 1996). Schulte-Sasse's analysis focuses on individual film texts and key genres; I am extending that analysis here to encompass the broader reception context. For discussion of the need for aesthetic integration of the filler programme with the main feature, which produces, it is argued, 'the miracle of refined and tasteful entertainment', see, for example, Walter Stang, 'Film im Dienst kultureller Werbung', FL, 20 January 1934.

57. This is not a 'propaganda film' in the ideological sense, but a public service advertisement of the kind common in cinemas of the time.

58. Holmes, 'Hamburg Cinema', pp. 19–20.

59. Corinna Müller, *Frühe deutsche Kinematographie. Formale, wirtschaftliche und kulturelle Entwicklungen* (Stuttgart and Weimar: Metzler, 1994), pp. 209–14.

60. Heinrich Stümcke, 'Kinematograph und Theater', *Bühne und Welt* 4, April 1912; cited in Müller, *Frühe deutsche Kinematographie*, p. 215.

61. David Welch points out that it was not until 1943 that Goebbels imposed a ban on cinema entry after the start of the newsreels. By this point in the war, newsreel coverage of the war was losing credibility with German audiences, who 'were actually lingering outside the cinema until the newsreels were over': David Welch, *The Third Reich. Politics and Propaganda* (London and New York: Routledge, 1993), p. 119. Until this point, the closed programme appears to have been enforced, as Holmes suggests, by 'tabu' rather than formal legislation.

62. See Boberach, *Meldungen aus dem Reich*.

63. Balázs, *Der Geist des Films*, p. 6.

64. Iros, *Wesen und Dramaturgie*, p. 111.

65. Ibid., pp. 108 and 101.

4

Personality and the *Völkisch* Sublime: Carl Froelich and Emil Jannings

In December 1937, the Ufa artistic committee met to consider scripts and treatments for future seasons. A treatment for the proposed *Pharao*, described by Ludwig Klitsch as 'an improbable, low-quality thriller, with the Egyptians and the pyramids as backdrop', was unanimously rejected, but Mathias Wieman seized his chance to draw to the group's attention a treatment by director Erich Waschneck. Adapted from a popular novel by John Knittel, *Der blaue Basalt* (*Blue Basalt*) told the story of a European Egyptologist who, 'having collapsed exhausted in the pharaoh' burial chamber, brings the mummy to life in a dream as an enchanting woman and lover'. Against objections from Ufa production chief Ernst Hugo Correll (he dubbed the narrative 'necrophiliac'), Wieman argued that '*Blue Basalt* rises to a truly sublime finale that is fully in keeping with recent findings on Egyptian beliefs ...'.[1]

Wieman's championing of this narrative's 'sublimity' won the day, and the treatment was accepted for further consideration at a later meeting. This was, moreover, more than a passing incident. As we have seen throughout this book, the transition to National Socialism was marked by renewed efforts to establish film as legitimate art. That battle was waged in film theory and criticism by a return to neo-Kantian aesthetic theory as the foundation for a revitalised art of film. It is out of this context that Wieman's comments on *Blue Basalt* are generated. Between 1933 and 1940 – the period in which Wieman himself rose to prominence as Staatsschauspieler, Ufa bureaucrat, lecturer, critic and active NSDAP member – his contemporaries drew extensively on canonical conceptions of the sublime as the foundation for a revitalised art of film. Ernst Iros, for instance, drew in particular on Kant's third *Critique* to elaborate a distinction between the beautiful and the sublime that would underpin his proposal for a modernised, yet idealist reception aesthetics of film. In the *Critique,* Kant had drawn a distinction between the beautiful and the sublime as two distinct modes of access to precisely that spiritual truth which, for some Third Reich theorists at least, was mediated by the art of film. Günter Groll's notion of true film art as bypassing sense perception, for instance, is clearly indebted to Kant's comments on the experience of beauty as dependent on a disavowal of vulgar sense perception (ideal beauty, he claims, allows 'no sensory charm to be mixed into the satisfaction in its object') and an engagement instead with the 'moral ideas' of which the beautiful is the formal expression.[2]

Neo-Kantian concepts of the sublime were also widely mobilised in defence of the aesthetic status of particular films, personalities and film-cultural practices. The sublime, for Kant, had been, like the beautiful, not a category of sense perception, but of the mobilisation of reason (*Vernunft*) in pursuit of the idea. In its encounter with the sublime, the 'mind', he claimed, is prompted 'to abandon sensibility, and to occupy itself with ideas that contain a higher purposiveness'.[3] Naming as the aesthetic realisation of the sublime a number of qualities of both aesthetic artifacts and of Nature – a certain 'formlessness', a transcendence of time and space constraints, an extension into infinity – Kant concluded that, while the beautiful evokes mere 'pleasure' in the beautiful object, the sublime triggers a response closer to 'respect' in the face of the 'absolutely great'.[4]

In the National Socialist appropriation of Kant, this notion of the sublime as a mode of aesthetic experience demanding 'respect' was redefined to encompass a reverential submission to the sublime object. We have seen Mathias Wieman using the term in this way to argue his case for *Blue Basalt*. The term was also regularly used to describe figures of political supremacy, especially the *Führer*. In one of numerous calls for German film to align itself not just politically, but aesthetically with the Nazi state, one Josef Kugel, for instance, a Munich cinema owner, called in *Film-Kurier* early in 1933 for a reform of exhibition practices (his reference was to the double bill) that would bring German cinema into line with 'the sublime work of our *Führer*'.[5] Ernst Iros similarly locates an experience of the sublime as the prelude to those Nietzschean acts of will commonly identified with the Nazi state when he writes, 'anyone who has confronted his emotions after experiencing the enjoyment of a great work of art, will bear witness to the fact that pure pleasure in the aesthetic becomes combined with a mood of sublime religiosity ... that can become intense enough to effect a spontaneous ethical act'.[6]

If, then, as we saw in the preceding chapter, the feature film itself was located within the cinema programme as the apex of an aesthetic experience that constituted the film audience as microcosm of the *Volk*, then the filmic mode that best realised this aesthetic apotheosis seems to have been the cinematic sublime. More than this: in a film art structured, as I tried to show in Chapter 1, around the artistic 'personality', then it was likely to be through this figure that the audience's experience of the sublime was orchestrated.

In the rest of this chapter, I want to explore that possibility in an analysis that I have organised around what at first glance is a rather mundane example of mid-1930s narrative film. Carl Froelich's *Traumulus* is an unmemorable melodrama, a (for Froelich) characteristically pompous screen adaptation of a play by Arno Holz and Oskar Jerschke. The film has been largely ignored by post-war critics, despite its recent revival on video by Taurus-Film. In what follows, however, I shall treat *Traumulus* as one example of an attempted injection into German narrative film of precisely that sublime quality after which Wieman and others strove. My analysis focuses on two aspects of the foregrounding of 'personality' in the film. First, I consider its director, Carl Froelich, as a prominent film auteur of the period, and look at particular aspects of his film style – specifically, camera and light – that show Froelich striving to achieve that 'sublimity' which was the desired spectatorial effect of the assertion of personality in film. Moving on then from the auteur-personality, I consider the actor Emil Jannings as a second bearer of the personality aesthetic in *Traumulus*: a figure emblematic, I will finally suggest, of a mode of spectatorship I will call the *völkisch* sublime.

CARL FROELICH AS AUTEUR-PERSONALITY

In 1939, for the second time in his Third Reich career, Carl Froelich was awarded the National Film Prize, this time for his 1938 melodrama with Zarah Leander, *Heimat*. Firmly ensconced by now in leadership positions within the Nazi film-industrial hierarchy (Froelich already chaired the Ufa artistic committee, and stood on the threshold of his appointment as head of the *Reich* Film Chamber), the fifty-four-year-old director could look back with satisfaction on a six-year career under the *Reich* in which he had risen to prominence as a premier auteur-director. Among the mechanisms the Film Censorship Office developed to draw public attention to the Nazis' favoured films was, for instance, the 'predicate' (*Prädikat*) system, which awarded such distinctions as 'artistically valuable', 'culturally valuable', 'politically and artistically especially valuable' and so on to films deemed particularly fit for audience consumption.[7] By 1945, Froelich regularly outstripped his rival directors in terms of the number and range of predicates his films attracted (see Tables 6 and 7).[8] The large number of Froelich's films deemed culturally or artistically valuable suggests that his films enjoyed a position in Third Reich cinema as exemplary models of Nazism's new popular film art. That impression is reinforced by his status as the only director among the twelve figured in the statistics to have twice been awarded the State Film Prize, first for his 1936 *Traumulus* (*Little Dreamer*) – a comedy starring Emil Jannings in a schoolmaster role reminiscent of his part in

Table 6: Top twelve directors, ranked by total number of 'Prädikate', 1933–45

Director	skbw	sbw	kbw	sw	kü	küw	Kuw	jw	vw	FN	Lf	ST	vb	aw	Total
Veit Harlan	4	–	2	–	–	7	3	3	4	2	–	1	2	1	29
Carl Froelich	2	1	3	1	2	8	2	–	2	–	–	2	1	–	24
Hans Steinhoff	3	–	–	1	–	7	2	2	3	1	–	–	2	–	21
Wolfgang Liebeneiner	2	–	1	1	–	7	1	2	2	1	–	–	1	1	19
Gustav Ucicky	3	–	3	1	2	5	–	1	–	1	–	1	–	–	17
Arthur Maria Rabenalt	–	–	–	3	–	5	–	1	3	–	–	–	–	–	12
Paul Verhoeven	–	–	2	1	–	5	2	–	1	–	–	–	–	–	11
Fritz Peter Buch	–	–	–	1	–	4	–	2	3	–	–	–	–	–	10
Erich Waschneck	–	–	–	1	2	4	–	1	1	–	–	–	–	–	9
Paul Martin	–	–	–	–	–	5	–	–	4	–	–	–	–	–	9
Victor Tourjansky	–	–	–	–	–	8	–	–	–	–	–	–	–	–	8
Erich Engel	–	1	–	–	–	6	–	–	–	–	–	–	–	–	7

Source: Gerd Albrecht, *Nationalsozialistische Filmpolitik. Eine soziologische Untersuchung über die Spielfilme des Dritten Reichs* (Stuttgart: Ferdinand Enke, 1969), pp. 545–57).
Key:
skbw = *staatspolitisch und künstlerisch besonders wertvoll* (politically and artistically especially valuable) (5 November 1934 – 1 September 1942)
sbw = *staatspolitisch besonders wertvoll* (politically especially valuable) (from 1 April 1939)
kbw = *künstlerisch besonders wertvoll* (artistically especially valuable) (from 1 April 1939)
sw = *staatspolitisch wertvoll* (politically valuable) (from 7 June 1933)
kü = *künstlerisch* (artistic) (until 5 November 1934)
kuw = *kulturell wertvoll* (culturally valuable) (throughout period)
jw = *jugendwert* (valuable for youth) (from 21 November 1938)
vw = *volkstümlich wertvoll* (of popular value) (from 1 April 1939)
FN = *Film der Nation* (Film of the Nation) (from 1939)
Lf = *Lehrfilm* (throughout period)
ST = *National (Staats-)Preis für Film* (National/State Film Prize) (from 1933)
vb = *volksbildend* (of popular educational value) (throughout period)
aw = *anerkennenswert* (worthy of note) (from 1 September 1942)

Table 7: Top twelve directors[1]

Directors	Film title, date (number of predicates and/or skbw)
1. Carl Froelich	*Ich für Dich – Du für mich*, 1934 (2); *Traumulus*, 1936 (2, incl. skbw); *Wenn wir alle Engel wären*, 1936 (skbw); *Heimat*, 1938 (2); *Es war eine rauschende Ballnacht*, 1939 (2); *Das Herz einer Königin*, 1940 (2); *Familie Buchholz*, 1944, Part 1 (2), Part 2 (2)
2a. Veit Harlan	*Der Herrscher*, 1937 (2, incl. skbw); *Jud Süss*, 1940 (2, incl. skbw); *Der grosse König*, 1942 (6, incl. skbw); *Immensee*, 1943 (3); *Kolberg*, 1943/44 (7, incl. skbw)
2b. Gustav von Ucicky	*Flüchtlinge*, 1933 (2); *Das Mädchen Johanna*, 1935 (skbw); *Aufruhr in Damaskus*, 1939 (2); *Mutterliebe*, 1939 (skbw); *Heimkehr*, 1941 (3, incl. skbw)
3. Hans Steinhoff	*Der alte und der junge König*, 1935 (2, incl.skbw); *Robert Koch, der Bekämpfer des Todes*, 1939 (4, incl. skbw); *Die Geierwally*, 1940 (2); *Ohm Krüger*, 1941 (6, incl.skbw)
4. Wolfgang Liebeneiner	*Ziel in den Wolken*, 1938 (2); *Bismarck*, 1940 (2, incl. skbw); *Ich klage an*, 1941 (2); *Die Entlassung*, 1943 (7, incl. skbw)
5a. Fritz Peter Buch	*Jakko*, 1941 (3); *Menschen im Sturm*, 1941 (2); *Gefährtin meines Sommers*, 1943 (2)
5b. Arthur Maria Rabenalt	*...reitet für Deutschland*, 1941 (2); *Fronttheater*, 1942 (2); *Zirkus Renz*, 1943 (2)
5c. Paul Verhoeven	*Der grosse Schatten*, 1942 (2); *Die Nacht in Venedig*, 1942 (2); *Philharmoniker*, 1944 (3)
6a. Paul Martin	*Das war mein Leben*, 1944 (2)
6b. Victor Tourjansky	*Feinde*, 1940 (3)
6c. Erich Waschneck	*Die Affäre Roedern*, 1944 (2)
7. Erich Engel	–

Source: Gerd Albrecht, *Nationalsozialistische Filmpolitik. Eine soziologische Untersuchung über die Spielfilme des Dritten Reichs* (Stuttgart: Ferdinand Enke, 1969), pp. 545–57.
1. Ranked by numbers of films with two *Prädikate* or more and/or with the highest *Prädikat*, skbw.

Sternberg's *Blue Angel* (1930) – and two years later, for *Heimat* (1938), the Third Reich's prototypical *Heimatfilm*.

In what follows, I want to consider one of these titles, Froelich's 1936 *Traumulus*, as an example of the authorial style that positioned him not as an auteur in the sense in which that term is understood in either Hollywood, or European art cinema, but in terms of the celebration of 'personality' that was, I have proposed, characteristic of Third Reich film. My focus here will be on two elements of Froelich's aesthetic: his handling of camera, and his use of light. In the former case, I will suggest, Froelich positions himself as the representative of a national aesthetic reconstructed in the spirit of National Socialism through his embracing of conventions from a lost period of German cinematic greatness:

the period of the Wilhelmine silents, of which Froelich was an early pioneer. In the latter instance, I consider how that assertion of national tradition was reinforced by a use of light that defined Froelich's national style both through its opposition to Hollywood, and through a construction of the actor-personality as the 'sublime' object that is the organising centre of film art.

FROELICH AND CAMERA

In his work on F. W. Murnau as one of Weimar cinema's most gifted exponents of 'modernist camera', Marc Silberman explores how, in his *Der letzte Mann* (*The Last Laugh*, 1924), Murnau and the cameraman Karl Freund exploited the possibilities of Weimar's unchained camera to 'place the spectator in the mise-en-scène instead of in front of a set'[9]. As Silberman indicates, the fragmentation of perspective and mobile identifications produced by the handling of camera in Murnau's film evoke that more profound 'crisis of the subject' that was the product of the multiple cultural, social and economic transitions of Weimar modernity. *Der letzte Mann* is 'modernist', then, not only in its visual style, but in the experience that style evokes of the 'loss of stable identities' that preoccupied modernist artists, writers and film-makers throughout the turbulent Weimar years.[10]

Froelich's *Traumulus*, by contrast, bears the hallmarks of its director's oft-expressed desire to invent for the Third Reich a film style that evoked the

Figure 10: *Traumulus* (1936) – von Zedlitz' death in tableau

'plenitude and harmony' to which proponents of a new film art aspired after 1933. That desire is visible, first, in Froelich's stylistic disavowal of modernism, and his indebtedness to pre-Weimar cinematographic traditions. One major source of Froelich's prestige status after 1933 was his reputation as an early film pioneer. Lauded by Third Reich commentators as one of Germany's first 'explorers of the *terra incognita* of film', Froelich drew in his sound films on his early film experience to develop a style that explicitly referenced the Wilhelmine silents he had helped to pioneer.[11] He was, for instance as likely to use as his basic element of narrative the single shot tableau (see Figure 10); the mannered graphics and ornamental script of his film credits recall the opening titles of his early Henny Porten collaborations; deep staging and slow cutting regularly replace the analytical editing and short shot length that were the 'hallmarks of cinematic sophistication and modernity' from the late 1910s on.[12]

Among the most striking features of *Traumulus*, however, is its refusal of what Silberman identifies as Murnau's 'modernist' handling of the look. The film's narrative and its use of Jannings as star position it from the outset as a direct riposte to the cinematic modernism of the Weimar period. Though ostensibly a theatrical adaptation from Holz and Jerschke, *Traumulus* was also recognisable as a remake of what the film historian Oskar Kalbus, as late as 1935, was still calling 'a glittering victory for German sound film', von Sternberg's *Der blaue Engel* (1930).[13] Like *Der blaue Engel, Traumulus* stars Emil Jannings as a benevolent but misguided boarding-school headmaster, Professor Niemeyer, whose blind faith in his morally wayward boys, as well as his naive bedazzlement by women of dubious virtue and intent – his second wife Jadwiga (Hilde Weissner), and the actress Lydia Link (Hilde von Stolz) – lead him, as they do in von Sternberg's film, to financial ruin and personal despair.

Numerous features of *Traumulus* situate the film, however, in opposition both to Sternberg's modernist aesthetic, and to a mode of address that engages the spectator through multiple identifications and shifting narrative perspectives. Froelich's treatment of dialogue offers a relevant example here. In an early sequence, four male municipal dignitaries – a doctor, a major, and two officers of the regional administration – meet at a Sunday *Stammtisch* (a barroom table for regulars) to exchange men's gossip over a pre-lunch glass of wine. Emil Jannings as Niemeyer is late, and the dastardly *Landrat* (regional administrator), von Kannewurf (Herbert Hübner), seizes the opportunity to spread malignant rumours of moral impropriety at Niemeyer's school. After a rehearsal of a play they are preparing for the Kaiser's birthday celebrations, one of Niemeyer's pupils, Kurt von Zedlitz (Hannes Stelzer), has been spotted cavorting with Lydia Link at a local inn. In exchanges charged with anticipation of Niemeyer's impending public shame, the men debate the possible outcome when the news of von Zedlitz' misdemeanours breaks.

Yet the visual treatment of the sequence displays nothing of its potential emotional tension. Most striking is Froelich's abandonment of the classical (Hollywood) conventions that both establish continuity in space and time, and situate the spectator as a participant in intersubjective exchanges. Following a cursory establishing shot – a pan leftwards from the bar's decorative stained-glass window to the seated men – the sequence proceeds with alternating medium shots of talking heads, interspersed with occasional high-angle and long shots that establish the *Stammtisch* and the bar pictorially as the scene of action. Here as elsewhere in *Traumulus*, however, there is apparent contempt for the cinematic conventions of space/time continuity that film historians have conventionally assumed to have been well entrenched not only in Hollywood, but in German popular cinema of the first sound decade. This sequence is remarkable for the camera's unwillingness to establish lines of action, its infringement of the 180-degree rule, its refusal of eyeline match, and in particular the virtual absence of point-of-view editing. The spectator's eye is aligned instead with a largely static objective camera that places faces at medium distance and in centre-frame, and locates the four participants in this otherwise animated debate as the objects of a detached spectatorial gaze.

Figure 11: light as border in *Traumulus* (1936)

The address here, then, is to a spectator whose cultural competence in reading classical cinematic codes is downplayed in favour of a capacity to decipher static composition within a symmetrical and bounded frame. This emphasis on the pictorial frame as the origin and limit of spectatorial pleasure is, moreover, reinforced by other visual features of this film. The wholly static opening sequence displays title and credits in ornamental script with a decorative border that evokes both theatre (the proscenium arch), and the graphic conventions of pre-modernist popular art.[14] This graphic reinforcement of the boundaries of the image frame is reproduced as the film progresses by, for example, Froelich's obsessive decoration of studio flats with framed images – portraits and landscapes whose shapes echo the camera frame and reinforce its border status. His apparent impulse to contain meaning within the image frame is further evident in theatrical sets whose borders are the frontier of narrative action in most sequences, as well as in a use of light that seems designed – perversely enough – not to illuminate figures in the *mise en scène*, but rather (see Figure 11) to delineate borders around the profilmic space and accentuate the frontier status of the image frame.

In a 1939 article on 'Carl Froelich's *oeuvre*', the popular magazine *Filmwelt* reflected on the origins of the director's 'artistic characteristics':

> During film's turbulent early years … when few had yet grasped its potential, or its intrinsic power, [Froelich] was one of the rare figures whose presentiment of film's greatness and future development led him to embark on a process of research, enquiry, discovery. By the time war broke out, he had already filmed the life of Richard Wagner. He worked on the General Staff during the World War, and became the inventor of aerial photographs in serial form. … When he moved later into film direction, he created such high-calibre works as Dostojewski's *Die Brüder Karamasoff* [*The Brothers Karamasov*] and *Idioten* [*The Idiots*], as well as numerous films with Henny Porten, who rose to prominence under his direction to one of the most significant of film actresses.[15]

Filmwelt's rooting of Froelich's art in his experiences in early film is empirically accurate both in terms of his role in early technical experiments, and, as we saw above, of the stylistic debt he owes to Wilhelmine film. But the magazine's lyrical celebration of the medium's infant years situates Froelich also as the putative bearer of a nationally specific tradition in film art. Third Reich film commentators eager to displace Weimar modernism from its film-historical throne constructed in the film press, as well as in popular and scholarly film-historical works, a narrative of the German cinematic heritage that located the work of early cinema pioneers – the Skladanowsky brothers, Oskar Messter, Carl

Froelich himself – as the wellspring of excellence in German film art. Hence, for instance Otto Kriegk's celebration of Froelich in an Ufa history published for the studio's twenty-five-year jubilee. Froelich's positioning here, alongside Paul Wegener, as a vanguard figure in efforts 'to show the German people [*Volk*] how to fashion from film an art and a profession of faith' is echoed by *Filmwelt* when it dubs Froelich 'a model of purposeful creation in the field of film art ... [Germany's] foremost director of film'.[16]

Froelich's stylistic construction of his films around conventions from the early silents can be seen, therefore, as one element in a larger cinematic discourse that located his films as models for a revived (anti-modernist, pictorial, Wilhelmine) German film tradition. Importantly in our present context, they are models too for a mode of spectatorship that facilitates an experience of film not as entertainment, but as 'art'. Froelich's emphasis on the bounded frame, combined in his films with frontal acting and balanced composition within the *mise en scène*, acts to dislodge the viewer from any affiliation to the oscillating gaze of cinematic modernism, and to re-situate her/him instead as the detached and centred subject of pictorial perspective. Froelich, it seems, frankly rejects the opportunities offered by mobile camera, point-of-view editing and other devices for an absorption of the spectator into the diegetic space. But the contemplative distance thus established between spectator and text is precisely a prerequisite for that more elevated experience of the cinematic sublime that, I want now to suggest, is one desired effect of Froelich's *Traumulus*.

FROELICH AND LIGHT

In a work on which the film theorist Ernst Iros substantially draws, the Wilhelmine aesthetician Johannes Volkelt wrote of the sublime that it involved an experience of 'the superhuman, the superior, the excessive'. It was this awakening in the perceiving subject of forces more powerful than her/himself that produced that 'effect on the soul' and enhancement of 'spiritual energy' that was many years later to become the desired subject effect of Third Reich film.[17]

In Carl Froelich's aesthetic as exemplified by *Traumulus*, the distancing conventions of camera and editing discussed above function in part to prepare the spectator for an encounter with textual objects whose very remoteness situates them, to borrow Volkelt's terms, as 'superior' or 'excessive'. But it is Froelich's use of light that contributes most to an aesthetic of sublimity in which 'personality' is located as the privileged source of Volkelt's 'spiritual energy'.

The importance of *Traumulus* for the new Third Reich film art was underlined in 1940 by one admirer, the would-be screenwriter Carl Müller, when he wrote to the director (in his new capacity as *Reich* Film Chamber President):

Your creative work in film, which I have followed with passionate concentration, has inspired me with overwhelming respect. *Traumulus, Wenn wir alle Engel wären* [*If All of Us Were Angels*], *Heimat* and *Es war eine rauschende Ballnacht* [*One Glittering Night at the Ball*], have furnished me with a revelation of the path I must pursue: it is in this way and no other that film *must* be shaped if it is to conform to its own indefinable laws.[18]

As 'indefinable' as the 'laws of film' might have seemed to Carl Müller, Froelich's authorial style nonetheless gained definition in the most concrete sense in the insistent use of the pictorial frame which, I have suggested, characterised *Traumulus*, and indeed much of Froelich's subsequent work. But his debt to pictorialism was also evident in his use of light. In an early sequence in *Traumulus*, the sixth-former and favourite of Niemeyer, Kurt von Zedlitz, is shown in the early hours of the morning leaving the bedroom of Lydia Link. We first see the couple as a dark shadow cast when Lydia opens her door (screen left) and her bedroom light projects their dual silhouette onto the wall beyond. The chiaroscuro lighting and low-angle camera appear at first to evoke the shadowy terrors of Weimar expressionism. But there are key differences. Caught in a lovers' kiss, the figures etched against the wall are too obviously mobilised as signifiers of romance to evince some hidden terror in the room offscreen behind the door. If there is a reference in this shot to silent cinema, then it is not to expressionism, but to Lotte Reiniger's puppet silhouettes, whose 'heraldic stylisation' (Lotte Eisner) is emulated by Froelich in an image that uses shadow to ornamental, not sinister effect.[19]

We see here, then, a referencing, yet subsequent disavowal of Weimar modernism that was as evident in *Traumulus*, as it had been in Froelich's earlier titles.[20] Here, a lighting mode developed to heighten spectatorial anxiety – the chiaroscuro effect of Weimar expressionism – is appropriated and transformed to become a decorative embellishment. Chiaroscuro, in other words, becomes the ornamental frame to a visual tableau presented for the spectator's pleasurable, if detached contemplation.

Froelich's pictorial penchant is further underlined by a subsequent sequence that uses light to demarcate a space for the human body as an object of pleasurable yet, again, distanced and disinterested contemplation. The shot that closes the opening romance sequence discussed above uses non-naturalist lighting – as in pictorial photography – to establish and mark as extraordinary the space occupied by the aesthetic artefact (here, the actor's body) that is the object of the spectator's gaze. When von Zedlitz descends from his lover's bedroom, the sequence cuts from a medium long shot of the couple at opposite ends of the stairwell, to a long shot in which the foreground is occupied by an oven in the bakery below Lydia's room, and the background by the bottom of the stair-case. A pool of light with no obvious source spreads across the floor beyond the last step. Von Zedlitz descends the stairs, pauses in the light, gestures a final farewell to Lydia, then runs towards the (barely lit) foreground to make his escape. A single key light is used here, then, to demarcate a space for actorly performance in the background of the studio set. A mix of conventions from the early silents (deep staging, spotlighting), still photography and theatre are drawn upon, in other words, to situate Froelich's film in a tradition that bypasses both Hollywood and Weimar, and connects *Traumulus* to an older (Wilhelmine) heritage of artistic representation.

But there is more. If Froelich's use of camera and light enacts a disavowal of Weimar modernism, then there is evident in his lighting style a repudiation also of a second representational mode seen as inimical to the German national style, namely Hollywood. Froelich's lighting style was characterised, as we saw above, first by a studied ornamentalism, and second, by a use of light to frame and delineate the space around the aesthetic object. Importantly, this emphasis on light as ornament and frame led him to abandon established (Hollywood) star lighting conventions in favour of lighting set-ups that emphasised the aesthetic ensemble, not the star, as the source of visual pleasure within the camera frame.

FROELICH VERSUS HOLLYWOOD: STAR LIGHTING IN *TRAUMULUS*

An example from *Traumulus* is Niemeyer's first confrontation with von Zedlitz when news is leaked of the student's affair. As in other key scenes of dramatic confrontation in the film, staging occurs here in a dual plane. While the fore-ground is occupied by two figures (von Zedlitz and Niemeyer), the background is brought to the spectactor's attention by its vivid and complex interplay of light and shade. In Niemeyer's study, lights across the studio flats behind the actors pick out an array of props: an architectural painting of classical columns, a mar-ble cherub on the mantelpiece, a classical bust, a line of books on the dresser. The spotlighting casts shadows that dynamise the space around each object, lending it symbolic significance as an externalised representation of Niemeyer's inner traits: his antiquated morality, his affiliation to intellect, not action, and so on (Figure 12).

In Hollywood melodrama of the period, that use of lighting as one element in a *mise en scène* that speaks the muted realities of stars' inner worlds would have been reinforced cinematographically by a combination of close shots, and a complex system of key, fill and kicker lighting designed, in the words of one contemporary Hollywood cinematographer, John Alton, to 'bring ... out char-acter never suspected'.[21] In his 1949 book, *Painting with Light*, Alton offered a series of guidelines for good lighting and camera practice drawn from his own

two-decade Hollywood career. In a chapter on star lighting for close-up, he recommended a system of no less than eight lights – key, fill, filler, clothes light,
backlight, kicker, eyelight and background lighting – for the proper illumination
of faces in close shot. The (entirely gendered) function of the multiple lights in
Alton's schema is, in the case of a 'feminine close-ups', to 'accentuate beauty',
and for male actors, to highlight 'the character of the individual'.[22]

For *Traumulus*'s male protagonists, by contrast, the use of star lighting in
close-up to accentuate character is eschewed. In the Hollywood context as
described by Alton, the shift from long to close shot must be accompanied by a
change in lighting set-up. Overhead lights are replaced by floor lighting, and key
lights supplemented with fill and other lights that 'counterbalance unwanted
shadows' and 'assure … that no surface of the field of view of the lens will
remain without light'.[23] The Niemeyer–von Zedlitz sequence, by contrast, is
shot in a series of long takes, and the lighting set-up remains constant throughout. As the two actors move around the set, their often only partially lit faces
pale sometimes into insignificance against the starkly illuminated studio set that
is the backdrop to each shot. Froelich's refusal of the Hollywood use of key lighting on the actor's face to reinforce character, mood or star quality is especially
striking in a crucial two-shot midway through the sequence. This is von Zedlitz'
moment of truth, as Niemeyer challenges him to admit to his sexual liaison. The

Figure 12: illuminated props in *Traumulus* (1936)

absence of a frontal key light, however – the men are lit from a single overhead light source towards the back of the set – places their faces in shadow, in contrast to the bust behind them, which remains brilliantly illuminated, and thus a focus of spectatorial attention.

In this sequence, then, the emphasising through key lights of the classical artefacts that people Niemeyer's study suggests an equality of these with the actors, indeed a privileging of them over Jannings as star within the *mise en scène*. This is, moreover, by no means an isolated instance of a use of light in Froelich that displaces the spectator's gaze from the actor-star, to a set drenched with symbolic significance. Froelich worked during his Third Reich career with many of the period's most prominent stars: Heinz Rühmann, Zarah Leander, Heinrich George and even, in the one film she made in Germany, Ingrid Bergman. As we saw already in Chapter 2, his Bergman film, *Die vier Gesellen* (*The Four Companions,* 1938) is notable for its studied refusal of Hollywood star lighting conventions. Bergman is cast here in the leading female role as a graphic artist apparently seeking an independent career in partnership with three female friends, but secretly hankering after romance with her ex-teacher (Hans Söhnker). Designed as a launch pad for the Swedish actress into German stardom, the film is striking for the absence throughout of the frontal key lighting that was, for such as Alton, the *sine qua non* of female star representation. Prominent too in *Die vier Gesellen* is the same sculptural lighting of props and studio flats as was evident in *Traumulus*: a use of light, then, that lends to lifeless objects a symbolic significance equal, even superior to that of Bergman as actress-star.

This visual positioning of Bergman, like Jannings in *Traumulus*, as one only among an ensemble of symbolically freighted objects within a pictorial *mise en scène* is, on the one hand, symptomatic of Froelich's hostility to an Enlightenment aesthetics that situated the bourgeois individual at its heart. In both Hollywood and European art cinema, the 'stylistic touches' that are said to be characteristic of the film auteur act to promote audience identification with the 'expressive individual' who is the 'source of meaning' in the work of film art.[24] In Third Reich film culture, by contrast, it is not as creative individual that either the film auteur or the star are celebrated. As the film theorist Bruno Rehlinger wrote of what he called films of 'community' (among which he included Froelich's 1934 title *Ich für Dich – Du für mich/Me for You – You for Me*), 'the individual is here of no significance; he becomes or is made prominent only in so far as he is characteristic of the collectivity'.[25] Rehlinger concludes that 'the value of the film actor is in relative terms no greater than that of any other object that is brought into play in film'; and it is precisely that visual equivalence between actor and inanimate object which we have seen realised in Froelich's work.

PERSONALITY VERSUS STAR: JANNINGS AND WEISSNER

Yet Froelich's refusal, in his treatment both of Bergman and Jannings, of Hollywood conventions of star representation, is indicative of something more than a generalised anti-individualism in his visual style. Froelich is actively committed also to a representation of 'personality' that can displace and undermine the star aesthetic as one manifestation of individualism at the level of film style.

That positive espousal of the aesthetics of personality is best exemplified in *Traumulus* by the contrast between Froelich's treatment of Emil Jannings, and of Hilde Weissner, who plays opposite Jannings/Niemeyer as Jadwiga, Niemeyer's physically attractive, but morally repugnant second wife. Jadwiga is marked from the outset as a figure of difference by Froelich's use of precisely those conventions of star representation from which he otherwise abstains. Apart from her extravagant costume and heavy, non-naturalist make-up, Jadwiga is signalled cinematographically from the moment of her first appearance as a 'star' in the Hollywood mode. In the sequence immediately preceding the Niemeyer–von Zedlitz confrontation discussed above, Jadwiga's distinctiveness is signalled by a (for Froelich) rare medium close-up on her frontally presented face. The combination of frontal key light, and of top and backlighting to create the halo that lends her the aura of star, was uncharacteristic not only for Froelich, but for much contemporary German genre film. As one writer on film lighting, A. von Barsy, wrote in 1936, German cinematography was notable for its combination of a 'sparing use of diffuse light' with a 'criss-cross of spotlights for illumination'.[26] The use of backlighting to 'pick out figures and faces from the background' was, by contrast, a feature so closely associated with Hollywood that von Barsy coins the term 'America' for a lighting mode in location shooting that combines spotlight and sunlight to produce 'the halo so beloved of [US] studio-based film'.[27]

What is remarkable about Froelich's use for Jadwiga of the halo and related cinematographic conventions is that they are employed entirely negatively, as markers of her otherness and irredeemable difference. The close shots, soft-focus and diffuse use of light that pervaded Hollywood female star representation were in any case often decried by contemporary German critics as modernist effects that created disjunctive moments of spectacle in Hollywood's otherwise seamless narrative system.[28] Just such a disjunction is clearly apparent in the close shot of Jadwiga/Weissner discussed above. The combination here of close camera and high key frontal illumination contrast sharply with an immediately subsequent, sparsely lit medium shot of the film's 'true' star, Jannings/Niemeyer. Jadwiga's first appearance thus introduces a disruptive moment of 'kitsch' Hollywood spectacle into a narrative that otherwise refuses classical Hollywood visual conventions.

But it is towards the end of *Traumulus* that Froelich's desire to supplant star codes with the representational conventions of 'personality' becomes most evident. As the narrative approaches dénouement, a final scene with Jannings and Weissner poses against Jadwiga/Weissner's flaunting of the attributes of Hollywood stardom a rival visual encoding of Jannings as actor-personality in the required Third Reich mode. By this point Niemeyer/Jannings – who refused at first to believe rumours of von Zedlitz' liaison with Lydia Link – has been forced to recognise the truth of his pupil's guilt. Von Zedlitz repents; but Niemeyer remains blind to his pupil's loyalty, and banishes him from the school. Heartbroken, von Zedlitz seeks solace in suicide. Realising too late that he has destroyed one of the few young men of principle under his care, Niemeyer returns home in search of consolation from his wife.

That he will find little comfort here has been intimated earlier in the film, when we see Jadwiga spending Niemeyer's hard-earned cash, mistreating his beloved sixth-formers, or trading secrets with her husband's dissolute son. Her degeneracy is finally proven, however, only in this concluding sequence. When Niemeyer signals his intention to resign – the affair with von Zedlitz has left him a broken man – a horrified Jadwiga finally rebels. Unbeknown to Niemeyer, she has plunged him into debt through profligate spending on elegant dress and

Figure 13: Hilde Weissner and Emil Jannings – star versus personality

fancy living. Furious now at the prospect of a retirement in penury, she breaks
the news of their debt. 'Where?' stammers Niemeyer. 'Where do we owe
money?'

Jadwiga's riposte – 'What world is it that you live in anyway?' – is wholly
appropriate to Froelich's treatment of this sequence; for *mise en scène* and camera indeed situate Jadwiga and Niemeyer in separate representational 'worlds'
(Figure 13). Take Jadwiga first. We see her initially before a mirror in medium
shot, titivating a new hat with the assistance of her maid. Placed behind Jadwiga
and at medium distance, the camera captures props and costume accessories
that symbolise her extravagant living – fur wrap, feathered hat, expensive mirror – as well as Jadwiga's mirror image, the double of a woman absorbed in
self-adornment and narcissistic self contemplation.

Costume and set construct Jadwiga from the outset, then, as what Bruno
Rehlinger terms, 'the face of film ... according to ... American conception': a
conception bound, he continues, to 'the demands of beauty, style, make-up and
mask-like standardisation', and fatally linked to the 'cult of the beautiful star'.[29]
It is, moreover, more than set and costume that situate Jadwiga in a star representational mode. The use of toplighting, key and fill lights to suffuse the space
around her with light and enhance her glamour image equally recall those light-

Figure 14: Emil Jannings – lighting for effect

ing conventions that John Alton among others considered indispensable to Hollywood female star representation. Here as elsewhere in *Traumulus*, however, star lighting is used for a woman constructed throughout the film as an entirely negative figure of female profligacy and feminine deceit. Once again, then, Froelich turns star lighting on its head, using codes widely recognised in the contemporary context as 'American' to locate Jadwiga not as Alton's model of 'feminine beauty', but as a sinister femme fatale.

Contrast now the lighting of Jannings/Niemeyer. As in *Traumulus*' opening sequence, one is tempted to dub 'Expressionist' the use here of chiaroscuro, and of underlighting that distorts Jannings' features and displays the inner torment of a man bereft (Figure 14). Read against German lighting practice of the period, however, these are better defined as what was termed 'lighting for effect' (*Effektlicht*), whose function was not so much to suggest personalities split between surface 'normalities' and hidden terrors – as in Expressionism – but to heighten 'atmosphere' (*Stimmung*) and accentuate actorly genius. In a 1935 article on film lighting in the journal *Filmtechnik*, the critic Heinz Umbehr writes, for instance on just such a use of what he calls 'illogical lighting effects' in another Jannings vehicle, *Der alte und der junge König* (*The Old and the Young*

Figure 15: illogical lighting effects in *Der alte und der junge König* (1935)

King, 1935). Defending a sequence in which a candelabra carried by the king casts not light, but shadow on the wall behind (Figure 15), Umbehr writes: 'At first, we see only individual objects surfacing one after another into the candle-light. Then the King's shadow appears on the wall, accompanied at the same time by the candelabra shadow – an illogical lighting effect, in other words.' This effect, Umbehr continues, is however 'quite intentional'; for it 'renders ... extraordinarily effective' a scene which, if differently lit, 'would doubtless have achieved little of its force'.

Umbehr concludes his plea for a lighting mode that privileges 'atmosphere' over 'realism' with a discussion of the execution scene in which the 'Young King', Crown Prince Frederick, witnesses the death of Katte, his ally and friend. Again defending the use of artificial lighting 'simply for effect', Umbehr pleads for a cinematography that uses light to 'accentuate ... performance' – here, the performance of Werner Hinz as future Prussian king.[30] An anti-naturalist, pictorial lighting mode is endorsed here, in other words, as a (specifically German) response to Hollywood conventions of star representation: a mode that dispenses with Hollywood's kitsch preoccupation with surface image, and penetrates instead to the emotional depths touched by the high-calibre performance of such as Jannings.

EMIL JANNINGS AS SUBLIME PERSONALITY

But in what sense, finally, might *Traumulus*' concluding husband-and-wife sequence illustrate not merely a disavowal of Hollywood star codes, but also an embracing of the sublime as the mode of experience evoked by the audience's encounter with the actor-personality? The Kantian sublime, as we saw earlier, is an emotional state, or state of mind that is produced in the contemplation of objects or vistas that appear to have a capacity to break out beyond the bounds of aesthetic form and stretch forth into infinity. Part of Kant's distinction between the beautiful and the sublime rests on a notion that beauty can be located in artistic form, but that the sublime may transcend form; thus he writes of formlessness (*Formlosigkeit*), limitlessness (*Unbegrenztheit*), and a movement towards infinity (*das Unendliche*) as qualities that evoke sublimity.[31]

In histories of visual representation in Germany, early Romantic painting is regularly identified as a realisation of the Kantian sublime. In film history, Eric Rentschler has traced the further development of the Romantic sublime through German silent and early sound cinema, the latter exemplified most notably, for Rentschler, in the late Weimar mountain films of Leni Riefenstahl and Arnold Fanck.[32] In both cases, the link between representations of boundlessness and the Kantian sublime is clearly evident: witness Caspar David Friedrich's perspectives that fade to infinity, or Fanck's mountain vistas that transcend the boundaries of familiar space and human perception.

Figure 16: sublimity in the mountain film – Arnold Fanck's *Die weisse Hölle der Piz Palü* (1929)

In both Friedrich and Fanck, light plays a crucial part in this extension of human perspective into infinity. In Friedrich's paintings, natural light illuminates horizons, obscuring the vanishing point of Renaissance perspective and directing the viewer's gaze instead into limitless space. In Fanck's films, similarly, low-angle shots of mountain vistas orient the spectator's eye towards infinite skies that stretch forth beyond the bounds of vision (Figure 16). The mountain films, to this extent, are quite distinct from Froelich's oeuvre, with its cramped studio aesthetic and its use of light as boundary and frame. Yet Froelich's fettering of light, his emphasis on stark contrast and bounded space, is not synonymous with an abandonment of sublimity in cinematic representation. On the contrary, Froelich's visual handling of Jannings and other contemporary stars shows him at pains to rescue traditions of Romantic representation for a Third Reich aesthetic that imports into 'personality' the same transcendent qualities that Caspar David Friedrich located in landscape and Nature.

The case for seeing Emil Jannings in *Traumulus* as a representative of precisely that 'sublime' mode of aesthetic experience exemplified in the person of Froelich as cinematic auteur is explicitly and energetically made by one contemporary admirer, the art critic and anti-Semite Richard Bie. In his 1936 study of Jannings, Bie wrote that his 'name stands for an achievement that is indivisibly connected to the history of German film and its development ... into an art form'.[33] Like Rentschler, Bie situates the origins of German cinema's development in fine-art traditions extending back to the early 19th century and beyond. Prefiguring Rentschler again, he names Caspar David Friedrich as the figure who best demonstrates the role of pre-cinematic art in facilitating what he terms 'the revelation of the real'. It was, Bie further claims, Friedrich's landscapes in particular – his 'great field of corn straddled by a rainbow, deserted sand dunes ... ice-bound ruins' – that first provided 'symbols' that 'imbued with new and greater life our contemplation of the visible world'.[34] But – unlike Rentschler this time – it is for Bie not in the mountain film or other cinematic representations of landscape that Friedrich's legacy to the film medium is evident. In his wholly teleological history, fine art's progressive 'revelation of the real' – a progression to which Romantic landscape painting significantly contributes – is unthinkable without the 'concept of autonomous personality' that has underpinned artistic creation since the Renaissance. From the late 19th century onwards, Bie claims, however, concepts of personality have been superseded by a 'bankrupt individualism' whose effect has been to 'isolate the artist and alienate him from the spirit [*Sinn*] of the *Volk*'.[35]

In Bie's tendentious account, it is National Socialism that finally brings redemption to art, personality and *Volk*. Naming film as one of two art forms (the other is architecture) that can 'shape the mass and give generalised expression to the inner desires of our time', he ascribes to that medium the capacity to 'reveal and portray contemporary man [*der Mensch der Gegenwart*] as a ... political type', and thus to displace the 'private type' which formed the epicentre of the 20th century's now 'bankrupt', bourgeois individualist representational mode.[36] It is in this context that, for Bie, Emil Jannings comes to prominence as a 'model for the German people', a man who 'sets the standard' for a new behavioural mode.[37] In Jannings' films, he further claims, the exterior landscapes of early Romantic painting are replaced as a focus for popular contemplation by Jannings' face as it 'repeatedly reveals new landscapes of the soul', and thus – like Friedrich's painting – offers glimpses of the infinite.[38]

Bie himself names *Traumulus* as one film in which Jannings' performance mirrors in its 'spiritual depth' the spatial transcendence of the Romantic sublime. Jannings' actorly genius, he enthuses, generates around itself a 'perfect illusion of space'; for over and above his 'unique and magnificent capacity' to 'metamorphose' into humanly authentic characters, Jannings has, claims Bie, the ability 'to invigorate the most inanimate of props', and 'magically to extract from decorative objects ... a life-meaning'. Jannings' performance, indeed, possesses nothing less than the capacity to imbue with 'soul' the physical space within the camera frame.[39]

The actor's body becomes, then, for Bie, the site of precisely that spatial transcendence that was the hallmark of Romantic representation from the early 19th century onwards. It is, moreover, exactly this sense of the actor's body as landscape of the soul that Froelich evokes in his chiselled use of lighting to mark out on Jannings' face what Bie terms the 'summation of life' and the 'passion' visible in this, as in other faces of actorly genius. For Froelich as for Bie, the furrowed complexity of Jannings' face, accentuated by 'lighting for effect', marks him as the fundamental opposite of star images à la Jadwiga/Weissner. From these, Bie concludes, 'all true traces of character are gradually obscured', leaving only the 'fabricated, doll-like beauty' of the 'mask' that is the face of the star.[40]

JANNINGS, SPECTATORSHIP AND THE SUBLIME

In the cultural theorist Slavoj Žižek's exposition of aesthetic theory from Kant to Lacan, he traces a historical development in which the Kantian emphasis on the sublime as the space of infinity gradually gives way to a Hegelian conception of the material object as locus of sublimity. In Kant, writes Žižek,

> the feeling of the sublime is evoked by some boundless, terrifying, imposing phenomenon (raging Nature and so on), while in Hegel we are dealing with a miserable 'little piece of the real' ... the State as the rational organisation of social life *is* the idiotic body of the Monarch....[41]

In absolutist or totalitarian societies, Žižek continues, it is to the body of the leader – in absolutism, the king – that the materially embedded sublime of which Hegel writes is attributed. It is, he suggests, 'as if he [the king] possesses, beyond his ordinary body, a sublime, ethereal, mystical body personifying the State'.[42]

In her analysis of the Third Reich's Fridericus (Frederick the Great) cycle, Linda Schulte-Sasse uses Žižek to highlight these films' Hegelian 'obsession with the body of the King' as 'a sublime object ... at the centre of social being', a 'necessary hallucination' that helps the spectator maintain a sense of social and psychic coherence.[43] Above, by contrast, we have seen the sublime object embodied not in specific characters in *Traumulus*, but in the 'star' (Jannings) who is not a star in the Hollywood sense, but an actor-personality who features as both the vehicle for an experience of the sublime, and as an instrument for the displacement of this film's other, the (Hollywood) star.

Jannings own pre- and post-1933 career enacts precisely this process of displacement and ultimate elimination of the symbolic figure of the 'star' that he himself had once been. In his early Weimar career, Jannings reached international star status when he worked under Ernst Lubitsch in a series of internationally fêted historical epics. Jannings' *Madame Dubarry* (1919), *Anna Boleyn* (1920) and other titles achieved unprecedented Broadway success, and laid the foundations for Jannings' invitation to Hollywood in the mid-1920s. During his Hollywood period, Jannings' spectacular success continued. The first actor to receive an Oscar – for his performance in Victor Fleming's *The Way of all Flesh* (1928) – he collected further US accolades, including a second Oscar for his role in von Sternberg's *The Last Command* (1928) before returning to Germany in 1929.

In contemporary accounts of Jannings' career following his return home, the story is repeatedly rehearsed of a 'master' initially eclipsed by the emergent idols of German sound film – most famously Marlene Dietrich, who stole Jannings' show in von Sternberg's *Der blaue Engel*. But Jannings re-emergence in Third Reich biographies as the symbol of 'an achievement ... indivisibly linked to the history of German film' shows how, in a set of stylistic shifts intimately linked to the broader development of Goebbels' new film art, Jannings contributed to the forging of an anti-star aesthetic in post-1933 film. Again, it is Richard Bie who highlights the broader implications of Jannings' changing image when he traces his stylistic development from Weimar to the mid-1930s. Whereas in his Lubitsch films in particular, Jannings works, writes Bie, in a 'Jewish' mode that privileges the 'effectiveness of the mask' over authentic 'human expression', he has, by 1936, embarked on a new route towards a 'filmic reality in which mask and face are no longer distinguishable'.[44]

Three facets of Jannings position him by this stage, for Bie, as a source of Nazi film's 'new expression of the will to life'.[45] The first, as we have seen, is an acting style that refuses 'Jewish', 'Hollywood' modes of star performance and masquerade in favour of what we saw in Chapter 2 defined as the 'mime': a performance mode that 'closes the gap between consciousness and Nature, understanding and emotion, mask and face'.[46] What Jannings represents through body, face and gesture is, furthermore, not the inner dynamics of the individual psyche. As we also saw in Chapter 2, the 'personality' that speaks through the actor's body as conceptualised in Nazi acting theory is a biologically determined entity, the essence of *Volk*. Thus the inner self revealed by actors of Jannings' stature is the property of a racially defined, *völkisch* collective. As Bie writes of Jannings, his parental origins, on his father's side supposedly in the Brandenburg Marches, on the maternal side in Magdeburg, bequeath to Jannings the 'dowry' of a specific 'landscape and nature'; and there is, he continues, in Jannings' roles, an 'obvious' rooting in 'that breed of Low German' that he 'embodies' in the 'great historical persons' his roles portray.[47]

In the film of personality (as opposed to the star vehicle) as conceptualised by Bie, Jannings' body becomes, then, the site of representation of a geographically specific 'landscape', and of the racially defined essence of certain 'breed of Low German'. This functionalising of the actor's body as the express-

Figure 17: Emil Jannings'
mobile physiognomy in *Varieté*
(1925)

ive vehicle of a blood and soil aesthetic is visible, thirdly, in developments in Jannings' acting style from Weimar to the Third Reich. In the opening shot of E. A. Dupont's *Varieté* (1925), a twitch of Jannings' shoulder speaks a whole world of inner turmoil in the character he plays (a trapeze artist jailed for his lover's murder, Figure 17). In the films Richard Bie most admires, by contrast – *Traumulus, Der alte und der junge König* – Jannings returns to a performance style organised around climactic moments of static pose and symbolic gesture. In the Jadwiga/Niemeyer scene discussed above, Jannings slumps across a chaise longue, his body largely immobile, his face presented for the most part frontally to a camera that situates it centre frame, in a series of studied tableaux. Here, as elsewhere in his most fêted Third Reich titles, Jannings is represented as a body drained of individual significance; he figures instead as what Bie terms that inanimate 'landscape of the soul ... that the great actor reveals'.[48]

In Kant's *Critique of Judgement*, the encounter with the sublime led ultimately to knowledge of what he termed 'ideas that contain a higher purposiveness'.[49] For such as Caspar David Friedrich, that idea was God – whereas for the fascists, it was the idea of the *Volk*, organised under the supreme authority of the *Führer* as fascism's godhead figure. In *Traumulus*, I have suggested, Jannings is positioned as the embodiment of the gendered and racialised ideal that was the sublime artistic 'personality' – the pinnacle of the *völkisch* heritage as represented in the German man of genius. I have tried to show how Carl Froelich's adherence to that *völkisch* ideal leads him in *Traumulus* to repudiate established modes of star representation. But Froelich's cinematographic treatment of Jannings sheds important light, too, on the mode of star spectatorship preferred in Third Reich film. Studies of Third Reich stars to date regularly assert that it was through an 'intensification of identification' with stars that Third Reich propagandists sought to instrumentalise the star cult as 'the initiator of the desired [propaganda] effect of film'.[50] Film theorists in 1933 and after, by contrast, conceptualised rather differently the cinematic processes involved in star spectatorship. For Ernst Iros, for instance, the spectator's relation to what I described in Chapter 3 as the Third Reich's cinema of experience was best described as a 'state of unconscious, unwilled receptiveness', a 'surrender to an Other', a 'submerging' of the self in an 'alien becoming'.[51] Iros' further comment that the 'aesthetic experience' he here describes depends entirely on 'elements of perfection and harmony' in the film text itself can be read as legitimising precisely the representational mode we have seen realised in *Traumulus*. Froelich's ornamental film style, his impetus towards stasis, are conjoined in *Traumulus* with a studied inflexibility in Jannings' performance style to produce precisely that visual 'synthesis' to which Iros' *Wesen und Dramaturgie des Films* repeatedly aspires.[52] Iros' reference to unconscious 'surrender' (*not* identification) as his preferred model for audience engagement with film is, moreover, of relevance to the audience's relation with Third Reich stars. In Johannes Volkelt's *System der Ästhetik,* the author notes that the aesthetic experience which his disciple Iros also celebrates is not limited to 'feelings' – the conscious or unconscious desires, anxieties and pleasures that are the focus of theories of identification in Third Reich film. 'Feelings', writes Volkelt, 'often end, as it were, on a bodily note. If the effect of a piece of music is to rejuvenate us and bring us peace, then it is also the case that we experience a physical refreshment and calm. We breathe more easily; thus this spiritual warmth seems also to translate itself into its bodily equivalent.'[53]

In Chapter 3, we saw how shifts in exhibition practice through the 1930s involved the Third Reich audience in the bodily experience of individual submission within a hierarchically organised and racially defined collective. Volkelt's comments, finally, suggest that what is involved in the personality (*not* star) cult of Third Reich film is an effort to reproduce in the spectator's engagement with the film text the same bodily submission to a dominant ('sublime') Other as that promoted by the temporal and spatial organisation of the cinema auditorium itself after 1933. Certainly, contemporary film commentary speaks repeatedly in bodily metaphors of a necessary submission to an overpowering physical force when it writes of the 'shattering' (*erschütternd*), 'gripping' (*ergreifend*) or 'overpowering' (*überwältigend*) effect of star performance.

There remain, however, a number of open questions. To what extent did the transformation of audience response from star adulation, to reverential submission to personalities of genius, actually take effect in German film after 1933? To what extent did there remain a popular ambivalence towards the figure of the star, a reluctance to participate in self-abasing celebrations of what I have termed the cinematic sublime?

In the next chapter, these issues are explored in a study of one émigré star, Marlene Dietrich, whose reception both in the Third Reich and subsequently identifies her as an object of precisely such ambivalence – a figure of difficulty and disturbance who upsets the applecart of the sublime aesthetic as embodied, I have proposed, in Jannings' and Froelich's *Traumulus.*

NOTES

1. R109I 5252 504–505.
2. Immanuel Kant, *Critique of the Power of Judgement*, Paul Guyer (trans. and ed.), and Eric Matthews (trans.) (Cambridge: Cambridge University Press, 2000, orig. 1790), p. 120.
3. Ibid., p. 129.
4. Ibid., pp.140–1 and 150. The original German has it that the beautiful leads the

viewing subject to 'love' (*lieben*) its object. In the Cambridge translation cited here ('the beautiful . . . must *please* without any interest'), Kant's point loses something of its force.

5. Josef Kugel, 'Wir alle sind Schuld! Ehrliches Theaterbesitzer-Bekenntnis zum Zweischlager-Programm', *Film-Kurier* (FK), 27 April 1933.

6. Ernst Iros, *Wesen und Dramaturgie des Films* (Zürich and Leipzig: Max Niehaus, 1938), p. 114.

7. Launched under 1923 legislation on entertainment tax, the *Prädikat* system gave tax bonuses to producers of 'quality' films, as well as emphasising to audiences the artistic quality and cultural status of any given film. Amendments to the 1933 legislation in June 1933 replaced Weimar's three attributions of 'high cultural quality' (*kulturell hochstehend*), 'public education' (*volksbildend*) and 'educational film' (*Lehrfilm*) with the more overtly political trio 'public education' (*volksbildend*), 'culturally valuable' (*kulturell wertvoll*) and 'politically valuable' (*staatspolitisch wertvoll*). As the decade progressed, the quality ratings became yet more complex with the addition of such categories as 'politically and artistically especially valuable' (*staatspolitisch und künstlerisch besonders wertvoll*), 'artistically valuable (*künstlerisch wertvoll*), 'politically especially valuable' (*staatspolitisch besonders wertvoll*), 'nationally valuable' (*volkswert*) and others. By 1939, the highest distinction, 'politically and artistically especially valuable', carried full exemption from entertainment tax; but, as David Welch among others has claimed, even distinctions involving lesser tax relief 'greatly enhanced a film's status' and 'helped to establish the appropriate expectations and responses on the part of cinema audiences'. See David Welch, *Propaganda and the German Cinema 1933–1945* (Oxford: Clarendon, 1983), p. 21.

8. A further useful list of film favourites, albeit for 1935 only, and drawn from 'semi-official best seller lists', appears in Boguslaw Drewniak, *Der deutsche Film 1938–1945. Ein Gesamtüberblick* (Düsseldorf: Droste, 1987), p. 630. Alongside *Traumulus*, Drewniak lists Peter Hagen's *Freisennot* (*Friesland's Time of Need*), and Gerhard Lamprecht's *Der höhere Befehl* (*Order from Above*) as hits for 1935.

9. Marc Silberman, 'The Modernist Camera and Cinema Illusion: Friedrich Wilhelm Murnau's *The Last Laugh*', in idem, *German Cinema. Texts in Context* (Detriot: Wayne State University Press, 1995), p. 25.

10. Ibid., p. 33.

11. Quote from 'Zum zweiten Male Filmpreisträger. Carl Froelich und sein Werk', *Filmwelt* (FW), 14 May 1939.

12. Quote from Thomas Elsaesser, 'Early Film Form. Introduction', in idem (ed.), *Early Cinema. Space, Frame, Narrative* (London: BFI, 1990), p. 11. The use of deep space, and slow cutting, are the two characteristics identified by Ben Brewster in Elsaesser's volume as specifically European characteristics of the early

silents. See Ben Brewster, 'Deep Staging in French Films 1900–1914', in Elsaesser, *Early Cinema*, p. 49.

13. Oskar Kalbus, *Vom Werden Deutscher Filmkunst. 2 Teil: Der Tonfilm* (Hamburg: Cigaretten-Bilderdienst Altona-Bahrenfeld, 1935), p. 15.

14. For examples of nineteenth-century popular graphics, see Tom Cheesman, *The Shocking Ballad Picture Show. German Popular Literature and Cultural History* (Oxford and Providence: Berg, 1994), especially pp. xviiff.

15. 'Zum zweiten Male Filmpreisträger. Carl Froelich und sein Werk', FW, 12 May 1939.

16. Ibid., and Otto Kriegk, *Der deutsche Film im Spiegel der Ufa. 25 Jahre Kampf und Vollendung* (Berlin: Ufa, 1943), p. 49.

17. Johannes Volkelt, *System der Ästhetik* (Munich: Beck, 1910), vol. 2, p. 110.

18. Letter from editor Carl Müller to Carl Froelich, 8 December 1940. BA R56VI 5a 438.

19. Lotte Eisner, *The Haunted Screen: Expressionism in the German Cinema and the Influence of Max Reinhardt* (London: Secker & Warburg, 1973, orig. Fr.1952), p. 133. The German translation of Eisner traces the impulse towards decorative stylisation to Reiniger. The reference to Reiniger is absent, however, from the English version.

20. Froelich's *Reifende Jugend* (1933), for instance – a tale of romantic adventure in a modern mixed-gender sixth-form – had revealed a director torn between an eagerness to display his mastery of Weimar's modernist techniques and, on the other hand, an allegiance to his origins in silent film. Thus *Reifende Jugend* sets a high-tempo pace in an opening cycling sequence whose mobile framing and rapid montage directly reference such unlikely Weimar precursors as Ruttmann's *Berlin Symphony* (1927), or even *Kuhle Wampe* (1932). The casting of *Kuhle Wampe*'s leading actress, Hertha Thiele, in *Maturing Youth*'s starring role, cements the link between Froelich's title and Weimar film. Yet as the narrative proceeds, so too the film's Weimar origins are progressively disavowed, as Froelich returns repeatedly to the static, distanced camera and tableau composition of early silent film. My thanks to Johannes von Moltke for drawing to my attention the structure of disavowal involved in this gesture towards, then brusque repudiation of the Expressionist heritage.

21. John Alton, *Painting with Light* (Berkeley and Los Angeles: University of California Press, 1995, orig. 1949), p. 92.

22. Ibid., pp. 94 and 96.

23. Ibid., p. 97.

24. David Bordwell, 'The art cinema as a mode of film practice', *Film Criticism* vol.4, no.1, 1979, paraphrased here by Pam Cook, in 'Authorship and Cinema', in Pam Cook and Mieke Bernink (eds.), *The Cinema Book*, 2nd edn. (London: BFI, 1999), p. 237.

25. Bruno Rehlinger, *Der Begriff Filmisch* (Emsdetten: Lechte, 1938), p. 61.

26. A. von Barsy, 'Die Grundlagen der Szenenbeleuchtung', FT, 3 July 1936, p. 133.

27. A. von Barsy, 'Grundtypen der Freilichtbeleuchtung', FT, 1 October 1936, p. 172.

28. See Curt Emmermann, 'Zum Kapitel "Soft Focus" ', FT, 30 June 1935, pp. 251–2.

29. Rehlinger, *Der Begriff Filmisch*, p. 63.

30. Heinz Umbehr, 'Aufnahmetechnik neuer Filme. *Der alte und der junge König*', FT, 23 February 1935, p. 37.

31. Kant, *Critique of the Power of Judgement*, pp. 131, 140 and 138. See also Chapter 7 in this book.

32. Eric Rentschler, 'Hochgebirge und Moderne: eine Standortbestimmung des Bergfilms', *Film und Kritik*, 1, June 1992, pp. 8–27.

33. Richard Bie, *Emil Jannings. Eine Diagnose des deutschen Films* (Berlin: Frundsberg, 1936), p. 5.

34. Ibid., p .6.

35. Ibid., p. 9.

36. Ibid., p. 10.

37. Ibid., title page.

38. Ibid., p. 24.

39. Ibid., p. 64.

40. Ibid., pp. 21–3

41. Slavoj Žižek, *The Sublime Object of Ideology* (London and New York: Verso, 1989), p. 204.

42. Ibid., p. 145.

43. Linda Schulte-Sasse, *Entertaining the Third Reich*, pp. 94–6.

44. Bie, *Emil Jannings*, p. 36.

45. Ibid., p. 47.

46. Ibid., p. 26.

47. Ibid., p. 35. Jannings in fact claimed hybrid parentage: American on his father's side, Russian-born German on his mother's; see Emil Jannings, *Theater, Film – Das Leben und ich* (Berchtesgaden: Zimmer & Herzog, 1951), p. 7.

48. Bie, *Emil Jannings*, p. 39.

49. Kant, *Critique of the Power of Judgement*, p. 129.

50. Quote from Andrea Winkler-Mayerhöfer, *Starkult als Propagandamittel. Studien zum Unterhaltungsfilm im Dritten Reich* (Munich: Ölschläger, 1992), p. 113.

51. Iros, *Wesen und Dramaturgie*, p. 108. As so often, Iros acknowledges a debt to Ludwig Klages in this passage.

52. Ibid., p. 107.

53. Volkelt, *System der Ästhetik*, p. 164.

5

Marlene Dietrich: From the Sublime to the Beautiful

Like so many stories about Marlene Dietrich, the one that follows is well known. In August 1929, the Austrian émigré director Josef von Sternberg arrived in Germany from Hollywood. Von Sternberg himself attributed his German sojourn to 'a flattering cable from Emil Jannings asking me to guide him in his first sound film'. Under commission from Ufa's Erich Pommer, and in consultation with Jannings, von Sternberg lighted on Heinrich Mann's 1905 novel *Professor Unrat* as the source for the literary adaptation that was to become Jannings' next star vehicle.

The dual-language film, which von Sternberg titled *Der blaue Engel (The Blue Angel)*, told the story of a middle-aged teacher, Immanuel Rath, who meets his moral and professional nemesis in the person of the cabaret singer, Lola-Lola. Jannings, an actor whose 'forte was to portray the zenith of personal misfortune', was a perfect Immanuel Rath.[1] But he objected strongly to von Sternberg's choice of the relatively unknown actress and cabaret artiste Marlene Dietrich to play opposite him as the film's femme fatale. Perhaps Jannings saw the writing on the wall; for when the film premiered in Berlin's Gloria-Palast on 1 April 1930, it was Dietrich, not Jannings, whom audience and critics adored. Kurt Pinthus, admittedly, praised Jannings' 'incredibly credible characterisation', but he bemoaned the occasional 'ponderousness' that marked Jannings' performance here, as in previous films. Dietrich, by contrast, was 'thrilling' in her 'vulgarity', in the 'passivity of her sex appeal', and the 'low and throaty depths' to which her voice descended in such frankly suggestive numbers as *Ich bin die fesche Lola, Einen Mann, Einen richtigen Mann*, or *Ich bin von Kopf bis Fuß auf Liebe eingestellt*.[2] The day after the premiere, the Vossische Zeitung echoed Pinthus in rebuking Jannings for the 'fussiness' of a style that 'unwittingly recalls his theatre roles'. Dietrich, on the other hand, had a 'vulgarity' that derived from filmic presentation alone. 'Everything here is film, not theatre ... Extraordinary!'[3]

Max Brod and Rudolf Thomas' conclusion, in their 1930 volume *Liebe im Film (Love in Film)*, that *Der blaue Engel*, though initially a Jannings vehicle, 'remains

in the end only a film of and by Dietrich', sets the tone both for the study of Dietrich on which we now embark, and for my ensuing discussion of our last Third
Reich star, Zarah Leander, as 'Dietrich's ghost'.[4] We saw in the previous chapter
how the *völkisch* aesthetics of Third Reich film located the auteur-director Carl
Froelich, and in particular the actor Emil Jannings as embodiments of what I
termed Third Reich film's *völkisch* sublime. In this chapter, by contrast, we will
consider Marlene Dietrich as the representative of a nagging tension in the aesthetic schema of Third Reich film. Already in 1930, as comments from Pinthus,
Brod, Thomas and the rest indicate, Dietrich had displaced Jannings as *Der blaue
Engel's* major star. As we see in more detail below, Dietrich's popularity in Germany continued unbroken, at least until the mid-1930s. In that context, her
image operated for 1930s audiences, I shall suggest, as the emblem of multiple
challenges to a film aesthetics structured around a masculine and 'Aryan' high
cultural norm. Those challenges were rooted in part in Dietrich's exhibitionist
flouting of conventions of gender (she famously courted gender ambiguity), of
sexuality (her bisexuality and open eroticism were legend), and of 'race' (increasingly, she claimed a hybrid identity as European–American). But they relate also
to the specifically cinematic difficulty of incorporating Dietrich's image into the
neo-idealist aesthetic discourses that were the structuring framework for Third
Reich film. The place allotted to femininity in aesthetic discourse since Kant and
his contemporaries has in any case not been that of the sublime personality (to
this height only the male artist can aspire), but of the beautiful as the representational mode for which women are predestined by Nature. Below then, I move
first to a discussion of the beautiful as the preferred discursive location in Third
Reich neo-idealism for the female image. Second, I consider film coverage in the
1930s German fan and daily press: the prime context, I argue, for official efforts
to reconfigure popular taste around an appreciation of the cinematic 'beautiful'
and 'sublime'. Thirdly and finally, I return to the case of Marlene Dietrich, whose
reception in 1930s Germany I represent as one (failed) attempt to recuperate for
the cinema of personality its best-loved émigré stars.

GENDER IN THE CINEMA OF PERSONALITY: THE BEAUTIFUL
VERSUS THE SUBLIME

We saw in Chapter 4 how Froelich and Jannings, gained a symbolic position in
German cinema after 1933 as personalities of genius through the textual construction, in Froelich's case, of his authorial style, in Jannings', of his star image.
Not least through their contextualisation within the temporally and spatially
reorganised exhibition space analysed in Chapter 3, these two figures, I
suggested, became the objects of that mode of spectatorship I have called the
völkisch sublime.

There is, however, clearly a point at which the audience experience of personality can no longer be encapsulated within an aesthetic of the sublime. In aesthetic theory from Burke to Kant and Schopenhauer, the sublime is regularly described as the product of an encounter with genius.[5] That discourse of genius, as Christine Battersby has pointed out, works by a 'rhetoric of exclusion' that pits the genius figure in opposition to a whole array of figures of difference. Thus men of supposedly lesser talent or ambition, as well as categories of person excluded by gender (women), generation (children) or 'race' ('primitives') become symbolic figures of otherness against whom the category of genius gains definition as male creativity 'made sublime'.[6]

The efforts charted in previous chapters to establish after 1933 as the aesthetic framework for German film a racialised version of this hierarchical discourse of genius beg the question of the status of those 'other' figures – male stars of significant talent, but not genius, as well as 'foreigners' and women – within the Third Reich cinematic system. What, for example, of such actors as Heinz Rühmann, remembered today as the 'archetypal' male German star? Rühmann's career spanned Weimar to the Third Reich and beyond, yet he never appeared, as Stephen Lowry has commented, as either a 'nationalist hero' or a 'fated genius'.[7] What too of the male leads of the Third Reich's staple fare of comedies, musicals and romantic melodramas: Willy Fritsch as the legendary dream partner of Lilian Harvey in such films as Paul Martin's *Schwarze Rosen* (*Black Roses*, 1935) and *Glückskinder* (*Lucky Kids*, 1935); or the 'foreigner' Johannes Heesters, who like Fritsch played the Platonic better half to a popular female star, this time to the Hungarian Marika Rökk, in the early titles that catapulted her to musical stardom (*Gasparone*, 1937; *Hallo Janine*, 1939)?

And what, most particularly, of the women? Battersby has identified in the concept of genius an 'explicit and implicit gender bias' that positions the sublime woman genius as 'an unbeautiful, and unnatural freak who is disobeying nature and aping the genius of ... her lord and master'.[8] Battersby's identification of Kant as an important figure in the elaboration of this gendered vision is, moreover, especially illuminating for any history of 1930s German film. In previous chapters, I have traced the neo-Kantian impulse that was evident, I have suggested, in contemporary theoretical discourse on Third Reich film. In both post- and pre-1933 writings, the debt owed by film aethetics to Kant is explicit. Thus Rudolf Arnheim, for example, described his work as 'fastening on to what may be called a Kantian truth ... according to which even the most elementary processes of vision do not produce mechanical recordings of the outside world but organise the sensory raw-material creatively according to the principles of simplicity, regularity and balance'.[9]

Arnheim's reference here is to Kant's idea of the beautiful, which privileges inner balance and stasis as the desired products of beauty's contemplation. In the *Critique of Judgement*, Kant follows Burke in identifying three possible modes of aesthetic experience: the sublime, the beautiful and the 'agreeable' or entertaining. The three are distinguished by the nature of the aesthetic objects from which they proceed, by the subjective faculties that they mobilise, and by the subject effect that each engenders. The sublime, as we have seen, derives from an encounter with a masculine and superordinate other power; it is accessible through the imagination, but only if imagination and fantasy act in tandem with the reason that is the property of civilised man (*sic*). The Kantian sublime, to quote Terry Eagleton, is a 'chastening, humiliating power'; it works by dissolving the subject 'into an awesome awareness of its finitude'.[10]

The sublime provokes, then, that very dissolution of the viewing subject that was, I suggested in Chapter 3, one desired outcome of the post-1933 reorganisation of film exhibition and reception. In Kant's model, however, this subjective chaos may also be the product of a second mode of aesthetic reception: of the viewing subject's encounter, that is, with the merely entertaining. In idealist aesthetics from Kant onwards, entertainment has appeared as a base form engaging neither reason nor fantasy, but the body and the senses. As Kant writes in the third *Critique*, entertainment arises from 'inclination' (*Neigung*), not contemplation; it produces purely sensory 'charms' (*Reiz*) and 'enjoyment' (*Genuss*) that remain unregulated by the rational faculties, and that thus – unlike objects of beauty – provide no foundation for those common values ('truth, propriety ... [or] justice') that ground enlightened social organisation.[11]

It was this understanding of entertainment that underpinned countless onslaughts on film, at least in its most popular manifestations, from the Wilhelmine period to mid-century.[12] Even the modernist Rudolf Arnheim reproduced in his *Film as Art* the emphasis common among conservative cultural critics on entertainment as sensory chaos, the product of primitive cultures, and of technology, not art. In a 1934 essay, Arnheim, moreover, singled out von Sternberg as the epitome of the 'brutal' aesthetics of a contemporary sound cinema that displaced 'the enjoyment of art as disinterested pleasure', and reduced 'pleasure to sex-appeal, disinterest to frigidity'.[13] Arnheim's further claim that in von Sternberg, 'California unmasks Kant', was echoed only too readily by the anti-modernists who rose to prominence after 1933 – among them Fedor Stepun, who singled out von Sternberg's *Der blaue Engel* as an example of the 'primitive eroticism' and formal hybridity of much sound film.[14] Stepun was adamant in his denunciation of the mass art of film as embodied in *Der blaue Engel*; but other Third Reich critics saw in a third category of aesthetic experience the promise of redemption.

In Kant's *Critique*, both base entertainment and the sublime are contrasted to the beautiful as a third key mode of aesthetic reception. Most pertinent to 1930s film commentary were Kant's distinctions between the beautiful and the merely entertaining. The seven sets of bipolar opposites around which both the *Critique*, and Kant's subsequent essays on the beautiful are structured, are worth enumerating here, since they functioned as points of reference, as we shall see, for Dietrich reception after 1933. They are as follows:

1. The beautiful is allied to Nature, the entertaining to artifice and mechanical intervention. Hence Kant's distinction between 'agreeable' entertainment and 'beautiful art', and his insistence that the latter must 'look to us like Nature'.[15]

2. The beautiful is accessible through a combination of imagination and reason, and has a relation to the ethical. Beauty is distinguished from entertainment by the dependence of the latter on the senses; thus 'the correctness of [any given] ideal of beauty is proved by the fact that no sensory charm is allowed to be mixed into the satisfaction in its object'.[16]

3. The beautiful is a class-bound category in the sense that it belongs in the bourgeois realm of autonomous art. Entertainment, by implication, belongs in the lower-class domains of commerce and wage labour. As Kant writes, 'beautiful art must be free art [in the sense] that it must not be a matter of remuneration, a labour whose magnitude can be judged, enforced, or paid for in accordance with a determinate standard'.[17]

4. The beautiful is a gendered category, insofar as it is primarily to women that Kant attributes the beautiful ideals of 'prettiness, harmony, good proportions and formal perfection'.[18] The 'prevalence of emotion and sympathy in [women's] moral make-up' apparently endows them, moreover, with a greater sensibility than men for the beautiful in art and nature. Kant's gendering of aesthetic sensibilities is most explicit in an essay that precedes the *Critique*, *Observations on the Feeling of the Beautiful and the Sublime* (1764). Here, Kant comments that women have a 'strong inborn feeling' for the beautiful, whereas in masculinity, by contrast, both women and men perceive a nobility that is the unique province of the male gender.[19]

5. There is, however, a mode of femininity that is not beautiful, but merely stimulating, and that is femininity in its manifestation as the object of a purely sensual pleasure. Again, it is in Kant's early essay on beauty and the sublime that he most clearly specifies the limits of beauty's designation as feminine. Kant here insists both that beauty is determined by its relation to virtue, and that it is perceptible primarily in a femininity that is 'very cleanly, and very delicate in respect to all that provokes disgust', (which latter includes a lack of chastity, of 'neatness', or an indulgence of 'the sort of vulgar jests called obscenities').[20] Contrast the image of Dietrich as Lola-Lola (Figure 18), the embodiment of an erotic, vulgar femininity whose links to virtue and bourgeois morality are

indubitably tenuous. Kant's model is of an eighteenth-century bourgeois femininity not yet challenged by mass-cultural icons à la Lola-Lola. As feminist critics have often observed, however, cultural modernisation after Kant, and specifically the emergence of mass culture (including, latterly, film) through the 19th and early 20th centuries, produced a splitting of femininity in post-Enlightenment cultural discourse between the bourgeois ideal espoused by Kant, and a subterranean mass-cultural feminine. The encoding 'mass culture as Woman', as Andreas Huyssen observes, 'has its primary historical place in the late 19th century'.[21] As Huyssen further comments, the same equation, mass culture = woman, persists well into the 20th century; and the relevance of Huyssen's contention to Dietrich is demonstrated in the essay by Arnheim cited earlier, where he writes that Dietrich represents 'the unsurpassable incarnation of the type in which von Sternberg's American style culminates': a type in which, as Arnheim wrote, 'California unmasks Kant', and the disinterested pleasure that beauty evokes gives way to the 'art without roots' that is modern mass entertainment.[22]

6. A sixth dichotomy that structures the opposition between beauty and entertainment is that of the 'cultured' versus the 'primitive'. Primitivism in Kant is the product not so much of national, ethnic or 'racial' difference. (Kant is a cultural relativist insofar as he allows 'the Negro' a 'different', but not intrinsically

Figure 18: Marlene Dietrich as Lola Lola in *Der blaue Engel* (1930)

inferior conception of the beautiful.) Instead, the 'barbaric' quality of
entertainment derives from its appeal to the emotions and sensory charms.[23]
Herein lies what will emerge in what follows as among the most significant of
Kant's distinctions for Third Reich film reception, which is the following.

7. Unlike entertainment, beauty involves a refusal of the senses, and requires instead
a disinterested mode of aesthetic contemplation. Most important for the Third
Reich context is the subject effect that this detached encounter with the beautiful
produces; for where the sublime disrupts and the entertaining disorganises, the
beautiful reconfigures and stabilises the viewing subject as part of the collective.

The Kantian conception of the beautiful as elaborated above was attractive for
Third Reich film theory on two grounds. First, it offered a resource for the articulation of aesthetic norms specific to cinematic representations of femininity
(see point 4 above): norms of formal construction (point 1), of class (point 3),
of taste (points 2 and 5), and of 'race' (point 6). In the concluding sections of
this chapter, I thus consider 1930s German commentary on 'Dietrich the beautiful' as one example of this attempted mobilisation for cinematic femininity of
a post-Kantian bourgeois aesthetic. My focus here will be on the specifically aesthetic issue of Dietrich's film image, and its availability (or otherwise) as an
emblem of the beautiful in film art.

But there is secondly, of course, already in Kant an important cultural-political dimension to beauty: a dimension relating to the particular reception mode
(point 7) that it putatively inspires. Kant himself made frequent reference to
'common sense' as the collective sensibility that underpins subjective judgments
of the beautiful; and Third Reich film theory recognised only too clearly the
capacity of a film art constructed around 'common sense' to regulate what was
otherwise deemed a dangerously chaotic process of film reception.[24] In the aesthetic paradigm plundered by 1930s film theory from Kantian idealism, the
beautiful figures as a mode of reception that captures and fixes within ordered
form the unruly pleasures that flow between the aesthetic object (in our case,
film) and its spectators. Weimar cultural theory had already explored the socio-
cultural disorganisation that cinema helped induce; note, for instance, Siegfried
Kracauer's insistence that modernity's 'ineluctable' social transformations produced as film's primary audience the 'homogeneous' and 'cosmopolitan' mass.[25]
Conservative film theory before and after 1933 concurred that it was in what
Alfred Brühl termed the 'relation of the masses to cinema' that 'a considerable
portion of the social reality of our civilised world is contained'.[26] Brühl and his
Third Reich contemporaries inherited from Weimar film theory, in other words,
a post-Kantian reception aesthetic that saw modern cultural values as emanating not from the artwork itself, but from the audience as mass.[27] What they

repudiated, of course, was the Weimar theorists' political response. While abhorring modern mass entertainment's subservience to capitalist values, Siegfried Kracauer's dialectical method, for instance, had allowed him to validate as 'truthful' – and, in that sense, as profoundly ethical – the working masses' abandonment of such 'unreal' values as beauty and depth in favour of a 'distraction' that acknowledged contemporary society's 'actual state of disintegration'.[28] The fascist response, by contrast, was to attempt, through a regulation and reordering of the mass, a recuperation for popular film of those idealist aesthetic values, refracted through *völkisch* ideology, that I have suggested were embodied for instance in Third Reich cinema's evocation of a masculine *völkisch* sublime.

We saw that response exemplified in Chapter 3 in a spatial and temporal reconfiguring of exhibition spaces that aimed to remodel the amorphous mass audience as microcosm of the *Volk*. A further intervention into the field of reception designed to recapture a Kantian appreciation of beautiful form is evident in a second aspect of Third Reich reception discourse, namely the treatment in trade press and newspaper commentary of single films and contemporary stars.

FILM COMMENTARY *CONTRA* THE MODERNIST MASS

Among the more striking cultural characteristics of pre-1933 Germany was the diversity of its film press. The Weimar industry supported two daily trade titles – *Film-Kurier*, the organ of the *Reich* Association of German Exhibitors, and the independent *LichtBildBühne* – alongside trade weeklies (*Der Film* and the *Reichsfilmblatt*, among others); technical journals (*Filmtechnik* and others); confessional and party-political titles, from the Catholic *Deutsche Filmzeitung*, to the leftist *Arbeiterbühne und Film*; and a flourishing fan press, including such titles as *Neue Illustrierte Filmwoche*, *Deutsche Filmwoche*, *Die Filmwoche* and *Filmwelt*. The liberal-democratic *Frankfurter Zeitung*, the vehicle for many of Kracauer's early essays on film, was, moreover, by no means the only newspaper to devote regular attention to the moving image. By 1930, the Republic boasted between forty and fifty regional and national dailies with dedicated film sections, while significantly more carried (usually weekly) film supplements with extensive news, feature and review coverage of contemporary film.[29]

The post-1933 restructuring of the film press proceeded, characteristically for the period, through a complex interplay between state regulation and repression, and the self-subordination of cultural practitioners and their professional associations to fascist ideologies and the Nazi state. Following the foundation of the *Reich* Press Chamber (RPK) in September 1933, compulsory licensing for editors, journalists and other practitioners allowed the state swiftly to expel from the industry 'racially' or politically undesirable personnel. While the NSDAP-controlled Eher Verlag tightened its grip on newspaper ownership (by 1939, it is estimated to have controlled two-thirds of the nation's press), newspaper content was regulated through the RMVP's daily press briefings, as well as its regular and detailed directives on the desired form and focus of press coverage of named issues and events.[30] Legislative measures, meanwhile, reproduced the privileging of cultural politics over commerce that pervaded the RMVP's film-industrial interventions. The 1933 Editors' Law (*Schriftleitergesetz*) made editors directly responsible for implementing state directives. David Welch has observed that the law 'in effect … reversed the roles of the publisher and editor, reducing the publisher to the position of business manager'.[31] Its successful realisation, moreover, depended on the industry's willingness to promote to positions of editorial responsibility figures committed to the Nazi *Weltanschauung* and sharing Nazism's concomitant cultural-revolutionary aspirations.

That willingness was clearly demonstrated in respect of editors and journalists with specific responsibilities for film. The 'Aryanisation' of the press in 1933 drove into exile some of the Weimar Republic's most influential film critics – Kracauer, of course, alongside such figures as Rudolf Arnheim and E. A. Dupont. By November 1936, when the RMVP finally prohibited film criticism *tout court* on grounds of its 'Jewish … distortion', the film press landscape had already been irrevocably transformed, as Kracauer *et al.* ceded place to a new generation of writers committed to what the Nazi state would henceforth dub 'film commentary' (*Filmbetrachtung*).

The 1936 RMVP directive named film commentary as a journalistic mode that operated 'in the spirit of National Socialism' and sustained 'a proper attitude' to film art.[32] The emphasis here on film commentary's artistic project fuelled an already live debate on the relation of press film coverage to Joseph Goebbels' larger designs for a National Socialist film art. Stung perhaps by 'scholarly' critiques of press commentary's alleged inattention to the aesthetic (one 1937 doctoral dissertation, for instance, excoriated 'professional film commentators' for operating with 'a concept of film art deriving from unclarified interpretations of opinions absorbed through superficial readings whose validity is automatically accepted'),[33] editors of the national and regional broadsheets wrote or commissioned numerous features on such issues as 'Film content and audience taste', 'Does film need the literary author [*Dichter*]?', 'Film and literature – a consideration of the role of film' or 'The experience of the image'.[34]

Two guiding principles underpinned this rash of journalistic disquisitions on the aesthetic theory and practice of film. The first involved an elaboration of the role of the film editor or critic as a 'film-critical personality' (*Filmbetrachterpersönlichkeit*) who functioned to intervene in, reorder and regulate the otherwise anarchic process of mass film reception.[35] Such figures as Hans Karbe, film editor of the NSDAP organ, the *National-Zeitung*, Eberhard Schulz, the party fellow-traveller who took over film editorship of the *Frankfurter Zeitung* after 1933, or Werner Kark at one of Germany's most long-lived national dailies, the *Deutsche Allgemeine Zeitung*, were thus lauded by the media analyst Kurt Wortig as figures who rose above the mass (the film commentator, wrote Wortig, 'never himself belongs to the mass'), and as individuals with 'the courage when necessary decisively to challenge' audience tastes and preferences.[36]

The first function of the film writer was, then, to fracture and reconfigure the relationship between the mass audience and film. Her/his assumed second function – which Wortig succinctly identified as the 'education and formation of public taste' – was by no means uniquely the product of National Socialism; the Weimar modernists themselves were engaged, after all, in what Balázs, for instance, termed the education of the mass public to 'critical enjoyment' as the highest form of spectatorial pleasure.[37] What characterised the transition from Weimar modernism to National Socialism was rather the efforts of Karbe, Kark, Wortig, Schulz and others to refocus critical practice around a reformulated understanding of the source and function of aesthetic pleasure in film.

For Kracauer and other Weimar critics, film stars, Marlene Dietrich among them, had functioned as emblems of a singularly modern aesthetic of surface and show. Dietrich's press reception after 1933 offers a symptomatic and contrasting case of film-critical efforts to roll back modernity's advances by repositioning its cultural products within a neo-Kantian aesthetic field. In relation to Dietrich, that roll-back took the form of a symbolic repositioning of her star image within press commentary as a prototype of the beautiful in contemporary film art: a repositioning first discernible in the press reception of *The Scarlet Empress*, 'Marlene's' first release in Nazi Germany, and the first case study to which we now turn.

DIETRICH AS ICON OF BEAUTY: *THE SCARLET EMPRESS* (1934)

In Kant, as we have seen, a de-eroticised and de-sensualised femininity functioned as the embodiment of bourgeois culture's beautiful ideals of harmony and formal perfection. With accelerating speed through the early decades of the 20th century, mass cultural conceptions of feminine 'beauty', however, conceived now as the commodified product of modern technologies of cultural production – fashion, cosmetics, photography, film – competed with and increasingly displaced older ideals of feminine beauty as the product of an inner ethical sense, or of Nature. Siegfried Kracauer related this 'quiet change' in prevailing taste codes to larger processes of socio-cultural change when he identified the 'mass ornament' (emblematised in the mass-cultural feminine icon of the Tiller girl) as reflecting 'the entire contemporary situation' in its foregrounding of the capitalist values of mass production, spatio-temporal regulation, and the standardised production of what Adorno and Horkheimer would later term 'the eternal same'.[38] Kracauer was, furthermore, entirely correct to observe that capitalist mass-cultural production had irrevocably shattered the values of 'Nature', 'community' and 'personality' around which National Socialist efforts to recuperate the beautiful in film art would later pivot.

Commodity production in what Kracauer had identified as a quintessentially modern mode continued apace under National Socialism, as women's magazines and advertising unabashedly perpetuated the commercial myth of a 'natural beauty' dependent on the commodified products of the beauty industry: eye make-up, face powder, hair colourant, and the remaining paraphernalia of twentieth-century 'beauty care' (*Schönheitspflege*). Hans Dieter Schäfer has identified as characteristic of the Third Reich's 'split consciousness' in relation to mass cultural femininity Nazism's simultaneous ideological reduction of femininity to its biological value as reproductive instrument – thus women's role was primarily to breed children for the *Volk* – and the state promotion of a feminine 'naturalness' that was in fact the highly artificial product of modern technologies of commodity representation. Schäfer here references state provision of cosmetics and beauty care training through, for example, the Deutsche Arbeitsfront (German Labour Front, DAF), or the Bund Deutscher Mädel (League of German Girls, BDM), whose courses on '*Glaube und Schönheit*' (Belief and Beauty) combined 'social studies' training in National Socialist values with instruction in cosmetics, ballroom dancing, riding, tennis, and what the BDM grandiosely termed the 'homage to the body's beauty' that was sunbathing.[39]

The oscillation evident here between a fascination with, and an impetus towards the aesthetic/ideological regulation of the mass-cultural feminine, is prevalent, too, in Third Reich representations of our case study in this chapter, Marlene Dietrich. 'Marlene' had left Germany on the night of *Der blaue Engel*'s Berlin premiere; yet her name remained a guarantor of German box-office success. Of the eight titles Dietrich made for Paramount between 1930 and 1936, seven were released in Germany. A memorandum from Washington's 'film diplomat' in Berlin, George Canty, cites *Shanghai Express* (1931) and *Blonde Venus* (1932) among the top ten German box-office hits for 1932; and the film historian Markus Spieker draws on data on the duration of first runs in Berlin premiere cinemas to highlight Dietrich's 'unbroken popularity' among German audiences after 1933.[40] First runs for both *The Scarlet Empress* and *Desire* (1936) were thus double the average length for German titles (twenty-eight days as against fourteen), while *The Devil is a Woman* (1935) broke the one-month barrier with a Berlin first run of thirty-two days.[41] Dietrich's significance for German audiences was further evidenced by Paramount's decision to stage *Desire*'s world premiere in Berlin, not New York, and by reviews that continued to celebrate her as a 'great actress' who explored in such films as *Desire* the 'full range' of her talents as Germany's premier émigré star.[42]

Especially striking in press coverage of Dietrich's image and performance in her post-1933 films is its reference to larger debates on the nature of the beautiful under National Socialism. Thus in press commentary on *The Scarlet Empress*, Dietrich's first release in the Nazi state, she won effusive accolades for her embodiment of qualities that were 'not only beautiful', but that 'take possession of the beauty of the moment'.[43] Abstruse as this distinction may seem between a formal beauty, and a beauty that transcends modernity by arresting the transience of the moment, it had clear resonance with the yearning that ghosts through much contemporary cultural critique for a mass culture capable of generating the 'unified and harmonious totality' considered the source of the beautiful in high art.[44] A feature on shop-window dummies as 'beautiful phantoms', for instance, pleaded less than two weeks before *The Scarlet Empress'* release for a popular aesthetics capable of identifying the 'human beauty of the everyday', and thus of defining for women in particular a 'norm' for the cultivation of beauty among the mundanities of mass-cultural femininity. The writer's concomitant plea for a transformation of the fashion dummy into a figure that displayed 'her own personality' indeed 'what one it tempted to call soul and character' may verge on the absurd; but it finds echoes in contemporary coverage of the mass reproduction of woman-as-image in advertising, photography, beauty culture, and such popular cultural ephemera as star postcards, film programmes and cigarette card collections (of which latter, in the context of a cigarette manufacturer's competition for photos of Berlin's '300 most beautiful women', one bemused commentator opined that their 'endless' proliferation undermined all certainty over 'what one might understand by the term "beautiful Berlin women"'.)[45]

For this writer, then, National Socialism has failed to restore order to a mass culture that repeatedly evades Nazism's neo-idealist aesthetic norms. In reviews of *The Scarlet Empress*, by contrast, Marlene Dietrich emerged as the emblem of the potential to recuperate precisely that consensual conception of beauty after which Third Reich cultural commentators strove. Coverage of the film repeatedly stressed its conformity to Nazi standards for film as popular art, and related its artistic value to what the *Hamburger Nachrichten*, for instance, dubbed *Empress'* quasi-painterly management of image and montage.[46] Reviews in the trade press and broadsheets, similarly, commented on the censors' award of the *Prädikat* 'artistically valuable', which they approved on the particular grounds of the film's masterly handling of 'a hundred magical close-ups of the star'.[47] This emphasis on the close-up was repeated in an advertising campaign that foregrounded Dietrich's face as the film's trademark; by numerous references in reviews to 'repeated close-ups' of a face 'which we never tire of contemplating'; and indeed by the film text itself, which, as Barry Salt has calculated, pushed von Sternberg's fascination with Dietrich's face to new heights by featuring an extraordinary seventy-two narratively unmotivated close-ups of his most favoured female star.[48]

That it was *The Scarlet Empress'* handling of the close-up in particular that located Dietrich in that film as an object of beauty in the high art sense, is evidenced by further press comments on Dietrich's face in the film. For the *Berliner Tageblatt*, von Sternberg's predilection for the close-up revealed Dietrich as an actress of 'astounding' talent, capable of expressing 'every nuance, from virginal dismay, to caustic ridiculing of her surroundings'.[49] In an article by Hans-Joachim Hahn the following day on 'The secret of the close-up', the same newspaper, perhaps unconsciously echoing Béla Balázs, designated the close-up the 'very language of film', and continued: 'The long and medium shot are of course also necessary; yet it is surely only the close-up that facilitates the organic fusion of single scenes into a unified, harmonious whole.'[50]

Repeatedly emphasised in trade and popular coverage of *The Scarlet Empress* was its success in achieving just such a fusion into aesthetic totality that was the source for the spectator (or for what was more often termed the *Beschauer*, literally, 's/he who contemplates') of the beautiful in film. An especially wordy newspaper advertisement related *Empress'* art-film status first to von Sternberg's virtuoso handling of camera and montage ('the action develops with a fluidity that sweeps the viewer along at breathtaking tempo, and engulfs him with its urgent, suggestive power'). But it was not purely to von Sternberg that the capacity was attributed to provoke in the spectator an aesthetic experience of the integration of surface and inner essence. Dietrich, too, with her 'fine acting' and 'expressive face', was seen to trigger what the text insisted was a 'cinematic experience [*Erlebnis*] ... of such force that even the highest expectations are surpassed'.[51]

Apparently, then, *The Scarlet Empress* met the demands of contemporary film criticism for a construction of the film text that, in subordinating the star close-up (here, close-ups of Dietrich) to the visual whole, allowed them to function as vehicles of a spectatorial pleasure that derived from an experience of the harmonious, the ordered and the beautiful. To prevailing demands for the placing of close-ups 'in the correct relation to each other, i.e. in a harmonious relationship determined by the totality of the film' (*Filmwelt*), von Sternberg was seen to have responded with a film that achieved aesthetic totality through a rhythmic and fluid montage that fused close-ups of Dietrich's face into an 'art-historically magnificent' unity distinguished in particular by its 'dramatic construction ... vibrant scene development, rhythmic dramatic resolution, enchanting use of the dissolve and superimposition'.[52]

EROTICISM AND AMBIGUITY: CHALLENGES TO BEAUTIFUL FORM

The extent of critics' success in channelling audience response towards an appreciation of Dietrich in *The Scarlet Empress* as beautiful object is, of course, open to question. The film displays stylistic characteristics that militate strongly against its interpretation as an object of disinterested contemplation. As Mary Ann Doane has observed, the sequence in which Catherine weds the lunatic Tsar Peter offers one of many examples of the challenge Dietrich's film image poses to a metaphysics of beautiful form.[53] Certainly, von Sternberg's handling of camera and light do position the star at points as an icon of beauty in Kant's sense. The wedding narrative is thus punctuated by serial close-ups of Dietrich in which minute adjustments in shot length, light and framing offer to the spectator the promise of an unmediated encounter with the 'harmony, good proportions and formal perfection' which Kant identifies as the key attributes of beauty in feminine form. The camera's move from a first medium close-up, to extreme close-ups towards the sequence's end, suggest, first, the possibility of penetration to some inner core or essence of the image of the star. That

Figure 19: Dietrich the beautiful in *The Scarlet Empress* (1934)

inference is reinforced by a shift in lighting from chiaroscuro in the opening close-up (where Dietrich's brow and eyes especially are shaded), to toplighting that accentuates the perfect symmetry of her sculpted eyebrows, her flawless skin, her luminous eyes. The transition from oblique framing in the first close-up in this sequence – a shot that situates the spectator as omniscient observer within a wedding narrative – to the frontal and symmetrical composition of the second shot, further reinforces the capacity of Dietrich's image to facilitate a spectatorial encounter not with a climactic narrative moment (the wedding), but with the visual harmony and formal balance that the aesthetics of the beautiful demands (Figure 19).

Yet throughout the wedding sequence, those visual features that establish Dietrich as a beautiful icon are undermined by aspects of *mise en scène* and performance that infringe the Third Reich's neo-Kantian precepts and norms. An idealist appreciation of beauty, as we saw earlier, demands a disavowal of the senses, a repudiation of the erotic, the sexual and the primitive, and an embracing instead of contemplation as a 'disinterested' reception mode. Dietrich's performance throughout the wedding sequence, however – in particular the parted lips and exaggerated eyelash-fluttering with which she responds to her spurned lover Alexei – remind the spectator of a sexual narrative that dislocates *The Scarlet Empress* from its relation to highbrow art, situating the film instead in the realm of the sensual, the erotic, base entertainment. The studied close-ups that apparently claim Dietrich as an object of disinterested contemplation thus offer the star simultaneously (as Laura Mulvey famously observed) as the object par excellence of a voyeurism that is the very hallmark of Hollywood film entertainment.[54] The exoticism of von Sternberg's *mise en scène*, its proliferation of fabulous costumes, candles, incense burners, bodies, screens and decorative sets, moreover, not only further destabilise neo-Kantian norms in the fascination they evoke for the 'barbaric' and the 'primitive'. The use of veils, incense, curtains and other obstructions (Dietrich's face, for instance, is veiled, even in extreme close-up, throughout the wedding sequence) undermines the possibility of an integration in Dietrich's image between surface and inner essence – an integration which, as we have seen, contemporary film commentary considered pivotal to the 'cinematic experience' (*Film-Kurier*) of the beautiful in film art.

The reading of the Dietrich of *The Scarlet Empress* in the Third Reich film press as an emblem of neo-Kantian transcendence reveals, in sum, very little of the rather complex and ambiguous conjunction of elements that characterised Dietrich's star image in that film. What that reading does illuminate is the opportunistic disavowal in contemporary film commentary of the erotic, 'primitive' and anti-realist potential of a star image which – to borrow a phrase from Thomas Elsaesser – 'provide[d] in [its] moments of inauthenticity' (its use of the veil, Dietrich's anti-realist performance style) the 'surest sign' of a challenge to the idealist precepts of Third Reich film art.[55]

DIETRICH AND THE MASQUERADE: *THE DEVIL IS A WOMAN* (1935)

That challenge was, by contrast, very clearly recognised in Third Reich responses to the second Dietrich title released in Germany after 1933, *The Devil is a Woman*. Launched in June 1935 as *Die spanische Tänzerin* (*The Spanish Dancer*), the film enjoyed the long first run characteristic of Dietrich titles after 1933.[56] Despite its popularity with film audiences, however, *The Devil* attracted critical censure on grounds that reveal the mounting difficulties Dietrich's image now posed for the film aesthetic of the Third Reich.

The Devil cast Dietrich as the femme fatale Concha Perez, a cigarette factory-worker turned variety artiste, whose fatal charms spell ruin for various suitors, including the aristocratic soldier Don Pasqual (Lionel Attwill) and the rebel republican Antonio (Cesar Romero). The film was already politically dubious in the Third Reich context, since its plot circulated around a Spanish fighter in the republican underground, and his relation to Dietrich as society 'whore'. *The Devil*'s modernist propensities were apparent, too, in its bizarrely disjointed scripting by John dos Passos – a figure already suspect in Germany for his literary experimentalism and Communist affiliations. But it was the film's visual style that attracted the greatest opprobrium – particularly in relation to the image of Dietrich. Like many of von Sternberg's films, *The Devil* was attacked by critics for its 'emptiness' and 'lack of meaning'. This was a film in which visual signifiers were released from their referents in the real; Dietrich's image was split, fragmented, rendered unrecognisable as it became 'two (kilo)metres of lipstick-laden lips on screen, amongst a sea of streamers and massed balloons'. But the image was not only fractured, released from the 'illusion of wholeness' that Linda Schulte-Sasse suggests was pivotal to Third Reich representations of identity.[57] Dietrich was detached too from the 'soul' that should infuse her; she was the 'shadow of a costumed vamp' in a film with a 'corpse-like absence of soul'.[58]

The split between surface image and inner soul that this reviewer so abhors is evident from the first moments of *The Devil*. The film opens with a police parade in which the Chief of Police, Don Paquito (Edward Everett Horton), briefs his men on the annual carnival scheduled to open the following day. Here as later in the film, Don Paquito is heavily caricatured, his slapstick acting style, the pomposity of the parade and the absurdity of his men's excessive handlebar moustaches combining to announce *The Devil* from the outset as a film constructed not around narrative verisimilitude, but artifice and spectacle. *The Devil*'s anti-realist commitment is further underscored in Don Paquito's explicit reference to the masquerade when he warns 'tomorrow the carnival begins.

Unfortunately every crook within a 1000 miles, every political offender and exile will try to take advantage of the masquerade.'[59]

The ambivalence of Don Paquito's response to carnival and masquerade – in the same breath, he suggests shooting masked men caught stealing ('Less trouble afterwards'), and announces 'I definitely do not want any interference with the people's pleasures' – sets the stage for the persistent play throughout *The Devil* between, on the one hand, the pleasure of the masks and surfaces that are the stock-in-trade of popular entertainment (in *The Devil*, of the carnival, which can be read as an allegorical figuring of popular film itself), and on the other, the sadistic aggression that the masquerade evinces. From the police parade, the film cuts to an establishing shot of a multi-storey tenement seething with the bodies of carnival revellers, their identities obscured by masks, bizarre costumes, swirling flags, streamers, balloons and garlands. Here, as in much of von Sternberg's work, baroque ornamentation in the foreground of the shot bars the camera's access to the photographed object, emphasising *The Devil*'s concern with formal decoration and multi-layered surfaces beyond which – as the *Film-Kurier* reviewer quoted above rightly insists – no inner content or essence can be perceived.

It is, however, in *The Devil*'s portrayal of Dietrich as Concha Perez that the film most clearly reveals both its commitment to the masquerade, and its challenge to the metaphysics of presence championed in Third Reich film commentary. Dietrich/Concha first appears in a point-of-view shot from Antonio (Romero). A long tracking shot following the masked Antonio's trajectory through the surging crowd, his eyes searching, as he tells us, for a 'pretty girl', cuts to a similarly probing shot in which the camera tilts downwards towards a horse and carriage in long shot, its passenger a masked and veiled woman gesturing playfully to the crowd. Once again, the the camera plays with a spectator who anticipates a visual encounter with Dietrich, but is confounded both by the balloons and streamers that obscure her figure from view, and by a second carriage passing across her and barring the camera's access to her image.

Only after this reminder of the mediated nature of our access to the image of the star are we granted a close-up of a Dietrich searching the crowd, like Antonio/Romero, for an appropriate object for her sexual teasing. Yet even here, Dietrich appears not as an image of that beautiful depth celebrated in a contemporary *Film-Kurier* feature on fans and stardom, which notes Dietrich's capacity to represent 'beauty unbounded'.[60] Rather, the Dietrich of *The Devil* stands as the emblem of a femininity whose identity resides in masquerade and mask, surface not essence.

Mary Ann Doane has discussed this sequence in *The Devil* in the context of a broader exploration of femininity and the masquerade.[61] In cultural theory since Freud, Doane identifies a dominant conceptualisation of femininity 'in terms of a certain closeness, the lack of a distance or gap between sign and referent'.[62] That trope of an essential proximity between the female body and its image was also pervasive in Third Reich theorising of the image of the star. Bruno Rehlinger, for instance, roundly denounced the artificiality of the 'cult of the beautiful star': a cult that associates beauty with 'style [*Aufmachung*], make-up and mask-like typification'. The corrective to the artifice of the star is the European actress-personality (his examples are Greta Garbo and Paula Wessely) who abandons this 'fracturing of personhood', and devotes herself instead to the 'unmediated, elemental expression of unfeigned life'.[63] In a similar celebration of women's proximity to bodily essence, Rudolf Bach, in his 1937 treatise on the woman as actress, opines that women 'find it less difficult than men to penetrate to their true core; for as women, they *live* more unified lives, and are more *present*'. Hence, Bach continues, 'the polarity of outside and inside, soul and body, body and spirit almost never becomes [in women] the source of that ... ambivalence, which the young actor experiences'.[64]

Mary-Ann Doane draws on Joan Rivière's psychoanalytic account of the masquerade to offer a different account of the nature of actorly femininity. Rivière's essay focuses on a woman intellectual who, Rivière argues, feels compelled to compensate for her 'masculine' social status by, as Doane puts it, 'overdoing the gestures of a feminine flirtation'. Thus what Rivière calls 'womanliness' is 'assumed and worn as a mask, both to hide the possession of masculinity and to avert the reprisals expected if she was found to possess it'. Doane, like other feminist critics, initially reads the masquerade as a practice of resistance, a defamiliarising of femininity that drives a wedge between 'woman' and her assumed bodily essence, and constitutes 'an acknowledgement that it is femininity itself which is constructed as mask – as the decorative layer which conceals a non-identity'.[65] It is in this spirit that she and others have often read Dietrich's star image. Silvia Bovenschen comments on Dietrich's performance mode that it foregrounds the fictive nature of her image: 'the myth appears and demonstrates itself as self-produced'.[66] Bovenschen's reference is to Dietrich's stage performances during her second career as a variety star. For Doane, by contrast, Dietrich already demonstrates in the much earlier *The Devil is a Woman* the significance of the masquerade as a critique of metaphysical conceptions of feminine stardom à la Rehlinger and Bach. Focusing her discussion on the film's use of the close-up and the veil, Doane first recalls the conventional status of the facial close-up both as an important narrative device to establish character and identity, and as a significant mechanism in the star system, insofar as it guarantees 'the recognisability of each star'. In *The Devil*, by contrast, the first close-up reveals a Dietrich 'doubly obscured by a filigreed mask which surrounds her eyes, and an elaborately tufted veil which cages the head' (Figure 20).[67] Here

Figure 20: Dietrich and the masquerade – *The Devil is a Woman* (1935)

as in other 1930s Dietrich titles that foreground issues of disguise and masquerade in Dietrich's image (in her roles in *Dishonored* [1931] as a female spy, for instance, or as a conwoman and jewel thief in *Desire*), 'tropes of the mask, fan and veil' signal 'a dangerous deception or duplicity attached to the feminine'.[68]

Doane's analysis of Dietrich and the masquerade pinpoints one source of the unease that Dietrich's star image generated in Nazi Germany. We saw in Chapter 3 how high a premium was placed in Third Reich acting theory on 'mime', not 'mask'. *The Devil*, by contrast, reveals its allegiance to the splitting of image (mask) from body that Doane defines as the masquerade, not only in its opening sequence, but throughout the film. Dietrich's acting style is unremittingly anti-realist; frontal acting and self-conscious preening, studied erotic poses and knowing winks repeatedly signal the status of 'Concha' as performed identity. When, therefore, at the end of the film, 'Concha' adopts an assumed name and a false passport to cross the border from Spain to France, this merely underscores in narrative what the spectator already knows from her/his encounter with the image of Dietrich – which is that there is no metaphysical truth or essence that underlies her star presence in *The Devil*.

THE MASQUERADE IN CLOSE-UP: RACIAL READINGS

But there is more. In a more recent essay, 'Masquerade Reconsidered', Doane revises her conception of the masquerade. In her early work, she had read it as a subversive alternative to a femininity discursively confined within the body-as-essence. This is certainly to an extent the function of Dietrich's masquerade in the reception context of the Third Reich. Doane later concludes, however, that her first reading of the masquerade as discussed by Rivière was incomplete. Certainly, Rivière analyses 'womanliness' as a 'mask' assumed as a form of defence against an over-identification of the 'masculine' intellectual woman with the male gender. But Rivière continues: 'The reader may now ask how I define womanliness or where I draw the line between genuine womanliness and the "masquerade". My suggestion is not, however, that there is any such difference; whether radical or superficial, they are the same thing.'

In this description, as Doane underlines, the femininity that is assumed as a mask by Rivière's patient does not challenge conventional assumptions of gender primarily by its reference to a female identity that implicitly has some more authentic existence in other realms. Instead, the masquerade of femininity has no referent in the real: it is 'in actuality non-existent – it serves only as a disguise ... and as a deception'.[69]

Rivière's account as read by Doane shares with contemporary post-modern feminist criticism a conception of femininity – or 'womanliness' – as constructed and/or performed entirely in and through representation.[70] As Doane further points out, moreover, Dietrich's image, particularly as constructed by von Stern-berg, prefigures this post-modern refusal of referentiality by its persistent highlighting of its own status as simulation. We have already seen how it was in von Sternberg's use of close-ups of Dietrich that the capacity of her image to disturb, through masquerade, the Third Reich's metaphysics of presence was most evident. That this disturbance results from the radical refusal in Dietrich's image of *any* ontological certainty regarding the feminine is clear from dis-cussions of the close-up in 1930s German discourses of star reception. In the idealist model around which those discourses pivoted, the close-up featured as the primary mode of filmic representation of essential identities. As we have seen, writers like Rehlinger, Iros and Groll turned, paradoxically perhaps, to the Marxist Romantic Balázs as the source of their conception of the close-up's aes-thetic function. For Balázs, famously, the close-up was the most significant of film's aesthetic innovations (he called it 'the new territory of this new art', its unique 'poetry').[71] At the same time, the close-up of the human face in particular played a key part for Balázs in film's transformation of perceptions of human identity, allowing the viewer access as it did to the invisible depths of selfhood that lay concealed beneath the material surface of the face.

   In Balázs' physiognomy, the primary concern was with the 'soul' or occasion-ally, the 'unconscious' as the latent content of the actor's film image. 'Close camera', he asserted, 'can photograph the unconscious'.[72] But Balázs' further comment that the face, at such proximity, becomes a 'document' to be read 'as graphologists read writing' gives a foretaste of the racial perversions to which his work on the close-up would be subject under National Socialism. From the early 1930s onwards, graphology developed apace as a branch of the new racial physiognomy that drew inferences regarding biological and racial identities from surface phenomena – in the case of graphology, from handwriting.[73] Analo-gously, film-theoretical writing re-inflected Balázs' reading of the close-up as window on the actorly unconscious or soul, and began to conceptualise it instead as a key to biological or racial essence. Rehlinger, for instance – who cited Balázs' *Der Geist des Films* as 'the only extant example of an aesthetics of film' – repro-duced Nazism's interpretation of the human face as the distilled essence of a *völkisch* personality rooted in blood and soil when he celebrated the peasant roots of lay actors featured in such films as an *Man of Aran* (1934) and *Triumph of the Will* (1935):

> The camera may attempt to interpret the secret reality of these authentic examples
> of humanity . . . – a reality that derives from their rooting in the landscape, their
> uninhibited yet emotionally reticent quality, their diversity – but it can never
> cheapen them.

'Only the close-up', Rehlinger continues, has been able to reveal the 'miracle' of faces such as these in their 'finest nuances of expression'.[74]

A comment on the face of Dietrich from the Berlin evening paper *8 Uhr Abendblatt* puts the case for a racial reading à la Rehlinger of her use of masquerade more bluntly. The paper compares the faces of Garbo and Dietrich as receptacles for an essence of race, the latter perceived as a 'unity to which the whole person belongs: body and spirit'. Garbo, the *Abendblatt* asserts, must be counted in this context as 'primarily' of 'Nordic' extraction (albeit with the proviso that 'she may appear on closer inspection to display certain East Baltic features'). Marlene Dietrich, by contrast,

> must be decisively rejected. Her facial profile and the colour of her hair and eyes may perhaps exactly resemble those of the Nordic race. Her performances, as well as her behaviour during the 'system era' [*Systemzeit*] and her particularly intimate intercourse with the Jews (Sternberg!) have nothing in common with the Nordic way of life. In her case, it is a matter of relative certainty that her phenotype [*Erscheinungsbild*] is deceptive; for the hybrid nature of the German population produces a situation ... in which Nordic appearance does not in any sense always allow one to assume the same inner [*seelisch*] characteristics. Nordic appearance may be conjoined with non-Nordic soul, as non-Nordic appearance may equally be combined with Nordic soul.[75]

Contrast *8 Uhr Abendblatt*'s comments with a contemporary letter to 'Marlene' from one enraptured fan. For 'Trude Häck, Berlin', the star's 'fabulous beauty' as Concha in *The Devil* was as 'unforgettable' as 'your so uniquely beautiful achievements in *Scarlet Empress*, *Blonde Venus*, *Shanghai Express*, *Morocco* and *Der blaue Engel*'.[76] The gulf dividing Häck from the pro-Nazi *Abendblatt* illustrates what was becoming by 1935–6 a mounting tension between hostility to Dietrich from regime ideologues, and popular acclaim. For the former, Dietrich occasioned a discomfort deriving not least from her embracing of a modernist aesthetic that radically divided 'form' and 'content', 'face' and 'soul'. Hence the numerous references in reviews to her 'emptiness' in her role as Concha, her transition from a 'German Garbo' whose face was 'the mirror of her soul', to what the Nazi organ *Völkischer Beobachter* termed 'a world champion in seduction and vice'.[77] It was, moreover, repeatedly on racial grounds that the disjunction in Dietrich's image between appearance and essence was condemned. In the neo-Kantian aesthetic schema on which Third Reich film commentary drew, the artifice that Dietrich mobilised for her version of the masquerade in *The Devil* was already implicitly racialised through its inclusion in the category of 'primitive' and 'barbaric' popular entertainment. Nazi film commentary then substituted for Kant's rather more benign cultural relativism (see point 6 in my account of Kant on beauty above) a reading of the masquerade as a racial perversion, an offence against 'Nordic soul'. Small wonder, then, that *The Devil* was banned barely three months after its release in the 'Reich', in part in response to a row between Paramount and the Spanish government over the film's portrayal of the Spanish police, but in part surely also on account of its flagrant celebration of an aesthetic of mask, artifice, kitsch and show.[78]

DESIRE (1936): RETURNING HOME TO NARRATIVE

Despite the censors' hostility to the Dietrich of *The Devil*, however, even her sternest critics were forced to concede on the film's release that 'this film will be guaranteed greater than average popularity ... [among] German audiences'.[79] It was, then, in part in recognition of Dietrich's continuing domestic pulling power that just one more film featuring the star was allowed an airing in Nazi Germany.

July 1936 saw the release of Dietrich's last title shown under NSDAP rule, Frank Borzage's romantic comedy *Desire*. Dietrich here plays a sultry Parisian jewel thief, Madeleine de Beaupré, who steals a priceless pearl necklace, then heads across the border to Spain to join her accomplice, Carlos (John Halliday). A chance encounter with a wet-behind-the-ears American motor engineer, Tom Bradley (Gary Cooper) initiates a moral transformation in Madeleine/Dietrich. Swept along by the emotion of a burgeoning romance, she returns the necklace, and exits to a blissful future as Tom/Cooper's wife.

Desire was Dietrich's first film following her very public split with von Sternberg; and among German critics, her apparently simultaneous farewell to Sternberg's kitsch modernist aesthetic won her high praise indeed.

> No longer is Dietrich the centre of some techno-aesthetic experiment à la Sternberg. Here, she is simply one actress amongst others; she plays a role that has a genuine beginning and end, a meaning and a content – a comedy role, moreover, whose possibilities are recognised and exploited so convincingly by Dietrich that it is towards her above all that the applause at the end of the film is directed.[80]

This *Film-Kurier* review set the tone for what was to become widespread critical acclamation of Dietrich in *Desire*. We have seen in this chapter how the Third Reich's neo-Kantian aesthetic privileged harmony, balanced proportions and formal perfection as attributes of the beautiful in film art. Dietrich's image in *Desire* was considered by *Film-Kurier* and others to embody in four distinct ways the cinematic attributes of the beautiful. First, her performance was seen to depart from the self-referential acting mode that Dietrich had adopted in her work with von Sternberg, in which her mannered acting style pointedly drew attention to her own status as star. A Dietrich who situated herself in *Desire*, by contrast, as 'simply one actress among others' was viewed as committing herself to an ensemble aesthetic valued by Third Reich critics, as we saw also in Chapter 2, for its achievement of artistic balance through the integration of stars into the actorly whole.

This ensemble commitment was seen as reinforced, second, by Borzage's dramaturgical privileging of narrative over spectacle. This was, after all, a romantic comedy with 'a genuine beginning and end'. *Film-Kurier* here echoed a recurrent trope in Third Reich film theory, which celebrated what Ernst Iros, for instance, termed the 'harmonious perfection' of rounded narrative for its realisation of the transcendent 'idea' that underpinned all art. As Iros elaborated, 'only [this] idea, and never mere directorial play with form, can be the bearer of a work of art'.[81] In this context, he continued, it is incumbent on the actor or actress to abandon the 'personal motives' that animate stardom, and to 'submit themselves' in their very 'soul' to the 'idea' that forms film art.[82]

Film-Kurier's view of Dietrich in *Desire* as meeting the demands of idealist theories à la Iros that posited the narrative integration of star images as a prerequisite for the realisation of the beautiful, was not universally shared. The *Berliner Tageblatt*, for instance, saw Dietrich's performance as contributing 'relatively little' to what was otherwise the 'simply delightful' harmony of elements that Hollywood comedies attained.[83] Less contentious was the third aspect that prompted *Film-Kurier* to such enthusiasm for *Desire*. The *Film-Kurier* reviewer singled out for special praise Borzage's abandonment of a Sternbergian mode of star close-up that froze Dietrich into a status as the object of spectacle and visual pleasure, in favour of an integration of shots of Dietrich into the narrative flow. In *Desire, Film-Kurier* contended,

> it is the plot and its protagonists that are prioritised. Certainly, the camera lingers willingly when it occasionally pauses to allow the audience to gaze on fabulous shots of Dietrich, but it does so … without Dietrich becoming uniquely dominant within the image. … In the end, then, this is a delightful film, which stands and falls by its own merits, rather than by those of an international star.[84]

Karsten Witte, in his important work on Third Reich popular film, has identified as a common stylistic feature of that cinema what he terms its 'inhibition' of the visual pleasure of film spectacle.[85] Witte's focus is on film texts themselves; but the same impulse towards a restraining of spectacular pleasures is visible in the broader field of film commentary. *Film-Kurier*'s praise for *Desire* as a film that integrates star close-ups of Dietrich into the narrative flow thus echoed

Figure 21: *Desire* (1936)

wider critical debates on the close-up's function in narrative film. I cited above
Hans-Joachim Hahn's 1934 article on 'The secret of the close-up', in which he
argued for a stylistic integration of the 'harmonious trilogy' of long, medium and
close shot; an integration that achieved an 'organic fusion of individual scenes
into a unified, harmonious whole'.[86] Echoes of Hahn's insistence on narrative
integration as a guiding principle of visual construction are apparent in numerous contemporary film-theoretical deliberations; witness, for instance, Günter
Groll ('the artistic film must ... display a visual style that allows organic integration through montage'), or Johannes Eckhardt, film adviser to the Berliner
Kulturfilmbühne (Berlin Documentary Film Association), whose (undoubtedly
premature) claim for National Socialist film art was that it had 'begun to instil
order in the excess of sense impressions that daily overwhelm us; for our struggle is one for inner connections, for deeper knowledge, for the essence of
ultimate pheonomena, not of superficial sensation'.[87]

If *Desire* was seen, fourth and finally, to achieve precisely the integration into
narrative totality that Third Reich film theory so admired, then this was attributed
in reviews not only to Borzage's montage, but to shifts in Dietrich's performance
style. In her collaborations with von Sternberg, as we have seen, Dietrich flaunted

Figure 22: Dietrich as jewel thief in *Desire* (1936)

an anti-realist commitment to an aesthetics of masquerade and mask. In Borzage's film, by contrast, Dietrich's talents as a 'great actress' (*Film-Kurier*) were realised through the harnessing of her capacity for masquerade to realist narrative. Thus in *Desire*, the masquerade, drawn upon in *The Devil* to heighten the ambiguity of Dietrich's image, was both narratively motivated, and negatively valued. The success of Madeleine/Dietrich's criminal mission depended, firstly, precisely on her capacity for disguise. Redemption was possible, however, if the masquerade was relinquished – an inference emphasised in the film's dénouement, when Dietrich dons a demure A-line skirt and workaday jacket to confess her crime to her would-be fiancé, Tom/Cooper (Figure 21). Earlier in the film, too, the ambivalence that emanates from the masquerade – its capacity to destabilise or fracture identity – had been deflected by its comedic treatment. In the opening sequences, Dietrich's ability to pull off her crime depended on her disguise as the wife of two men, a psychiatrist and a jeweller. A subsequent scene, in which the two men confront each other, each convinced that Dietrich is the other's wife, is not only among the funniest in the film, it is also noticeably lengthy – as if it took this long to defuse the threat to artistic integrity posed by Dietrich's slippage across identities through masquerade (Figure 22).

DIETRICH THE PRODIGAL DAUGHTER[88]

In press coverage of *Desire*, in sum, Dietrich's image was recuperated for a Third Reich film aesthetic that privileged the beauty of narrative order over the duplicitous surface attractions of visual spectacle and the masquerade. This aesthetic reintegration of Dietrich was paralleled, finally, by film-critical commentary that sought to relocate the biographical narrative that framed her star persona within the narrative and genre conventions of popular cinema German-style. Recurrent in contemporary German melodrama was, for instance, the trope of the prodigal daughter, and the narrative of her return. Detlef Sierck/Douglas Sirk's *Schlußakkord* (*Final Chord*, 1936), for instance, told the story of an émigré mother who returned to Germany seeking reunion, not only with her child, but – through her romance with a prominent conductor – with German cultural tradition. That same year, one of German cinema's most popular rising stars, Marika Rökk, scored a hit with *Und Du, mein Schatz, fährst mit* (*Come with me, my love*), the tale of an operetta-singer-turned-variety-star who abandons a brilliant American career in favour of wifely duties in her German home. The formula was perfected in the Zarah Leander vehicle *Heimat* (1938), one of the most successful melodramas of the pre-war period. Based on a novel by Hermann Sudermann, *Heimat* achieves resolution in a return home by an actress whom one reviewer dubbed

> the great figure of homecoming, a woman who fled the rigidity of her paternal home and the confines of small-town living, then endured the bitterest of personal sacrifices before reaching maturity as a great singer and returning to the home she has always loved and never forgotten. . . . [89]

The contrast, both with Dietrich's films, and with her biography, is stark. Rarely in her early films does narrative resolution involve homecoming. The final frame of *Morocco* (1930), for instance, shows Dietrich disappearing across the horizon to begin life as a desert vagrant. Similarly, though the dénouement of *Shanghai Express* returns Dietrich to her British lover, there is no suggestion that they will now leave China for less exotic European climes. *Blonde Venus*, too, depicts a vagrant Dietrich: a figure certainly returned finally to her marital home, but denounced nonetheless by German censors for her 'whorish' performance, and her 'improbable' representation of an ultimate commitment to maternal love.[90]

The territorial dispersion in her films of Dietrich's image was matched in her biography by the star's repeated refusals to return home. Werner Sudendorf lists at least three approaches from German production companies – Ufa in 1933, Tobis and Syndikat-Film in 1936 – designed to recapture Dietrich for productions at home.[91] These were as unsuccessful as were the advances of the Berlin theatre impresario Henry Pless, who corresponded energetically between December 1937 and May 1938 with Dietrich's husband and manager, Rudolf Sieber, on the possibilities of guest appearances by Dietrich on the German stage.[92] Doubtless unbeknown to Pless, Goebbels himself sent to Paris in November 1937 one of his most prominent cultural functionaries, the director of the Deutsches Theater, Heinz Hilpert, to negotiate a passage home for the renegade star.[93] He met the same negative response as industry and theatre entrepreneurs, as well as the numerous German reporters who had visited Dietrich on her European trips to persuade Dietrich of the benefits of a passage home; for it was in the event not until 1944–5 that Dietrich would re-enter the country, this time as an American citizen and US army entertainer.[94]

The fact that Ufa waited until March 1939 before confirming in an internal memorandum to Director-General Klitzsch that Dietrich 'seems to wish finally to renounce the use of her person in Germany', tells us much of the strength of official desires to retain this most alluring of German stars for the national industry.[95] Hence, undoubtedly, the quasi-hysterical repetition in film commentary on Dietrich from 1933 to 1939 of a melodramatic narrative of national return. Until mid-decade at least, the trade press regularly (mis)reported Dietrich's supposedly imminent German visits. On 3 January 1933, twenty-seven days before the Nazi takeover, *Film-Kurier* confidently announced Dietrich's plans for a February trip.[96] That those plans were shelved was not finally confirmed until July of the same year, in a report that also noted with teeth-gritting irritation that Dietrich would shortly be visiting Cannes (and could thus, by implication, have made a detour to Germany without difficulty).[97] By July 1934, when Dietrich was reported to have called off a planned Viennese tour, the rancour surrounding her continued absence was evident; thus for the first time, 'Marlene' became 'Frau Dietrich' in an article that noted with injured irony that 'already last year, Frau Dietrich noticeably omitted to grace her German homeland and us un-modern Berliners with her presence'.[98]

The same article went on confidently, if contradictorily to assert that Dietrich would indeed shortly revisit her 'homeland' and her native Berlin. The piece displays many of the narrative and stylistic features of what was at this stage still a recurrent news story of Dietrich's imminent return. Defending the star against attacks in the German popular press, the *Film-Kurier* declares:

> Though we never try to obscure what is often the emptiness of her performance, its superficial and vapid quality, we nonetheless do not believe that the standards of the *Tribüne* or other Berlin weekend papers can be used to condemn or dismiss such a film phenomenon as Dietrich. 'God is glad of the repentant sinner . . .'. And Marlene Dietrich is a beautiful sinner indeed. She will visit Germany this autumn and will renounce, entirely of her own accord, the reserve and disgruntlement that she currently considers the best response to the serious nervous condition she has developed in Hollywood.[99]

The analogy that was only implicit in much contemporary reporting is here clearly articulated. The biblical allusion – 'God is glad of the repentant sinner' – situates Dietrich as a prodigal daughter whose offences will be forgiven, if only she comes home. In 1930s Germany, of course, it was not primarily in Christianity that the narrative of the prodigal daughter was ideologically located, but in Nazi myths of ethnic unity within the territory of the *Reich*. A key focus of early Nazi propaganda was the return of ethnic Germans to their homeland ('*Heim ins Reich*'). The incorporation of all Germans into the *Reich* was a 'positive part of racial policy and . . . one of the earliest features of Hitler's political thought': hence Hitler's comment in *Mein Kampf* that 'German-Austria must be restored to the great German Motherland . . . People of the same blood should be in the same *Reich*. The German people will have no right to engage in colonial policy until they shall have brought all their children together in one State.'[100]

Mein Kampf's phrasing here is typical of right-wing nationalist prose in its use of a key trope from melodrama – the return of the child to the mother's bosom – to articulate the racial ideology of *Heim ins Reich*. The same *topoi* surfaced repeatedly in contemporary reportage on Dietrich's return. Press reports had regular recourse to the great melodramatic motifs: desire (Germany's for Dietrich), transgression (hers, in Hollywood), guilt (Dietrich is a 'beautiful sinner'), redemption (achieved by her return home). Those motifs are embedded, too, in the classical narratives of family melodrama: Dietrich is the 'child'[101] who has sinned, her German audience a 'loyal' public that will 'forgive its favourites much; for it takes more than a single error for one who is truly loved to fall out of favour'.[102]

Towards the end of the decade, hopes of Dietrich's return were fading; but the strength of the desire that fuelled the narrative of her homecoming revealed itself in a fantasy sighting of an *ersatz* Dietrich at the Ufa studios: the Swedish actress Karin Albihn, who apparently auditioned with Ufa in winter 1937, but never made her career in Germany. Albihn was presented by *Film-Kurier* in a moment of wishful thinking as 'Marlene Dietrich's *Doppelgänger* in Babelsberg'.[103] In the event, though, it was neither the case that Karin Albihn made it to a career in Germany – she sunk without trace – nor did Dietrich return for a last pre-war appearance on German screens. *Desire* was the last of her Hollywood films to achieve Third Reich release. Selznick's *The Garden of Allah* (1936) is thought by Markus Spieker to have been refused a licence because of the 'envy' of the Propaganda Minister, whose diaries report his admiration for what he erroneously believed to be Hollywood's first full-colour film.[104] Whatever the motive, *The Garden* failed to past the quota barrier and, like Dietrich's three subsequent titles – *Knight without Armour*, *Angel* (both 1937) and *Destry Rides Again* (1939) – never played to German audiences under the *Reich*. As we shall see in this book's next chapter, it was left instead to a generation of what I have termed 'Dietrich's ghosts' to attempt to realise, in a Nazi Germany, which Dietrich herself had repudiated, the cinematic legacy of this most international of 1930s German stars.

NOTES

1. Josef von Sternberg, 'Introduction', in idem, *The Blue Angel* (London: Lorrimer, 1968), p. 9.
2. Kurt Pinthus, 'Hinreissend ordinär', in Lars Jacob (ed.), *Apropos Marlene Dietrich* (Frankfurt am Main: Neue Kritik, 2000), p. 85. The song titles are translated by von Sternberg, in the order in which they appear here, as 'My Name is Naughty Lola', 'The Real Man, the Right Kind for Me', and 'Falling in Love Again': see von Sternberg, *The Blue Angel*.
3. 'Diesen Film werden ein paar hundert Millionen Menschen sehen!', *Vossische Zeitung*, 2 April 1930. Reproduced in Gerd Albrecht and Deutsches Institut für Filmkunde (eds), *Die großen Filmerfolge. Vom blauen Engel bis Otto, der Film* (Ebersberg: Edition Achteinhalb, 1985) p. 14.
4. Max Brod and Rudolf Thomas, 'Sanfte Erotik', in Jacob, *Apropos Marlene Dietrich*, p. 86.
5. Christine Battersby cites among many examples Schopenhauer's essay 'On Women' (1851), William Duff's *Essay on Original Genius* (1767), *Critical Observations* (1770), and especially Duff's *Letters on the Intellectual and Moral Character of Women* (1807): Christine Battersby, *Gender and Genius. Towards a Feminist Aesthetics* (London: Women's Press, 1989), p. 6. On Burke's sublime, articulated as what Terry Eagleton calls a 'phallic swelling' (Burke, *Philosophical Inquiry into the Origin of our Ideas of the Sublime and the Beautiful* [1757]), see Terry Eagleton, *The Ideology of the Aesthetic* (Oxford: Blackwell, 1990), p. 54.

6. Battersby, *Gender and Genius*, pp. 4–5.

7. Stephen Lowry, 'Heinz Rühmann – the Archetypal German', in Tim Bergfelder, Erica Carter and Deniz Göktürk (eds), *The German Cinema Book* (London: BFI, 2002), p. 81.

8. Battersby, *Gender and Genius*, pp. 11 and 112. Battersby's comment relates particularly to Kant's *Observations on the Feeling of the Beautiful and the Sublime*, John T. Goldthwait (trans.) (Berkeley, Los Angeles and London: University of California Press, 1981, orig. 1764). She points out here that 'Kant does not deny that some individual women might be capable of masculine intellectual pursuits', yet that he observes (Kant, *Observations*, p. 78) that '[d]eep meditation and a long-sustained reflection are noble but difficult, and do not well befit a person in whom unconstrained charms should show nothing else than a beautiful nature'. Battersby concludes from this that, for Kant, 'for a woman to aim at the sublime makes her merely ridiculous'.

9. Rudolf Arnheim, *Film as Art* (Berkeley, Los Angeles and London: University of California Press, 1971, orig. 1957), p. 3.

10. Eagleton, *The Ideology of the Aesthetic*, p. 90. The term 'shattering' (*Erschütterung*) was often deployed by Third Reich critics to describe the 'experience' (*Erlebnis*) of the sublime work of art. I am grateful to Christine Battersby for pointing out to me just how selective is this Third Reich appropriation of Kant; he uses *Erschütterung* only once in relation to the sublime, preferring such terms as *Achtung, Schauer, Furcht, Grausen, Schreck, Verwunderung, Bewunderung, Enthusiasmus, Schwärmerei* and *Schwung*.

11. Immanuel Kant, *Critique of the Power of Judgement*, Paul Guyer (trans. and ed.), and Eric Matthews (trans.) (Cambridge: Cambridge University Press, 2000, orig. 1790), pp. 184 and 173.

12. A comprehensive survey of those responses to the film medium is Sabine Hake's *The Cinema's Third Machine. Writing on Film in Germany, 1907–1933* (Lincoln and London: University of Nebraska Press, 1993).

13. Rudolf Arnheim, 'Josef von Sternberg', in Peter Baxter (ed.), *Sternberg* (London: BFI, 1980), p. 36.

14. Ibid.; see also Fedor Stepun, *Theater und Kino* (Berlin: Bühnenvolksbundverlag, 1932), p. 12.

15. Kant, *Critique of the Power of Judgement*, p. 184.

16. Ibid., p. 120.

17. Ibid., pp. 198–9.

18. Battersby, *Gender and Genius*, p. 111.

19. Kant, *Observations*, pp. 77 and 81.

20. Ibid., pp 77–85.

21. Andreas Huyssen, *After the Great Divide. Modernism, Mass Culture and Postmodernism* (London: Routledge, 1986), p. 62

22. Rudolf Arnheim, 'Josef von Sternberg', pp. 36 and 39.

23. Kant, *Critique of the Power of Judgment*, p. 119 and 108.

24. As Kant writes, 'The condition of the necessity that is alleged by a judgment of taste is the idea of common sense', ibid., p. 122.

25. Siegfried Kracauer, 'Cult of Distraction', in idem, *The Mass Ornament. Weimar Essays*, Thomas Levin (trans. and ed.) (Cambridge, MA and London: Harvard University Press, 1995), p. 325.

26. Alfred Brühl, 'Der Film als soziale Wirklichkeit', *Deutsches Volkstum*, January 1936, p. 44.

27. Ibid. Among the numerous pleas for an understanding of the contemporary artwork in terms of reception aesthetics, many focused on the need to educate the audience in the distinction between 'art' and 'kitsch': see, for example, Sigmund Graff, 'Von Kunst und Kitsch', *Die Bühne* (BN), 1 September 1936, 'Kitsch cannot be objectively established, but only subjectively experienced', p. 527; and A. E. Frauenfeld, 'Kitsch und Kunst', BN, 15 March 1937, especially his comment, p. 138, that 'every work of art is repeatedly formed anew in an act of creation by that person who truly experiences it'.

28. Kracauer, 'Cult of Distraction', pp. 326–8.

29. Figures are from a *Zeitungsverlag* survey, Nr. 10, 1928, cited in Kurt Wortig, *Der Film in der deutschen Tageszeitung* (Frankfurt am Main: Moritz Diesterweg, 1940), p. 101. Wortig also quotes a 1935 survey in *Film-Journal* (14 April 1935) listing eighty daily titles with film supplements. On the Weimar film press, see Helmut H. Diederichs, 'Über Kinotheater-Kritik, ästhetische und soziologische Filmkritik. Historische Aspekte der deutschsprachigen Filmkritik bis 1933', in Irmbert Schenk, (ed.), *Filmkritik. Bestandsaufnahmen und Perspektiven* (Marburg: Schüren, 1998), pp. 22–42; also Helmut Korte, *Der Spielfilm und das Ende der Weimarer Republik. Ein rezeptionshistorischer Versuch* (Göttingen: Vandenhoek & Ruprecht, 1998), pp. 136–41.

30. For a more detailed overview of the Nazi *Gleichschaltung* of the press, see David Welch, *The Third Reich. Politics and Propaganda* (London and New York: Routledge, 1993), pp. 34–8.

31. Ibid., p. 37.

32. Text of Goebbels' ban on art criticism, 27 November 1936: translated and reproduced in Welch, *The Third Reich*, p. 169.

33. Karl August Götz, 'Der Film als journalistisches Phänomen', unpublished dissertation, Düsseldorf 1937, pp. 42ff: cited in Wortig, *Des Film in der deutschen Tageszeitung*, p. 53.

34. Hans-Walter Betz, 'Filmstoffe und Publikumsgeschmack – Eine vergleichende Betrachtung über Filme in aller Welt', *Berliner Tageblatt* (BT), 24 October 1937; anon., 'Braucht der Film den Dichter?', *National-Zeitung* (NZ), 6 April 1939; 'Film und Literatur – Eine Betrachtung über die Aufgabe des Films', *Kölnische Zeitung* (KZ), 28 February 1937; 'Das Bilderlebnis', *Rheinisch-Westfälische Zeitung* (RWZ), 27 November 1937.

35. The reference to the *Filmbetrachterpersönlichkeit* occurs, among other places, in Wortig, *Der Film in der deutschen Tageszeitung*, p. 54.

36. Vring Wiemer of the *Preussische Zeitung* (PZ) was positively effulgent in his elaboration of the film commentator's responsibility to 'direct the audience away from the superficial and the commonplace ... and towards a genuine experience [*Erlebnis*] of art' (Vring Wiemer, 'Im Spiegel von Kunstbetrachter und Öffentlichkeit', PZ, 22 November 1938, cited in Wortig, *Der Film in der deutschen Tageszeitung*, p. 65). In similar vein, Hans Karbe concluded a review of Veit Harlan's *Das unsterbliche Herz* (*The Immortal Heart*, 1939) with a reference to his own 'unshakeable will to construct a genuine and serious film art' (NZ, 2 February 1939, cited in Wortig, *Der Film in der deutschen Tageszeitung*, p. 75).

37. Béla Balázs, *Der sichtbare Mensch oder die Kultur des Films* (Vienna and Leipzig: Deutsch-österreichischer Verlag, 1924), p. 15.

38. Siegfried Kracauer, 'The Mass Ornament', in idem, *The Mass Ornament*, pp. 75 and 78–9. The 'eternal same' is my translation of Adorno and Horkheimer's 'das Immergleiche'. John Cumming gives this as 'constant sameness'; see Max Horkheimer and Theodor W. Adorno, *Dialectic of Enlightenment*, John Cumming (trans.) (London: Allen Lane, 1973, orig. 1944), p.134.

39. Hans Dieter Schäfer, *Das gespaltene Bewußtsein. Deutsche Kultur und Lebenswirklichkeit 1933–1945* (Munich and Vienna: Hanser 1981) p. 124ff.

40. Markus Spieker, *Hollywood unterm Hakenkreuz. Der amerikanische Spielfilm im Dritten Reich* (Trier: Wissenschaftlicher Verlag, 1999), p. 114. On the dearth of statistical data relating to foreign film exhibition under the Third Reich, see Joseph Garncarz, 'Hollywood in Germany. Die Rolle des amerikanischen Films in Deutschland 1925–1990', in Uli Jung (ed.), *Der deutsche Film. Aspekte seiner Geschichte von den Anfängen bis zur Gegenwart* (Trier: Wissenschaftlicher Verlag, 1993), p. 172.

41. Spieker, *Hollywood unterm Hakenkreuz*, pp. 108 and 114.

42. 'Sehnsucht', FK, 3 April 1936.

43. 'Die grosse Zarin. Der neue Marlene-Dietrich-Film', *Hamburger Nachrichten* (HN), 14 September 1934.

44. Quote from Hans-Joachim Hahn, 'Das Geheimnis der Grossaufnahme', BT, 16 September 1934.

45. 'Grete träumt am Fliederstrauch ... Die 300 schönsten Berlinerinnen werden für Zigarettenbilder gesucht', BT, 14 September 1934.

46. 'Every scene, every image breathes, appearing for all the world like a photographic painting': 'Die grosse Zarin', HN.

47. 'Die grosse Zarin', FK, 15 April 1934.

48. Barry Salt, 'Sternberg's Heart Beats in Black and White', in Baxter, *Sternberg*, p. 110. Salt counts, by contrast, only sixteen star close-ups in *Der blaue Engel*, and thirty-two in *Morocco*.

49. 'Die grosse Zarin', BT, 15 September 1934.

50. Hans-Joachim Hahn, 'Das Geheimnis der Grossaufnahme', BT, 16 September 1934.

51. 'Die grosse Zarin' HN.

52. Quotations, in the order in which they appear here, from 'Aus dem Werden eines Films II', FW, 30 May 1937; 'Die grosse Zarin im Marmorhaus', FL, 15 September 1934.

53. Mary Ann Doane, *Femmes Fatales. Feminism, Film Theory, Psychoanalysis* (London: Routledge, 1991), p. 56.

54. Laura Mulvey, 'Visual Pleasure and Narrative Cinema', in Leo Braudy and Marshall Cohen (eds), *Film Theory and Criticism: Introductory Readings* (New York: Oxford University Press, 1999), pp. 833–44.

55. Thomas Elsaesser, *Weimar Cinema and After. Germany's Historical Imaginary* (London; Routledge, 2000), p. 43.

56. Spieker estimates the first run at thirty-two days: see Spieker, *Hollywood unterm Hakenkreuz*, p. 352.

57. Linda Schulte-Sasse, *Entertaining the Third Reich. Illusions of Wholeness in Nazi Cinema* (Durham and London: Duke University Press, 1996).

58. 'Die spanische Tänzerin', FK, 29 June 1935.

59. The English dialogue is quoted here, since the film was released in a subtitled, not dubbed version.

60. 'Ein Wort über die Star-Verehrung', FK, 12 January 1933. The full quotation rather unconvincingly equates a fetishistic 'adoration' of stars' gloves and autographs with a love of 'beauty itself': 'love and adoration [of film stars] involves a love of something beautiful and glittering – and behind this lies a love of beauty itself, which we should surely treat with greater care and delicacy. When Christian Morgenstern's hero, Herr Palmström, is seized, at the sight of his "great red handkerchief", by a love of the world's beauty unbounded, then surely we too should allow young men and women to adore Käthe Dorsch's autograph, or Marlene Dietrich's gloves . . .'.

61. Doane, *Femmes Fatales*, p. 49

62. Ibid., p. 18.

63. Bruno Rehlinger, *Der Begriff Filmisch* (Emsdetten: Lechte, 1938), pp. 59–61.

64. Rudolf Bach, *Die Frau als Schauspielerin* (Tübingen: Rainer Wunderlich, 1937), p. 10. His emphasis.

65. Joan Rivière, 'Womanliness as a Masquerade', in Hendrik M. Ruitenbeek (ed.), *Psychoanalysis and Female Sexuality* (New Haven: College and University Press, 1966, orig. 1929), cited in Doane, *Femmes Fatales*, p. 25.

66. Silvia Bovenschen, 'Mythos in eigener Regie', in Jacob, *Apropos Marlene Dietrich*, p. 134. Mary Anne Doane also makes reference to Bovenschen's work on feminine aesthetics as one source of her own reflections on Dietrich: see Silvia Bovenschen, 'Is there a Feminine Aesthetic?', *New German Critique* no. 10, winter 1977, p. 129; cited in Doane, *Femmes Fatales*, p. 26.

67. Doane, *Femmes Fatales*, p. 46.

68. Ibid., p. 49.

69. Ibid., p. 34: see Rivière, 'Womanliness as a Masquerade', p. 213.

70. As Judith Butler puts it in a critique of the 'metaphysics' of gendered substance, '[t]here is no gender identity behind the expressions of gender; ... identity is performatively constituted by the very 'expressions' that are said to be its results'. Judith Butler, *Gender Trouble. Feminism and the Subversion of Identity* (London: Routledge, 1990), p. 25.

71. Balázs, *Der sichtbare Mensch*, pp. 73 and 78.

72. Béla Balázs, *Der Geist des Films* (Halle: Knapp, 1930), p. 5.

73. Important fora for debates on the development of physiognomy and graphology as racial sciences were the *Zeitschrift für Menschenkunde* and the *Zentralblatt für Graphologie* (which eventually merged), as well as the *Zeitschrift für angewandte Psychologie*: see for example F. M. Huebner, 'Die Zeichensprache der Seele', *Zentralblatt für Graphologie*, no. 3, September 1933, pp. 137–57; idem, 'Die Zeichensprache der Seele. Von Auge und Antlitz', *Zeitschrift für Menschenkunde*, vol. 9, no. 2, 1933, pp. 77–91; Richard Detlev Loewenberg, 'Der Streit um die Physiognomik zwischen Lavater und Lichtenberg', *Zeitschrift für Menschenkunde*, vol. 9, no. 1, 1933, pp. 15–33; Willy Hellpach, 'Das Antlitz des Volkstums', *Zeitschrift für Menschenkunde*, vol. 11, no. 1, 1935, pp. 1–7; Rudolf Luck, 'Rassenforschung und Charakterkunde', *Zeitschrift für Menschenkunde und Zentralblatt für Graphologie*, vol. 12, 1936/7, pp. 1–5.

74. Rehlinger, *Der Begriff Filmisch*, p. 64.

75. 'Das Gesicht der Rasse im Film', *8 Uhr Abendblatt* (AA), 8 May 1936.

76. Letter from Trude Häck, 17 September 1935 (Marlene Dietrich Collection [MDC], Fanpost).

77. 'Die grosse Zarin', HN, and 'Die spanische Tänzerin', *Völkischer Beobachter* (VB), 30 June 1935.

78. In autumn 1935, *Film-Kurier* reported on a diplomatic row between the US and Spain. The dispute had allegedly erupted around *The Devil*'s caricatured portrayal of the Spanish police. After Spain threatened a general import ban on all Paramount titles, the studio apparently agreed that all copies of the film should be

withdrawn, and the master copy destroyed. See 'Spanische Regierung wird energisch', FK, 9 November 1935, and 'Dietrich-Film soll verbannt werden', FK, 11 November 1935. *The Devil* was banned in Germany by the Oberprüfstelle (Central Censorship Office, OP) on 26 November, apparently on the express command of Goebbels; see Spieker, *Hollywood unterm Hakenkreuz*, p. 166.

79. 'Natürlich zieht Marlene', FK, 3 July 1935.

80. 'Sehnsucht', FK, 3 April 1936.

81. Ernst Iros, *Wesen und Dramaturgie des Films* (Zürich and Leipzig: Max Niehaus, 1938), pp. 127 and 123.

82. Ibid., p. 137.

83. 'Sehnsucht', BT, 3 April 1936.

84. 'Sehnsucht', FK, 3 April 1936.

85. Karsten Witte, *Lachende Erben, Toller Tag* (Berlin: Vorwerk 8, 1995), pp. 177ff, on 'gehemmte Schaulust'. This section of Witte's book is extracted and translated in 'Visual Pleasure Inhibited. Aspects of the German Revue Film', J. Steakley and Gabriele Hoover (trans.), *New German Critique*, no. 24–5, fall/winter 1981/2, pp. 238–63.

86. Hahn, 'Das Geheimnis der Grossaufnahme'.

87. Günter Groll, *Film. Die unentdeckte Kunst* (Munich: C. H. Beck, 1937), p. 24; Johannes Eckert, 'Zum Sehen geboren, zum Schauen bestellt', FL, 22 December 1934.

88. This is an edited version of my 'Marlene Dietrich – the Prodigal Daughter', in Tim Bergfelder, Erica Carter and Deniz Göktürk (eds), *The German Cinema Book* (London: BFI, 2002), pp. 71–80.

89. Felix A. Dargel, '*Heimat* im Ufa-Palast', *Berliner Lokal Anzeiger* (BLA), n.d., 1938: reproduced in Albrecht, *Die großen Filmerfolge*, p. 32.

90. '*Die Blonde Venus* durch Oberprüfstelle verboten', FK, 4 July 1933. The preoccupation with returning 'Marlene' to a symbolic position within a narrative of nation is also evidenced by the ferocity of responses when her films were seen to infringe national cinematic norms. Witness, for example, the harsh treatment meted out not only to *Blonde Venus*, but to Rouben Mamoulian's 1934 *Song of Songs*. In March 1934, the Oberprüfstelle upheld the Berlin censors' invocation of Paragraph 7 of the newly reformed *Reichslichtspielgesetz* (*Reich* Cinema Law) to ban *Song of Songs* outright. A literary adaptation from the nineteenth-century novelist Hermann Sudermann, *Song of Songs* was described by *Film-Kurier* as centring 'on a German colonel who buys himself a girl for one thousand marks. Though he does marry her, he boasts in the most vulgar manner of having trained her up as a society lady, and cynically reveals – in the presence of her former lover – that he enlisted the latter's aid and used devious means to gain possession of her. The role of the female lead sinks to the same base level. A

simple and unspoilt country girl at the beginning of the film, she then becomes the lover of a sculptor, later a colonel's wife, an adulteress, a woman of the street, and finally once again the sculptor's lover. The bearer of this role is a *German* actress, whose preferred roles in America are those of whores, and who is known the world over as a German.' *Song of Songs* was duly banned on the grounds of its offence against 'moral or artistic feeling', and in particular, its jeopardising of 'German prestige' through its portrayal of low life in a German setting: see 'Oberprüfstelle über *Song of Songs*', FK, 16 March 1934.

91. Werner Sudendorf, *Marlene Dietrich* (Munich: Deutscher Taschenbuch Verlag, 2001), pp. 121ff.

92. Letters from Henry Pless to Rudolf Sieber, 8 December 1937, 3 January 1938, 2 March 1938 (MDC, personal correspondence).

93. Diary entry, 7 November 1937, in Elke Fröhlich (ed.), *Die Tagebücher von Joseph Goebbels. Sämtliche Fragmente*, part 1, vol. 3 (Munich, New York, London and Paris: K. G. Saur, 1987), p. 328.

94. For full biographies – which deliver a variety of often conflicting accounts – see Franz Hessel, *Marlene Dietrich. Ein Porträt* (Berlin: Das Arsenal, 1992, orig. 1931); W. K. Martin, *Lives of Notable Gay Men and Lesbians. Marlene Dietrich* (New York and Philadelphia: Chelsea House, 1994); Maria Riva, *Marlene Dietrich by her Daughter* (London: Bloomsbury, 1992); Sudendorf, *Marlene Dietrich*; Donald Spoto, *Dietrich* (London: Bantam Press, 1992); Alexander Walker, *Dietrich. A Celebration* (London: Pavilion, 1999, orig. 1984); and among Dietrich's autobiographical accounts, her memoir *Ich bin, Gott sei Dank, Berlinerin. Memoiren* (Marlene D. par Marlene Dietrich), Nicola Volland (trans.) (Berlin: Ullstein, 1997, orig. Fr. 1984).

95. Internal memorandum to Klitzsch, Greven *et al.*, 15 March 1939: BA R109I/5465 41.

96. 'Paramount klagt gegen Marlene', FK, 3 January 1933.

97. 'Marlenes Pläne. Kein Besuch in Deutschland?', FK, 15 June 1933.

98. 'Marlene Dietrich befindet sich nicht in Wien', FK, 4 July 1934.

99. Ibid.

100. Quotes from David Welch, *Propaganda and the German Cinema 1933–1945* (Oxford: Clarendon, 1983), p. 132; Adolf Hitler, *Mein Kampf*, Ralph Manheim (trans.). (London: Hutchinson, 1974, orig. 1925/6), second edition, p. 17.

101. 'What have they done to you, my child?' is the pathetic question that concludes *Film-Kurier*'s review of *The Devil*: see 'Die spanische Tänzerin', FK, 29 June 1935.

102. 'Natürlich zieht Marlene', FK, 3 July 1935.

103. 'Doppelgängerin Marlene Dietrichs in Babelsberg', FK, 11 December 1937.

104. Spieker, *Hollywood unterm Hakenkreuz*, p.150.

6

Zarah Leander: From Beautiful Image to Voice Sublime

In May 1960, Marlene Dietrich returned for her first and, it transpired, also her last stage tour of the post-war Federal Republic. Though enthusiastically embraced by some, not least as a result of her principled anti-Nazi stance during World War II, Dietrich was vilified by many among the German press and public as a renegade who had turned her back on wartime Germany. She re-entered voluntary exile after the tour, and returned to the country of her birth only in death, for a Berlin funeral in May 1992.

Perhaps in a gesture of atonement for the public hostility Dietrich had endured in the Federal Republic after 1945, the Berlin Senate moved swiftly after her death to buy up her estate, and to preserve as archive material her multitudinous collection of letters, press cuttings, posters, books, stage costumes, furniture and other ephemera. Among the personal effects now permanently housed in the Berlin Film Museum's 'Marlene Dietrich Collection' are a handful of letters to the star dating from her 1960 German tour. They include the following from one Heinz C., Frankfurt am Main. Recalling a letter he had penned 'many years ago – I think it was 1935', Heinz C. writes:

> I carried your response around with me for years, until it was taken from me by the *Gestapo*, along with other papers and my passport. ... I remember that the letter I wrote at the time – and it was a long letter – dealt with your absence from Germany, and that I ended by asking you to reconsider and return. I didn't fully understand your position at the time – I think I felt 'abandoned', left alone to suffocate in a sinister, brown-shirted world.[1]

There has been little historical work on the relation between fans and stars in Nazi Germany. Such studies as do exist draw on sources ranging from industry surveys and secret police reports, to anecdotes, autobiographies, novels, fan mail and personal correspondence, to conclude, with Sabine Hake, that 'official claims about a fundamental change in audience tastes' often remained 'wishful thinking'.[2] Certainly, Heinz C.'s letter to Dietrich suggests that, far from delivering that experience of imaginary plenitude after which Third Reich theories of spectatorship aspired, film images of stars might have functioned in some cases to evoke in their viewers an experience of abandonment, disorientation ('I didn't fully understand your position'), lack, absence and loss. Those sentiments derived most particularly from the savage campaign the Nazis pursued against many of the film industry's best-loved creative personnel. In his March 1933 Kaiserhof speech, Joseph Goebbels had named as his goal the 'root and branch' eradication of 'ideas' unrooted in 'National Socialist soil'.[3] The ensuing rash of anti-Semitic and anti-leftist film initiatives by or on behalf of the Nazi state included compulsory licensing for all film personnel, and hence the exclusion from the industry of Jews and other undesirable figures; the re-classification as non-German of films made with Jewish participation (thus 'Jewish' films produced in Germany became subject to quota restrictions on 'foreign' films); the massive extension of censorship, including to films that offended against 'National Socialist … feeling'; and the organisation by Nazi activists of 'spontaneous' protests against 'Jewish' films. The results are well known. The years immediately following the Nazi seizure of power in 1933 saw an unprecedented exodus of film artists from Germany. Many headed for European destinations – Vienna, Paris, London, Prague, Amsterdam, Budapest. Later, as Nazi annexation or conquest became a palpable threat, some sailed for the US, joining an exile community in Hollywood said to have numbered, at its highest point, as many as 800 figures, including directors, producers, screenwriters, editors, composers, cinematographers, sound engineers, agents, cinema entrepreneurs – and an estimated 200 or so actors and actresses.[4]

In a star system thus eviscerated through Nazi persecution and enforced mass flight, fan culture after 1933 was haunted by the anxiety over abandonment and loss that Heinz C.'s letter to Dietrich encapsulates. His sentiments find echoes, for instance, in the fan weekly *Filmwelt*, which ran a contact column responding to queries on star biographies (age, birth date, career plans, even private address), and pointed readers towards merchandising sources for autographs, star postcards, calendars, song texts, and so on. That the audience/star relation the magazine fostered was in any case structured around a separation between fan and star was already clear from the column's insistence that readers sustain polite distance from the artist-personalities of German film.[5] Hence, for instance, the magazine's repeated warnings to fans over excessive questioning ('It simply defeats your object if you divide every question into four sub-questions.

We answer four, and four only.'),[6] or its strictures on lines of enquiry deemed inappropriate to the actorly arts ('Why ask questions of peripheral detail, questions which have no bearing at all on the artistic value and the artistic impact that any personality evokes?').[7]

It was in their assumed function as guardians of codes of appropriateness in fans' relation to the stars, moreover, that *Filmwelt* and cognate titles deflected, rebuffed or ridiculed audience requests for contact with stars temporarily or permanently absent from public view. Anxieties expressed over such figures as Martha Eggerth, who shuttled for a time between the US and Germany before finally emigrating in 1938; or Adolf Wohlbrück, whose emigration to England was the subject of rumour from January 1936 onwards, were greeted with assurances that their sojourn abroad was 'temporary', or in Wohlbrück's case – as one issue of *Filmwelt* confidently, if erroneously asserted – that readers need 'have no fear', for the star would 'continue filming' for the foreseeable future in Germany.[8] When a pregnant Brigitte Helm withdrew for the duration of her confinement from public view, a more forthright *Filmwelt* lambasted one reader with 'in heaven's name, have we not repeated a dozen times already that [Frau Helm] now wishes to live as a private individual. Who are we to dictate how she should or might lead her life?'[9]

More energetic still were the rebuttals to readers' enquiries after exiles from the *Reich*. Too numerous to cite in full are references in *Filmwelt*'s letter pages to unnamed artists who, as 'non-Aryans' now 'no longer film in Germany', or whose films 'no longer play' in German theatres. Fruitless therefore the readers' quest for star autographs, gramophone records, intimate details of those stars' émigré lives: 'further details unknown', stonewalls *Filmwelt* to 'film fan Paula', since 'the actress you name is non-Aryan', and has 'long since left'.[10]

LEANDER AS UNCANNY DOUBLE

It is a contention of contemporary, post-Freudian cultural analysis that painful experiences of loss or absence – in 1930s German fan culture, the loss of a whole generation of émigré stars – are compensated in fantasy by disavowal of that loss, and by the substitution of the lost object with a fantasised double, copy or facsimile.[11] I return in Chapter 7 to psychoanalytic accounts of the double, and to the issue of their applicability in relation to creative personnel in Third Reich film. For now, it suffices to note the undoubted pervasiveness in 1930s German star representation of the uncanny double as image and narrative trope. In some cases, promising new talent was explicitly figured as a substitute for, or copy of, this or that émigré star. Hence, for instance, *Film-Kurier*'s 1937 coverage of Karin Albihn (see Chapter 5) as 'Marlene Dietrich's *Doppelgänger* in Neubabelsberg ... a young Swede ... of whom one might have sworn at first glance that she was indeed Marlene Dietrich', so 'deceptively similar' was her external appearance to that of the Hollywood star.[12] Albihn was, moreover, one of a procession of figures trumpeted 'with astrological certainty' as substitutes for absent idols, only to reveal themselves, to quote *Hamburger Tageblatt*, as 'insignificant comets whose powers of illumination were in the end too weak to hold an audience for even the briefest moment'.[13] Liselott Klingler, Charlotte Gerda, Angela Salloker and many more; who now remembers these erstwhile emblems of 'genuine' artistic quality and/or star potential?[14]

This is not to say that regime and industry were idle in attempting to compensate for the dearth of star talent in 1930s German film. The recruitment efforts of the Ufa-Lehrschau, later the Deutsche Filmakademie (Chapter 1), represented a concerted attempt, in the words of Ufa Director-General Ludwig Klitzsch, to foster an artistic 'blossoming' of creative talent groomed for the new German film art.[15] More haphazard, though perhaps more fruitful, were the activities of industry scouts and talent competitions (*Nachwuchswettbewerbe*) which brought to German screens such celebrated figures as Kristina Söderbaum, Lida Baarova and Marika Rökk.[16]

Karsten Witte has noted how many such new recruits functioned as copies of, or doubles for, counterparts rendered inaccessible to domestic audiences as a result of censorship or exile after 1933. Witte's focus is on the modelling of German stars on such Hollywood favourites as Eleanor Powell (explicitly emulated by Marika Rökk), Spencer Tracy (Hans Söhnker), Katharine Hepburn (Marianne Hoppe) – the latter 'pure figures of *ersatz*', notes Witte drily, 'who never fully suppressed the memory of the gap that had been created in their name'.[17] It was not, however, in respect of US-born talent that the regime, in tandem with Ufa, recruited the figure who was to become the jewel in its mid-1930s firmament of rising stars. When the Vice-President of the *Reich* Film Chamber, Hans-Jakob Weidemann, travelled to Vienna in autumn 1936, he sought a substitute not for Jeanette MacDonald or Eleanor Powell, but for Hollywood's two rivals for the position of most celebrated European émigré: Greta Garbo, and Germany's own Marlene Dietrich.

RECRUITMENT FOR THE *REICH*, 1936

Weidemann's target in Vienna was the Swedish-born operetta and revue diva Zarah Leander – perhaps at first glance an unlikely candidate for a future career as international cinema star. Contemporaries of Leander recruited to German film included such fresh-faced starlets as Marika Rökk, contracted to Ufa at the tender age of twenty-one for a role in Werner Hochbaum's *Leichte Kavallerie* (*Light Cavalry*, 1935); or the Austrian actress and cabaret artiste Heidemarie Hatheyer, who played alongside Leander in Vienna revue before debuting for cinema at age nineteen in Luis Trenker's *Der Berg ruft* (*The Mountain Calls*, 1937). Leander, by contrast – on the brink of turning thirty in 1936 – already boasted a dazzling career in her native Sweden; yet her major triumphs had been as stage diva, rather than in her less successful sorties into Swedish film. Between 1929 and 1934, Leander had starred in a dozen Swedish revue, operetta and theatre titles, most famously alongside Gösta Ekman in Karl Gerhard's celebrated 1931 production of the Franz Léhar operetta *The Merry Widow*, but also previously in such titles as *Rolfs Revue* (1929), *Det glada Stockholm* (*Merry Stockholm*, 1930) and *Vasans nyarsrevy* (*New Year Revue at the Vasa Theatre*, 1931).

It was Leander's established persona as stage diva, indeed, that brought her to Vienna in 1936 to play the tempestuous film idol Gloria Miller in Ralph Benatzky's new musical *Axel an der Himmelstür* (*Axel at Heaven's Gate*). Leander's magisterial performance of herself in that production as a star of international stature was, moreover, the source of her allure for German Film Chamber functionaries and studio bosses who sought, alongside such vernal talents as Rökk, Hatheyer and their ilk, a cinematic grande dame capable of doubling for Dietrich and Garbo. Leander seemed perfect, not least because her revue roles had explicitly foregrounded her capacity to replicate and parody her two most celebrated rivals in Hollywood film. Leander herself, for instance, later attributed her Stockholm breakthrough in the 1931 revue *Stockholm blir Stockholm* (*Stockholm Remains Stockholm*) in part to audience acclaim for her Swedish version of Marlene Dietrich's 1930 *Der blauer Engel* hit 'Falling in Love Again' (in Swedish as '*Från topp till tå ewtt kärlekstundens barn*').[18] That the Dietrich label stuck is suggested by Leander's further account of Vienna rehearsals for *Axel an der Himmelstür*; slopping around the dressing rooms in slippers, dark glasses and men's slacks, she earned a reputation for haughtiness and sartorial laxity, summed up by fellow cast members in the nickname 'Marlene from Karlstad'.[19]

As in previous roles, the Leander of *Axel* combined these ambivalent tributes to Dietrich with similarly ambiguous acts of homage to 'Marlene's' MGM rival, Greta Garbo. Leander capitalised on the 'Garbo complex' that pervaded European popular theatre and film by incorporating into her Swedish revues such stage tributes as the 1934 song '*Farväl, farväl, lilla Greta*' ('Farewell, Farewell Little Greta'), or by playing the Gloria Miller of *Axel an der Himmelstür* as a thinly veiled parody of Garbo herself, whose notoriously imperious aloofness was lampooned in the opening song, '*Kinostar!*' ('Cinema Star').

The song lyrics are instructive for the insight they allow into Leander's pointed manipulation in her stage persona of her status as Garbo facsimile. The song runs:

I am a star, a great star, moods and all,
So runs the judgement, gentlemen, does it not?
But you err, gentlemen – why be astounded?
What do I gain, after all, from being a star?
A cinema star, the desire of girls in their thousands.
Cinema star, idol of today.
Metres-high are the tributes of the smallest small towns
To your fame, your beauty, your uniqueness.
Cinema star, idol (*Abgott*) of the century!
It is the wish of all to take your place.
Yet harsh spotlights
Hide my true face from the world.
In the depths of my heart
I am alone.

Ich bin ein Star. Ein grosser Star, mit allen Launen
So heisst das Urteil, meine Herren, is das nicht wahr?
Das ist ein Irrtum, meine Herren, wozu das Staunen?
Was hab ich schon so viel davon, dass ich ein Star?
Ein Kinostar, die Sehnsucht tausender Mädchen
Kinostar, Idol der heutigen Zeit.
Meterhoch verkünden die kleinsten Städtchen
Deinen Ruhm, deine Schönheit, deine Unvergleichbarkeit.
Kinostar, du Abgott diese Jahrhunderts!
Jeder wünscht an deiner Stelle zu sein.
Doch das grelle Scheinwerferlicht
Verbirgt der Welt mein wahres Gesicht.
Im Grunde meines Herzens bin ich allein.[20]

'Kinostar!' alludes unambiguously to the Garbo myth in its references to the 'moods' of its protagonist, her melancholia ('what do I gain?'), her solitude ('in the depths of my heart I am alone'), and her uniqueness ('*Unvergleichbarkeit*'). But its lyrics also – and contradictorily – foreground the mass character of star images when they dub film stars 'the desire of girls in their thousands', and observe how 'the smallest small towns' display 'tributes ... metres-high/To your fame'. For star images were, of course, from the moment of their first emergence in European and Hollywood cinematic systems in the 1910s the very emblem of what Walter Benjamin termed the 'mechanical reproducibility' of the art work in modernity.[21] The elaborate publicity and merchandising apparatus that developed around cinema stars, coupled with the ubiquity of what was after all a technological artefact, their film image, produced – to quote Knut Hick-ethier – a progressive 'detachment of the actorly product from the person ... a reification of performance that was of a piece with the industrial transformation of culture in general, and that paved the way for an infinite reproducibility of actorly performance itself'.[22]

That capacity for an endless doubling or multiplication of the star image pro-duced a simmering cultural unease at the star's challenge to 'genuine' performance skill and actorly art. Hence, for instance, the ambivalence towards star appreciation evident in the German text of 'Kinostar!', which shifts from the neutral presentation of its narrator as '*Idol*' (line 6), to the '*Abgott*' ('false idol') of line 9, her 'true face' obscured by the 'spotlight' of media attention. Yet Leander herself had less grounds to mistrust the star system's recurrent impulse to reproduce prototypes of existing popular stars, an impulse deriving in part from the star system's very nature as an apparatus of film-industrial mass reproduction, but expressing itself in 1930s Germany with special urgency in the wake of mass emigration and the resultant talent drain. In her revue career, as we have seen, Zarah Leander had turned to her own advantage the status of the star image as copy, not original, profiting from stars' inauthenticity by replicating in her stage roles the persona, and indeed the popular success of her two alter egos, Garbo and Dietrich. The success of Leander's mimicry among audiences in Vienna, Stockholm and elsewhere was, moreover, enough to convince Ufa to offer an unusually generous contract for her work in German film. On 28 October 1936, Ufa production chief Ernst Hugo Correll signed an agreement engaging Leander for leading roles in three titles scheduled for production between 1 February 1937 and 31 January 1938. The contract was unprecedented not only for its largesse (RM200,000 were promised for the year 1937–8: compare Chapter 2, Table 3), but for the manner of Leander's payment (30 per cent only of her fee would be paid in RM, the remaining 70 in Swedish krone). Ufa further retained the option of extending Leander's contract for two more years, with an agreed augmenting of her fee by RM100,000 yearly (i.e. to a total of RM400,000 by 1939).[23]

LEANDER IN GERMAN-LANGUAGE FILM, 1936–43

Zarah Leander, then, entered the German film industry as what Lutz Koepnick terms 'a mere copy measured against what she was supposed to replace'.[24] Her arrival was certainly timely in respect of Marlene Dietrich. Leander signed her Ufa contract a mere three months after the release of Dietrich's last film in Nazi Germany, *Desire*. In that context, the Swedish star may appear simply to have assumed the mantle Dietrich cast off when she so adamantly refused to return to work in Germany after 1933.

And yet: did 'Zarah' function unambiguously as a facsimile 'Marlene', manu-factured by Ufa as a double for the German star? In Chapter 5, I detected within reception discourse around Dietrich – the film and daily press, film history and theory, the state censors – an impulse to recuperate those elements of her star image deemed capable of stimulating in Third Reich audiences an experience of the beautiful in film art. Third Reich film culture created for Dietrich's image a reception context that I have presented in this book as structured around gen-dered and racialised bourgeois aesthetic norms. In this context, that image was made the target (unsuccessfully, as it turned out) of efforts to establish as an ideal for Third Reich star femininity the prettiness, harmony, good proportions and formal perfection that Kant had suggested were the pre-eminent attributes of feminine beauty in both Nature and art (see p. 139).

Leander's case, I will propose in what follows, was different. Tracing a devel-opment from Leander's first German-language film (*Premiere*, 1937), through the range of Ufa titles in which she starred between 1937 and 1943, I explore what I suggest was a developing tension between her visual image, and a voice to which Third Reich commentators attributed not the qualities of the beauti-ful, but of a feminised sublime. That development is traced in part through an analysis of Leander's narrative and visual construction in her German-language films, in part through her reception in the film and daily press, as well as in popu-lar biographical volumes on leading stars. In Chapter 7, I turn then finally to the physical space of the cinema, and to a consideration in this context of Leander's films after 1939, especially of the association forged by the film programmes' staple fare of newsreel and documentary war coverage between Leander's voice, and the 'sublime' imagery of a fascist war.

PREMIERE (1937)

Let us begin, then, with Leander's first German-language film, an Austrian pro-duction which predated the star's engagement by Ufa, Gloria-Syndikat-Film's *Premiere* (1937). Already in production during the closing months of *Axel an der Himmelstür*, *Premiere*, filmed under the seasoned direction of the operetta and revue film veteran Géza von Bolváry, featured elaborate musical sequences which showcased Leander's talents as revue queen. Hanging its lengthy musi-cal numbers around a mildly implausible crime narrative involving the murder of the unpopular theatre owner Reinhold (Walter Steinbeck), the film cast Leander in the role of stage prima donna Carmen Deviot, and featured Karl Martell (later, Leander's partner in Detlef Sierck's *La Habanera*, 1937) as Deviot's former lover, who is initially the prime murder suspect, though he is later rehabilitated as Deviot's sweetheart in the inevitable happy ending.

As in her performance of Garbo in *Axel*, the Leander of *Premiere* finds

Figure 23: the chorus line, and Leander as body and backdrop image in *Premiere* (1937)

herself caught between contradictory imperatives, on the one hand simulating her own star image (which figures ubiquitously within the *mise en scène* as poster, photograph or mirror image), and on the other, presenting herself as diva, a figure incomparable, transcendent, unique. Hence the film's abundant references to Leander's reproducibility as image (see Figures 23 and 24), from the posters of Deviot that populate backstage sets, through star portraits ranged across the theatre foyer, to the massive still of Leander's face in close-up that forms the backdrop to the closing song, '*Merci, mon ami*'. At the same time, the threat posed by technologies of mass image reproduction to the myth of singularity underpinning Leander's star identity is underlined both by the ubiquity in *Premiere*'s narrative sequences (and this is of course a generic characteristic of the backstage musical) of a disruptively chaotic mass of chorus girls, and (in a narrative move specific to *Premiere*), by the explicit figuring of the chorus line as the source of mortal danger (it is under the cover of a mock shoot-out in one revue sequence that Reinhold's murder takes place).

Premiere seems, then, to identify in Leander's star persona a tension between her status as mass-produced simulacrum (Dietrich copy, Garbo facsimile), and the more embodied essence of stardom towards which the film aspires. Hence *Premiere*'s visual construction of Leander's star image as the emblem of some distinct and singular aesthetic truth. The film's two numbers, the lightly

Figure 24: Leander's image multiplied in *Premiere* (1937)

syncopated '*Merci, mon ami*' and the love ballad '*Ich hab' vielleicht noch nie geliebt*' ('I Have Perhaps Never Truly Loved'), are sung against backdrop images of mass-cultural femininity: in the latter case, the chorus line, in the former, an inflated star portrait of 'Carmen Deviot' herself. Leander is singled out from the backdrop through a combination of central framing, close-up, and an immobile performance style that detaches her body from the visual totality of the *mise en scène*, establishing her visually as a figure at odds with what Siegfried Kracauer would have termed the 'pure externality' of mass-cultural femininity on screen.[25]

LEANDER AT UFA: THE VOICE SUBLIME

It is in the Leander's early Ufa titles, however, that the specific qualities of the challenge she is made to pose to mass culture become most clear. Between 1937 and 1939, Leander starred in a total of six Ufa films: two in 1937 under director Detlef Sierck, *Zu neuen Ufern* (*To New Shores*) and *La Habanera*; in 1938, *Heimat* (under Carl Froelich) and *Der Blaufuchs* (*Arctic Fox*); and in 1939, Froelich's *Es war eine rauschende Ballnacht* (*One Glittering Nicht at the Ball*) and Paul Martin's *Das Lied der Wüste* (*Desert Song*). Reviews of all six titles, as well as star biographies and critical accounts, repeatedly emphasise as the source of Leander's uniqueness her (admittedly singular) voice and singing style. Though that voice is technically merely an unusually rich contralto, writers grasping for a description that renders its androgynous quality and thrilling resonance regularly dub it either baritone or bass. The legend of Leander's low pitch and masculine timbre was sustained in the period through the regular recycling of tales of the necessary transposition of Leander's part in *The Merry Widow* two octaves down, from soprano to contralto; or of composer Ralph Benatzky's alleged response when Leander claimed a capacity to pitch 'deeper and deeper, right down to bass'. Benatzky in response: 'I shall start by going home and writing completely new songs, composed especially for ... the first [true] contralto I have ever met in my life.'[26]

Contemporary reviews focus equally on Leander's deep pitch, but they are concerned too with her voice's capacity to stimulate what is often described as a thoroughly enveloping somatic experience. Hence, for instance, the references to a range of senses – touch, taste and sight as well as sound – in one *Berliner Lokal-Anzeiger* review of *Zu neuen Ufern*: 'What dominates the film is the shimmer of [Leander's] voice: a voice as intoxicating as heavy, dark wine ... as powerful as the sound of an organ ... as transparent ... as glass, as deep as metal. Everything is in this voice: jubilation, happiness, the drunken melody and the wild pain of life.'[27]

Noteworthy in this reviewer's representation of the aesthetic effects of Leander's voice on the film spectator is his selection of qualities that bourgeois aesthetics attributes not to the beautiful, but the sublime. Accounts of the sublime since Kant have emphasised both its dynamism (the Kantian sublime 'moves', whereas the beautiful produces 'quiet contemplation'), and its

Figure 25: Wegena lingerie advertisement, c. 1941

ambivalence (hence the Kantian *Abgrund*, or abyss).[28] Leander's voice, this review suggests, operates in similar mode, stirring the very body of a spectator in whom it produces 'jubilation', certainly, but also jubilation's darker aspects: 'drunken melody', 'wild pain'.

Elsewhere in Leander reception, there is, moreover, evidence that her star image was made increasingly to pivot around that *völkisch* version of sublimity which I have suggested was the desired reception mode for Third Reich film. In Chapter 2, I showed how rare was the female star who occupied a position as 'personality', and thus as the embodiment of a *völkisch* sublime. Contrast, however, the following. In March 1941, Ufa found itself acting on Leander's behalf in a minor but illuminating copyright dispute. An advertisement for women's corsets in the sales catalogue of the Berlin-based *Wegena* had juxtaposed Leander's portrait with the images of two young women resplendent in *Wegena* corsets – and nothing more (Figure 25). A letter of complaint from Ufa met the following response (addressed to Leander herself): 'The high esteem in which your artistic and humane personality is held by all colleagues here must lead us to express profound regret [for any harm] caused by the use of this photo in a catalogue published by ourselves.'[29]

This small incident, and above all its culmination in a homage to the 'artistic personality' of the Swedish star, tells much of a process that had indeed led by 1941 to Leander's repositioning in film-aesthetic discourse as 'personality', not star. I have suggested that a repudiation of stardom's mass aesthetic of surface and show was achieved in *Premiere* by Leander's visual detachment within the *mise en scène*, and the concentration of spectatorial attention therefore on her singing voice. Her later films for Ufa continued to explore the tension in Leander's star persona between image and voice. On the one hand, Ufa invested much in Leander's visual construction after 1937 as 'not just a star, but *the* star' of Third Reich film.[30] The Ufa publicity chief Carl Opitz, orchestrated an extensive media campaign that paved the way for Leander's runaway success in *Zu neuen Ufern* and subsequent titles, while Franz Weihmayr, a seasoned cinematographer who worked on all of Leander's Ufa films, collaborated with Ufa costume and make-up departments to model a diva image from Leander's face.

Of that face, Detlef Sierck had remarked that it had 'the same flat quality as the face of Garbo: … it's a feature of many Swedish women, and we young filmmakers called it a cow face because of its quiet eyes … and a tranquillity which made it curiously fascinating for the camera'.[31] To capture that fascination, Weihmayr made extensive use of star close-ups; yet his use of light, by contrast, recalled *Premiere*'s repudiation of surface glitter as a source of Leander's star allure. As noted in Chapter 4, German cinematographers were often reluctant to replicate the multiple lighting systems mobilised for Hollywood stars, and

Figure 26: lighting in *Zu neuen Ufern* (1937)

Weihmayr in particular was known for his canny use of 'numerous clever tricks' to reproduce Hollywood effects, but 'with the simplest of technical tools'.[32] Thus in *Zu neuen Ufern*, back, top and side lighting were combined with skilfully deployed props and costume accessories – a mirror, a lace fan, a flickering flame, a white veil – to create around Leander both the halo effect common to Hollywood stars and, across her face, enchanting filigrees of dappled light (Figure 26). For *La Habanera*, Weihmayr and Sierck relied similarly on make-up, costume and performance to enhance the effect of what was by Hollywood standards an often meagre lighting apparatus. Hence Leander's careful moves towards frontal light sources at moments of dramatic tension in the film – her first meeting with her future husband Don Pedro, for instance, when she tilts and turns her face into the light to allow the camera to register her emerging erotic desire.

Star lighting in Hollywood famously lent to the faces of Garbo, Dietrich and their contemporaries a shimmer that fractured the realism of the film image, and drew attention to the star as fabrication, surface image and show. In Leander's films, by contrast, the rejection of Hollywood star aesthetics in the visual construction of her screen image went hand in hand with a narrative repudiation of visual excess. The opening number of *Zu neuen Ufern*, Ralph Benatzky's 'Yes Sir!', features a Leander glittering in sexually suggestive lace crinoline, and dominating both the diegetic audience (the song is set in a studio reconstruction of the packed auditorium of London's Adelphi Theatre), and a film spectator to whom Detlef Sierck's suggestively roving camera displays every detail of her erotic charms.

The contrast with the closing song, *'Ich steh' im Regen/und warte auf Dich'* ('I Stand in the Rain/and Wait for You) could not be greater. Exhausted by a prison sojourn, and defeated in love, Leander delivers the song as a melancholy lament for possibilities now lost – including the possibilities for feminine self-fulfilment that she herself represented as the visually excessive Gloria Vane of the film's opening song. At the film's dénouement, concomitantly, a persona that circulates around visual pleasure is finally renounced, when Gloria/Leander embarks with palpable reticence on a marriage of convenience to Henry Hoyer (Viktor Staal) – an ideologically suitable, but romantically unpromising man of (Australian) blood and soil.

This masochistic narrative pattern of a voluntary denial of visual pleasure is repeated in *La Habanera* when, as the Swedish tourist on Puerto Rico, Astrée Stjernhelm, Leander falls in love with the figure her aunt and travelling companion terms a 'filthy Carib', Don Pedro (Ferdinand Marian), only to be finally rescued by the film's emblematic man of intellect, not image, Dr Sven Nagel (Karl Martell). In this film, moreover, a devotion to the image is implicitly racialised through the figure of Don Pedro, Leander's first object of desire. Marian's casting opposite Leander is interesting, since he represented precisely that mode of mass-cultural representation, which Leander's films ultimately deny. In the twenty-two films in which he starred between 1933 and 1945, Marian's star image increasingly came to circulate around his figuring as one of the Third Reich's prototypical racial others and screen villains. His Austrian accent, dark hair and eyes, and heavy features facilitated his casting as all-purpose alien, from white Russian emigré in *Ein Hochzeitstraum* (*Wedding Dream*, 1936), to French seducer of Pola Negri in *Madame Bovary* (1937), Puerto Rican baron in *La Habanera* (1937), then on – via an improbable casting as Scandinavian fur trapper in the unmemorable *Nordlicht* (*Northern Lights*, 1938) – to propaganda roles as British colonial master in *Der Fuchs von Glenarvon* (*The Fox of Glenarvon*, 1940), *Ohm Krüger* (1941), and of course as the Jew Josef Süss Oppenheimer in Veit Harlan's notorious *Jud Süss* (1940).

In *La Habanera*, Marian was cast, as ever, as ethnically marked villain – the corrupt and tyrannical Don Pedro. Importantly, moreover, here as elsewhere, Marian's racial transgression is closely associated with his commitment to visual excess. Thus, for instance, the film's first image of Don Pedro, a low-angle point-of-view shot from Astrée's perspective as he intervenes early in the film to rescue Astrée (Leander) and her aunt from an altercation with local police, allows Don Pedro to dominate the frame, resplendent in ornate costume and broad-brimmed hat (Figure 27). At the same time, Marian/Don Pedro's image is negatively coded, both by visual and verbal references to his identity as 'Carib', and by the signalling through flamboyant dress and, later, interior shots of the palatial fortress that is his ancestral home, of a penchant for luxury that, to quote one reviewer, contradicted the 'voice of the blood and the heart' that was ultimately to recall Astrée to her Swedish home.[33]

Marian's image in *La Habanera* both embodies, then, the aesthetic qualities Leander repudiates in *Premiere* and *Zu neuen Ufern* – mass-cultural commercialism, cosmopolitanism, erotic attraction, visual excess – and encodes them racially through the figuring of Don Pedro as Caribbean master of a Puerto Rican home. Contrast Leander's positioning within the visual and aural landscape of this film. On the one hand, her construction as Astrée draws on the conventional techniques of star representation, including extensive close-ups, as well as costume, make-up and lighting, to locate her as the film's primary source of visual allure. Her myriad costume changes in the film, moreover, suggest an ethnic fluidity that allows the star to shift from the braided hair and pith helmet of the Nordic-rationalist tourist, through the lace mantilla of the Puerto Rican bride, to the improbably exotic Hispanic/gypsy identity she assumes in her closing rendition of the film's title song.

Figure 27: Don Pedro (Ferdinand Marian) in *La Habanera* (1937)

The multidimensionality of Leander's image is countered, however, by her use of voice. Leander's first number in *La Habanera* is the 'snow song', a lyrical portrait of a Swedish snow scene, which she sings to evoke for her son, Juan, the cool beauty of her Scandinavian home. Leander/Astrée's dogged faith in her music's capacity to transcend the reality of the image is conveyed here by the scene's disjuncture between image and voice. Gazing wistfully across the semitropical environs of her marital home, Leander intones a song whose opening lines ('the whole garden is full of snow') and aesthetic structure – that of Romantic *lied,* not *habanera* – evoke a snowscape apparently more real to her than the visible landscape of her island home. That capacity of Leander's voice to root both singer and audience in the fantasised space of an originary (European, Germanic, racialised) identity is re-emphasised in her closing performance of the *habanera*. The island's Chief of Police misrecognises in her rendition a simulation of Caribbean identity when he declares 'never have I heard the *habanera* sung like this, not even by a native'. In fact, though, Leander's emphasis in her performance on the song's melody and expressive dynamics (the latter in its closing crescendo, for instance), locate her version of the *habanera* less in Cuban folk, than in that version of classical European musical tradition favoured by Nazi ideologues for its privileging of melody, tonality and harmony over the 'primitive' rhythms of folk or non-European dance.[34]

Unlike Marian, in sum, Leander demonstrates a proximity to *völkisch* values in *La Habanera* through a performance style that uses her singing voice to pierce the surface of the star image, presenting voice, not image, as the vehicle of the deepest of aesthetic, if not indeed racial truths.

HEIMAT (1938): LEANDER'S VOICE IN FLIGHT

If Leander's early Ufa films established her voice as the primary source of spectatorial pleasure, then it was her later films that began to establish her as a figure of sublimity in the *völkisch* sense I outlined in Chapter 4. The summer of 1938 brought a turning point in Leander's career. June 25 saw the premiere of *Heimat*, the first of three titles in which she was to star under the direction of that much-trumpeted master of the artistic film, Carl Froelich. As chairman of Ufa's artistic committee, NSDAP member, 'Professor' and future *Reich* Film Chamber president, Froelich lent to Leander's name a political legitimacy it could never have gained through her association with the more maverick, and (following his flight into exile) now officially discredited Detlef Sierck. *Heimat*, moreover, an adaptation of a Hermann Sudermann novel, began a process that was to shift Leander's star persona for the latter part of her Ufa career towards the personality aesthetic, and the musical sublime.

From *Heimat* on, Leander played a succession of diva figures celebrated for their fusion of highbrow musical cachet with popular acclaim: the international opera star Maddalena dall'Orto (*Heimat*); the high bourgeois grande dame and would-be operetta singer Ilona (*Der Blaufuchs*); the Tschaikovsky lover and muse Katya (*Es war eine rauschende Ballnacht*); Grace Collins, the singer-daughter of English colonial aristocrat Sir Herbert (*Das Lied der Wüste*); the eponymous heroine in Froelich's 1940 Mary Queen of Scots biopic *Das Herz der Königin* (*The Heart of the Queen*); and Hanna the variety diva in Leander's crowning Ufa success, *Die grosse Liebe* (*The Great Love*, 1942).

That this new image sat more comfortably with regime aspirations for a star aesthetic imbued with the values and affects of high bourgeois art is evident from the official tributes accorded to *Heimat* on its release. Credited as 'politically and artistically valuable', the film also won the coveted State Film Prize for 1938, and was hailed by critics as – to quote the *Berliner Lokal-Anzeiger* – a title '[whose] unity of form [*Guss*] and particular human stance, as well as its deployment of music and character development, are only thinkable in Germany ... a German film in the best sense of the word'.[35]

Heimat cast Leander in the role of 'Magda' (stage name Maddalena), a daughter disowned after a youthful affair, but redeemed when she returns from a brilliant American career to sing, among other pieces, an aria from that 'pinnacle of ... German culture', Bach's *St Matthew Passion*.[36] Reputed to have attended her first ever singing lessons for the part of Magda, Leander was rewarded with accolades for a vocal performance that was said to touch artistic heights hitherto unprecedented in German sound film. One review from the period is worth citing here at length, since it reproduces many of the central tropes of 'Zarah's' critical reception from *Heimat* on. In late 1937, the critic Hans-Joachim Schlamp visited the set of *Heimat* for a preview that included a live performance of Leander singing Bach, as well as a private viewing of the rushes for an aria from Gluck's *Orpheus and Eurydice*, the latter screened for Schlamp in the company of the film's musical director, Theo Mackeben. In his account of that experience, Schlamp first notes how Leander's voice has been the defining attribute of her German stardom from the mid-1930s on. Her chansons from *Axel an der Himmelstür*, he notes, 'were sung all around Vienna's streets and squares, and gramophone records soon arrived in Germany'. Concluding that 'strange as it may sound, Zarah Leander's voice was known well before her first photographs arrived in Germany', Schlamp notes of her Austrian film *Premiere* – which he otherwise dismisses as a thriller 'of no particular beauty' – that it nonetheless cemented Leander's reputation for artistic merit. He quotes in this connection one Vienna critic who, as unmoved as Schlamp himself claimed to be by the film's handling of narrative and image, resolves instead to close his eyes and 'listen only to ... a voice that seethes and burns like fire, deep and unfathomable ... [only to be] borne aloft by primitive forces'.[37]

The *Premiere* review foreshadows many in its deployment of spatial metaphors to capture the specific qualities of Leander's singing voice. Here is Schlamp again, this time relating his experiences of Leander's voice on the *Heimat* set. On the *St Matthew Passion*, he rhapsodises: 'her voice ... swells, its notes rising in untrammelled passion like a flock of liberated birds: a writhing lament that swirls stormily upwards, then suddenly falls back, plunging into the depths, bending in humility, and fading away.' Of Leander's voice in 'Orpheus', Schlamp records in similar vein that it

> flow[s] across the room like an expansive stream, sweeping along everything in its path, bubbling forth freely and easily from within her ... Then we find ourselves standing again in the body of the cathedral, looking up to the gallery, hearing the choir singing and the organ play. Once again Zarah Leander's powerful voice rings out across the studio. 'Reu und Buss' ... the prodigious sound of a last, threatening warning.[38]

Metaphors of flight, images of a voice disembodied, detached from the image ('I close my eyes'), then propelled through space by 'primitive forces': these discursive figures, recurrent in Leander reviews, will be shown in Chapter 7 to situate Leander's voice as a vehicle of that very specific mode of sublime experience delivered to cinema audiences, I shall suggest, through their cinematic encounter with world war. But let us look first more closely at the ways in which Leander's cinematic treatment in her Ufa titles laid the foundations for an association of Leander's voice with the experience of war. They did so, I want to suggest, by increasingly foregrounding her voice's transcendent quality, its capacity to traverse the space of narrative and explode into untrammelled flight.

MUSICAL GENRE

The relation between Leander's voice and spatial transcendence was evident in three significant aspects of her voice as deployed in her Ufa films. The first aspect relates to Leander's capacity to range across multiple musical genres and styles. In the opening number of *Zu neuen Ufern*, 'Yes Sir!', the star deploys what will become a characteristically broad spectrum of singing styles as she moves from the melodic (the operetta-style trills of the song's opening lines), through the declamatory or cabarettistic (when she speaks or shouts the 'Yes, Sir!' of the refrain), to the song's *faux* operatic dénouement in a triumphant 'Halleluya!' This stylistic eclecticism was to become a hallmark of Leander's singing. Among the thirty or so hit songs that emerged from 'Zarah's' six-year Ufa career, the critic Ulrike Sanders identifies stylistic influences ranging from European operetta or classical tradition (Sanders counts eight *Lieder*, five waltzes, and one march), to such distinctly profane modern sources as Euro-American jazz (the foxtrot was Leander's favourite), Latin-American tango and *habanera*, or central European folk and/or gypsy dance (the polka, and the *csárdás*, the latter in Tourjansky's *Der Blaufuchs*, 1938).[39] The spatial mobility suggested by Leander's songs – their internationalism, as well as their effortless shifts across boundaries between high culture and low – was accentuated in her two Sierck films by her visual treatment in song. In *Zu neuen*'s 'Yes, Sir!', for example, vertiginous pans and tilts, coupled with rhythmic editing, dynamise the space around the star, accentuating her voice's liquid quality, its capacity to flow through space and envelop its audience on- and offscreen in pleasurable sound. Similarly, in the *habanera* that she performs in the film of that name – 'Der Wind hat mir ein Lied erzählt' ('The Wind has Told Me a Song') – a slow pan across a rapt onscreen audience heightens the foreboding that emanates both from the song's lyrics (the 'wind' of the title will shortly reveal itself as the bearer of a putrid fever from which her husband will die), and from Leander's *rubato* delivery, as her slow phrasing cuts across the dance rhythms of the *habanera*, lending the song the quality not of dance, but of agonising lament.[40] Here, moreover – as frequently in the low-tempo moments that punctuate even the most upbeat of Leander's songs – her low pitch produces a resonance that allows her voice to traverse and fill both the diegetic space, and the cinema auditorium (of which latter more below).

THE DISEMBODIED VOICE

A second feature of Sierck's handling of Leander's voice relates similarly to its fracturing and/or extension of cinematic space. When sound cinema first emerged in the late 1920s, debate on the new medium was polarised between the realists, who favoured a naturalistic treatment of sound – dialogue or song that was largely synchronous with the image, and emanated from objects perceptible within the camera frame – and modernist or avant-garde practitioners keen to explore the aesthetic possibilities of image/sound asynchronicity, including by exploiting the potential of offscreen sound. That debate was spurred throughout the early 1930s by advances in film sound technology, beginning with the development of smaller and more mobile microphones, and recording equipment that extended the range of volume and frequency that could be captured for reproduction on film. Editing techniques, too, were gradually enhanced by new mixing units for soundtracks, and sophisticated synchronising devices that extended the aesthetic choices available in determining the relation between sound and image in the finished film.[41]

As Wolfgang Mühl-Benninghaus has noted, the realists triumphed, at least in narrative film, deploying the new technologies to enhance the authenticity and proximity to 'Nature' of cinematic sound.[42] A signal exception, however, in Germany as elsewhere, was the musical genre, which – as observed by one contemporary commentator on the 'creative' potential of sound film technology – reversed the aesthetic hierarchy of a realist cinema that privileged image and narrative over sound, operating instead in a mode in which 'music becomes content', and the image a mere 'visionary accompaniment' to recorded sound.[43]

Detlef Sierck's deployment of Leander's voice in his musical melodramas locates those films within this latter, tendentially modernist mode. Leander's second number in *Zu neuen Ufern*, 'Ich steh' im Regen' ('I Stand in the Rain'), was post-synchronised for a scene depicting Gloria/Leander at the farewell party that presages the departure for Australia of her lover, Finsbury. In a song dripping with the pathos of parting and loss, Leander's voice derives melodramatic intensity from the use of close sound, and the absence of ambient noise. Once synchronised with the image, the song also breaks the film's realism, not only by blending out the idle chatter of party guests, but by its antagonistic relation to the sequence's visual representation of narrative space. While the film crosscuts at the level of the image between two spaces of action, the parlour where Leander performs, and her host's study – the scene of an altercation between Finsbury and 'Pudding', the friend whom he will shortly defraud to the tune of £600 – the volume of her voice remains unchanged. Detached here from the narrative, it becomes instead a transcendent presence that dominates both narrative spaces in equal measure, and fractures the Aristotelian unity of place that is the *sine qua non* of realism in theatre and film. This figuring of Leander's voice as a spatially dislocated, phantom or uncanny presence is reinforced later in the film, first when Finsbury's new lover, Mary, unwittingly conjures up her rival's spectre when she tinkles her way through a piano rendering of 'Yes, Sir!'; and second – more ominously – when the voice returns to superimpose itself on images of a now distraught Finsbury, who has learned too late of Gloria's self-sacrifice, and who will shortly be driven to kill himself in a final gesture of guilty humiliation and shame.

In her important essay on 'The Voice in the Cinema', Mary Ann Doane offers perspectives on the relation between voice and cinematic space that are illuminating here. Noting how, in the transition to sound, filmic techniques including the manipulation of room tone, reverberation and sound perspective were developed 'to spatialize the voice, to localize it, give it depth', Doane goes on to identify three spaces relevant to the cinematic treatment of voice: the 'space of the diegesis', the 'visible space of the screen', and the 'acoustical space of the theater or auditorium'.[44] Doane's further contention that 'the voice is frequently related to the body as a form of narrative closure' is, moreover, pertinent to an extent to an analysis of Leander in her Ufa films. The visual figuring of

Leander as singing body, and her narrative positioning as, variously, revue or opera diva, recording artiste and music-hall star, reproduce in her 1930s films that 'image of corporeal unity' between body and voice that Doane suggests is a key source of the 'auditory pleasure' that early sound cinema evokes. The harmonious integration of spectator and film text through the fixing of voice to body image within diegetic and visual space is reinforced, moreover, in Leander's case, by her voice's capacity for depth and resonance: qualities that embrace the cinema audience within the 'sonorous envelope' identified by Doane within the auditorium or film theatre as the third space of articulation between body and voice.[45]

First published in 1980, Doane's account, however, shares with other structuralist film analyses of its period a privileging of narrative cinema that renders it only partially applicable in Leander's case. Doane's focus is on the voice in dialogue in narrative film; a voice she sees, even in the apparently disembodied form of the voice-over, as 'submitted to the destiny of the body' (Pascal Bonitzer) because it '*belongs* to a character who is confined to the space of the diegesis, if not the visible space of the screen'.[46] Leander's *singing* voice, by contrast (and this is indeed a genre characteristic of the musical's use of voice in song), breaks the link between body and voice, both by a spatial treatment that ruptures their unity, and by a textual structure that situates the musical number, not the narrative, as the fulcrum of dramatic development.

VOICE IN THE CINEMATIC PUBLIC SPHERE

Leander's success as a musical star depended, then, on a detachment of her voice from her body image on film: a fracturing of the unity between image and sound that was the prerequisite for what Schlamp and other contemporaries described as her voice's capacity for explosion into flight. That splintering of the unity of image, body and voice in Leander's films becomes yet more evident if we consider a third space of cinematic representation that is not discussed by Doane, but that is surely pivotal to the more historically grounded account of acoustic aesthetics and spectatorship that I am attempting here.

In an essay contemporaneous with Doane's, but written from within feminist film history, not textual theory, Miriam Hansen drew on Oskar Negt and Alexander Kluge's writings on the public sphere to develop an account of cinema (in her case, of early German film) as a socio-cultural as well as a textual space: a domain therefore in which the 'raw material of human experience' is worked on and transformed through the operation of those apparatuses, institutions and practices that constitute the broader 'public sphere' of film-cultural representation. While concurring with the exponents of textual apparatus theory à la Doane that the film medium's historical development involved a 'systematic improvement of cinematic techniques' – an improvement that guarantees what Doane terms the 'unity', or, in Hansen's terms, the 'absorption of the spectator into the fictional world of the film' – Hansen insists that such integration be seen as the product of socio-cultural as well as textual forces: of changing exhibition practices, shifting mass markets, larger shifts in the understanding of the 'public' in mass-cultural modernity – in Hansen's case study, shifts that arise for instance via the drive for gender equality, or via cinema reform debates on mass-cultural taste, and whose specific contours must be traced in detail if we are to comprehend film's historical relationship to the cinema experience and to spectatorship.[47]

Though not explicitly indebted to Hansen, recent historians of Third Reich film have similarly stressed the importance to Nazi film culture of what Goebbels termed the 'orchestra principle': a principle which Eric Rentschler, for instance, sees embodied in the 'orchestrated diversions (radio programs, mass rallies, gigantic spectacles, holidays and commemorations)' that pervaded everyday life under National Socialism, and situated Third Reich films within that wider experiential domain which Hansen terms the cinematic 'public sphere'.[48] In the case of Zarah Leander, there are compelling historical reasons to argue that it was within that sphere that her voice began to operate as that pervasive, disembodied or phantom acoustic presence that I will later call sublime. The dispersal of Leander's voice into public space occurred from the late 1930s on through the operation of (at least) two mass-cultural apparatuses of representation: genre, and popular music, the latter in its manifestation as the *Schlager*, a nationally specific mode of commercial popular song.

Genre

In 1930s German understandings of the musical genre, both the film operetta and the so-called *Schlagerfilm* (a vehicle for mass musical hits whose narrative links to the film text were minimal at best) were excoriated by some precisely for that dislocation of musical performance from the film text, which I have presented as a characteristic of Leander's films. Hence, to cite one symptomatic critique, Joseph Gregor's denunciation of the *Schlagerfilm* for its rupturing of that 'higher unity' between sound and image which, for him, constitutes the bedrock of film aesthetics in the era of sound.[49]

Recognising the dangers of associating Leander – the jewel in the crown of the Ufa star stable – with the *Schlagerfilm*'s reputation for kitsch aesthetics and lowbrow taste, her directors, Froelich in particular, attempted a positioning of the star within the revue genre (*Zu neuen Ufern, Die grosse Liebe*), the musical melodrama (*La Habanera, Der Blaufuchs*), or the so-called *Musikfilm*, the latter a sub-genre distunguished from the *Schlagerfilm* by a symphonic dramaturgy that supplanted narrative with music as the source of an aesthetic unity between voice and body, image and sound. Thus in his *Musikfilm*, *Es war eine rauschende Ballnacht*, for instance, Carl Froelich structures the opening sequences visually and narratively around successive arrangements of Tchaikovsky compositions. Here, a combination of diegetic and extra-diegetic music function contrapuntally with dialogue to develop the film's unfolding biographical narrative, to introduce its main protagonists, and to locate Tchaikovsky's music as the organising principle that structures editing, actorly performance and dramatic composition in the film.

Even Froelich's doggedly cohesive textual construction falters, however, at the climactic moment of Leander's vocal performance in the film. In the role of Katya, Tchaikovsky's fictional lover-turned-anonymous-patron, Leander is figured giving an impromptu performance for her much-loathed husband Michael (Aribert Wäscher) and assembled guests at a *soirée* on the eve of Tchaikovsky's wedding to Katya's rival in love, Natascha (Marika Rökk). Unaware of Katya's amorous attachment to the composer, the guests clamour for a rendering of a Tchaikovsky song. 'Katya' refuses, and chooses instead her own 'song of love', the Theo Mackeben composition and enduring Leander hit, '*Nur nicht aus Liebe weinen*' ('Don't Cry for Love').[50]

Though integrated narratively into the body of the film through its mirroring of Katya's own predicament – her loveless marriage, her estrangement from Tchaikovsky – the song's mix of Russian folk musical style with Weimar *chanson* sits uneasily with the Tchaikovsky compositions that structure the opening of the film. The number marks a generic shift of *Es war eine*, in other words, however briefly, into proximity with the *Schlagerfilm*. This genre slippage from *Musikfilm* or revue to *Schlagerfilm* was, moreover, evident on other occasions in Leander's early Ufa films. In *Zu neuen Ufern*, for instance, awkward edits and barely credible narrative motivation (the song's implausible figuring as a worksong accompanying basketweaving activities among prison inmates) situate one number, '*Ich sehn' mich nach Dir*' ('I Long for You'), at an uneasy tangent to the film narrative. Crasser still is the disjunction in *Der Blaufuchs*, or in *La Habanera*, between visual style and character development in the body of the film, and the contrived staging and studied performance that characterise the films' rendering of their major Leander hits, '*Der Wind hat mir ein Lied erzählt*' ('The Wind has Told Me a Song') (*La Habanera*) or '*Auf der Puszta will ich träumen*' ('I Long to Dream on the Puszta' (*Der Blaufuchs*).

Popular music: the *Schlager*

It is in these moments of stylistic fracture that Leander's voice begins to detach itself from the diegetic and visual spaces of the film text, and to assume the identity it possesses within the public space of mass culture as a disembodied acoustic presence. For if the first apparatus of representation that displaces Leander's voice from its location in the individual film text is genre, then the second is the culture of the *Schlager*, or hit song itself as it developed within the popular music industry in tandem with sound film.

Historians have often highlighted Zarah Leander's significance as a model case of National Socialism's exploitation of the interpenetration of mass-produced popular music and sound film. Lutz Koepnick, for example, notes that Leander's songs were usually broadcast on radio weeks before their film premiere: a marketing strategy already common in the early sound era, but that was refined after 1933 with the spread of radio to allow such figures as Leander, as Koepnick puts it, to 'enter German hearts and minds through ... performance on screen as much as over the *Volksempfänger*'.[51] Leander herself points out in her autobiography that her recording career began well before her appearances on German screens. A 'lifelong' contract to the Odeon recording studios began in Sweden in 1930; Leander earned her first royalties from foreign sales during her Vienna season in *Axel an der Himmelstür*, months before shooting began for her first German-language film, *Premiere*; and she herself commented on her film career that, even were she to remain, in her capacity as film star, a mere 'footnote' to film history, she would be 'truly saddened' were future historians to 'forget or obscure' the memory of her voice, her musical performances and her much-loved hit songs.[52]

Leander's ubiquity in popular music has led existing critics to attribute to her voice – much as I have done above – a specific geographical extensiveness, a capacity, via technologies of sound reproduction, to traverse social, symbolic and physical space. Brian Currid, for instance, situates Leander's voice as the emblem of what he terms a 'national acoustic', the *sound* of a nation, as embodied in the voice one of its most enduring singing stars.[53] Certainly, this was indeed in part Leander's function, in particular (as Currid also notes) in those recurrent musical passages in her films when she leads a male chorus, often a soldier audience, in vigorous renderings of popular hymns to national community and collective strength. Thus, for instance, Leander's rendering in *Die grosse Liebe* of the rousing 'Davon geht die Welt nicht unter' ('Not the End of the World') engenders in both the diegetic audience (the soldiers who join her in song), and in the audience in the cinema auditorium and beyond, an 'affective and temporal experience' of that mode of collective belonging associated under National Socialism with nation and *Volk* (Figure 28).

Writing in a different context, however, Currid himself has analysed the *Schlager* as a form that is more ambiguously situated in relation to discourses of nation. Underlining the *Schlager*'s transnationalism, its construction of

Figure 28: 'Davon geht die Welt nicht unter' – *Die grosse Liebe* (1942)

audiences that are as dispersed geographically as their musical consumption is temporally asynchronous, Currid concludes of the early twentieth-century *Schlager* that it represented a transformation 'on a *global* scale' of popular experiences of space, time, and the acoustic aesthetic.[54] Currid derives that perception from his analysis of a 1933 Richard Oswald title, *Ein Lied geht um die Welt* (*A Song Goes Round the World*), a musical which reproduced both in its *mise en scène* (including its Venice setting), and in its casting of the popular radio tenor Joseph Schmidt in its leading role, that association of the *Schlager* with transnational travel, which Currid claims is a feature of modern popular song.

In Leander's films, the same association of song with travel is evident. Recurrent in her Ufa films, for instance, is a tourist motif that takes her first, as the Swedish tourist Astrée, to Puerto Rico, later to a sand-swept sojourn in the North African milieu that she inhabits briefly in the period of her 'desert song' (*Das Lied der Wüste*). Equally prominent is an association between Leander's songs, and modern technologies of spatial displacement – the boats, planes and automobiles that figure in all her films from *Zu neuen Ufern* onwards. Leander's rendering of *La Habanera*'s 'The Wind has Told Me a Song' is foreshadowed for instance when she is treated to an improbably operatic rendering of the song by an indigenous taxi driver, his eyes disconcertingly turned to his backseat passengers as his car speeds across the landscape of his island home. *Das Lied der Wüste* cements the connection between technologies of modernity (in *La Habanera*'s case, back projections of 'Puerto Rico'), modern transport, and Leander's voice in song with an opening image of an airborne Grace Collins (Leander), resplendent in pilot's goggles, and negotiating her landing in the North African desert to the accompaniment of a gramophone record playing one of her own popular hits.

Through its relation to technologies of sound reproduction in the popular music industry, as well as through Leander's visual and narrative encoding with touristic travel, her voice, in sum is released into a mass-cultural public space that is, importantly, potentially limitless, and certainly unbounded by the spatial constraints of nation. How then, finally, does this relate to Leander's place within Third Reich film aesthetics as a figure, I have suggested, of the post-Kantian sublime?

NOTES

1. Heinz C., Letter to Marlene Dietrich, Marlene Dietrich Collection, fan mail, no ref.

2. Sabine Hake, *Popular Cinema of the Third Reich* (Austin: University of Texas Press, 2001), p. 77. Hake's chapter on 'Film Audiences and the Problem of Spectatorship' provides the most comprehensive account to date of Third Reich audience reception studies. Anna and Joachim Paech's *Menschen im Kino. Film und Literatur erzählen*, (Stuttgart: Metzler, 2000), also provides some useful pointers towards literary and autobiographical sources: see especially Chapter 11.

3. Goebbels' speech in the Berlin Kaiserhof, 28 March 1933. Reproduced in full in Gerd Albrecht, *Nationalsozialistische Filmpolitik. Eine soziologische Untersuchung über die Spielfilme des Dritten Reichs* (Stuttgart: Ferdinand Enke, 1969), pp. 439ff.

4. See Helmut Asper, *Etwas Besseres als den Tod . . .'. Filmexil in Hollywood. Porträts, Filme, Dokumente* (Marburg: Schüren, 2002), pp. 15ff, and Jan-Christopher Horak, *Fluchtpunkt Hollywood. Eine Dokumentation zur Filmemigration nach 1933* (Munich: MaKs, 1986), second edition, pp. 6ff. Among the audience favourites already exiled by January 1936 (the launch year of Dietrich's *Desire*) were the cabaret-artiste-turned-film-actress Rosa Valetti, who played alongside Dietrich in *The Blue Angel* as Guste the backstage manageress; the Austrian-born Luise Rainer, who was to make her mark internationally when she won two consecutive Oscars for her roles in *The Great Ziegfeld* (Robert Z. Leonard, 1936) and *The Good Earth* (Sidney Franklin, 1937); the theatre and film diva Elisabeth Bergner, whose rival portrayal of Dietrich's 'scarlet Empress', the Korda production *Catherine the Great*, appeared simultaneously with von Sternberg's film, and two years after Bergner's emigration to London; the singer Richard Tauber, who

dubbed the voice of Harry Liedtke for the title number in Dietrich's first excursion into sound film, *Ich küsse Ihre Hand, Madame/I Kiss Your Hand, Madame* (Robert Land, 1929); *M* star Peter Lorre; Weimar heartthrob Conrad Veidt; and many more. For biographical details of these and other émigrés, see Alastair Phillips and Ginette Vincendeau (eds), *Journeys of Desire. European Actors in Hollywood* (London: BFI, forthcoming).

5. References to 'politeness' abound, as for instance in *Filmwelt* (FW) 5, 2 February 1936: 'Artists do generally give autographs, if they are sent in with a brief and *polite* request, together with a postcard and stamped addressed envelope.' (My emphasis.)

6. Reply to R. Sch., Dresden, FW, 19 January 1936.

7. Reply to R. K., Weinheim, FW, 26 January 1936.

8. Letter on Martha Eggerth to H.R., Oberhausen, and on Adolf Wohlbrück to C.M.G., Chemnitz, FW, 2 February 1936.

9. Reply to Anon., Lankwitz 111, FW, 2 February 1936.

10. Reply to 'Filmfreundin Paula', FW, 19 January 1936. Other quotations are stock responses used repeatedly in notices to fans in FW issues from January and February 1936.

11. The source in Freud for this account of the double is his 1919 essay, 'The Uncanny', in Sigmund Freud, *Art and Literature*, James Strachey (ed.), Alix Strachey (trans.) (Harmondsworth: Penguin, 1985), pp. 335–75. Early psychoanalysis' account of the double was developed with specific relation to cinema in Otto Rank, 'Der Doppelgänger', in idem, *Psychoanalytische Beiträge zur Mythenforschung* (Leipzig and Vienna: Internationaler Psychoanalytischer Verlag, 1919), pp. 267–354.

12. 'Doppelgängerin Marlene Dietrichs in Neubabelsberg', *Film-Kurier* (FK), 11 December 1937.

13. 'Tip auf ein wirkliches Talent,' *Hamburger Tageblatt* (HT), 15 July 1939.

14. Ibid. For other references to actresses now forgotten, but once tipped as possible successors to more illustrious forbears, see, for example, Käthe Brinker's account of one Charlotte Gerda as Garbo's double: Brinker, *Nordische Filmsterne. Zarah Leander, Kristina Söderbaum, Ingrid Bergmann* (sic), *Greta Garbo* (Berlin: Mölich, 1938 , p. 21; and on the 'expatriate German' (*auslandsdeutsche*) newcomer Angela Salloker as a 'new partner' to Emil Jannings (and in this sense a successor to Dietrich), see Hans-Joachim Schlamp, *Willy Birgel spielt mit Zarah Leander, Angela Salloker, Brigitte Helm* (Berlin: Mölich, 1937), p. 17.

15. 'Lehrschau der Ufa eröffnet', FK, 31 July 1936.

16. Söderbaum was awarded her first Ufa role in Erich Waschneck's *Onkel Bräsig* (1936) after winning a talent competition in Berlin; the Czech actress Baarova was recruited for Ufa by the studio's overseas director in Czechoslovakia; and Marika Rökk was spotted in 1933 by Ufa talent scouts in Budapest.

17. Karsten Witte, *Lachende Erben, Toller Tag* (Berlin: Vorwerk 8, 1995), p. 112.

18. Zarah Leander, *Es war so wunderbar! Mein Leben* (Frankfurt am Main: Ullstein, 1984, orig. 1973), p. 77.

19. Ibid., p. 120.

20. '*Kinostar!*', lyrics: Hans Weigel, music: Ralph Benatzky, 1936.

21. 'Reproducibility' is a more accurate rendering of the original German *Reproduzierbarkeit* than 'reproduction', though the latter term has become standard. See Walter Benjamin, 'The Work of Art in the Age of Mechanical Reproduction', in idem, *Illuminations*, Harry Zohn (trans.) Hannah Arendt (ed.) (London: Fontana, 1973), pp. 211–44.

22. Knut Hickethier, 'Vom Theaterstar zum Filmstar. Merkmale des Starwesens um die Wende vom neunzehnten zum zwanzigsten Jahrhundert', in Werner Faulstich and Helmut Korte (eds), *Der Star. Geschichte, Rezeption, Bedeutung* (Munich: Fink, 1997), pp. 45–6.

23. Minutes of Ufa board, 10 November, 1936, BA R109/1031b 1195; see also Memorandum to Klitzsch, 8 August 1939, BA R109 I 2874, for a breakdown of Leander's actual and projected fees from 1937–9.

24. Lutz Koepnick, *The Dark Mirror. German Cinema between Hitler and Hollywood* (Berkeley and Los Angeles: University of California Press, 2002), pp. 81–2.

25. Siegfried Kracauer, 'Cult of Distraction', in idem, *The Mass Ornament. Weimar Essays*, Thomas Levin (trans. and ed.) (Cambridge, MA and London: Harvard University Press, 1995), p. 326.

26. Cited in Leander, *Es war so wunderbar!*, p. 115.

27. *Berliner Lokalanzeiger* (BLA), n.d., cited in Paul Seiler, *Zarah Leander. Ich bin eine Stimme* (Berlin: Ullstein, 1997), p. 34.

28. Immanuel Kant, *Critique of the Power of Judgement*, Paul Guyer (trans. and ed.) and Eric Matthews (trans.) (Cambridge: Cambridge University Press, 2000, orig. 1790), p. 141.

29. *Wegena*: letter to Zarah Leander, 24 March 1941: BA R109 I 2874.

30. Cornelia Zumkeller, *Zarah Leander. ihre Filme – ihr Leben* (Munich: Heyne, 1991), p. 70.

31. Detlef Sierck, cited, n.d., n.s., in ibid., p. 74. See also Leander, *Es war so wunderbar!*, p. 145.

32. Heinz Umbehr, 'Aufnahmetechnik neuer Filme. *Hermine und die Sieben Aufrechten*' Filmtechnik (FT), 26 January 1935, p. 13.

33. S. Pfankuch, 'Im Schloße Don Pedros de Avila', *Filmwoche* (FLW), 8 December 1937.

34. See Michael Meyer, *The Politics of Music in the Third Reich* (New York: Peter Lang, 1991), especially pp. 253ff.

35. Felix A. Dargel, 'Heimat im Ufa-Palast. Begeisterter Beifall für einen grossen

Film', BLA, 2 November 1938. Reproduced in Gerd Albrecht (ed.), *Die grossen Filmerfolge Vom Blauen Engel bis Otto, der Film. Die erfolgreichsten Filme vom Beginn des Tonfilms bis heute* (Ebersberg: Edition Achteinhalb, 1985), p. 32.

36. See Celia Applegate, 'Bach Revival, Public Culture, and National Identity. The *St. Matthew Passion* in 1829', in Scott Denham, Irene Kacandes and Jonathan Petropulos (eds), *A User's Guide to German Cultural Studies* (Ann Arbor: University of Michigan Press, 1997), p. 142. Applegate here charts the revival of the piece as part of a larger, early nineteenth-century effort to establish the specificity of a German national identity, a process in which, as she convincingly demonstrates, what she terms German 'musiconationalism' played a significant role.

37. Quote from anon., n.d., n.s., in Schlamp, *Willy Birgel*, p. 12.

38. Schlamp, *Willy Birgel*, pp. 11–14.

39. Ulrike Sanders, *Zarah Leander – Kann denn Schlager Sünde sein?* (Cologne: Pahl-Rugenstein, 1988), pp. 34–9. See also Koepnick, *The Dark Mirror*, pp. 82–4.

40. The term *'rubato'* refers to performances that depart from the music's prescribed tempo in order to enhance its expressive quality.

41. See Alfred Schneider, 'Zehn Jahre deutscher Tonfilm', FT, 16 September 1933, pp. 209–11.

42. Wolfgang Mühl-Benninghaus, *Das Ringen um den Tonfilm. Strategien der Elektro- und der Filmindustrie in den 20er und 30er Jahren* (Düsseldorf: Droste, 1999), p. 232; see also E. von Löhlöffel, 'Schöpferische Mitarbeit der Tonfilmtechnik', *Der Film* (FL), 9 May 36, pp. 87–8.

43. Von Löhlöffel., 'Schöpferische Mitarbeit', pp. 87–8.

44. Mary Ann Doane, 'The Voice in the Cinema. The Articulation of Body and Space', in Leo Braudy and Marshall Cohen (eds), *Film Theory and Criticism. Introductory Readings* (Oxford and New York: Oxford University Press, 1999), fifth edition pp. 364 and 366.

45. Ibid., p. 368.

46. Ibid., p. 366. Doane's quote from Bonitzer is her translation of a passage in his 'Les silences de la voix', *Cahiers du Cinéma,* February–March 1975, p. 25.

47. Miriam Hansen, 'Early Cinema – Whose Public Sphere', in Thomas Elsaesser and Adam Barker (eds), *Early Cinema. Space, Frame, Narrative* (London: BFI, 1990), pp. 228–46.

48. Eric Rentschler, *The Ministry of Illusion. Nazi Cinema and its Afterlife* (Cambridge, MA and London: Harvard University Press, 1996), p. 20.

49. Joseph Gregor, *Das Zeitalter des Films* (Vienna and Leipzig: Reinhold, 1932), second edition, p. 124: see also Bruno Rehlinger, *Der Begriff Filmisch* (Emsdetten: Lechte, 1938), p. 36.

50 Translation of Zarah Lerander's, *'Nur nicht aus Liebe weinen'* (*Es war eien rauschende Ballnacht*, 1939)

It really doesn't matter who we love
And who ends up breaking our hearts
We are tossed on the winds of fate
and the result is always sacrifice.
We believe and we hope and we think
That one day there will be a miracle.
But when we finally give ourselves away
It's the same old story

(Refrain)
Don't cry for love.
There's more than one man on this earth.
There are so many men in the world.
I love any man who pleases me.
And so today, I want to belong to you,
And you must swear to love me and be faithful
Even if I know it's a lie
I shall lie too – and be yours.

We came from the South and the North
With hearts so silent and stange,
And so I became yours,
though I can't tell you why.
For when I lost myself to you
I was thinking of another
So the lie was born
that very first night.

51. Koepnick, *The Dark Mirror*, p. 83. On media cross-fertilisation in the early 1930s, see Wolfgang Mühl-Benninghaus, *Das Ringen um den Tonfilm*.
52. Leander, *Es war so wunderbar!*, pp. 60, 124 and 147.
53. Brian Currid, ' 'Es war so wunderbar!' Zarah Leander, ihre schwulen Fans, und die Gegenöffentlichkeit der Erinnerung', *montage a/v*, vol. 7, no. 1, 1998, pp. 57–94.
54. Brian Currid, ' "A song goes round the world": the German *Schlager*, as an organ of experience', *Popular Music*, vol. 19, no. 2, 2000, p. 149. My emphasis.

7

Leander as Sublime Object

Let us return one last time to Kant. It is in his observations on the sublime that Kant's writings resonate most strongly with those late 1930s cinematic discourses that situated Leander's voice as the vehicle of a potentially limitless spectatorial pleasure. In the *Critique of Judgement*, Kant distinguishes as follows between the qualities of the beautiful and the sublime: 'The beautiful in nature concerns the form of the object, which consists in limitation; the sublime, by contrast, is to be found in a formless object, insofar as *limitlessness* is represented in it, or at its instance.'[1]

Elsewhere in the *Critique*, Kant reinforces the association between the sublime and boundlessness when he stresses not only the 'formlessness' that can be attributed to 'that which we call sublime', but also its 'immeasurable' quality, its magnitude, its evocation of what he calls the 'idea of infinity'.[2] The sublime, then, is distinguished from the beautiful by precisely that capacity for limitlessness which Leander's voice apparently displayed in its aptitude for border-crossing of both a symbolic and a topographical kind. Third Reich commentary on Marlene Dietrich, as we saw in Chapter 5, attributed to her image a range of aesthetic qualities – its formal perfecion, its inner authenticity, etc. – that (allegedly) contained that image within the boundaries of the beautiful as one desired quality within Third Reich star aesthetics. Is it the case, then, as I have implied so far, that Leander is distinguished from Dietrich by a displacement from image to voice that situates her, not as icon of 'beautiful' form, but, by virtue of her voice's capacity for boundlessness, as a vehicle of the Kantian sublime?

Not quite. Throughout the third *Critique*, Kant refuses any account of the sublime, or indeed the beautiful, in terms of formal properties considered inherent in the aesthetic object itself. Even formlessness, he reminds us, is a formal property of a given object, insofar as it is by reference to form (even if only by its absence) that formlessness is recognised as the characteristic quality of any given object of aesthetic pleasure. The beautiful and the sublime, Kant by contrast insists, are experiential, not formal phenomena: experiences that derive from the mind's capacity to transform an encounter with, say, formless objects, into an idea of the boundlessness that is embodied (or perhaps more accurately, disembodied) in the sublime. To put this another way, an experience of the sublime is possible only through the mobilisation of the *subjectivity* of the spectator: a deployment of her/his imaginative powers in a way that permits consciousness 'to occupy itself with *ideas*' (ideas of boundlessness, ineffability, infinity) that contain that 'higher purposiveness' evoked by the sublime.[3]

WAR AND THE SUBLIME

At various points in this book, I have discussed those Weimar cultural theorists – in particular Siegfried Kracauer – whose materialist re-readings of Kant led them to conceptualise modern film culture as a set of practices and institutions whose specificity was located primarily in new modes of spectatorship and reception. Following Kant, in other words, they located the aesthetic not in film as cultural object, but in subjectivity – though this was not, of course, the transcendental subjectivity of the Kantian model, but a radically historicised subjectivity understood as produced in a determinate and specific context of film reception. Hence Kracauer's focus, for instance, on distraction as a perceptual practice particular to mass-cultural modernity, or on exhibition space (the 'mass-ornamental' quality that characterised not only the film text, but the Weimar film palace) as a key location for Weimar modernity's broader transformation of film spectatorship.[4] The National Socialists, I have contended, became, paradoxically, the heirs to Weimar Marxism's materialist development of Kant when they embarked after 1933 on a programme not primarily for the analysis of the cinema aesthetic, but for a material transformation of that aesthetic through practices of reception that would – they hoped – relocate film as an aesthetic vehicle for the experience of the Kantian beautiful and/or the sublime.

In this context, Leander's voice could be identified as sublime not merely through the 'boundless' qualities evoked by its acoustic form (its depth, its resonance, its use of radio and gramophone to gain unlimited passage across mass-cultural public space), but rather, through its embedding in a reception context that produced in the listener an association between Leander's acoustic 'boundlessness', and other modes of 'sublime' experience with which her voice (literally) resonated. Of particular interest here are those Leander titles whose launch coincided with a disconcerting shift in German audiences' perceptual and symbolic relation to the border-crossings evoked, I have suggested, by her voice. Leander's early Ufa films appeared in the boom period of Third Reich tourism; thus we may read her adventures here in exotic foreign climes in part at least as feeding popular appetites for frontier-crossing in the (relatively) benign form of touristic travel across and beyond the borders of the *Reich*.[5] Five subsequent titles, *Es war eine rauschende Ballnacht*, *Das Lied der Wüste*, *Der Weg ins Freie* (1941), *Das Herz der Königin* and *Die grosse Liebe*, by contrast, spanned the period that marked a shift from mass overseas tourism, to frontier transgressions of a more sinister kind. The most spectacular of these occurred on 1 September 1939, with the launch of Germany's military assault on Poland, the opening salvo in a series of violent onslaughts on national borders first eastwards, then north, west and south. Prefigured first in the occupation of the demilitarised Rhineland in March 1936, later in the 1938 annexation of Austria, the Sudeten region, the Memel, and the rest of Czechoslovakia (March 1939), the German invasion of Poland unleashed successive waves of military aggression that brought under German rule first Denmark, Norway, Belgium and the Netherlands, and finally France, with whom an armistice was signed on 22 June 1940, a mere nine months after German armies launched their opening offensive on Polish soil.

As Hitler's *Blitzkrieg* raged, Leander sang on. *Es war eine* premiered on 15 August 1939, two weeks before Germany invaded Poland. Following *Das Lied*'s premiere on 11 November, German audiences waited a further twelve months before the launch of the Carl Froelich title *Das Herz der Königin* on 1 November 1940: twelve months that were to see Germany triumph in successive military campaigns to east, west and south. *Das Herz* appeared in a momentary lull in Germany's devastating military storm; the Franco-German armistice was five months back, and German armies months away from new offensives to the south (Greece and Yugoslavia), and again to the east. Leander's last film in this cycle, *Die grosse Liebe* (1942), by contrast, situated her star image firmly in the context of German aggression abroad. The film explicitly locates its fictional love affair between the revue star Hanna (Leander) and the *Luftwaffe* officer Paul Wendtland (Viktor Staal) in the context of the June 1941 German invasion of the Soviet Union, and makes a case in that context for popular forbearance in the face of Germany's mounting difficulties on the Eastern Front.[6]

In three preceding titles, however, *Die grosse Liebe*'s narrative link between war and Leander is presaged, I would suggest, by a less tangible association between her singing voice, and a war aesthetic. We saw above how Kant makes the experience of the sublime contingent upon the generation within the subject of set of ideas that evoke sublimity. Those ideas include a capacity of the mind to conceive of infinity as an experience that 'surpasses every standard of sense'.[7] This movement beyond sense perception, Kant further elaborates, is the source of the profound ambivalence that haunts sublimity: that mix of pleasure and unpleasure, desire and fear that is evoked by any encounter with the 'abyss' (*Abgrund*) which lurks in the sublime space beyond the body and the senses. Emphatically stressed, moreover, in Kant's account, is the *violence* that characterises subjective experience of the sublime. What he at one point calls the sublime's 'vibration' (*Erschütterung*) of the subject is, he insists, by no means always benign; indeed it finds one source in the organised violence of a war experience that 'has something sublime about it', and which indeed renders popular thinking 'all the more sublime', the more numerous are the dangers to which any people is exposed in the course of war.[8]

Though few reliable accounts exist of audience experience in the Third Reich, we do have one source (albeit a uniquely corrupted one) that illuminates in intriguing ways the capacity of war on film to produce that form of subjective instability which Kant dubs sublime. In 1936, the internal espionage wing of the SS, the Staatssicherheitsdienst (SD), began using its network of spies and informers to produce the first *Meldung aus dem Reich* (*Report from the Reich*). The *Meldungen* comprised eyewitness accounts of everyday life in the Third Reich, and were designed to give the regime minute and comprehensive insight into popular consciousness in all areas of social, political and cultural life – including cinema.

One regular comment in the period 1939–40 concerned the perceived clash between feature films, newsreel and documentary. After the German invasion of Poland, the subsequent outbreak of World War II and Germany's spectacular military successes on all fronts, the popularity of actuality forms (newsreel and documentary) soared. The *Meldungen* show them to have been valued not only for the news they brought of loved ones on battle fronts far from home, but for the vision they offered of German expansion, of a *Reich* exploding outwards on all fronts. Alongside the often lavish photographic sections of the broadsheet press, the newsreels and *Kulturfilme* (documentaries) that accompanied the main features were valued, reports suggest, for their insight into the 'variable nature' of 'German landscapes and peoples' newly incorporated into the *Reich* – the Austrian provinces of Carinthia and the Wachau, the Sudeten region, and so on.[9] In April 1940, the 'quieter war situation' gave SD reporters pause to reflect on a perceived need for film images from newly subjugated eastern territories, of which German audiences were said still to 'lack any concrete vision'.[10] By May, this more contemplative moment had passed. As German troops marched into the Netherlands and Belgium, they sent back newsreel footage whose 'technical brilliance' and up-to-the-minute immediacy were reported to have allowed home audiences 'for the first time to experience war as it actually is'.[11] That the source of the newsreel's popularity was in part its capacity to involve film spectators experientially in German imperial aggression was underlined by SD reports on colonial documentaries – *Sehnsucht nach Afrika* (*Longing for Africa*, 1940) and *Deutsches Land in Afrika* (*German Land in Africa*, 1940). Such titles were said to be playing to packed houses in provincial towns, whose populations displayed 'considerable interest' in 'the colonial idea'.[12]

For cinema audiences on the home front, then, the *Blitzkrieg* opened up the promise of potentially limitless new territories of audiovisual pleasure, forging imaginary bonds to 'new landscapes and peoples', while confirming all the while the roots in military aggression of what one contemporary observer, Herbert Karowski of *Filmwelt*, dubbed the '*Erregung*' (excitation of a strong emotional or sexual nature) that flows from documentary reportage in times of war.[13] The *Meldungen* further reveal, however, that the 'excitation' of which Karowski writes derived as much from fear, as from pleasurable identification or desire. Audience responses to newsreels of the Franco-German conflict are a case in point. Militarised Germany's ambivalence towards France as both desired exotic Other, and (alleged) military aggressor coalesced in twentieth-century war reportage around the figure of the black French soldier, an object of both desire and loathing, lust and fear.[14] Hence one 1940 SD report that the spellbound fascination of female spectators in particular with French POWs' 'coloured faces' dissolved in a moment when 'several among the audience' demanded loudly that the occupying army 'shoot the black beasts dead'.[15]

Less palpably aggressive, but equally ambivalent were audience responses to frontline reports. A favoured genre of 1939–40 was the aerial documentary, which, in its various manifestations from newsreel footage, to *Kulturfilm*, provided the 'most exciting visual documents' of German victories abroad.[16] Since World War I, the airborne camera had fulfilled simultaneous functions as wartime reconnaissance tool, and as a technological vehicle for new cinematic sensations among audiences at home.[17] Thus in the Third Reich, such titles as the much-celebrated *Kulturfilm Feuertaufe* (*Baptism of Fire*, 1940) were celebrated for aerial shots in which – to cite Karowski again – 'the spectator feels himself being literally swept downward in a furious nose-dive, at a speed of over 150 metres per second' (Figure 29).[18]

Compare Karowski's comments here with the observations by Hans-Joachim Schlamp cited in Chapter 6 on Leander's voice, as it 'swirls stormily upwards, then suddenly falls back, plunging into the depths, bending in humility, and fading away'. The vertiginous experience associated here with Leander's voice is 'sublime', both in its spatial transcendence, and in the ambivalent oscillation its reception produces between pleasure, awe and fear. Hence Schlamp's further comment on Leander's *St. Matthew Passion* as evoking both a fluid *jouissance* (it is an 'expansive stream'), and, in its more sinister aspect, 'the prodigious sound of a last, threatening warning'. It is not, moreover, solely the descriptive similar-

Figure 29: *Feuertaufe* (1940) – cameras were mounted on wings, nose and elsewhere
to situate the viewer in the midst of the aerial scene of action

ity between Karowski on aerial war photography, and Schlamp on Leander's
voice, that suggests that Leander's appeal, at least in the early wartime period
1939–41, might be seen as linked to that mode of 'sublimity' which Kant associated with the experience of war. The metonymic association evident in my
juxtaposition of Kurowski and Schlamp above of Leander with actuality war
footage in general, and in particular with aerial film, recurs throughout the period
in which her stardom coincided with the Third Reich's war of aggression in
Europe and beyond. In two wartime titles, for instance, that association is forged
through narrative links between Leander and war heroes. *Das Lied der Wüste* and
Die grosse Liebe cast Leander as the romantic counterpart to warmongering men
– Paul the *Luftwaffe* pilot in *Die grosse*, mining-engineer-cum-resistance-fighter
Howard Brenton in *Das Lied* – for both of whom the aeroplane technology that
delivered to Kurowski the special 'excitation' of vicarious aggression in flight represented a source both of military prowess and of romantic appeal. The narrative
link between Leander's desires, and airborne aggression, is cemented in *Das Lied*
when her lover, Brenton, uses air reconnaissance to plan an Arab uprising against
Sir Herbert Collins – a figure positioned in the film as the embodiment of the
corruption endemic in British colonial rule. *Die grosse Liebe*, as both Brian

Currid and Karsten Witte have noted, forges similar spectatorial attachments to the airborne technology of war, first through point-of-view editing from Paul's fighter-pilot perspective (as in his opening descent from the clouds to base), then later (after Hanna's first night with Paul, or in their final lover's kiss) through shots that align the viewer with the perspective of a Leander whose desiring gaze fluctuates between Paul and his warplanes, and hints therefore – as Karsten Witte suggests – at an erotic attachment to war.[19] (Figure 30) That association between Leander and war was reinforced, moreover, by the juxtaposition in fan magazines of Leander reviews with increasingly numerous features à la Kurowski on war actuality; by the increasing prominence of the war newsreels in the cinema programmes in which her films appeared; and by a film-critical discourse – press coverage for instance – that situated Leander titles metaphorically in the very midst of the war experience, as it clamoured for 'films that dare to leap straight to the heart of the powerful and dangerous life of our current times'.[20]

Most importantly in relation to our consideration here of reception aesthetics, Leander's capacity to disturb the acoustic conventions of classical cinema – a capacity resulting from her voice's fracturing of narrative cinema's conventional image/voice bond, its disembodied quality, and its facility for boundary-crossing of numerous kinds – was replicated at the visual level by war

Figure 30: Hanna (Leander) with her *Luftwaffe* lover Paul (Viktor Staal) in *Die grosse Liebe* (1942)

actuality, in particular aerial footage, both of which were reported by the SD to run the risk, through their use of aerial footage and thus their fracturing of narrative cinema's spatial conventions, of visually disorienting and thus 'exhausting' home-front audiences, even as they elicited 'genuine admiration' for the *Luftwaffe*'s military might.

The sublime ambivalence apparently evoked by both war actuality and Leander's voice, was, however, emphatically not equatable with what I called in Chapter 4 the *völkisch* sublime evoked by Carl Froelich's popular art film. In my discussion there, I suggested that what stabilised the viewing subject in her/his encounter with the shattering experience of the sublime was the perception of the *Volk* or *Führer* as sublime objects that seemed to promise some possible reintegration of self with collectivity. What Zarah Leander appears to have evoked, by contrast, was an experience of disintegration and disembodiment that was prolonged both spatially and temporally, and that, I have suggested, found one cognate cultural expression in the potentially limitless violence of the *Blitzkrieg*.

GENDER AND THE SUBLIME

The salient distinction between these two modes of the Third Reich's cinematic sublime, finally, is one of gender. Feminist critics have noted how, in his early *Observations on the Feeling of the Beautiful and the Sublime*, Kant's distinctions between the two are drawn along clearly demarcated gender lines. Meg Armstrong, for instance, has observed that, while for the Kant of the *Observations*, the experience of the sublime arises from that 'admiration' which is the product of a contemplation of manly 'strivings and surmounted difficulties', the experience of beauty is the product of the 'unconstrained charms' (unconstrained, among other things, by education to rationality) that are assumed as integral to a pre-given feminine nature.[21] As Armstrong further notes, the Kant of the later *Critique of Judgement* at first apparently abandons the 'gender-based differences' of his earlier discussion, and considers the sublime instead as an aesthetic mode involving both (masculine) reason and (feminine) imagination. Thus reason mobilises the imagination in an effort to represent to itself those aspects of the sublime object – its infinity, its magnitude, its power – that exceed the bounds of rational conception.

Yet even within Kant's later conception of the sublime in the third *Critique*, gender difference is eventually reasserted through Kant's notion of the 'supersensible' idea that is the ultimate product of sublime experience. As Armstrong writes, 'emblems of sublimity ... provoke reflexive moments in which Reason supersedes the imagination [and encompasses] the ... image at hand ... within a supersensible idea of the coherence of the scene or its (larger) purpose'.[22] As we saw in Chapter 4, this 'supersensible' idea was embodied within the National

Socialist political aesthetic in the image of a racialised *Volk*, whose 'coherence' was guaranteed by its hierarchical organisation under, and subservient to the will of the *Führer*. To borrow terms from Deleuze and Guattari: if National Socialism promised 'sublimity' in the form of an infinite 'deterriorialisation' of social, geographical and symbolic space, then the space of the sublime was 'reterritorialised' through the reassertion of the body of the *Führer* as a symbolically bounded embodiment of the values of *Volk* and *Reich*.[23]

In the specific cinematic context that concerns us in this chapter, by contrast – Zarah Leander's films, considered in the particular reception context of the *Blitzkrieg* – what is evoked, I have suggested, in the interplay between Leander's vocal performance, and actuality footage of war is a sublime experience that exceeds symbolic representation, suggesting instead the possibility of an *infinite* 'deterritorialisation' of territorial and symbolic space in National Socialism's bloody war of aggression from 1939 on.

But this is only half the story. As we saw in SD reports of audience responses to newsreel footage of black French POWs, cinematic images of war provoked not only awe and admiration for German military prowess abroad; they also induced in audiences at home states of loathing and fear in the face of images of that terror that lurks beyond the fractured boundaries of war – the terror of the enemy, realised most particularly in the black soldier as the emblem of those further symbolic and actual boundary-transgressions (racial mixing, miscegenation) that may follow in the wake of war. In actuality reportage, the 'coherence' which Armstrong suggests is the product of a (masculine) reassertion of the *ratio* in the face of sublime terror was achieved through pervasive (and hugely popular) representations of a range of processes that 'reterritorialised' sublime experience within the national and racial boundaries of National Socialism's *völkisch Reich*. Hence, arguably, the popularity in Third Reich cinemas of actuality coverage of such events as the exhibitions of 'degenerate' art and music that preceded the outbreak of war: events that elaborately staged a popular encounter with the racial other, in order more effectively to 'reterritorialise' that figure – to contain its ambivalence – first through the internal policing of racial boundaries (the Nuremberg Laws 1935, the 'Aryanisation' of business and public life), and later, through the murderous eradication of racial difference in the Nazi death camps. Hence also audience acclaim for such documentary features as the 1939 title *Westwall (The Siegfried Line)*, a film much lauded for its invigorating portrayal of a Germany shored up against enemy incursion by a western defence wall that appeared to reaffirm the solidity of German frontiers, even as the nation prepared for the violent fracturing of national boundaries that would result from its aggressive onslaughts on neighbouring countries after 1939.[24]

In the face of the sublimity both of the racial other, and of the war experi-

ence, Third Reich documentary, then, reasserted the perverse 'rationality' of the
Nazi racial state through a return to representations that confirmed the solidity
of that state's internal and external, actual and symbolic boundaries. In relation
to Leander's voice, a cognate process of 'reterritorialisation' took place; but it
was a process that took a more conventionally feminine form. I have argued that
Leander's voice functioned as the auditory vehicle for an audience experience
of a 'sublime' extension into infinity: a spatial transcendence which, in the
moment of the *Blitzkrieg*, became associated also with the violent boundary-
crossing that opened Hitler's war. The ambivalence that resulted from the
spatial and symbolic dislocations evoked by Leander's voice was countered,
however, not by 'bringing it within the bounds of reason' (a reflex which
Christine Battersby attributes to the rational *man* who is the paradigmatic subject of Kant's sublime), but through a more clearly feminine mode of bounding
and symbolic containment.[25] In all her Ufa titles, what Eric Rentschler terms the
'impossible desire' that Leander's voice evokes is contained at the narrative level
by plot structures that bind her sometimes within the confines of (loveless) mar-
riages – to Henry Hoyer in *Zu neuen Ufern*, Sven the colourless Swedish doctor
in *La Habanera*, Michael the stuffed-shirt aristocrat in *Es war eine*, and so on –
and always within structures of sexual renunciation (*viz.* the endless deferral of
Hanna's union with Paul in *Die grosse Liebe*, or the suicide that banishes all hope
of a sexual consummation in *Der Weg ins Freie*). This assertion of narrative
boundaries that relocate Leander's transgressive voice within the symbolic
bounds of a masochistic, and often (most prominently in *Heimat* and *La
Habanera*) maternal femininity, is reinforced in Leander's vocal performances,
moreover, by a pervasive oscillation between, on the one hand, an assertion of
her voice's androgyny, its stylistic range, its dislocation from her image, and on
the other, moments of containment within the bounds of a more conventional
singing style. Thus Leander's shift from melody to emphatic declamation in such
songs as 'Yes, Sir' (*Zu neuen*), '*Auf der Puszta*' (*Der Blaufuchs*) or '*Nur nicht aus
Liebe weinen*', may distantly recall the androgynous voice of Dietrich, with its
mix of husky female eroticism and masculine self-assertion. Ultimately celebrated in Leander's delivery, however, is the defeat of Dietrich and the cabaret
tradition. Musically, '*Nur nicht aus Liebe weinen*', for instance, may well evoke
the polymorphous sexualities, the exotic ethnic affiliations and gender transgressions of Weimar, but the lyrics remind Leander's listeners of the imperative
that such desires end in renunciation: '*Das Ende ist immer Verzicht*' ('The End
is always Sacrifice').

That same message is underlined by Leander's body language as she sings;
she stands statuesque and frozen, as if to fix and immobilise the longings to
which her voice gives vent. Leander's songs, in conclusion, may well extend a

promise of a possible extension of the territories of the self that is at least analogous to the newsreels' vision of their audience as participants in an infinitely expanding *Reich* and nation. What the singing Leander as performing body and narrative figure also enacts, however, is a drama of the (often brutal) coercion and control of the others encountered at the borders of the self: a drama that evokes for Leander's German listeners the (imperialist) utopia of an infinite extension of self, only to underscore the centrality of female bodies and female agency in policing the internal borders of gender and racial identity in an extended nation and *Reich*.[26]

THE STAR SYSTEM AFTER DIETRICH: MARLENE'S GHOSTS?

As we saw in Chapter 6, it is common in discussions of Zarah Leander to note her status as copy, facsimile, uncanny double for two of Hollywood's most prominent émigré divas, Garbo and Dietrich. Leander, moreover, as I also stressed, was only one of numerous figures recruited after 1933 to shore up a star system violently depleted following the persecution and/or flight into exile of whole generations of German-speaking stars. What Andrea Winkler-Mayerhöfer has termed Third Reich cinema's 'politics of role typage' demanded a panoply of star figures capable of spanning the full range of male and female ideal types; thus Zarah Leander occupied only one small corner of an expansive female role typology that extended from such girl-next-door figures as Lilian Harvey or Ilse Werner, through the tomboy characters of Käthe von Nagy or Marika Rökk, the mystery heroine (Sibylle Schmitz) and the European grande dame (Olga Tschechowa), to Kristina Söderbaum as Third Reich melodrama's emblematic female victim.[27] Star studies from Winkler-Mayerhöfer on have mapped similar topographies for Nazi cinema's leading men, beginning with Heinz Rühmann as German national cinema's most enduring embodiment of the 'little man', through the prototypical 'man of action' (Hans Albers), or such comic bunglers as Hans Moser and Theo Lingen, to the youthful charmer Carl Raddatz, or Willy Birgel as Nazism's cinematic emblem of the unflinchingly authoritarian soldier male.

Regularly noted in existing histories, moreover, are processes of ideological 'repression' whereby images of stars after 1933 first recall apparently subversive elements of Weimar stars, only to contain or accommodate those elements within the constricted narrative and symbolic conventions characteristic of National Socialist film. Hence, for instance, Stephen Lowry's account of Heinz Rühmann as a figure whose Third Reich films play out a drama of ideological and aesthetic integration into dominant narrative – as, for example, in Rühmann's *Die Umwege des schönen Karl* (*Handsome Karl's Roundabout Ways,*

1937), which Lowry convincingly interprets as a parody that first recalls, then disavows the pleasures of Weimar film style.[28] Similar processes are evident in the narrative personae of such female stars as Lil Dagover or Pola Negri, whose Third Reich film roles first recall the vamp stereotype these actresses had themselves embodied in Weimar film, only symbolically to obliterate that image in the actual or symbolic death of the characters they portray. Witness in this context Lil Dagover's eventual suicide in her role as the adulteress Charlotte in Detlef Sierck's *Schlußakkord* (*Final Chord*, 1937): a death which, as Sabine Hake has shown, enacts a symbolic repression of the Weimar femme fatale whom Dagover emblematises in favour of an altogether more fitting female role model, the fresh-faced young widow Hanna (Maria von Tasnady).[29]

The ambivalence that is as much a quality of Dagover in *Schlußakkord* (Hake decsribes her as the 'libidinal center' of the film, even while her suicide rehearses the demise of the Weimar eroticism her image evokes), as it is of Rühmann in his Third Reich films (*viz.* Lowry's notion of the 'double character' of Rühmann's image as oppressed little man, but also 'model figure and male lead') may suggest that we should see these and cognate 1930s stars, like Leander, as 'ghosts' of figures politically extirpated from the image repertoire of Third Reich film. Certainly, film's capacity for the mechanical reproduction of images ('doubling') locates the medium in general as a vehicle for the fantasised restitution of lost objects – in Third Reich cinema, the lost stars of the Weimar screen. Certainly, too, as Robert Kiss has shown of the Wilhelmine silents, and as Siegfried Kracauer claimed of Weimar film, the double figure is pervasive enough in pre-1933 German film history for it to be legitimate to seek in Third Reich film some continuation of a cinematic tradition in which the *Doppelgänger* functions as imaginary substitute for objects traumatically lost or suppressed from view.[30] Most importantly, accounts from Hake, Lowry and others of the psychic ambivalence surrounding the star images of Dagover, Rühmann and similar stars position these as figures emblematic of a psycho-historical 'return of the repressed', recalling as they do simultaneously the moment of traumatic loss (the loss in Dagover's case of the Weimar period's erotic freedoms, in Rühmann's of the autonomy of the little man), while at the same time enacting a fantasised compensation of that loss, in *Schlußakkord* through substitution (of Charlotte by Hanna), in Rühmann's case, through the star's narrative transition from oppressed little man, to the triumphant hero that he becomes in the dénouements of his Third Reich films.

The reception history of Third Reich stars that I have attempted in this book delivers, however, a second and rather different reading of the function of these ghosts or doubles of counterparts on the Weimar screen. In psychoanalytic accounts, the uncanny double appears as the product of conflicting psychic forces: the repressive apparatus on the one hand, pitched on the other against unconscious, tabooed or traumatically suppressed memories, anxieties and desires. Third Reich film commentary lays similar stress on what it terms the 'struggle' (*das Kämpferische*) that is the necessary prelude to the production of any image of German stars. As the critic Harry Weinschenk writes for instance, in his preface to one popular star biography collection, 'each of these individuals has pursued a different path, just as experience itself is always of differing kinds. But one thing is common to the lives of all, and that is [their background in] struggle.'[31]

In his more theorised account of the creative process underpinning star representation, Ernst Iros writes analogously of the 'filmic artwork' as demonstrating 'the eternal interior struggle in which the individual is caught between the voluntarism of the drives and a reason [*Vernunft*] that demands order and discipline, between untrammelled desire, and the obligations of the aesthetic'.[32] It is typical that Iros makes explicit earlier in this passage the debt he owes to Kant in his depiction of the film image as the product of a struggle between the imagination (or, for Iros, the 'drives' and 'desire'), and reason. His comments help us pinpoint more precisely the *historical* sense in which Leander and her contemporaries were perceived as creative substitutes for their antecedents in Weimar film. The repeated references in Iros' book to a post-Kantian predecessor, Johannes Volkelt, place his work in a theoretical tradition that was both more accommodating than Kantian aesthetics itself to the ideological programmes of National Socialism, and that operated at a tangent to Freudian notions of the double image as 'return of the repressed'. Volkelt's three-volume *System der Ästhetik* (*System of Aesthetics*) was published between 1905 and 1914 and, as Jutta Müller-Tamm has shown, owes many of its insights to nineteenth-century developments in aesthetic theory that conceive both the production and reception of the artwork not in terms of a return of repressed material, but of acts of projection in which 'the ego projects itself into an object perceived theoretically as lacking its own personality and soul, but within which [the ego] finds its own soul'.[33] For Volkelt, this fusion through projection of aesthetic object and human 'soul' is achieved through 'aesthetic empathy': a process initiated not through identification with the aesthetic object, but through an 'emotion-laden act of looking' that reconstitutes the intrinsically lifeless aesthetic object is an 'embodiment of the soul'.[34]

Iros' *Wesen und Dramaturgie des Films* draws on a heady mix of Volkelt's empathy theory, with the vitalism of Nietzsche and Ludwig Klages, to conceptualise both film production and reception as engendering a 'sinking' of the viewing subject into the 'alien becoming' that is the visual image on film.[35] For him, therefore, the star image on film appears not as the trace of memories or desires lost, 'forgotten' or repressed, but as the projection of a creative fantasy (an 'empathetic imaginative perception')[36] whose origins lie not at the level of representation, but in the 'soul' of the viewing subject's contemporary life-world.

The ideological dimensions of Iros' projection theory of star images are evident when he specifies that what film art acquires through this process of empathetic projection is a capacity to 'represent the steel-hard rhythms and mechanical beat of our time'.[37] Nor was Iros the only writer to perceive both the production and reception of star images as involving the subjective projection of an assumed collective will. Witness, for instance, the less theoretically elaborate accounts of such critics as Weinschenk, or Rudolf Bach (see Chapter 3) of the 'inner struggle' that was the necessary prelude to the formation of the image of the star. Read through these accounts, my analysis of Leander's sublime voice appears as one manifestation of what Third Reich commentators apparently took to be a capacity of the star image to function as a projection screen for contemporary fantasies of the 'steel-hard' and 'mechanical' rhythms of the *Blitzkrieg*. That Leander's image and voice functioned quite differently for film audiences in other historical moments and spaces – gay audiences in post-war Germany for instance – has been amply demonstrated elsewhere; but the changing patterns of Leander reception may also lend some credence to Iros' theory of projection, not identification, as one of the processes through which she engaged German audiences from 1937 on.[38] Certainly, contemporary accounts of Leander as a star engaged in active creative struggle on behalf of the *Reich* situate her less as the re-embodiment of a lost presence (a 'ghost' of 'Marlene'), than as a projective fantasy of fascist will in times of war. Ultimately, however, the conclusions of this present study must remain limited. I have concerned myself in this and the preceding chapter with Zarah Leander as only one instance of a lost star's ghostly return. It remains open to other studies to explore the extent to which other star figures functioned similarly as projective fantasies of the Third Reich's will to the creative production not of the merely entertaining, but of the beautiful and the sublime.

NOTES

1. Immanuel Kant, *Critique of the Power of Judgement*, Paul Guyer (trans. and ed.) and Eric Matthews (trans.) (Cambridge: Cambridge University Press, 2000, orig. 1790), p. 128.

2. Ibid., pp. 131, 140, and 138.

3. Ibid., p. 129.

4. See Siegfried Kracauer, 'Cult of Distraction' and 'The Mass Ornament' in idem., *The Mass Ornament. Weimar Essays*, Thomas Levin (trans. and ed.) (Cambridge, MA and London: Harvard University Press, 1995), pp. 323–30 and 75–88.

5. On the pre-war tourist boom, see Hans-Dieter Schäfer, *Das gespaltene Bewußtsein.*

Deutsche Kultur und Lebenswirklichkeit 1933–1945 (Munich and Vienna: Hanser, 1981), pp. 120ff. On the implications for tourism of Germany's war of aggression in Europe, and particularly the need for a marketing focus on destinations closer to home, see for example, Wilhelm Seelemeyer, 'Was wird aus dem Fremdenverkehr?', *Deutsche Allgemeine Zeitung* (DAZ), 29 September 1939.

6. For a detailed reading of *Die grosse Liebe* in terms of its ideological address, see Stephen Lowry, *Pathos und Politik. Ideologie in Spielfilmen des Nationalsozialismus* (Tübingen: Niemeyer, 1991), pp. 116–201.

7. Kant, *Critique of the Power of Judgement*, p.138 and 141.

8. Ibid., p. 146. Paul Guyer's translation of *Erschütterung* with 'vibration' is entirely correct in this context, but does not render the connotations that surround the term in German, where it can also be used to describe a particularly violent shaking or even 'shattering'.

9. Heinz Boberach, (ed.) *Meldungen aus dem Reich. Die geheimen Lageberichte des Sicherheitsdienstes der SS 1938–1945* (Herrsching: Manfred Pawlak, 1984), p. 829: report dated 1 March 1940.

10. Ibid., p. 978: 10 April 1940.

11. Ibid., p. 1179: 27 May 1940.

12. Ibid., p. 740: February 1940.

13. Herbert Karowski, 'Film im Flug', *Filmwelt* (FW), 24 November 1939.

14. See in this context Tobias Nagl, 'Die Entscheidungsschlacht für den deutschen Grossfilm. *Ohm Krüger* (1941) und der historische Nazi-Blockbuster', in Jan Distelmeyer (ed.), *Tonfilmfrieden/Tonfilmkrieg. Die Geschichte der Tobis vom Technik-Syndikat zum Staatskonzern* (Munich: edition text+kritik, 2003), p. 176. On the black French soldier in the wake of World War I as an embodiment of fascist anxieties, see Klaus Theweleit, *Male Fantasies*. vol. 1, Stephen Conway, Erica Carter and Chris Turner (trans.) (Oxford: Polity, 1987), pp. 90ff.

15. Boberach, *Meldungen aus dem Riech*, p. 1221: 6 June 1940. The violence of this response matches the extremity of the audience's ambivalence towards the black other, an ambivalence characteristic, Homi Bhabha has suggested, of colonial discourse on the black other, and which erupts in violent disavowal of this kind. See Homi Bhabha, 'The Other Question. The Stereotype in Colonial Discourse', *Screen*, vol. 24, no. 6, 1983, pp. 18–36.

16. Karowski, 'Film im Flug'.

17. Cf. Tiziana Carrozza, 'The Eye Over the Hill. Aerial Photography up to the First World War', *Kintop* 3, 1994, pp. 117–28; Wolfgang Mühl-Benninghaus, 'Oskar Messters Beitrag zum Ersten Weltkrieg', *Kintop* 3, 1994, pp. 103–15.

18. Karowski, 'Film im Flug'.

19. Brian Currid, ' "Es war so wunderbar!" Zarah Leander, ihre schwulen Fans, und die

Gegenöffentlichkeit der Erinnerung', *montage/av*, vol. 7, no 1, 1998, especially pp. 61ff; Karsten Witte, *Lachende Erben, Toller Tag* (Berlin: Vorwerk 8, 1995), pp. 201–2.

20. Cited in 'Das deutsche Filmschaffen. Die Filme der *UFA*', FW, 6 September 1940. The article includes a short preview of Leander's *Der Weg ins Freie*, 1941. On negative audience responses to the progressive lengthening of the newsreels after 1939, see for example Boberach, *Meldungen aus dem Reich*, p. 1123; and for a sample of one fan magazine's war actuality coverage, see, for example 'Filme, die wir sahen: *Feuertaufe*', FW, 19 April 1940; 'Die Wochenschau des Sieges', FW, 12 July 1940; Günther Schwark, 'Die Wochenschau. Dokument der Geschichte. Gespräch mit Dr. Fritz Hippler', FW, 19 July 1940; Erwin Kirchhof, 'Die Kamera. Waffe der Wahrheit', FW, 23 August 1940; Feliz Henseleit, 'Die neue Epoche des Kulturfilms', FW, 30 August 30.

21. Meg Armstrong, ' "The Effects of Blackness". Gender, Race, and the Sublime in Aesthetic Theories of Burke and Kant', *Journal of Aesthetics and Art Criticism*, vol. 54, no. 3, summer 1996, p. 222; Immanuel Kant, *Observations on the Feeling of the Beautiful and the Sublime*, John T. Goldthwait (trans.) (Berkeley, Los Angeles and London: University of California Press, 1960, orig. 1764).

22. Armstrong, ' "The Effects of Blackness" ', p. 226. Kant's idea of the supersensible refers to an experiential field that 'is inaccessible … for our faculty of cognition', and that we therefore 'must … occupy with ideas': Kant, *Observations*, p. 63.

23. Gilles Deleuze and Felix Guattari, *Anti-Oedipus. Capitalism and Schizophrenia*, Robert Hurley, Mark Seem and Helen R. Lane (trans.) (Minneapolis: University of Minnesota Press, 1983), especially pp. 244ff. Deleuze and Guattari's discussion of deterritorialisation and reterritorialisation, related in their their account to the 'social field' of capitalism, is developed with reference to German fascism in Theweleit, *Male Fantasies*, pp. 264ff.

24. See Boberach, *Meldungen aus dem Reich*, p. 818.

25. Christine Battersby, 'Terror, Terrorism and the Sublime: Rethinking the Sublime after 1789 and 2001', unpublished paper, November 2002.

26. Women's complicity in the gender and racial politics of National Socialism has been extensively discussed in feminist history in recent years. For a helpful overview, see Adelheid von Saldern, 'Victims or Perpetrators? Controversies about the Role of Women in the Nazi State', in David Crew (ed.), *Nazism and German Society 1933–1945* (London and New York: Routledge, 1994), pp. 141–65.

27. Andrea Winkler-Mayerhöfer, *Starkult als Propagandamittel. Studien zum Unterhaltungsfilm im Dritten Reich* (Munich: Ölschläger, 1992), p. 100.

28. Stephen Lowry, 'Heinz Rühmann – the Archetypal German', in Tim Bergfelder, Erica Carter and Deniz Göktürk (eds), *The German Cinema Book* (London: BFI, 2002), p. 84.

29. Sabine Hake, *Popular Cinema of the Third Reich* (Austin: University of Texas Press, 2001), pp. 107–27.

30. Robert Kiss, *The* Doppelgänger *in Wilhelmine Cinema (1895–1914). Modernity, Audiences and Identity in Turn-of-the-Century Germany* (unpublished doctoral thesis, University of Warwick, 2000); Siegfried Kracauer, *From Caligari to Hitler. A Psychological History of the German Film* (Princeton: Princeton University Press, 1947), especially his discussion of film as 'an outward projection of psychological events', in his analysis of Robert Wiene's *Das Cabinet des Dr Caligari (The Cabinet of Dr Caligari*, 1919), pp. 71ff.

31. Harry E. Weinschenk, *Schauspieler erzählen* (Berlin: Wilhelm Limpert, 1941), p. 5.

32. Ernst Iros, *Wesen und Dramaturgie des Films* (Zürich and Leipzig: Max Niehaus, 1938), p. 125.

33. Jutta Müller-Tamm, *Abstraktion als Einfühlung. Zur Denkfigur der Projektion in Psychophysiologie, Kulturtheorie, Ästhetik und Literatur der frühen Moderne* (professorial dissertation, Technische Universität, Berlin, 2002), p. 201.

34. Johannes Volkelt, *System der Ästhetik* (Munich: C. H. Beck, 1905–1914), vol. 1, pp. 387 and 394.

35. Iros, *Wesen und Dramaturgie*, p. 108.

36. Ibid., pp. 108 and 281.

37. Ibid., p. 109.

38. See, for example, Alice Kuzniar, ' "Now I have a Different Desire". Transgender Specularity in Zarah Leander and R. W. Fassbinder', in idem, *The Queer German Cinema* (Stanford: Stanford University Press, 2000), pp. 57–87; and Brian Currid, ' "Es war so wunderbar!" Zarah Leander, ihre schwulen Fans, und die Gegenöffentlichkeit der Erinnerung', *montage/av,* vol. 7, no 1, 1998, pp. 57–93.

Bibliography

Agde, Günter, *Flimmernde Versprechen. Geschichte des deutschen Werbefilms im Kino seit 1897* (Berlin: Das Neue Berlin, 1998).

Albrecht, Gerd, *Der Film im Dritten Reich. Eine Dokumentation* (Karlsruhe: Schauburg, 1979).

———, *Nationalsozialistische Filmpolitik. Eine soziologische Untersuchung über die Spielfilme des Dritten Reichs* (Stuttgart: Ferdinand Enke, 1969).

Albrecht, Gerd and Deutsches Institut für Filmkunde (eds), *Die großen Filmerfolge. Vom Blauen Engel bis Otto, der Film. Die erfolgreichsten Filme vom Beginn des Tonfilms bis heute* (Ebersberg: Edition Achteinhalb, 1985).

Alton, John, *Painting with Light* (Berkeley and Los Angeles: University of California Press, 1995, orig. 1949).

Anon., *Der Deutsche Film 1943/44. Kleines Film-Handbuch für die deutsche Presse*, n.pl., n.d.

Applegate, Celia, 'Bach Revival, Public Culture, and National Identity. The *St. Matthew Passion* in 1829', in Scott Denham, Irene Kacandes and Jonathan Petropulos (eds), *A User's Guide to German Cultural Studies* (Ann Arbor: University of Michigan Press, 1997), pp. 139–62.

Armstrong, Meg, ' "The Effects of Blackness". Gender, Race, and the Sublime in Aesthetic Theories of Burke and Kant', *Journal of Aesthetics and Art Criticism*, vol. 54, no. 3, summer 1996, pp. 213–36.

Arnheim, Rudolf, *Film as Art* (Berkeley, Los Angeles and London: University of California Press, 1971, orig. 1957).

———, 'Josef von Sternberg', in Peter Baxter (ed.), *Sternberg* (London: BFI, 1980), pp. 35–41.

Ascheid, Antje, Hitler's Heroines: Stardom and Womanhood in Nazi Cinema (Philadelphia: Temple University Press, 2003).

Asper, Helmut, *'Etwas Besseres als den Tod . . .'. Filmexil in Hollywood. Porträts, Filme, Dokumente* (Marburg: Schüren, 2002).

Bach, Rudolf, *Die Frau als Schauspielerin* (Tübingen: Rainer Wunderlich, 1937).

Bach, Steven, *Marlene: Life and Legend* (New York: William Morrow, 1992).

Balázs, Béla, 'Der Fall Dr. Fanck', *Film und Kritik* , no. 1, 1992, pp. 4–7.

———, *Der Geist des Films* (Halle: Knapp, 1930).

———, *Der sichtbare Mensch oder die Kultur des Films* (Vienna and Leipzig: Deutsch-österreichscher Verlag, 1924).

Baron, Cynthia, 'Crafting Film Performances. Acting in the Hollywood Studio Era', in Alan

Lovell and Peter Krämer (eds), *Screen Acting* (London and New York: Routledge, 1999), pp. 31–45.

Bathrick, David and Eric Rentschler (eds), *German Film History* (New York: Telos, 1993).

Battersby, Christine, *Gender and Genius. Towards a Feminist Aesthetics* (London: Women's Press, 1989).

———, 'Terror, Terrorism and the Sublime. Rethinking the Sublime after 1789 and 2001', unpublished paper, November 2002.

Bauer, Alfred, *Deutscher Spielfilm-Almanach 1929–1950* (Munich: Filmladen Christoph Winterberg, 1976).

Baur, Eva Gesine, *Göttinnen des Jahrhunderts* (Berlin: Ullstein, 1999).

Baxter, Peter (ed.), *Sternberg* (London: BFI, 1980).

Bechdolf, Ute, *Wunsch-Bilder? Frauen im Nationalsozialistischen Unterhaltungsfilm* (Tübingen: Tübinger Vereinigung für Volkskunde, 1992).

Beddow, Michael, 'Goethe on Genius', in Penelope Murray (ed.), *Genius. The History of an Idea* (Oxford: Blackwell, 1989), pp. 98–111.

Belach, Helga (ed.), *Wir tanzen um die Welt. Deutsche Revuefilme 1933–1945* (Munich: Carl Hanser, 1979).

Benjamin, Walter, *Charles Baudelaire. A Lyric Poet in the Era of High Capitalism*, Harry Zohn (trans.) (London: Verso, 1997).

———, 'The Work of Art in the Age of Mechanical Reproduction', in idem, *Illuminations*, Harry Zohn (trans.), Hannah Arendt (ed.) (London: Fontana, 1992, orig. 1936).

Bergfelder, Tim, Erica Carter and Deniz Göktürk (eds), *The German Cinema Book* (London: BFI, 2002).

Berkefeld, Wolfgang, *Untersuchungen zur Theorie der Schauspielkunst auf dem Boden der Forschungen von Ludwig Klages* (Dresden: Dittert, 1937).

Beyer, Friedemann, *Die Ufa-Stars im Dritten Reich. Frauen für Deutschland* (Munich: Heyne, 1991).

Beyfuss, Edgar, *Grundzüge einer Dramaturgie des Films* (Berlin: Zentral Verlag, 1925).

Bhabha, Homi, 'The Other Question. The Stereotype in Colonial Discourse', *Screen*, vol. 24, no. 6, 1983, pp. 18–36.

Bie, Richard, *Emil Jannings. Eine Diagnose des deutschen Films* (Berlin: Frundsberg, 1936).

Bitomsky, Hartmut, 'Der Kotflügel eines Mercedes Benz. Nazikulturfilme, Teil I: Filme von 1933 bis 1938', *Filmkritik*, vol. 27, no. 10, 1983, pp. 443–74.

Boberach, Heinz (ed.), *Meldungen aus dem Reich. Die geheimen Lageberichte des Sicherheitsdienstes der SS 1938–1945* (Herrsching: Manfred Pawlak, 1984).

Bock, Hans-Michael and Michael Töteberg (eds), *Das Ufa–Buch. Kunst und Krisen; Stars und Regisseure; Wirtschaft und Politik* (Frankfurt am Main: Zweitausendeins, 1992).

Böhm, Wilhelm, *Die Seele des Schauspielers* (Leipzig: E. A. Seemann, 1941).

Bordwell, David, 'The Art Cinema as a Mode of Film Practice', *Film Criticism*, vol. 4, no. 1, 1979, pp. 56–64.

Bowie, Andrew, 'Critiques of Culture', in Wilfried van der Will and Eva Kolinsky (eds), *The Cambridge Companion to Modern German Culture* (Cambridge: Cambridge University Press, 1998), pp. 132–52.

Ben Brewster, 'Deep Staging in French Films 1900–1914', in Thomas Elsaesser and Adam
    Barker (eds), *Early Cinema. Space, Frame Narrative* (London: BFI, 1990), pp. 45–55.

Brinker, Käthe, *Nordische Filmsterne. Zarah Leander, Kristina Söderbaum, Ingrid Bergmann*
    (sic), *Greta Garbo* (Berlin: Mölich, 1938).

Brockett, Oscar, *History of the Theatre* (Boston: Allyn and Bacon, 1977), third edition.

Brühl, Alfred, 'Der Film als soziale Wirklichkeit', *Deutsches Volkstum*, January 1936,
    pp. 44–9.

Bullivant, Keith (ed.), *Culture and Society in the Weimar Republic* (Manchester: Manchester
    University Press, 1977).

Bullock, Alan and Oliver Stallybrass (eds), *The Fontana Dictionary of Modern Thought*
    (London: Fontana, 1977).

Butler, J. G. (ed.), *Star Texts: Image and Performance in Film and Television* (Detroit: Wayne
    State University Press, 1991).

Butler, Judith, *Gender Trouble. Feminism and the Subversion of Identity* (London: Routledge,
    1990).

Cardinal, Roger, *German Romantics in Context* (London: Studio Vista, 1975).

Carrozza, Tiziana, 'The Eye Over the Hill. Aerial Photography up to the First World War',
    Kintop 3, 1994, pp. 117–28.

Carter, Erica, 'Marlene Dietrich – the Prodigal Daughter', in Tim Bergfelder, Erica Carter
    and Deniz Göktürk (eds), *The German Cinema Book* (London: BFI, 2002), pp. 71–80.

———, 'The New Third Reich Film History', *German History*, vol. 17, no. 4, 1999,
    pp. 565–83.

Cascardi, Anthony J., 'From the Sublime to the Natural. Romantic Responses to Kant', in
    idem, ed., *Literature and the Question of Philosophy* (Baltimore and London: Johns
    Hopkins University Press, 1987), pp. 101–31.

Caughie, John (ed.), *Theories of Authorship* (London: Routledge & Kegan Paul, 1981).

Chamberlain, Houston Stewart, *Foundations of the Nineteenth Century*, John Lees (trans.)
    (London: The Bodley Head, 1910, orig. 1899).

Charney, Leo and Vanessa R. Schwartz (eds), *Cinema and the Invention of Modern Life*
    (Berkeley, Los Angeles and London: University of California Press, 1995).

Cheesman, Tom, *The Shocking Ballad Picture Show. German Popular Literature and Cultural
    History* (Oxford and Providence: Berg, 1994).

Courtade, Francis and Pierre Cadars, *Histoire du Cinéma Nazi* (Paris: Eric Losfeld, 1972).

Crofts, Stephen, 'Authorship and Hollywood', in John Hill and Pamela Church Gibson
    (eds), *The Oxford Guide to Film Studies* (Oxford: Oxford University Press, 1998),
    pp. 310–23.

Currid, Brian, ' "Es war so wunderbar!" Zarah Leander, ihre schwulen Fans, und die
    Gegenöffentlichkeit der Erinnerung', *montage/av*, vol. 7, no. 1, 1998,
    pp. 57–93.

———, ' "A Song Goes Round the World". The German *Schlager*, as an Organ of
    Experience', *Popular Music*, vol. 19, no. 2, 2000, pp. 147–80.

Von Cziffra, Geza, *Es war eine rauschende Ballnacht. Eine Sittengeschichte des deutschen Films*
    (Frankfurt am Main and Berlin: Ullstein, 1987).

Davidson, John E., 'Working for the Man, Whoever That May be', in Robert C. Reimer
    (ed.), *Cultural History through a National Socialist Lens* (Rochester: Camdem House,
    2000), pp. 240–67.

Deleuze, Gilles and Felix Guattari, *Anti-Oedipus. Capitalism and Schizophrenia*, Robert
    Hurley, Mark Seem and Helen R. Lane (trans.) (Minneapolis: University of Minnesota
    Press, 1983).

Denzer, Kurt, *Untersuchungen zur Filmdramaturgie des Dritten Reiches* (unpublished doctoral
    thesis, University of Kiel, 1970).

Deutsche Filmakademie (ed.), *Deutsche Filmakademie mit dem Arbeitsinstitut für
    Kulturfilmschaffen* (Babelsberg-Ufastadt: Deutsche Filmakademie, 1938).

Diederichs, Helmut H., 'Über Kinotheater-Kritik, ästhetische und soziologische Filmkritik.
    Historische Aspekte der deutschsprachigen Filmkritik bis 1933', in Irmbert Schenk
    (ed.), *Filmkritik. Bestandsaufnahmen und Perspektiven* (Marburg: Schüren, 1998),
    pp. 22–42.

Dietrich, Marlene, *ABC Meines Lebens* (Berlin: Blauvalet, 1963).

———, *Ich bin, Gott sei Dank, Berlinerin. Memoiren (Marlene D. par Marlene Dietrich)*,
    Nicola Volland (trans.) (Berlin: Ullstein, 1997, orig. Fr. 1984).

———, *Nehmt nur mein Leben* (Munich: Bertelsmann, 1979).

Distelmeyer, Jan (ed.), *Tonfilmfrieden/Tonfilmkrieg. Die Geschichte der Tobis vom Technik-
    Syndikat zum Staatskonzern* (Munich: edition text+kritik, 2003).

Doane, Mary Ann, *Femmes Fatales. Feminism, Film Theory, Psychoanalysis* (London:
    Routledge, 1991).

———, 'The Voice in the Cinema. The Articulation of Body and Space', in Leo Braudy
    and Marshall Cohen (eds), *Film Theory and Criticism. Introductory Readings* (Oxford
    and New York: Oxford University Press, 1999), fifth edition, pp. 363–72.

Douglas, Mary, *How Institutions Think* (London: Routledge & Kegan Paul, 1987).

Drewniak, Boguslaw, *Der deutsche Film 1938–1945. Ein Gesamtüberblick* (Düsseldorf:
    Droste, 1987).

Drews, Wolfgang, *Die Großen des deutschen Schauspiels. Bildnisse aus zwei Jahrhunderten*
    (Berlin: Deutscher Verlag, 1941).

Dyer, Richard, *Heavenly Bodies. Film Stars and Society* (New York: St. Martins Press, 1986).

———, *Stars*, (London: BFI, 1998), second edition.

Eagleton, Terry, *The Ideology of the Aesthetic* (Oxford: Blackwell, 1990).

Eisner, Lotte, *The Haunted Screen. Expressionism in the German Cinema and the Influence of
    Max Reinhardt* (London: Secker & Warburg, 1973, orig. Fr. 1952).

Ellwood, David W. and Rob Kroess, *Hollywood in Europe. Experiences of a Cultural
    Hegemony* (Amsterdam: VU University Press, 1994).

Elsaesser, Thomas, 'Moderne und Modernisierung. Der deutsche Film der dreißiger Jahre',
    montage a/v, vol. 3, no. 2, 1994, pp. 23–40.

———, *Weimar Cinema and After. Germany's Historical Imaginary* (London: Routledge,
    2000).

Elsaesser, Thomas and Adam Barker (eds), *Early Cinema. Space, Frame, Narrative* (London:
    BFI, 1990).

Elsaesser, Thomas and Michael Wedel (eds), *The BFI Companion to German Cinema* (London: BFI, 1999).

Fachgruppe Filmtheater und Lichtspielstellen der Reichsfilmkammer (ed.), *Grundlagen für die Berufsausbildung des Filmtheaterbesitzers* (Berlin: Deutscher Zentraldruck, 1939).

Faulstich, Werner and Helmut Korte, *Der Star. Geschichte, Rezeption, Bedeutung* (Munich: Fink, 1997).

Field, Geoffrey C., *Evangelist of Race. The Germanic Vision of Houston Stewart Chamberlain* (New York: Columbia University Press, 1981).

Findahl, Theo, *Traumland Hollywood im Tageslicht. Eindrücke*, H. von Born-Pilsack (trans.) (Munich: F. Bruckmann, 1940).

Flinn, Caryl, *Strains of Utopia. Gender, Nostalgia, and Hollywood Film Music* (Princeton: Princeton University Press, 1992).

Forster-Hahn, Françoise, Claude Keisch, Peter-Klaus Schuster and Angelika Wesenberg, *Spirit of an Age. Nineteenth-century Paintings from the Nationalgalerie, Berlin* (London: National Gallery, 2001).

Freisburger, Walther, *Theater im Film. Eine Untersuchung über die Grundzüge und Wandlungen in den Beziehungen zwischen Theater und Film* (Emsdetten: Lechte, 1936).

Freud, Sigmund, 'The Uncanny', in idem, *Art and Literature*, James Strachey (ed.), Alix Strachey (trans.) (Harmondsworth: Penguin, 1985), pp. 335–75.

Frieden, Sandra, Richard W. McCormick, Vibeke R. Petersen and Laurie Melissa Vogelsang (eds), *Gender and German Cinema. Feminist Interventions* (Providence and Oxford: Berg, 1993).

Fritsch, Willy, *... Das kommt nicht wieder. Erinnerungen eines Filmschauspielers* (Zürich and Stuttgart: Werner Classen, 1963).

Garncarz, Joseph, 'Hollywood in Germany. Die Rolle des amerikanischen Films in Deutschland 1925–1990', in Uli Jung (ed.), *Der deutsche Film. Aspekte seiner Geschichte von den Anfängen bis zur Gegenwart* (Trier: Wissenschaftlicher Verlag, 1993), pp. 167–214.

——, 'Towards a Theory of Culturally Distinctive Star Systems' (unpublished paper, Stockholm 2001).

Geuter, Ulfried, 'Nationalsozialistische Ideologie und Psychologie', in Mitchell G. Ash and Ulfried Geuter (eds), *Geschichte der deutschen Psychologie im 20. Jahrhundert* (Opladen: Westdeutscher Verlag, 1985), pp. 146–71.

Gledhill, Christine, *Stardom. Industry of Desire* (London: Routledge, 1991).

Gomery, Douglas, 'Economic Struggles and Hollywood Imperialism. Europe Converts to Sound', *Yale French Studies*, no. 60, 1980, pp. 80–93.

Gramsci, Antonio, *Selections from the Prison Notebooks of Antonio Gramsci*, Quintin Hoare and Geoffrey Nowell-Smith (trans. and eds) (New York: International Publishers, 1971).

Gregor, Joseph, *Das Zeitalter des Films* (Vienna and Leipzig: Reinhold, 1932), second edition.

——, *Meister der deutschen Schauspielkunst. Krauß, Klöpfer, Jannings, George* (Bremen and Vienna: Carl Schünemann, 1939).

Gregor, Joseph and René Fülop-Miller, *Das amerikanische Theater und Kino. Zwei kulturgeschichtliche Abhandlungen* (Zürich, Leipzig, Vienna: Amalthea, 1931).

Griffin, Roger (ed.), *Fascism* (Oxford: Oxford University Press, 1995).

Groll, Günter, *Film. Die unentdeckte Kunst* (Munich: C. H. Beck, 1937).

Grunberger, Richard, *A Social History of the Third Reich* (Harmondsworth: Penguin, 1991).

Gunning, Tom, 'The Cinema of Attractions: Early Film, its Spectator and the Avant-Garde', in Thomas Elsaesser and Adam Barker (eds), *Early Cinema. Space, Frame, Narrative* (London: BFI, 1990), pp. 56–62.

Hagener, Malte and Jan Hans (eds), *Als die Filme singen lernten. Innovation und Tradition im Musikfilm 1928–1938* (Munich: edition text+kritik, 1999).

Hainge, Greg and Mark I. Millington (eds), *Fascist Aesthetics*: special issue of *Modern Studies*, vol. 42, 1999.

Hake, Sabine, *The Cinema's Third Machine. Writing on Film in Germany 1907–1933* (Lincoln and London: University of Nebraska Press, 1993).

———, *Popular Cinema of the Third Reich* (Austin: University of Texas Press, 2001).

Hansen, Miriam, *Babel and Babylon. Spectatorship in American Silent Film* (Cambridge, MA and London: Harvard University Press, 1991).

———, 'Early Cinema – Whose Public Sphere?', in Thomas Elsaesser and Adam Barker (eds), *Early Cinema. Space, Frame, Narrative* (London: BFI, 1990), pp. 228–46.

Hansen, Miriam Bratu, 'America, Paris, the Alps: Kracauer (and Benjamin) on Cinema and Modernity', in Leo Charney and Vanessa R. Schwartz (eds), *Cinema and the Invention of Modern Life* (Berkeley and Los Angeles: University of California Press, 1995), pp. 362–402.

Hauser, Rudolf, *Wille und Drang. Grundlinien zum Verstehen menschlicher Charaktere* (Paderborn: Schöningh, 1942).

Hefter, Rudolf, *Die moralische Beurteilung des deutschen Berufsschauspielers* (Emsdetten: Lechte, 1936).

Hehlmann, Wilhelm, *Persönlichkeit und Haltung. Rede gehalten auf der Tagung des NSD-Dozentenbundes der Martin-Luther-Universität Halle-Wittenberg am 13.Februar 1940* (Halle: Niemeyer, 1940).

Hellpach, Willy, 'Das Antlitz des Volkstums', *Zeitschrift für Menschenkunde. Blätter für Charakterologie und angewandte Psychologie*, vol. 11, no. 1, 1935, pp. 1–7.

Henseleit, Felix (ed.), *Der Film und seine Welt. Reichsfilmblatt-Almanach 1933* (Berlin: Photokino-Verlag, 1933).

Hessel, Franz, *Marlene Dietrich. Ein Porträt* (Berlin: Das Arsenal, 1992, orig. 1931).

Hickethier, Knut, 'Vom Theaterstar zum Filmstar. Merkmale des Starwesens um die Wende vom neunzehnten zum zwanzigsten Jahrhundert', in Werner Faulstich and Helmut Korte (eds), *Der Star. Geschichte, Rezeption, Bedeutung* (Munich: Wilhelm Fink, 1997), pp. 29–47.

Higham, Charles, *Marlene. The Life of Marlene Dietrich* (New York: Chelsea House, 1977).

Hinz, Berthold, *Die Malerei im deutschen Faschismus. Kunst und Konterrevolution* (Frankfurt am Main: Fischer, 1977).

Hippler, Fritz, *Betrachtungen zum Filmschaffen*. (Berlin: Max Hesses Verlag, 1942), second edition.

Hitler, Adolf, *Mein Kampf*, Ralph Manheim (trans.) (London: Hutchinson, 1974, orig. 1925/6), second edition.

Holba, Herbert, *Emil Jannings* (Ulm: Günther Knorr, 1979).

Holmes, Winifred, 'Hamburg Cinema. A Typical German Programme', *Sight and Sound*, no. 8, 1939, pp. 18–20.

Horak, Jan-Christopher, 'Exilfilm, 1933–1945', in Wolfgang Jacobsen, Anton Kaes and Hans Helmut Prinzler (eds), *Geschichte des deutschen Films* (Stuttgart: Metzler, 1993), pp. 101–18.

———, *Fluchtpunkt Hollywood. Eine Dokumentation zur Filmemigration nach 1933* (Münster: MAks, 1986), second edition.

Horn, Heinz, 'Zum Problem der Völkercharakterologie', *Zeitschrift für Menschenkunde und Zentralblatt für Graphologie*, vol. 12, no. 1, 1937, pp. 75–85.

Hubert, Ali, *Hollywood. Legende Und Wirklichkeit: Emil Jannings* (Leipzig: E. A. Seemann, 1930).

Huebner, F. M., 'Die Zeichensprache der Seele', *Zentralblatt für Graphologie*, vol. 4, no. 3, 1933, pp. 137–57.

———, 'Die Zeichensprache der Seele. Von Auge und Antlitz', *Zeitschrift für Menschenkunde*, vol. 9, no. 2, 1933, pp. 77–91.

Huhn, Thomas, 'The Kantian Sublime and the Nostalgia for Violence', *Journal of Aesthetics and Art Criticism*, vol. 53, no. 3, summer 1995, pp. 269–75.

Huyssen, Andreas, *After the Great Divide. Modernism, Mass Culture and Postmodernism* (London: Routledge, 1986).

Ihering, Herbert, *Emil Jannings. Baumeister seines Lebens und seiner Filme* (Heidelberg: Hüthig, 1941).

———, *Von Josef Kainz bis Paula Wessely* (Heidelberg, Berlin and Leipzig: Hüthig, 1942).

Iros, Ernst, *Wesen und Dramaturgie des Films* (Zürich and Leipzig: Max Niehaus, 1938).

Jacob, Lars (ed.), *Apropos Marlene Dietrich* (Frankfurt am Main: Neue Kritik, 2000).

Jacobs, Thomas, 'Visuelle Traditionen des Bergfilms: Von Fidus zu Friedrich oder das Ende bürgerlicher Fluchtbewegungen im Faschismus', *Film und Kritik*, no. 1, 1992, pp. 28–38.

Jacobsen, Wolfgang (ed.), *Babelsberg. Ein Filmstudio, 1912–1992* (Berlin: Stiftung Deutsche Kinemathek/Argon, 1992).

Jacobsen, Wolfgang, Anton Kaes and Hans Helmut Prinzler (eds), *Geschichte des deutschen Films* (Stuttgart: Metzler, 1993).

Jannings, Emil, *Theater, Film – Das Leben und ich* (Berchtesgaden: Zimmer & Herzog, 1951).

Jary, Michaela, *Ich weiß, es wird einmal ein Wunder gescheh'n. Die große Liebe der Zarah Leander* (Berlin: edition q., 1993).

John, Eckhard, *Musikbolschewismus. Die Politisierung der Musik in Deutschland 1918–1938* (Stuttgart and Weimar: Metzler, 1994).

Kalbus, Oskar, *Vom Werden Deutscher Filmkunst. 2 Teil: Der Tonfilm* (Hamburg: Cigaretten-Bilderdienst Altona-Bahrenfeld, 1935).

Kalbus, Oskar and Hans Traub, *Wege zum Deutschen Institut für Filmkunde*, ms., n.d., n.pl.

Kant, Immanuel, *Critique of the Power of Judgement*, Paul Guyer (trans. and ed.), and Eric Matthews (trans.) (Cambridge: Cambridge University Press, 2000, orig. 1790).

——, *Observations on the Feeling of the Beautiful and the Sublime*, John T. Goldthwait (trans.) (Berkeley, Los Angeles and London: University of California Press, 1981, orig. 1764).

Kauer, Edmund, *Der Film. Vom Werden einer neuen Kunstgattung* (Berlin: Deutsche Buch-Gemeinschaft, 1943).

Kern, Hans, 'Carl Gustav Carus als Erforscher der Seele', *Zeitschrift für Menschenkunde und Zentralblatt für Graphologie*, vol. 13, no. 4, 1937, pp. 171–82.

——, 'Das Werk von Ludwig Klages (zu seinem 65.Geburtstag am 10.Dezember 1937)', *Zeitschrift für Menschenkunde und Zentralblatt für Graphologie*, vol. 13, no. 4, 1937, pp. 169–70.

Kershaw, Ian, *The Hitler Myth. Image and Reality in the Third Reich* (Oxford and New York: Oxford University Press, 1987).

——, *The Nazi Dictatorship* (London: Arnold, 2002), fourth edition.

——, *Popular Opinion and Political Dissent. Bavaria 1933–45* (Oxford: Clarendon, 1983).

Ketelsen, Uwe-Karsten, *Heroisches Theater. Untersuchungen zur Dramentheorie des Dritten Reichs* (Bonn: Bouvier, 1968).

Kiss, Robert, *The* Doppelgänger *in Wilhelmine Cinema (1895–1914). Modernity, Audiences and Identity in Turn-of-the-Century Germany* (unpublished doctoral thesis, University of Warwick, 2000).

Klages, Ludwig, *Die Grundlagen der Charakterkunde* (Leipzig: Johann Ambrosius Barth, 1926), fourth edition.

——, *Persönlichkeit. Einführung in die Charakterkunde* (Potsdam: Müller & Kiepenhauer, 1928).

Klasen, Bernadette, ' "Eine Frau wird erst schön durch die Liebe". Ein Paradox. Zarah Leander in *Heimat*', in Joachim Schmitt-Sasse (ed.), *Widergänger. Faschismus und Antifaschismus im Film* (Münster: MAkS, 1993), pp. 38–58.

Klaus, Ulrich J., *Deutsche Tonfilme. Lexikon der abendfüllenden deutschen und deutschsprachigen Spielfilme (1929–1945)*, vol. 2, *Jahrgang 1931* (Berlin: Klaus, 1989).

Kleinert, Franz-Jürgen, *Das Herz der Königin – Maria Stuart. Die Adaption des klassischen Dramas im Spielfilm des Dritten Reichs* (Cologne: Pahl-Rugenstein, 1987).

Koch, Gertrud, 'Exorcised: Marlene Dietrich and German Nationalism', in Pam Cook and Philip Dodd (eds), *Women and Film: A Sight and Sound Reader* (London: Scarlet Press, 1992), pp. 10–15.

——, *Kracauer zur Einführung* (Hamburg: Junius, 1996).

Koch, Heinrich and Heinrich Braune, *Von deutscher Filmkunst. Gehalt und Gestalt* (Berlin: Scherping, 1943).

Koebner, Thomas (ed.), *Idole des deutschen Films* (Munich: edition text+kritik, 1997).

Koepnick, Lutz, *The Dark Mirror. German Cinema between Hitler and Hollywood* (Berkeley and Los Angeles: University of California Press, 2002).

——, 'Engendering Mass Culture: The Case of Zarah Leander', in Patricia Herminghouse and Magda Mueller (eds), *Gender and Germanness. Cultural Productions of Nation* (Providence and Oxford: Berghahn, 1997), pp. 161–75.

Korte, Helmut, *Der Spielfilm und das Ende der Weimarer Republik. Ein rezeptionshistorischer Versuch* (Göttingen: Vandenhoek & Ruprecht, 1998).

Kracauer, Siegfried, *From Caligari to Hitler. A Psychological History of the German Film* (Princeton: Princeton University Press, 1947).

——, 'The Mass Ornament', *New German Critique*, no. 5, 1975, pp. 67–76.

——, *The Mass Ornament. Weimar Essays*, Thomas Levin (trans. and ed.) (Cambridge, MA and London: Harvard University Press, 1995).

Kräh, Hans (ed.), *Geschichte(n): NS-Film – NS-Spuren heute* (Kiel: Ludwig, 1999).

Kreimeier, Klaus (ed.), *Die Metaphysik des Dekors. Raum, Architektur und Licht im klassischen deutschen Stummfilm* (Marburg and Berlin: Schüren, 1994).

——, *Die Ufa-Story. Geschichte eines Filmkonzerns* (Munich: Hanser, 1992).

Kriegk, Otto, *Der deutsche Film im Spiegel der Ufa. 25 Jahre Kampf und Vollendung* (Berlin: Ufa, 1943).

Krueger, Felix, 'Otto Klemm und das Psychologische Institut der Universität Leipzig. Deutsche Seelenforschung in den letzten drei Jahrzehnten', *Zeitschrift für angewandte Psychologie und Charakterkunde*, vol. 56, nos 5 and 6, 1939, pp. 253–346.

Kuhlmann, Walter, *Schule des Sprechens. Atmung, Stimm- und Lautbildung, Rechtlautung, Betonung* (Heidelberg: C. Winter, 1939).

Kuzniar, Alice, ' "Now I have a Different Desire". Transgender Specularity in Zarah Leander and R. W. Fassbinder', in idem, *The Queer German Cinema* (Stanford: Stanford University Press, 2000), pp. 57–87.

Lacoue-Labarthe, Philippe, *Heidegger, Art and Politics*, Chris Turner (trans.) (Oxford: Blackwell, 1990), p. 64.

Landesverband Berlin-Brandenburg-Grenzmark (ed.), *Filmtheaterführung. Die Vorträge des ersten Schulungsjahres 1934/35 der Fachschule der Filmtheaterbesitzer des Landesverbandes Berlin-Brandenburg-Grenzmark e.V. im Reichsverband Deutscher Filmtheater e.V.* (Berlin: Neue Film-Kurier Verlagsgesellschaft, 1935).

Leander, Zarah, *Es war so wunderbar! Mein Leben* (Frankfurt am Main: Ullstein, 1984, orig. 1973).

Lehnich, Oswald (ed.), *Jahrbuch der Reichsfilmkammer 1938* (Berlin: Max Hesses, 1938).

——(ed.), *Jahrbuch der Reichsfilmkammer 1939* (Berlin: Max Hesses, 1939).

Leiser, Erwin, *Nazi Cinema*, Gertrud Mander and David Wilson (trans.) (London: Secker & Warburg, 1975, orig. 1968).

Lenman, Robin, *Artists and Society in Germany 1850–1914* (Manchester and New York: Manchester University Press, 1997).

Lenssen, Claudia, *Blaue Augen, Blauer Fleck. Kino im Wandel von der Diva zum Girlie* (Berlin: Filmmuseum Potsdam/Parthas Verlag, 1997).

————, 'Sinnlichkeit abstrakt', *epd Kirche und Film*, vol. 34, no. 8, 1981, pp. 23–4.

————, 'Wissen, Mythen, Propaganda. NS-Kulturfilme', *epd-Film*, no. 12, 1998, pp. 16–17.

Lersch, Philipp, 'Grundriss einer Charakterologie des Selbst', *Zeitschrift für angewandte Psychologie*, vol. 46, nos 3 and 4, 1934, pp. 129–69.

Liebeneiner, Wolfgang, 'Film-Regie als jüngste Form künstlerischen Gestaltungswillens', in *Der deutsche Film 1943/44. Kleines Film-Handbuch für die deutsche Presse*, n.d., n.pl., pp. 38–40.

Locatelli, Massimo, *Béla Balázs. Die Physiognomik des Films* (Berlin: Vistas, 1999).

Loewenberg, Richard Detlev, 'Der Streit um die Physiognomik zwischen Lavater und Lichtenberg', *Zeitschrift für Menschenkunde. Blätter für Charakterologie und angewandte Psychologie*, vol. 9, no. 1, 1933, pp. 15–33.

Loiperdinger, Martin, 'Filmzensur und Selbstkontrolle', in Wolfgang Jacobsen, Anton Kaes and Hans Helmut Prinzler (eds), *Geschichte des deutschen Films* (Stuttgart: Metzler, 1993), pp. 479–98.

————, 'Kaiser Wilhelm II. Der erste deutsche Filmstar', in Thomas Koebner (ed.), *Idole des deutschen Films* (Munich: edition text+kritik, 1997), pp. 41–53.

Lovell, Alan and Peter Krämer (eds), *Screen Acting* (London and New York: Routledge, 1999).

Lowry, Stephen, 'Heinz Rühmann – the Archetypal German', in Tim Bergfelder, Erica Carter and Deniz Göktürk (eds), *The German Cinema Book* (London: BFI, 2002), pp. 81–9.

————, *Pathos und Politik. Ideologie in Spielfilmen des Nationalsozialismus* (Tübingen: Niemeyer, 1991).

————, 'Überlegungen zur NS-Unterhaltung anhand eines Rühmann-Films', *medium*, vol. 20, no. 3, 1990, pp. 27–30.

Luck, Rudolf, 'Rassenforschung und Charakterkunde', *Zeitschrift für Menschenkunde und Zentralblatt für Graphologie*, vol. 12, no. 1, 1937, pp. 1–5.

Lueken, Verena, 'Die unmögliche Frau. Ingrid Bergman in *Die Vier Gesellen*', *frauen und film*, no. 44–45, 1988, pp. 90–102.

Maltby, Richard, *Hollywood Cinema. An Introduction* (Oxford: Blackwell, 1995).

Martin, W. K., *Lives of Notable Gay Men and Lesbians. Marlene Dietrich* (New York and Philadelphia: Chelsea House, 1994).

Martini, Wolf G. (ed.), *Das Filmgesicht. Emil Jannings* (Munich: Curt J. C. Andersen, 1928).

Meyer, Eduard, 'Grundlagen der Persönlichkeitsgestaltung bei Nietzsche. Tragik – Eros – Wert', *Zeitschrift für angewandte Psychologie und Charakterkunde*, vol. 58, no. 4, 1940, pp. 236–45.

Meyer, Michael, *The Politics of Music in the Third Reich* (New York: Peter Lang, 1991).

Möhl, Walter, *Das deutsche Filmtheatergewerbe unter besonderer Berücksichtigung der Zusammenschlußbewegung* (Berlin: Lichtbildbühne, 1937).

Morgan, Paul, *Promin-Enten-Teich. Abenteuer und Erlebnisse mit Stars, Sternchen und allerlei Gelichter* (Berlin, Leipzig and Vienna: Amonesta, 1934).

Mühl-Benninghaus, Wolfgang, 'Oskar Messters Beitrag zum Ersten Weltkrieg', *Kintop 3*, 1994, pp. 103–15.

————, *Das Ringen um den Tonfilm. Strategien der Elektro- und der Filmindustrie in den 20er und 30er Jahren* (Düsseldorf: Droste, 1999).

Mühr, Alfred, *Die Welt des Schauspielers Werner Krauss* (Berlin: Brunnen, 1927).

Müller, Corinna, *Frühe deutsche Kinematographie. Formale, wirtschaftliche und kulturelle Entwicklungen* (Stuttgart and Weimar: Metzler, 1994).

Müller, Gottfried, *Dramaturgie des Theaters, des Hörspiels und des Films* (Würzburg: Konrad Triltsch, 1962, orig. 1942).

Müller-Tamm, Jutta, *Abstraktion als Einfühlung. Zur Denkfigur der Projektion in Psychophysiologie, Kulturtheorie, Ästhetik und Literatur der frühen Moderne* (professorial dissertation, Technische Universität, Berlin, 2002).

Munkepunke (*aka* Meyer, Alfred Richard), *1000% Jannings* (Hamburg: Prismenverlag, 1930).

Murray, Penelope (ed.), *Genius. The History of an Idea* (Oxford: Blackwell, 1989).

Nagl, Tobias, 'Die Entscheidungsschlacht für den deutschen Grossfilm. *Ohm Krüger* (1941) und der historische Nazi-Blockbuster', in Jan Distelmeyer (ed.), *Tonfilmfrieden/Tonfilmkrieg. Die Geschichte der Tobis vom Technik-Syndikat zum Staatskonzern* (Munich: edition text+kritik, 2003), pp. 167–81.

Naremore, James, *Acting in the Cinema* (Berkeley, Los Angeles and London: University of California Press, 1988).

Neumann, Carl, Curt Belling and Hans-Walther Betz, *Film- 'Kunst', Film-Kohn, Film-Korruption* (Berlin: Hermann Scherping, 1937).

Niessen, Carl, *Der 'Film'. Eine unabhängige deutsche Erfindung* (Emsdetten: Lechte, 1934).

Nightingale, Virginia, *Studying Audiences. The Shock of the Real* (London and New York: Routledge, 1996).

Noa, Wolfgang, *Marlene Dietrich* (Berlin: Henschelverlag, 1964).

Nowak, Karl, *Wie komme ich zum Film? Was muß ich vom Film wissen?* (Vienna: Karl Nowak, 1936).

Nowell-Smith, Geoffrey and Steven Ricci (eds), *Hollywood and Europe. Economics, Culture, National Identity 1945–95* (London: BFI, 1998).

Opfermann, H. C., *Die Geheimnisse des Spielfilms. Ein Buch für Filmer und Leute, die gern ins Kino gehen* (Berlin: Photokino-Verlag, 1938).

Osborne, John, 'Drama, After 1740', in H. B. Nisbet and Claude Rawson (eds), *The Cambridge History of Literary Criticism*, vol. 4. *The Eighteenth Century* (Cambridge: Cambridge University Press, 1997), pp. 184–209.

Paech, Anna and Joachim, *Menschen im Kino. Film und Literatur erzählen* (Stuttgart: Metzler, 2000).

Paschke, Gerhard, *Der Deutsche Tonfilmmarkt* (Berlin: Hoffmann, 1935).

Perinelli, Massimo, 'Die Geschichte des Herrn Liebeneiner', in idem, *Liebe '47 – Gesellschaft '49. Geschlechterverhältnisse in der deutschen Nachkriegszeit. Eine Analyse des Films* Liebe '47 (Hamburg: Lit, 1999), pp. 13–15.

Petley, Julian, *Capital and Culture. German Cinema 1933–45* (London: BFI, 1979).

Peukert, Detlef J. K., *Inside Nazi Germany. Conformity, Opposition and Racism in Everyday Life*, Richard Deveson (trans.) (Harmondsworth: Penguin, 1989).

Phillips, Alastair and Ginette Vincendeau (eds), *Journeys of Desire: European Actors in Hollywood* (London: BFI, forthcoming).

Pressedienst der Terra-Filmkunst, *Der Kunstausschuss der Terra-Filmkunst. Gespräch mit Karl Hartl, H. Paulsen, H. George, W. Liebeneiner und Th. Loose* (Berlin: Terra-Filmkunst, 1937).

Prieberg, Fred K., *Musik im NS-Staat* (Frankfurt am Main: Fischer, 1982).

Prümm, Karl, 'Historiographie einer Epochenschwelle. Der Übergang vom Stummfilm zum Tonfilm in Deutschland (1928–1932)', in Knut Hickethier (ed.), *Filmgeschichte schreiben. Ansätze, Entwürfe und Methoden* (Berlin: edition sigma, 1989), pp. 93–102.

Quaresima, Leonardo, 'Der Film im Dritten Reich. Moderne, Amerikanismus, Unterhaltungsfilm', *montage a/v*, vol. 3, no. 2, 1994, pp. 5–22.

Rabenalt, Arthur Maria, *Film im Zwielicht. Über den unpolitischen Film des Dritten Reiches und die Begrenzung des totalitären Anspruchs* (Hildesheim and New York: Olms, 1978).

———, *Joseph Goebbels und der 'Großdeutsche' Film* (Munich and Berlin: Herbig, 1985).

———, *Mimus ohne Maske. Über die Schauspielkunst im Film. Essay* (Düsseldorf: Merkur, 1945).

Rank, Otto, 'Der Doppelgänger', in idem, *Psychoanalytische Beiträge zur Mythenforschung* (Leipzig and Vienna: Internationaler Psychoanalytischer Verlag, 1919), pp. 267–354.

Rehlinger, Bruno, *Der Begriff Filmisch* (Emsdetten: Lechte, 1938).

Reimer, Robert C. (ed.), *Cultural History through a National Socialist Lens* (Rochester: Camdem House, 2000).

Rentschler, Eric, 'Expanding Film-Historical Discourse: Reception Theory's Use Value for Cinema Studies', *Cine-Tracts*, vol. 41, no. 1, 1981, pp. 57–68.

———, 'Hochgebirge und Moderne. Eine Standortbestimmung des Bergfilms', *Film und Kritik*, no. 1, June 1992, pp. 8–27.

———, *The Ministry of Illusion. Nazi Cinema and its Afterlife* (Cambridge, MA and London: Harvard University Press, 1996).

Richter, Hans, *Der Spielfilm. Ansätze zu einer Dramaturgie des Films* (Berlin: H. H. Richter, 1920).

———, *Filmgegner von heute – Filmfreunde von morgen* (Berlin: H. H. Richter, 1968, orig. 1929).

Riva, Maria, *Marlene Dietrich by her Daughter* (London: Bloomsbury, 1992).

Rivière, Joan, 'Womanliness as a Masquerade', in Hendrik M. Ruitenbeek (ed.), *Psychoanalysis and Female Sexuality* (New Haven: College and University Press, 1966, orig. 1929), pp. 209–20.

Robertson, J. G., *Lessing's Dramatic Theory* (Cambridge: Cambridge University Press, 1939).

Romani, Cinzia, *Tainted Goddesses. Female Film Stars of the Third Reich* (New York: Sarpedon, 1992).

Rothacker, Erich, *Die Schichten der Persönlichkeit* (Leipzig: Ambrosius, 1938).

Rudenski, Dyck, *Gestologie und Filmspielerei. Abhandlungen über die Physiologie und Psychologie des Ausdrucks* (Berlin: Hoboken, 1927).

Ruttmann, W. J., 'Das Erbgut im Gefüge des Charakters. Leitlinien zu einer Erbcharakterkunde', *Zeitschrift für Menschenkunde. Blätter für Charakterologie und angewandte Psychologie*, vol. 11, no. 4, 1936, pp. 181–207.

von Saldern, Adelheid, 'Victims or Perpetrators? Controversies about the Role of Women in the Nazi State', in David Crew (ed.), *Nazism and German Society 1933–1945* (London and New York: Routledge, 1994), pp. 141–65.

Salt, Barry, 'Continental Manners: Formal and Stylistic Features of French and German Cinema of the '30s and '40s', in Susan Hayward (ed.), *European Cinema Conference Papers* (Aston: AMLC, 1985), pp. 53–70.

———, *Film Style and Technology. History and Analysis* (London: Starword, 1983).

———, 'Sternberg's Heart Beats in Black and White', in Peter Baxter (ed.), *Sternberg* (London: BFI, 1980), pp. 103–18.

Sanders, Ulrike, *Zarah Leander – Kann denn Schlager Sünde sein?* (Cologne: Pahl-Rugenstein, 1988).

Sanders-Brahms, Helma, 'Zarah', in Hans Günther Pflaum (ed.), *Jahrbuch Film 81/82* (Munich: Hanser, 1981), pp. 165–72.

Saunders, Thomas J., *Hollywood in Berlin. American Cinema and Weimar Germany* (Berkeley, Los Angeles and London: University of California Press, 1994).

Schabert, Inge and Barbara Schaft (eds), *Autorschaft. Genius und Genie in der Zeit um 1800* (Berlin: Erich Schmidt, 1994).

Schäfer, Hans Dieter, *Das gespaltene Bewußtsein. Deutsche Kultur und Lebenswirklichkeit 1933–1945* (Munich and Vienna: Hanser, 1981).

Schenk, Irmbert (ed.), *Filmkritik. Bestandsaufnahmen und Perspektiven* (Marburg: Schüren, 1998).

Schlamp, Hans-Joachim, *Willy Birgel spielt mit Zarah Leander, Angela Salloker, Brigitte Helm* (Berlin: Mölich, 1937).

Schlegelberger, Franz, *Der Weg zur Persönlichkeit. Vortrag gehalten am 26.April 1938 vor den Rechtswahrern des Reichsschulungslehrgangs 1938 auf der Reichsschulungsburg Erwitte in Westfalen* (Berlin: Franz Dahlen, 1938).

Schlüpmann, Heide, *Abendröthe der Subjektphilosophie. Eine Ästhetik des Kinos* (Basel and Frankfurt am Main: Stroemfeld, 1998).

———, 'Faschistische Trugbilder weiblicher Autonomie', *frauen und film*, no. 44–5, 1988, pp. 44–66.

Schmidt, Jochen, *Die Geschichte des Genie-Gedankens 1750–1945* (Darmstadt: Wissenschaftliche Buchgesellschaft, 1985).

Schneider, Edmund, 'Empirisch-strukturpsychologische Untersuchungen über den Schauspieler', *Zeitschrift für angewandte Psychologie*, vol. 42, no. 4, 1932, pp. 285–356.

Schottky, Johannes, *Die Persönlichkeit im Lichte der Erblehre* (Leipzig: Teubner, 1936).

Schulte-Sasse, Linda, *Entertaining the Third Reich. Illusions of Wholeness in Nazi Cinema* (Durham and London: Duke University Press, 1996).

Schwartzmann, Karen, 'National Cinema in Translation. The Politics of Film Exhibition Culture', *Wide Angle*, vol. 16, no. 3, 1995, pp. 66–99.

Seiler, Paul, *Zarah Leander. Ein Kultbuch* (Reinbek bei Hamburg: Rowohlt, 1985).

———, *Zarah Leander. Ich bin eine Stimme* (Berlin: Ullstein, 1997).

Sennett, Richard, *The Fall of Public Man* (London and Boston: Faber & Faber, 1986).

Seydel, Renate, *Marlene Dietrich. Eine Chronik ihres Lebens in Bildern und Dokumenten* (Berlin: Henschelverlag, 1989).

Silberman, Marc, 'The Modernist Camera and Cinema Illusion: Friedrich Wilhelm Murnau's *The Last Laugh*', in idem, *German Cinema. Texts in Context* (Detriot: Wayne State University Press, 1995), pp. 19–33.

——— 'Zarah Leander in the Colonies', in Knut Hickethier and Siegfried Zielinski (eds), *Medien/Kultur. Schnittstellen zwischen Medienwissenschaft, Medienpraxis und gesellschaftlicher Kommunikation* (Berlin: Volker Spiess, 1991), pp. 247–53.

Silverman, Kaja, *The Acoustic Mirror. The Female Voice in Psychoanalysis and Cinema* (Bloomington: Indiana University Press, 1988).

Siska, Heinz W., *Wunderwelt Film. Künstler und Werkleute einer Weltmacht* (Heidelberg, Berlin and Leipzig: Verlagsanstalt Hüthig, n.d.).

Sontheimer, Kurt, *Anti-demokratisches Denken der Weimarer Republik. Die politischen Ideen des deutschen Nationalsozialismus zwischen 1918 und 1933* (Munich: Nymphenburger, 1962).

Spieker, Markus, *Hollywood unterm Hakenkreuz. Der amerikanische Spielfilm im Dritten Reich* (Trier: Wissenschaftlicher Verlag, 1999).

Spiker, Jürgen, *Film und Kapital* (Berlin: Volker Spiess, 1975).

Spoto, Donald, *Dietrich* (London: Bantam Press, 1992).

Spranger, Eduard, *Lebensformen. Geisteswissenschaftliche Psychologie und Ethik der Persönlichkeit* (Halle [Saale]: Niemeyer, 1930), seventh edition.

Stacey, Jackie, *Star Gazing. Hollywood Cinema and Female Spectatorship* (London and New York: Routledge, 1994).

Steinweis, Alan E., *Art, Ideology and Economics. The* Reich *Chambers of Music, Theater, and the Visual Arts* (Chapel Hill and London: University of North Carolina Press, 1993).

Stenzel, A., *Vom Kintopp zur Filmkunst. Menschen, die Filmgeschichte machten* (Berlin: Hermann Wendt, 1935).

Stepun, Fedor, *Theater und Kino* (Berlin: Bühnenvolksbundverlag, 1932).

von Sternberg, Josef, *The Blue Angel* (London: Lorrimer, 1968).

Strasser, Alex, *Filmentwurf, Filmregie, Filmschnitt. Gesetze und Beispiele* (Halle: Knapp, 1937).

Strathausen, Carsten, 'Nazi Aesthetics', in Greg Hainge and Mark I. Millington (eds), *Fascist Aesthetics*: special issue of *Modern Studies*, vol. 42, 1999, pp. 5–19.

Studlar, Gaylyn, *In the Realm of Pleasure. Von Sternberg, Dietrich and the Masochistic Aesthetic* (Urbana and Chicago: University of Illinois Press, 1988).

Sudendorf, Werner, *Marlene Dietrich* (Munich: Deutscher Taschenbuch Verlag, 2001).

Sydow, Barbara, *Zarah Leander, Marika Rökk und Kristina Söderbaum. Drei weibliche Stars im NS-Unterhaltungsfilm. Herausragende Karrieren im Dritten Reich* (unpublished dissertation, Friedrich-Alexander-Universität, Erlangen-Nürnberg, 1998).

Taylor, Brandon and Wilfried van der Will (eds), *The Nazification of Art. Art, Design, Music, Architecture and Film in the Third Reich* (Winchester: Winchester Press, 1990).

Theweleit, Klaus, *Male Fantasies*, vols 1 and 2, Stephen Conway, Erica Carter and Chris
   Turner (trans.) (Oxford: Polity, 1987–1989).

Tichelli, Kurt, *Wege zum erfolgreichen Tonfilm. Beobachtungen und Anregungen eines
   Kinodirektors* (Brig, Switzerland: Selbstverlag K. Tichelli, 1937).

Tilitzki, Christian, *Die deutsche Universitätsphilsophie in der Weimarer Republik und im
   Dritten Reich* (Berlin: Akademie Verlag, 2002).

Traub, Hans, *Als man anfing zu filmen. Ein geschichtlicher Abriß über die Entstehung des Films*
   (Munich: Eiserne Blätter, 1934).

Traub, Hans and Hanns Wilhelm Lavies, *Das deutsche Filmschrifttum. Eine Bibliographie der
   Bücher und Zeitschriften über das Filmwesen* (Leipzig: Hiersemann, 1940).

Traudisch, Dora, *Mutterschaft mit Zuckerguß? Frauenfeindliche Propaganda im NS-Spielfilm*
   (Pfaffenweiler: Centaurus, 1993).

von Trentini, Albert, *Erziehung zur Persönlichkeit. Ein Zyklus in acht Betrachtungen* (Munich
   and Berlin: Oldenbourg, 1935).

Uhlenbrok, Katja (ed.), *MusikSpektakelFilm. Musiktheater und Tanzkultur im deutschen Film
   1922–1937* (Munich: edition text+kritik, 1998).

Uricchio, William and Roberta Pearson, *Reframing Culture. The Case of the Vitagraph
   Quality Films* (Princeton: Princeton University Press, 1993).

Vasey, Ruth, *The World According to Hollywood 1918–1939* (Exeter: Exeter University
   Press, 1997).

Vincendeau, Ginette (ed.), *Encyclopedia of European Cinema* (London: BFI, 1995).

Virilio, Paul, *War and Cinema. The Logistics of Perception* (London: Verso, 1989).

Volkelt, Johannes, *System der Ästhetik* (Munich: Beck, 1910).

Wahnau, Gerhard, *Studien zur Gestaltung der Handlung in Spielfilm, Drama und Erzählkunst*
   (Rostock: Hinstorff, 1939).

Walk, Joseph (ed.), *Das Sonderrecht für die Juden im NS-Staat* (Heidelberg: C. F. Müller,
   1996), second edition.

Walker, Alexander, *Dietrich. A Celebration* (London: Pavilion, 1999, orig. 1984).

Warth, Eva, 'Hure Babylon vs. Heimat. Zur Großstadtrepräsentation im
   Nationalsozialistischen Film', in Irmbert Schenk (ed.), *Dschungel Großstadt. Kino und
   Modernisierung* (Marburg: Schüren, 1999), pp. 97–111.

Watt, Ian, *The Rise of the Novel. Studies in Defoe, Richardson and Fielding* (Harmondsworth:
   Penguin, 1963).

Webber, Andrew, 'Otto Rank and the *Doppelgänger*', in Edward Timms and Ritchie
   Robertson (eds), *Psychoanalysis in its Cultural Context* (Edinburgh: Edinburgh University
   Press, 1992), pp. 81–94.

Weinschenk, Harry E., *Schauspieler erzählen* (Berlin: Wilhelm Limpert, 1941).

———, *Unser Weg zum Theater* (Berlin: Wilhelm Limpert, 1942).

———, *Wir von Bühne und Film* (Berlin: Wilhelm Limpert, 1941).

Weis, Elisabeth and John Belton (eds), *Film Sound. Theory and Practice* (New York:
   Columbia University Press, 1985).

Weiss, Andrea, ' "A Queer Feeling When I Look at You". Hollywood Stars and Lesbian
   Spectatorship', in Diane Carson, Linda Dittmar and Janice R. Welsh (eds), *Multiple*

Voices in Feminist Film Criticism (Minneapolis: University of Minnesota Press, 1994), pp. 330–42.

Weissensteiner, Friedrich, *Publikumslieblinge. Von Hans Albers bis Paula Wessely* (Vienna: Kremayr & Scherlau, 1993).

Welch, David, *Propaganda and the German Cinema 1933–1945* (Oxford: Clarendon, 1983).

——, *The Third Reich. Politics and Propaganda* (London and New York: Routledge, 1993).

Wellek, Albert, 'Die Persönlichkeit im Lichte der Erblehre. Zu dem Sammelwerk von Johannes Schottky', *Zeitschrift für angewandte Psychologie und Charakterkunde*, vol. 59, nos 1 and 2, 1940, pp. 115–21.

Wesse, Curt, *Großmacht Film. Das Geschöpf von Kunst und Technik* (Berlin: Deutsche Buch-Gemeinschaft, 1928).

Williams, Christopher, *Realism and the Cinema* (London: BFI, 1980).

Williams, Raymond, *Marxism and Literature* (Oxford: Oxford University Press, 1977).

Winkler-Mayerhöfer, Andrea, *Starkult als Propagandamittel. Studien zum Unterhaltungsfilm im Dritten Reich* (Munich: Ölschläger, 1992).

Witte, Karsten, 'Introduction to Siegfried Kracauer's "The Mass Ornament"', *New German Critique*, no. 5, 1975, pp. 59–66.

——, *Lachende Erben, Toller Tag* (Berlin: Vorwerk 8, 1995).

——, 'Visual Pleasure Inhibited. Aspects of the German Revue Film', J. Steakley and Gabriele Hoover (trans.), *New German Critique*, nos 24–5, autumn/winter 1981/2, pp. 238–3.

Wollrab, Helmut, 'Aufschliessung der persönlichen Innenwelt. Formdeutversuche mit gestalteten Formkompositionen', *Zeitschrift für angewandte Psychologie und Charakterkunde*, vol. 58, nos 1–3, 1939, pp. 93–177.

Wortig, Kurt, *Der Film in der deutschen Tageszeitung* (Frankfurt am Main: Moritz Diesterweg, 1940).

Wottrich, Erika, *Deutsche Universal. Transatlantische Verleih- und Produktionsstrategien eines Hollywood-Studios in den 20er und 30er Jahren* (Munich: edition text+kritik, 2001).

Wulf, Joseph, *Theater und Film im Dritten Reich. Eine Dokumentation* (Frankfurt am Main, Berlin and Vienna: Ullstein, 1966).

Žižek, Slavoj, *The Sublime Object of Ideology* (London and New York: Verso, 1989).

Zumkeller, Cornelia, *Zarah Leander. ihre Filme – ihr Leben* (Munich: Heyne, 1991).

Index

Page numbers in *italics* denote illustrations; *n* = endnote.

LIST OF ILLUSTRATIONS

Whilst considerable effort has been made to correctly identify the copyright holders this has not been possible in all cases. We apologise for any apparent negligence and any omissions or corrections brought to our attention will be remedied in any future editions.

Figure 1: From Deutsche Filmakademie (ed.), *Deutsche Filmakademie mit dem Arbeitsinstitut für Kulturfilmschaffende*, inaugural brochure (Babelsberg-Ufastadt: Deutsche Filmakademie, 1938); **Figures 2, 23 and 24**: *Premiere*, Gloria Film GmbH, courtesy of Fotoarchiv Stiftung Deutsche Kinemathek; **Figure 3**: From Alex Strasser, *Filmentwurf, Filmregie, Filmschnitt. Gesetze und Beispiele* (Halle: Knapp, 1937), p. xxviii; **Figure 4**: *Die vier Gesellen*, Tonfilmstudio Carl Froelich & Co, courtesy of BFI Stills; **Figure 5**: *Casablanca*, Warner Bros., courtesy of BFI Stills: **Figure 6**: From G. O. Stindt, 'Bauten und Umbauten von Lichtspielhäusern', *Filmtechnik*, 31 December 1936, p. 226; **Figure 7**: From Werner Gabler, 'Das moderne Tonfilmtheater', *Filmtechnik*, 26 November 1932; **Figure 8**: Ufa-Palast am Zoo Berlin, 1936, courtesy of Landesbildstelle Berlin; **Figure 9**: Tauentzien-Palast Berlin, 1936, courtesy of Landesbildstelle Berlin; **Figure 10**: *Traumulus*, Carl Froelich – Tonfilm Produktions, courtesy of BFI Stills; **Figures 11–14**: *Traumulus*, courtesy of Fotoarchiv Stiftung Deutsche Kinemathek; **Figure 15**: *Der alte und der junge König*, Deka-Film, courtesy of Fotoarchiv Stiftung Deutsche Kinemathek; **Figure 16**: *Die weisse Hölle der Piz Palü*, H.R. Sokal-Film, courtesy of BFI Stills; **Figure 17**: *Varieté*, Ufa, courtesy of Fotoarchiv Stiftung Deutsche Kinemathek; **Figure 18**: *Der blaue Engel*, Ufa, courtesy of BFI Stills; **Figure 19**: *The Scarlet Empress*, Paramount Productions, courtesy of Filmmuseum Berlin – Marlene Dietrich Collection; **Figure 20**: *The Devil is a Woman*, Paramount Productions, courtesy of Filmmuseum Berlin – Marlene Dietrich Collection; **Figures 21 and 22**: *Desire*, Paramount Productions, courtesy of BFI Stills; **Figure 25**: *Wegena* lingerie advertisement, c.1941, Bundesarchiv Berlin-Lichterfelde, BA R1091/2874; **Figure 26**: *Zu neuen Ufern*, Ufa, courtesy of Fotoarchiv Stiftung Deutsche Kinemathek; **Figure 27**: *La Habanera*, Ufa, courtesy of Fotoarchiv Stiftung Deutsche Kinemathek; **Figures 28 and 30**: *Die grosse Liebe*, Ufa, courtesy of Fotoarchiv Stiftung Deutsche Kinemathek; **Figure 29**: *Feuertaufe*, Tobis, courtesy of Fotoarchiv Stiftung Deutsche Kinemathek.